BY POWER
AND SAIL

To the Memory of Vasco da Gama

1469–1524

A Quincentennial Tribute

Whose discovery of the all-sea passage to India
first caused the world as we know it today
to come into being

BY POWER AND SAIL

Sixty Years of World Travel

CHARLES BLOIS

UMBRIA PRESS

First published in 2024 by
Umbria Press
London SW15 5DP
www.umbriapress.co.uk

Designed by Louise Millar

Printed by Bell & Bain Ltd, Glasgow
bell-bain.com

ISBN 978 1 910074 47 3

I would like to thank my old friend,
Noel Bolingbroke-Kent for all that he has done
to assist me with this book over many years.
He has acted as my editor and helped to improve
the book immeasurably in many ways.

To Ali

We met at an RGS dinner where I mentioned
I was looking for a Spanish speaker to join
me on an adventure to the Orinoco;
her first words to me were "I'll come."

She was a wonderful partner and we created
amazing memories as travel companions on
SES, Earthwatch and personally over
the next 12 years until she went to work
with Médecins Sans Frontières.

To Sam and Clare

For beginning a lifelong friendship when meeting up
for the first time ever, sharing a glass of port and inviting
me to motorcycle across Ethiopia with them and then
traverse Canada and Alaska up to Prudhoe Bay.
We continue to travel together today.

TIMELINE

1939 Born, Crewe

1948 Stone House School

1953 Harrow School
Captain of Swimming

1958 Trinity College, Dublin

1961 Royal Agricultural College, Cirencester
Travelled in America for the first time

1963 Studied farming and travelled round Australia

1965 Travelled back from Australia via New Zealand, Fiji,
Tahiti, Central America, Miami at the time of Hurricane
Betsy, the Bahamas and Bermuda
Started farming at Red House Farm on family-owned land

1967 Married Celia Pritchett

1968 Sir Gervase Blois died
Bought sailing ketch *Caleta*

1969-75 Sailed around the Mediterranean to Black Sea

1971 Andrew Blois born

1974 Helen Blois born

1974 Confrontation with the Greek navy after Turkish invasion
of Cyprus

1976 Sailed the Atlantic to the Caribbean with *Caleta*

1976-82 Sailed round the Caribbean, South and Central America
and Florida

1984 Ordered *Caleta II* from Whisstock Boatbuilders, Woodbridge

1986 Sailed the Atlantic with *Caleta II* to Antigua

1987 Bought a Unimog on which to build a camping body

1989 Travelled to Morocco to test Unimog

1990 Travelled to Algeria in Unimog

1991 Travelled through West Africa to Cameroon in Unimog

1995 Travelled in Unimog through Yugoslavia to Turkey, Syria,
Jordan and Egypt

1996 Bought a Revenger, a rigid inflatable boat (RIB)

1997 Drove Unimog to Kazakstan via Moscow and back via Aral Sea, Ukraine, Crimea, Yalta Transnistru and Moldova

1998 Commissioned the building of *Ribaleta*, a purpose-built cruiser-racer rigid inflatable boat with two 315hp engines

1999 Maiden voyage of *Ribaleta* round Britain

2000 Sailed *Ribaleta*, single-handed, across the Bay of Biscay to Santander

2001 Joined Earthwatch crocodile expedition on the Zambezi River
Joined Scientific Exploration Society elephant expedition in Nepal
Cruised in *Ribaleta* from France to Tunisia
Met Alison (Ali) Criado-Perez at the Royal Geographical Society

2002 Divorced from Celia

2002 Shipped *Ribaleta* in a banana boat to St Lucia
Sailed with Ali in *Ribaleta* to Venezuela, round the Orinoco Delta, up the Caribbean and via the Bahamas to Baltimore, a total of 5,500 miles
White-water rafted down the Blue Nile doing research on wildlife

2003 Scientific Exploration Society expedition bringing clean water to a village in Meghalaya

2004 Cruised in *Ribaleta* with Ali down the Danube

2006 Won British Inflatable Boat Owners Association
World Championship in *Ribaleta*

2008 Met headhunters in Nagaland

2010 Support driver for Craig Bounds and Tamsin Jones in South America Dakar Rally in Nissan Patrol
Competed in Heroes Legend race from Paris to Dakar

2011 Supported South America Dakar Rally riding a Yamaha Transalp

2012 Support driver for Craig Bounds and Paul Jay in South America Dakar Rally in Nissan Patrol

2012 Rode a KTM motorcycle round Ethiopia

2013-14 Rode KTM motorcycle across Canada to Prudhoe Bay in Alaska and down through North America

2016-24 Travelled in North America by campervan and jet boat

2019-20 Travelled in Unimog from Namibia to Kenya via Zimbabwe, a total of 8,000 miles in ten countries

CONTENTS

FOREWORD

A true countryman and lover of travel and adventure, Sir Charles Blois has now written a fascinating memoir describing his many exciting and worthwhile ventures. The tales of his childhood, school days and early life are especially amusing and illustrate an age sadly passed.

Without doubt, he is a man with an unquenchable spirit of adventure, taking great pleasure in seeking new challenges in many remote regions of the world. Sailing, driving and motorcycling, he has undertaken numerous daring projects.

One can only admire someone who has sailed single-handed across the Bay of Biscay in a rigid inflatable boat, designed by himself, or who has travelled through little-known parts of Africa in an extraordinary vehicle called a Unimog, also designed by himself, or who, aged seventy, rode 6,000 miles on a motorcycle from London to Beijing.

Colonel John Blashford-Snell climbing the bank out of the Karnāli River on an elephant tour in Bardia National Park

Charles came with me on four expeditions of the Scientific Exploration Society, which I founded in 1969 to focus on discovery and research in remote parts of the world. The diversity of these expeditions appealed to him. They varied from riding elephants and walking in the jungle in Nepal where he actually saw the legendary king elephant Raja Gaj silently passing him at a distance of only 20 yards, to white-water rafting down the Blue Nile in Ethiopia where his team was held overnight by AK47-wielding bandits, to meeting the last of the head-hunters in Nagaland, a remote part of north-east India, where Charles was shown a collection of around 100 heads hidden in a canoe, to being involved in the installation of a solar-power pump in Meghalaya, a new state of India, bordering Bangladesh.

Charles has an unusually enquiring mind and clearly enjoys encouraging others to seek fulfilment through adventure. I cannot see him hanging up his boots for quite a while and trust others will be inspired by his remarkable stories.

Colonel John Blashford-Snell, CBE
Hon. President, Scientific Exploration Society

A view of the Pitons, two mountainous volcanic plugs, volcanic spires, located above Soufriere Town in St Lucia.

THE HAND OF GOD

The call from the port came at two o'clock in the morning. Ali and I walked out into the dark Caribbean night to navigate our way down the unlit streets. The St Lucian town of Castries seemed lifeless at that time, the bars and restaurants closed, the locals and tourists all retired to their beds, the only noise to be heard that of the cicadas. The air was fresh, a relief after the muggy heat of the day.

Then, as we rounded a corner, the docks appeared before us, all lit up and bustling with life even at this hour, shining out of the night like a beacon. I knew the name of the freighter we were looking for and, after winding through a maze of shipping containers, we found it. Its enormous hull rose from the water and towered high above my head.

A dockworker led us onboard, where we were warmly greeted by the captain and ushered down into the hold. There before us, wrapped in a protective polythene covering, was the reason we were in the belly of this freighter in the middle of the night, the reason we were in St Lucia at all – my boat: *Ribaleta*. For the next few months, this was to be our transport and our home as we ventured deep into the Orinoco Delta.

Ali and I unwrapped *Ribaleta* and readied the nylon strops and then I stepped into the boat and erected the A-frame. The hatch covers were removed, and, with a series of careful manoeuvres, I attached the three nylon strops that already shackled *Ribaleta* to the ship's crane hook. Back in Southampton I had watched as it had been hoisted from my trailer by a similar crane and placed into a wooden cradle in the bowels of the freighter so I knew what to expect – except that this time the process would be in reverse. The boat was to be hauled up out of the hold, swung over the side of the ship and then lowered gently into the sea.

I was still standing inside *Ribaleta* when the captain approached me to explain that someone would need to stay on the boat as it was lifted out and lowered into the water. Would I be happy to do it myself, he enquired?

I looked over his shoulder at the dockworkers clustered a few feet away and nervously staring at the ground. 'Shouldn't one of them do it?' I asked.

'They are too scared,' replied the captain, shrugging his shoulders.

I looked upwards, my gaze following the crane's winch wire up out of the hold to where, high above, I could just make out the boom head with nothing beyond it but the starlit sky. I have never had much of a head for heights – I am the sort of person who edges away from a cliff edge rather than peer over it. However, riding *Ribaleta* as it was winched up did not seem too frightening a prospect. And I rather liked the idea of becoming the only white dockworker in St Lucia.

'OK. I'll do it,' I told him.

The captain breathed a sigh of relief. He spoke to the men who, all smiles now, set about attaching ropes to the front and back of *Ribaleta* that would help them guide us safely out of the ship.

'Charles,' Ali said, 'are you sure this is a good idea?'

'It'll be fine,' I assured her, grabbing hold of the A-frame with one hand and the driver's seat with the other as, slowly and gently, the crane began to lift *Ribaleta*, and me with it, out of the hold and up into the open night air. It was done with careful precision, the dockworkers down below holding on tightly to the attached ropes and using them to guide and manoeuvre us clear of all the ship's deck superstructure.

Ribaleta and I gradually emerged from the hold, rising up past the shipping containers stacked on deck, and then finally clear above everything. I now found myself frighteningly high up, suspended some 60 feet in the air beneath the boom of the crane, and looking out towards the dock and the town behind it. Fearful of vertigo, I decided it would not be a good idea to look down!

The dockworkers below let go of the ropes, and then the crane operator swung *Ribaleta* out over the side of the ship to lower us down towards the water. It was at this point that things started to go wrong. There was a fair bit of wind, and as it caught *Ribaleta* it changed our trajectory: we were no longer swinging away from the boat; instead, the bow was swinging, so we were suddenly veering straight back towards the ship. Panic gripped me as we headed for what seemed like an inevitable collision.

I could not move, sheer terror freezing me to the spot. All I could do was watch in open-mouthed disbelief as the hull loomed larger and ever closer before me. I held my breath and braced myself for the impact – too terrified to move from the helm with the risk of falling 60 feet into the black Caribbean Sea.

Then, at the very last moment, there was a sudden change of direction, one so abrupt and unexpected that, had I not been holding on to the A-frame for dear life, it would have thrown me from my feet. What had happened? Somehow, I was now moving away from the ship, out into open air, still swinging but no longer on a potentially fatal collision course. I watched in astonishment as the enormous hull receded away from me. It was almost as if – and, as a non-religious man I do not say this lightly – it was almost as if the hand of God had plucked me from my fate.

The moment of danger having passed, the crane proceeded to lower *Ribaleta* once more. We eventually alighted safely in the water and I wasted no time before starting both engines. The reassuring rumble of the un-silenced diesels drowned out all the other sounds in the harbour, and I felt relief coursing through me, for I was now in full command of my boat. I was free from public transport, and the whole western ocean was my playground.

The crane operator lowered the winch wire a little further so that I could disengage the hook and motor back to the dock. Once there, reunited with Ali, I confessed my divine revelation to her. 'I was going to crash into the hull of the ship,' I said. 'But the hand of God saved me.'

Ali stared at me for a moment before breaking into a smile as she explained what had actually happed. After leaving the boat, she and the captain had watched the entire drama unfold from the safety of the dockside. Like me, she had been convinced that I was on a collision course with the ship and when, at the last minute, *Ribaleta* had suddenly changed direction, she had switched her horrified gaze to the cab of the crane, in which she could see the operator frantically working the controls, and swinging the boom as far out from the ship as he could.

'So, you see, it wasn't the hand of God at all, Charles,' she said. 'It was the hand of a very alert and quick-thinking Caribbean crane operator that saved you.'

Cockfield Hall, Yoxford, seat of the Blois family since 1693.

PART I:
EARLY YEARS

CHAPTER ONE

THE SCANDAL OF PEGGY WHITE

One of the things I have been blessed with is a family tree better recorded than most others in England. I could explain it in detail, elaborating on the lives and titles of my forebears, name-dropping Charlemagne here and William the Conqueror there, or King Alfred and King Stephen the Anarchist, or even throwing in some of the more amusing names – Charles the Bald or Louis the Stammerer – while remarking at length upon the baronetcy which has been passed down from father to son since 1686, and which now sits upon my shoulders.

But instead, I shall start far more recently, at the beginning of the twentieth century. My father, Sir Gervase Blois, was born in 1901. He went on to have a fairly illustrious military career. In the late 1920s, he was aide-de-camp to the governor of Bengal, and had the privilege of elephant-mounted tiger shoots, where he personally shot three tigers, in the days when they were plentiful. It was his duty to accept any invitation of the governor. While returning from India – no doubt 'posh' class, port out starboard home, to avoid the worst of the heat – he had the misfortune of mistiming a dive into the ship's pool just as the water surged away, hitting the bottom and breaking his neck.

Fortunately, he was well looked after and able to continue his military career. During the Second World War he served in north Africa at the Battle of El Alamein and later landed in Italy in time for the Battle of Anzio, earning the Military Cross, the Croix de Guerre and the Legion of Honour. He even marched behind Charles de Gaulle during the Liberation of Paris in 1944.

Not that I learnt all this from my father. Few people talked about their war experiences, and the only thing he ever personally told me was how, once, he 'fingered' his revolver to encourage some American soldiers to get their tank un-bogged and mobile so that they could shoot out a German Tiger tank. This was successfully achieved and the advance was able to proceed. As the saying goes, soldiers have rifles to shoot the enemy;

officers have revolvers to threaten their own men. My father was awarded his MC for his part in this action.

He met my mother, Audrey Johnson, before the war. They married in 1938 and I was born a year later. Throughout the war, he returned home frequently – my brother Rodney, born in 1941, and my sister Gillian, born in 1943, are evidence of that. Nevertheless, not long after the war – in 1948 in fact – their young marriage was over. The reason they divorced is mostly guesswork, but wartime separation must have played its part. My mother once told me that I would keep asking her when Daddy would be home, and she came to realise she needed to act. I know the decision was mutual, and I know that they were very different people with too large an age gap between them. When they married, my father was thirty-seven and my mother just twenty-one, so this was presumably a contributing factor. As for the rest of it, the few things I know for certain come from what my mother told me, for my father never spoke about it.

At that time, it was the husband who had to initiate divorce proceedings, so it was not something a woman could take responsibility for. My father knew it would have to fall to him. So, one night, he and his girlfriend, Lucy, stayed in a hotel together, and made sure that they were recognised. The ensuing scandal was enough to be used as grounds for divorce, and the marriage was soon legally over.

Not long after, my father married a woman called Peggy White. I was eight years old at the time, and it was not until my twenties that I discovered that my stepmother was the same woman who had shared that hotel room with my father all those years ago. She was the same 'Lucy', her middle name: the planned infidelity to obtain the divorce that my parents both wanted. When I shared this revelation with my mother, I was even more surprised to learn that she had never known either.

Captain Gervase Blois marching with General de Gaulle at the liberation of Paris in 1944

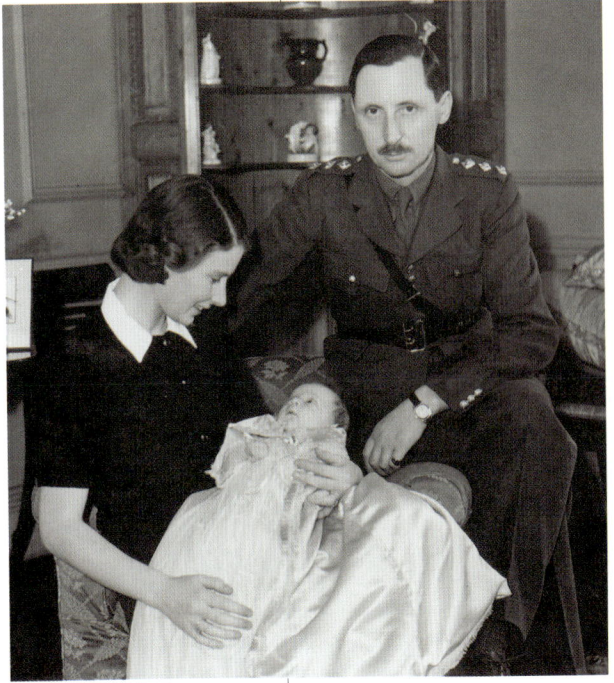

In Boden Hall, with my parents, 1940.

Boden Hall, Cheshire – birthplace of the Author.

The Blois family home was in Suffolk: Grundisburgh Hall, and later Cockfield Hall in Yoxford, inherited by Sir Charles Blois, 1st Baronet, in 1693. Remarkably, even though it stayed in my family until I was fifty-seven, I only lived there for, at most, three months.

We spent much of the war living in Staffordshire away from the bombs with my maternal grandfather. Then, following the divorce, my mother bought a house in Cheshire and we moved there. Rodney, Gillian and I would often spend our Easter holidays and two weeks of the summer holidays with our father. We did not stay in Cockfield Hall as it had been bombed during the war. All I can remember of that is seeing a pile of rubble several years after the war ended. A German plane had released its three bombs on its way home: one on a field, one on a barn, and the last on Cockfield Hall. It had been used by the army in the war and my father rented a house in Dunwich while it was being restored by the government; I don't have the happiest memories of those times. My father was a keen churchgoer, but we did not share his enthusiasm. I remember once that we were so determined to avoid it that we ran to the farm about half a mile away and hid in the back of a haystack to ensure we wouldn't be found and dragged off to church.

Sir Charles Blois
1st Baronet in 1737

A few years later, when I was fifteen years old, the three of us decided to run away. We didn't have any money, but we knew that our father had our train tickets back to Cheshire somewhere in the house. After searching high and low, we realised that the only place they could be was in his wallet. We devised a plan. The next day, I invited my father to a game of ping-pong, knowing this would encourage him to take off his jacket. As soon as he did so, it was Rodney's turn to become involved; he went through my father's jacket pockets to find the wallet and retrieve the tickets. Once we had them, it was on to the getaway stage of the plan. The three of us rode our bikes the mile to Darsham station, where we boarded a local train to Stowmarket, changed there and caught the Harwich–Holyhead train all the way to Liverpool and home. Our mother was not in so we made ourselves comfortable, relieved to be away from our father. Then the telephone rang. Our father had worked out what had happened and was calling our mother to find out if we had arrived. Rodney answered the telephone.

'No,' he told our father. 'We're not here.'

My mother and I were close and I lived with her into my early twenties. As a single parent bringing up three children after the war, she didn't have much of a social life, but what she did have was her ladies' cricket team. She never remarried and never even had another boyfriend, but this didn't matter to her. Apart from us children who were all at boarding school, her cricket team became her life.

She was an exceptional player in her 30s and was a regular choice for the North of England women's cricket team. She always felt that she could have played for England but her mother did not think cricket was suitable for ladies and kept that opportunity from her. Although the Cheshire women's cricket team that she joined had less experienced players, she thrived there amongst like-minded women. Her closest friend was the team's wicket keeper – also a single mother of three children, who were a similar age to us – and the two of them began to spend a lot of time together.

In 1959, she retired from cricket and wanted to live in the country, so she moved to Foxcote Grange in Gloucestershire. Just before we left Cheshire, she bought her brother's Jaguar XK140 – my dream car. I had saved all my Christmas money in the post office, so I took £200 out and gave it to my mother and asked for a third share of her car, which she kindly agreed to let me have. I spent those holidays as a nineteen-year-old driving the Jaguar as often and as fast as possible down the East Lancs Road trying, but never managing, to reach 100 miles an hour.

Once my mother moved to Gloucestershire, she turned her attention to horses, riding regularly. She had chosen the house as it had stables, two paddocks and a cottage. She could let the stables to keen show jumpers and help and support them when travelling to shows and as company when hacking out and exercising. I lived with my mother for four years while I attended the Royal Agricultural College at Cirencester and did my practical farm work.

CHAPTER TWO
SCHOOL DAYS

I started at my prep school – a boarding school called Stone House, in Kent – at the age of eight. I enjoyed it there: joining the cubs, learning Morse code, chopping wood, playing cricket. I remember how far away it was; it seemed to take forever to travel there. My mother drove us down from Cheshire to London with no dual carriageway and little power. Cars were rare in those days; I remember my mother and uncle talking about ordering a car for me when I was only ten years old, since the delivery time then was seven to eight years.

She put us on the school train – a steam train, of course – at Victoria station which would take us to Broadstairs, where the school was located. But the distance was not an issue for my mother. She had been determined that we would go to Stone House, the school which her brother, my uncle, had attended some twenty years earlier. Next door to it was a girls' school, which was where my mother had been educated. The schools were so close that she and my uncle had been able to stand on the boundary between them and talk to each other.

There were many prep schools in the area so we had good opportunities for sporting competition at every level. I remember one cricket match in which I was the bowler and the other side's batsman took an American baseball stance. He hit my first ball for four and my second ball for six, but then my third ball clean bowled him before he could cause any further upset to our traditional English game.

We had a small pool where we were all taught to swim before armbands were invented. We had a strop round our waist and were saved from drowning by a master supporting us with a long boom. I was a slow learner, largely because after passing the swimming test you always had to dive in. I did not like that idea at all so delayed passing my test. I finally decided I had to pass properly and ended up doing so in the middle of the pool, away from any possible help.

*Final leavers photo at
Harrow in 1958*

*Harrow Old School
Buildings*

If Stone House had any particular philosophy or focus, it was to send its pupils to a good public school. That, as prep schoolboys, was our primary objective – we had to do well in the Common Entrance exam. For me, this philosophy was, if anything, a little too successful. I excelled at maths but only at Common Entrance standard and nothing beyond that. Because of this, I was placed in entirely the wrong group when I went to Harrow, at scholarship level, two years above where I should have been, and completely out of my depth.

Nevertheless, I settled well into life at Harrow, and it was there that I first discovered my love of the water – a love which has continued to this day. Harrow's swimming pool at that time was an old kidney-shaped lake which had been concreted in, affectionately known as Ducker, after the custom of ducking other boys under the water for sport. It was so large that all of the school's 600 boys could swim in it on a Sunday. Nobody wore any clothes at Ducker, not even the teacher, or 'beak', in charge.

I learnt early on that, if I did life saving on the half-days we had every Tuesday and Thursday, I could spend the whole afternoon at Ducker rather than having to attend Bill, a Harrow tradition where you walked past in a pre-planned line and said 'Here, sir'. Not only that, but I could also have a Ducker bun for tea.

Of course, doing life saving meant that I did a lot of swimming and quickly became unusually good at it, which meant in turn that I was soon picked for the junior swimming team. The first time I was selected for an away match, I was the youngest on the team. On the bus to Stowe School, where the match was held, the others teased me mercilessly. I was told stories that the pool was just a lake and that we would have to walk round the edge on boards, or that a boy had dived from the high-diving board and ended up with his head stuck in the mud and was not missed but left to die. Unsure if it was all just a big joke for the new boys, I kept quiet – but, in fact, it all turned out to be true. I realised then how lucky we were that Ducker had concrete. I won a few of my races and, as a result, I earned my junior colours – the most obvious advantage being that I was allowed to wear swimming trunks. Quite a privilege when you're only fourteen years old and the other boys – even those who are seventeen and eighteen – have to swim naked.

After a year, I was promoted from the junior to the senior team, a great honour. At the end of the season – the last swimming race of the season – I managed to beat the number one swimmer *and* the head of house, which was a big surprise, and also meant being able to duck anyone I chose! The following year, I held the record for the 50 and the 100 yards. Also, because I had grown bigger and faster than everyone else, I had free rein at Ducker. Not surprisingly, I was a bit of a rebel, which annoyed some of the senior boys: when they came down to Ducker on Sunday, a friend and I could prevent them from swimming. One house monitor who we did not like sat on the side of the pool for the whole afternoon, managing to swim only one width. He kept watching us to see when we lost concentration – he knew that, if he was caught in the middle, he would be ducked mercilessly, and all the younger boys would see it and join in. On another occasion, all the house monitors were sitting on a poolside bench fully dressed, preening themselves and showing off their importance. We had some logs in the

Photograph published in the Tatler *showing Harrow School winners of the Champion Ducks competition. (1958, Charles Blois centre)*

Dr. R.L. James
19   58
Champion Ducks

A. J.H. Chisholm   C.N.G. Blois   J.P.V. Madjar

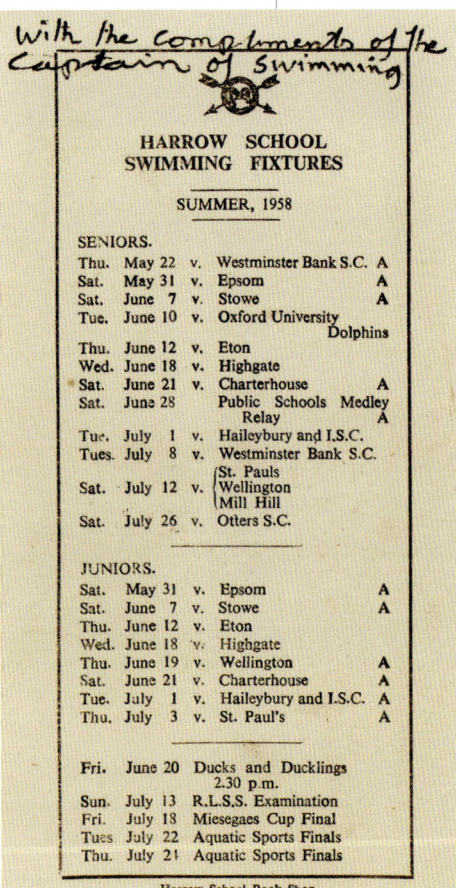

With the compliments of the Captain of Swimming

HARROW SCHOOL SWIMMING FIXTURES

SUMMER, 1958

SENIORS.

Thu.	May 22	v.	Westminster Bank S.C.	A
Sat.	May 31	v.	Epsom	A
Sat.	June 7	v.	Stowe	A
Tue.	June 10	v.	Oxford University Dolphins	
Thu.	June 12	v.	Eton	
Wed.	June 18	v.	Highgate	
Sat.	June 21	v.	Charterhouse	A
Sat.	June 28		Public Schools Medley Relay	A
Tue.	July 1	v.	Haileybury and I.S.C.	
Tues.	July 8	v.	Westminster Bank S.C.	
Sat.	July 12	v.	St. Pauls / Wellington / Mill Hill	
Sat.	July 26	v.	Otters S.C.	

JUNIORS.

Sat.	May 31	v.	Epsom	A
Sat.	June 7	v.	Stowe	A
Thu.	June 12	v.	Eton	
Wed.	June 18	v.	Highgate	
Thu.	June 19	v.	Wellington	A
Sat.	June 21	v.	Charterhouse	A
Tue.	July 1	v.	Haileybury and I.S.C.	A
Thu.	July 3	v.	St. Paul's	A

Fri.	June 20	Ducks and Ducklings 2.30 p.m.
Sun.	July 13	R.L.S.S. Examination
Fri.	July 18	Miesegaes Cup Final
Tues	July 22	Aquatic Sports Finals
Thu.	July 24	Aquatic Sports Finals

Harrow School Book Shop

Harrow School swimming fixtures, summer 1958

pool to play with and sit on. We floated them closer to the bench, lifted them up and then slammed them down on the water with such force that all the monitors, in their smart clothes, were soaked. There was nothing they could do about it – they were fully dressed, and if they had been in the water, they never would have caught us and we could have ducked them individually.

On the competitive side, I improved as I grew older and, by the end of my time at Harrow, I held all the school records from 50 yards to one mile. The swimming beak – a 24-year-old former half-blue at Cambridge – challenged me to a race. It ended up as a dead heat. I was later told that the beak had pushed himself so hard that he had been sick after our race. We also had a race against Cambridge University. They entered a team suitable for the school, because a race against a major university was clearly unfair. Nevertheless, they included their fourth best swimmer in their team to make sure they won, which they just did, but it was a good race overall. That was the last time I was beaten. In my final year, when I was captain of the team, we competed for the Ebrington Cup. We had lost the previous year and I was determined to win this time – my last chance before leaving Harrow for good. Not only did we win the cup, but the team also came third in the National Championship. We were all immensely proud of ourselves as a team, swimming in an old lake against schools with modern heated pools.

Perhaps my proudest moment of all came when, in 1955, Sir Winston Churchill, one of Harrow's most illustrious old boys, came to visit the school. After the traditional school songs which had been put on especially for Churchill, I rushed out on to the street to have a close look at him. Although I was still only fifteen years old, I was already at my full height of six feet two inches. I stood behind some older but smaller boys who – being somewhat unnerved by my size – asked me to join them as they preferred to have me with them than pushing from behind. I joined the front row and linked arms with the barrier of eighteen-year-olds, preventing the surge of boys who continued to jostle behind us. I still have the photograph taken by the *Daily Telegraph* of that occasion hanging in my hall. You can see me right in the front with Churchill. If you look

Despite being a Junior, due to my height and size I was invited to join the barrier line to protect Winston Churchill from the cheering boys of Harrow after songs. November 1955 (1955, Charles Blois far left)

closely enough, you will notice that my tie is different to that of all the other boys in the picture, for I was the only junior allowed to stand and be photographed so close to the great man.

At Harrow I was fairly lucky with the beaks I had. Stories abounded about them: some rather incredible for a young boy, such as the fact that the Ducker beak's father was the Archbishop of Canterbury; others somewhat more sinister, such as the story about my chemistry beak, an Olympic hammer thrower in his youth, who once made a bad throw with the hammer flying wild and killing a spectator.

I had suspected that I might be given a harder time from my beaks than I was, for I was the only boy who would not be confirmed. At my confirmation class I had a long discussion with the school chaplain, Rev. P.H.M. Bryant, known by the boys as Pumph, but not surprisingly I failed to persuade him that the Bible was just a fairy tale. I did not attend confirmation classes after that. I particularly liked my Beaks for physics and maths. Since I was in the top sets for both these subjects, I had the best beaks. I struggled in some other subjects, such as French, where beaks spoke French with an English accent. This was why I ended up, at the age of seventeen, taking my A levels in maths, physics and chemistry.

It was around this same time that plans at school turned to university, with Oxbridge being the number one choice for everyone. So, out of a

sense of duty rather than inclination, I applied to Cambridge, purely because I had always supported the light blue in university matches. I sat the entrance exam but failed miserably because it was far too hard. Luckily, it did not matter as two boys in my form, Charles Dewhurst and Noel Bolingbroke-Kent, had discovered something far more exciting. It was the possibility of studying abroad; not too far, but just far enough, at Trinity College, Dublin. We learnt that they would accept five O levels and on graduation one could pay £50 to add 'Cantab' or 'Oxon' after one's name. I was delighted when they accepted my application, and I was even more delighted when they made me an unconditional offer during my final summer term, as it meant I didn't need to take my S level exams. So, as you can imagine, I didn't – much to the justifiable annoyance of my beaks.

CHAPTER THREE
A YEAR IN IRELAND

Dublin was my first time abroad and the prospect of leaving Britain was an exciting one. I couldn't wait to go. Ireland was not entirely alien to me, for I had a contact there. My godmother lived just outside Dublin, and I would see her on occasional weekends. She had a fantastic house, one of those grand, old-world places where, even then in 1958, you tipped the maid looking after you and retired to bed with a candle. Sadly, soon after I left, this traditional way of life came to an end when the house was demolished – although, in 1963, my friends had one last party there where several hundred people danced until dawn.

It was my godmother who found me digs in Dublin, a house I shared with two other students. The plan was for me to live there for the first and second years, and then move into rooms in college for my third year. Once I had settled into my new house, I decided it was time to buy my first car: a wonderful little Ford Anglia which, I remember, had just three gears. That was the beginning of my love affair with cars. Not long after, I upgraded to an MG TD, of which I was extremely proud.

In my MG TD, participating in a sports car competition in Ireland, 1958.

Dr R.B. McDowell, Junior Dean, Trinity College, Dublin

Once, when I was cleaning and polishing it and painting the wheels white in the middle of the street, the Junior Dean, the legendary Dr R. B. McDowell, happened to come by. It turned out that he too had a love of cars, and when he saw my gleaming MG, he offered me a room in college and a space in the car park. I remember he called my car a 'lovely girl'. And he was right; she was.

My days in Dublin were always busy but little of my time was spent in lectures. Much of our time was passed in the social societies on campus, which revolved around games of billiards and snooker in grand and ornate rooms well suited to a totally relaxed atmosphere. When our games were finished, we could wander into the city and up Grafton Street to The Bailey for a pint of Guinness and know that there would always be fellow students there. The seven-week terms did not give us much time to be bored. I joined the swimming club for exercise and to find out if I was still competitive at university level. Luckily for me, I found that I was and only needed two hours a week to train when the pool was available. It seemed that this short time was normal and I maintained my unbroken record against all the Irish universities. I studied physics and chemistry, in the hope of becoming a scientist. We didn't do much work as we had done it all before at school, but when we sat for the physics exam, I found I had to write up a practical that I hadn't actually done. I passed with 43 per cent, not a good mark by any standards, but just scraping through. One of my friends beat me with 51 per cent – a particularly annoying result, for he hadn't put in a paper at all.

This arbitrary marking system may have contributed to my growing disillusionment with my course. After my first year, I realised that I no longer wanted to be a scientist or an engineer. Over the summer holidays, my father told me that the tenant on one of our farms hoped to retire, and in exchange for giving a retirement date my father would not increase his rent. I decided to use this opportunity to take up farming and do something I really wanted to do, so I switched to agriculture at the beginning of my second year.

Unfortunately, this new course was no better. The problem was that even as a first-year student I could tell that what they were teaching me was worthless. The course was seriously outdated, teaching how to mix fertiliser on the floor with a cement mixer, whereas in England it was all in pre-mixed in bags. At the same time, they told me I was not qualified to do the course because I didn't have an A level in biology. The decision for me to leave was mutual. The saddest thing about leaving was that I could not export my beloved MG from Ireland.

Trinity College, Dublin in 1795 by James Malton

I had enjoyed myself at Trinity College for much of the time, and I was sorry to be leaving it and Ireland itself. It was a lovely country to be young in, to drink Guinness and absorb the Irish pub life. I would miss my friends too. Often, we would go out shooting together, and on a Sunday we felt a bit out of place in our shooting clothes, loading the MG with our guns and cartridges outside College Chapel in front of the choir in their white gowns. When we turned up at a new farm and asked the farmer if there were any pheasants, he would invariably reply: 'Of course! Come with me and I'll show you.' And then he would take us around his farm with his dog to shoot his pheasants. It was a wonderful, old-fashioned and traditional way of life.

I bade farewell to my friends on my final night, which coincided with the Trinity Ball. The tickets were all sold out so I had to sneak in through a window. To make up for the lack of a ticket, my friends had instead arranged a blind date for me. It was a marvellous last night, and a fitting end to my year in Ireland. My friends continued to enjoy their life there, although one day they went a little too far and threw a piano out of a third-floor window. No one was expelled or hurt, but the Junior Dean, who was in charge of discipline, was not at all amused.

Polynesian outrigger canoes

PART II:
LEARNING TO FARM, LEARNING TO TRAVEL

CHAPTER FOUR
MUSTANGS AND MATADORS

Now that I had decided to become a farmer, I moved back to live with my mother in Gloucestershire and completed fifteen months' work of practical farming on neighbouring farms, to learn the basics of farming. I worked for a traditional colonel who was mostly interested in pedigree Herefords. I was only involved in the arable side of things, and remember having to plough with an overloaded tractor which meant that, when ploughing uphill, the front wheels would rear up into the air and remain there till the end of the field. Four-wheel drive had not arrived in those days, and you steered by braking each rear wheel. The harvest was mostly spent shovelling corn on and off the grain drier. I soon moved to another farm for more experience and was promoted to sprayer operator as I was better at spray calculation and mixing chemicals. The spray boom was mounted forward on a loader arm, which gave good visibility but meant I was always driving into the chemical I was spraying. This was not the healthiest way to work, but health and safety were not around then, and you did what you were told, although the chemicals were much simpler then.

I then began a two-year course at the Royal Agricultural College in Cirencester. I was much happier there as I felt I had found my calling. Most of the lecturers were excellent, although I do remember one in the second year who was pretty hopeless. His name was Neddy Weston and, because he went far too fast in his lectures, he earned the nickname Steady Neddy, which is what we would shout at him to make him to slow down. To liven up his lectures, we started throwing shotgun pellets at him when he wasn't looking. When we tired of this, we switched to throwing bags of flour. Unfortunately, as bags of flour were far more conspicuous than pellets, we had to stop when he realised who the culprits were. On one occasion, as it was the Royal Agricultural College, we had a royal visit. The Queen and Prince Phillip came and Neddy Weston was chosen to show them around the machinery, which he proceeded to do at a ridiculous speed. We could not resist shouting '*Steady Neddy!*' Poor Neddy stopped dead in his tracks, went absolutely crimson, and then proceeded to do the rest of the tour at half-speed. To this day, I am convinced my final grades suffered because Steady Neddy never forgave me for that.

Cirencester was the time when my future truly opened up. During those years, I was trained to farm and I travelled for the first time, realising how important both were for me. It was the college, of course, which qualified me to farm. And it was the time in between my studies, the summer holidays, which introduced me to travel.

The first big journey I ever undertook was in the summer holiday between my first and second years at Cirencester. At that time, there was an offer which young travellers could take advantage of called the '99', a ticket offered by the Greyhound bus chain that promised ninety-nine days of travel in America for just $99. I only had time to do forty-nine days in total, but, as a 22-year-old – although it would clearly be a rush – it was enough.

Back then, in the early 1960s, travelling to America was far more of an ordeal than it is today. The flight took place in three stages. First, we flew from London to Shannon, where the plane was refuelled, then to Gander in Newfoundland for more fuel, then finally to New York. Not only were

The route map for the six-week Greyhound bus tour of America in 1962

the flights longer then, but the pilots were also more honest. I remember that we were delayed in London for six hours, the penalty for cheap flights, and when we finally took off from Shannon, the pilot explained why over the intercom. 'We apologise for the delay. The crew were sitting drinking in a bar in Luxembourg, when we suddenly had an emergency call asking us to come back to London and take this flight to America. But no need to worry. We sobered up quickly.' At the time, I found his frankness amusing, but I would probably not feel the same way today.

In an effort to keep my American adventure as cheap as possible, I virtually lived on Greyhound buses. I never stayed in a hotel, and took night buses whenever I could so that I could sleep on their back seats. At some point in the journey, I managed to spend twenty-two consecutive nights on a bus. It was a wonderful adventure. There were the Cypress Gardens in Florida, where I saw acrobatic water-skiers for the first time, who skied barefoot or formed human pyramids. I went to Silver Springs, where – in the middle of a jungle – I found thousands of gallons per hour of the clearest water I had ever seen coming out of a huge spring. There was the OK Corral of Gunfight fame, where I watched a re-enactment of the famous fight in which the Earp brothers, Wyatt, Morgan and Virgil, and 'Doc' Holliday killed the cowboys Billy Clanton and Tom and Frank McLaury, sending them up to Boot Hill, so named as the burial place of those who died with their boots on. There was one grave marked 'George Johnson Hanged by Mistake'. He had been mistaken for a horse-rustler from whom he had bought the horse. Then there was the spectacle of looking into the Grand

In 1882 there was unfortunate mix-up of a stolen horse in Tombstone Arizona, which lead to the demise of innocent man, George Johnson

Canyon; there were the Hopi Indians performing their traditional dancing; there was Disneyland, where everything was so amazingly lifelike, more so than any other man-made things I'd ever seen; the giant redwoods of the Sequoia National Park with a roadway through one of the giant trees; Niagara Falls with all the noise, getting soaked from the spray in the boat that takes you below the Falls; and the Chicago Union Stockyards, so big I could not see the edge. I took them all in with amazement – the language may have been the same as my own, but this was a world far removed from the country in which I had grown up.

In California, I stayed with a college friend whose father was an airman. He took us to see the base, and I had the rare chance of seeing a B-52 bomber take off at close range, with black smoke coming out of all eight engines and an enormous roar. It was staggering to see the sheer

The P-51 Mustang kept polished for air races which Charles flew in. It was fitted with a hand-made Rolls Royce Merlin Engine used in the War, 1962

size of the plane. We were then told that a friend of his would take us up in his aeroplane, so we went out on the runway and saw an amazing P-51 Mustang which had been converted from a single-seater to a two-seater. I climbed quickly into the back seat before the engine overheated and the cockpit was closed and the pilot set off down the runway with a massive roar and climbed into the air. I was given a wonderful flight around the airfield and then, as he slowed the plane to come into land, I felt it was all over far too quickly. But then he opened up the throttles so that we experienced the never-to-be-forgotten thrust of the 27-litre Merlin engine. We flew at 400 miles an hour 100 feet off the runway and then he pulled the stick back into a vertical climb until we nearly stalled, before spinning round and taking us back for landing. It was the most amazing flight I've ever been on, and to listen to the Merlin engine at close range – which was a proper Rolls-Royce engine and not the less powerful American version, as they could not build to Rolls-Royce standard – was truly incredible.

America at that time, the early 1960s, was in the grip of the Cold War, but the tension which bubbled under the surface was never really noticeable to me. All the Americans I met were friendly and open, and the America I saw was largely rural, a land of wide spaces and small towns, all viewed from the window of a passing bus – an America which, away from the cities, is not all that different today, sixty years later.

I returned from my American adventure to college in Cirencester with a newfound sense of determination. They say that travel broadens the mind, and it certainly did for me – it broadened my mind in that I returned with the knowledge of precisely what I wanted to do with the rest of my life. I wanted to farm, and I wanted to travel. As I have proved over the last sixty years, the two are perfectly compatible.

I graduated from the Royal Agricultural College in 1963. To celebrate, a group of us took a two-week holiday in the south of Spain. The group comprised me, my first proper girlfriend, Anne Waterston, my good friend Noel Bolingbroke-Kent from Harrow and Trinity, his sister Gloria and her boyfriend George Wingfield. A few months before, I had bought a 14-foot lightweight speedboat for river cruising and water-skiing, and we decided it would be fun to tow it down to the Andalusian coast. As none of us had cars suited to the journey, my mother kindly lent us her Jaguar 3.4 Mark 2.

Along the way, we stayed in hotels. This meant having to find a new one each night, frequently driving late into the night to check in before they closed. They were often poor quality, and this is what gave me my lifelong aversion to hotels and is the reason I prefer self-contained living on my adventures. Trying to arrange for five people, a car and a boat to be ready to leave on time was a considerable challenge, one which we totally failed to achieve. By the time we arrived at Lydd airport, we were well over an hour late. Luckily for us, Lydd was a small airport and, as we were a large group, we had the aircraft all to ourselves with the car and the boat. It was the quickest and most pleasant Channel crossing I have ever made.

The highlight of our journey south was the stop at Pamplona, which we timed perfectly to coincide with the running of the bulls. As excited as we were about the event, I have to admit that we didn't fully understand it. We thought that if we ran *behind* the bulls rather than in front of them, we would be much safer. What we had not realised is that, often, the bulls make mistakes, hitting the walls with their horns and knocking themselves over. And, of course, when they stand up again, they've sometimes turned round, so they start running back into the crowd. As a result, those people who have chosen to follow the bulls from behind suddenly find themselves running directly towards the horns of an angry and disorientated animal, with a dense crowd preventing any way back. Fortunately, this didn't happen to us, and I was extremely glad when we followed the bulls into the arena. We then watched the Spaniards who had been running with us bravely acting as matadors by waving their jackets in front of the bulls and jumping away just in time. I saw how strong and fierce they were, even though the Spaniards had cut off the tips of their horns.

The drive into Málaga was rather frightening – I don't recommend driving a car with five people, fading brakes and a boat on tow down the twisting hill into the city – but we made it there. We had booked a villa in Fuengirola, about 20 miles down the coast from Málaga. These days, Fuengirola is a tourist resort filled with high-rise building and hotels, one of the Costa del Sol's leading holiday resorts, but back then it was just a small, dusty fishing village. Our villa was a few hundred yards from the beach, where we launched the boat.

The long drive had not suited the outboard and I spent the first day struggling to start the engine while trying to keep it clear of the breakers. I was badly sunburnt because I was only thinking about the engine. Then, when my helpers were momentarily distracted by some local topless girls, the boat was swept ashore and a wave broke over the unprotected engine. To my great surprise, after a rest and a beachfront lunch, the engine actually started at the first attempt, and we were finally able to enjoy it after our long drive down.

We spent our days swimming, getting sunburnt or water-skiing; at night, we went out sardine fishing with the local fishermen. It was my first experience of the Mediterranean, and I fell in love with the hot weather and warm sea. It was also the first time I visited Gibraltar – one of the two great crossroads of Europe, the other being Istanbul – where we went up to see the monkeys and learnt the legend that if they ever left the rock then so would the British. We took a tour of the tunnels blasted into the rock where the army positioned their guns to enable them to shoot down at the Spanish below. The guns had to be modified so that they could shoot downwards. We also went to a bullfight in La Línea, where we were excited to see the toreadors putting spears in the shoulders of the bulls to weaken them before giving the matadors a chance to show their skills in fighting from courageous well-trained horses.

After an enjoyable week with sun, boating, water-skiing and exotic Spanish meals, it was time to head home. We reached Paris, where I wanted to achieve my dream of taking the boat on the River Seine and under the famous bridges of the city. This, unfortunately, took longer than expected, and we missed seeing the Louvre, which disappointed Anne. Finally, Anne and I left the others to enjoy Paris and drove home via the ferry.

Arriving back in England once more, I bade farewell to Anne, who hoped it was only temporary. I learnt later that she had been telling people we were sort of engaged. One week later, I was on a boat bound for Australia. I would not return to England for another two years.

CHAPTER FIVE

DOWN UNDER

Having graduated from the Royal Agricultural College, I knew I had two years to wait before the tenant working my farm was due to retire and the farm would be handed over to me. It felt like a long time, and I decided to make the most of this freedom and see the other side of the world. I suppose it was what you might call a gap year today. I had a cousin in Australia with a farm so, with the vague notion that I might do some practical farming myself, I set off.

Back then, it was not as common for a young man to travel to Australia as it is now. Australia was desperately trying to attract white immigrants, offering to pay for people's passage out in the hope of populating the country. The subsidised boat fare was just £10. However, I knew I wasn't going to stay for the full two years and therefore wouldn't be eligible for the subsidised fare – I would only have to repay it – so I paid the full fare of £200.

The passage took five weeks on a vintage coal-burning steamship. Ninety per cent of my fellow passengers were older Australians who had

With the steam ship SS Stratheden *before leaving for Australia*

taken the same boat out, disembarked at Italy to tour Europe, and then returned to Australia. There were only two girls my own age. As such, life onboard was somewhat limited, but I contented myself by reading Eric Hiscock's book *Around the World in Wanderer III*, and dreaming of sailing to the countries and ports as he did.

On the way, we made regular stops: the first at Gibraltar, where I paid another visit to the monkeys and enjoyed the view of the town and harbour; and the next at Cairo, where many of the buildings had been destroyed during the Suez Crisis seven years earlier, and where locals came out towards the ship in dugouts to dive for the coins we threw to them from the upper decks. The Suez Canal took us from the Mediterranean to the Red Sea, and we went ashore in Aden, then a British colony, where I bought some Balkan Sobranie cigarettes. I liked the look of them – they were strong, exotic and brightly coloured – but just two puffs of one put me off smoking for good. Following that, we stopped at Colombo in what was then Ceylon, my first tropical island, and took a bus tour to Katukurunda Beach, where I walked for the first time in a tropical rainforest behind the sandy beach and had my first tropical swim – such a luxury. On the way to Perth on the west coast of Australia, we went down to the engine rooms and saw the stokers shovelling coal into the boilers to keep the steam up. The temperature was 75 degrees Centigrade so we didn't stay down there long. I was amazed at how the stokers could work in the tropics in these temperatures. We reached Perth and went ashore for my first experience of Australia. Both Australia and the Aussies were wonderful. We then crossed the Great Australian Bight and experienced the only rough sea before entering the Bass Strait, and sailed up the east coast before entering between the two heads of Sydney Harbour, where I saw the famous bridge. It had been an amazingly calm trip, and there had only been one day when my little outboard powerboat would not have been happy on the seas.

I went to stay with my cousin for a few days and, while I was there, I bought myself a split-screen VW campervan. It was completely bare inside, so I kitted it out with a bed, a chair, some curtains that I made in a little shop with hired sewing machines, and two primus cookers. I could now enjoy the freedom of living and camping in Sydney. It looked like a commercial VW van, so I could park it anywhere for free. It became my home for the rest of my time in Australia.

I went to work on my cousin's farm beyond the Blue Mountains. I lasted about three weeks, spending my days walking through the crops in wellington boots, moving irrigation pipes several times a day in mud, and then doing the washing up at night. It was not really to my taste, so I soon abandoned it. I then started looking for jobs which I could do while travelling – amongst them selling encyclopaedias and making jewellery. Unfortunately, I did not have the skills for sales of that kind, so I had to find a more regular job. I joined the Health Division of the Immigration Deaprtment of Sydney Harbour, working with a team which, amongst other things, was contracted to fumigate ships. This involved boarding a ship late in the afternoon when it was empty. Wearing special gas masks and protective clothing, we emptied out large tins of wood shavings impregnated with hydrogen cyanide into the holds and, in the cabins, we dropped hydrogen cyanide balls into bowls of hydrochloric acid. Once each ship had been properly fumigated, we finished by opening up everything and allowing the ship to ventilate. Waiting for the chemicals to work could take some time and, as the youngest member of the team, the others would often allow me to leave early. I would spend the time enjoying Sydney life, once taking a girl to a drive-in movie. During the interval, I looked at my watch and said to her: 'I've stopped being paid … now.' One job was especially nasty, and the others decided that I was too young to do it as it involved picking up all the dead rats killed by the fumigation. I was let off that, but not before I heard the rats screaming as they died falling down the pipes where they had been living. It is a sound I don't think I shall ever forget. The best job I had was crewing the patrol boat, which cruised around the commercial harbour, to check that all the ships had rat guards on their shore lines. These were round discs with a cut-out to go over the line and a big lip that the rats could not climb over. I remembered these many years later when, in Trinidad, we had to have a 'deratisation certificate'.

Inspired by the Hiscock book I had read on the voyage out, I took a sailing course and, before it was finished, I thought I knew enough to buy my first-ever sailing boat: an elegant 28-foot Herreshoff ketch, called *Verdandi*. I moored it outside my workplace in Sydney harbour and in slack times at work and lunch breaks I could get it in shape. At weekends, I would usually take it out to sail round the harbour and to Botany Bay with my girlfriend. I then changed jobs so I kept it further north on the Hawksbury River, where we discovered wild beaches and forested hills with no developments, and where we could sail out to sea for some adventure and then back to our deserted anchorages, all within 10 miles of Sydney. Later, when I was due to leave Australia and needed to sell the

Relaxing on the Hereschoff-designed ketch Verdandi, *Australia.*

boat, a South African offered me a diamond for it. As tempting as the offer was, I had no idea how much the diamond was worth, so politely declined. It was the Apartheid era of South Africa, and smuggling money out via diamonds was common. Luckily, the man sold his diamond and bought my boat for cash: enough to pay for my trip home.

The beauty of these casual jobs was that I could leave them and move my home round Australia. I drove up the east coast, camping at all the isolated beaches up to the Gold Coast, and then further north to the Barrier Reef, where I took a boat ride out to the reef islands. It was timed so that we arrived there at low water and could walk all over the reef, which was just above water. I think, looking back, that this should not have been allowed, because we broke off a lot of coral, but walking on the coral to see it close up was what the trip was about.

Then I visited the Whitsunday Islands with their beautiful beaches just a few miles off the coast. I went as far up the coast north of Cairns as possible until the roads ran out – the VW camper, which isn't an off-road vehicle, could go no further from there. So, at that point I changed direction and headed inland across the Queensland mountains to the rugged and desolate outback. After two days of driving on dusty roads, the engine's cooling fins had become solid with hard dust and the engine blew up. I was towed to a little town where the problem was diagnosed. It needed a new engine and the garage arranged for one to be flown in the following day.

I heard the plane fly in and was excited to be soon on my way, but when I went back to the garage, I was told that the pilot had forgotten to take the engine off, so I had another day walking around this desolate landscape. I wondered how people lived in this isolated and barren area. The next day, the engine was dropped off and fitted and I was glad to be back on the road.

I travelled on to see the Mount Isa Mines, which were then the largest in Australia, with about fifty dumper trucks hauling the minerals out. The trucks were all very basic – only about eight had self-starters, the rest had to be bump-started and just kept going all day. The slopes were so steep that if the driver changed gear the truck would be liable to tip over backwards, so they stayed perpetually in first gear. The mine was the biggest hole I've ever seen.

I then headed north, back into the tropics, to Darwin. This was a basic and out-of-the-way town with little attraction, so I drove south on a tarmac road which had been built by the Americans during the war so as to be able to protect the country from a possible Japanese invasion. It was here that I saw the massive road-trains which consisted of three trailers behind a huge truck. It was a long time before I plucked up the courage to overtake them. I then went down to Alice Springs for more supplies before heading out to the amazing monolith of Ayers Rock. There were virtually no tourists, no hotels, and only two other people there. The rock was just stuck right in the middle of the desert, with nothing else visible. After I managed to climb to the top and enjoy the view of the vast outback, I walked down to take a photograph but, unfortunately, I was late and the best light had gone, so I stayed another day to make sure I got a decent one.

Uluru, formally known as Ayers rock is the largest single rock known in the world which I managed to scale prior to climbing being banned.

I continued on to the Olgas, another amazing collection of blue rocks sticking out of the desert, all accessible only by sandy tracks through some narrow gorges that were at their best at noon when the sun was directly overhead. Then, as the Americans had had no need to go beyond Alice Springs, the road reverted to dusty gravel. The next stop was Coober Pedy: a basic opal-mining town populated solely by Greeks and Italians. The Greeks, who were the most hardy and used to the highest temperatures, lived in tin shacks above ground, whereas the Italians found it cooler to live down inside the mines. These mines were extremely crude, hand-dug and with everything hauled out by hand. There was no security around any of them. It was amazing to see people able to live and work in such hot, dusty conditions for such little reward.

That marked the end of the gravel road, so I went down to South Australia to Adelaide, before driving along the coast into Victoria past the gold-mining towns of Ballarat and Bendigo and then, eventually, to Melbourne. Melbourne had a frightening traffic system with trams and, at one point, I found myself stuck in a tramline with an irate driver behind me; from then on, I kept clear of all tramlines. My visit to Melbourne was brief: I found little attraction there, and much preferred Sydney. Then I went back up to Canberra to see the capital – still, at that time, a new city with lots of space and few buildings.

The road from Melbourne to Sydney was mountainous with steep drops and steep climbs. It was extremely dangerous in those days because the trucks freewheeled down the mountains at high speeds, the drivers letting the momentum take them as far as possible up the other side before engaging the gears and grinding slowly up to the top again. At the end of the road, back in Sydney once more, it was time for me to find another job. I found one as a soil engineer on a road-building project, where I had to make sure that the soil was compacted. It was an easy job out in the country which I much enjoyed. When the time came for me to leave Australia, I told my bosses that I had to return to England temporarily, and asked if they would keep the job open for me, to which they agreed. My time in Australia had been wonderful, and I would have been happy to come back if, for any reason, something happened to the farm in Suffolk.

Although I was sad to leave Australia, I was excited about the long journey home. Rather than repeat my passage out in reverse, I decided to keep moving east, on to New Zealand and the South Pacific and then to the Americas. It would be a complete circumnavigation of the globe.

CHAPTER SIX
COMING HOME

The flight from Australia to New Zealand was special. In the morning, as the sun rose we saw a partial solar eclipse from the plane in a perfectly clear atmosphere. After landing in Auckland, I hitchhiked down the North Island, stopping at the Waitomo Caves, where the entire roofs of the caves were lit with fluorescent insects. From there, it was on to Rotorua. As soon as I entered the town, I couldn't fail to smell the pungent sulphur-dioxide fumes which permeate the whole town. I went for a swim in a naturally heated swimming pool, warmed by the ground heat in this thermal basin. The temperature was perfect, but the smell of sulphur was inescapable.

Wairoki's geothermal steam bores, New Zealand

I travelled down to the South Island and took a boat to see the fjords and an incredible upside-down waterfall, where the water flowed into a cup-shaped hollow and then came out as a vertical spout. From there, I flew over to Mount Cook with an overenthusiastic pilot who did a very sharp turn coming in to land, sufficient to bend the plane and cause the outside door next to me to fly open. He straightened up and the wind flow shut the door, but not before I was able to enjoy the wonderful view of Mount Cook and the snowfields. I continued by hitchhiking, something at which I was quite successful as I never had to wait long to be picked up. When I asked drivers why they had chosen to stop for me, they said it was because I had the look of an Englishman – rather than that of a beach bum – and they knew I would be harmless.

My next stop was Fiji. I flew to Nadi on the west coast and booked into a hotel. These were the days before *Lonely Planet* and, without a guide, I had to find my own way round. Always attracted by the water, I went down to the harbour, to see a smart-looking private motor yacht, so I approached some men nearby and fell into conversation with them. They said the yacht was a charter boat. Normally, they took guests to a beautiful archipelago not far offshore called the Yasawa Islands, but unfortunately the engines were then being serviced. I liked the sound of the islands so went down to the local docks, where I talked to a fisherman who said he was going out the following day and offered to take me with him.

Naturally, I was thrilled, and was down there early the next morning to join the boat. We had a lovely sail out on an old wooden boat with cotton sails, full of cargo for the islands. As soon as we were on our way, the crew streamed fishing lines, hoping for a free meal. We caught a big mahi-mahi which was then gutted and stowed out of the sun. The wind steadily increased with the sailing becoming more exciting, especially

With Fiji welcome garland

when I noticed that, where it was fixed to the mast, the sail was tearing. Being a keen sailor, I was particularly interested to see how this gaff-rigged boat would reef. I was rather surprised when the only action taken was to bear off the wind to reduce the strain on the sail, so that we began to run with the wind behind us on a new course away from the Yasawas.

We arrived at the first inhabited island late in the afternoon, sailing the boat on to the beach and tying it to a palm tree. I followed the skipper and his crew to see the headman of the village. After a brief chat, we were invited to partake in the traditional Fijian welcoming ritual called the Kava ceremony –

Nosilas Fijian villages welcoming in front of a Bread Fruit tree

where the visitor drinks a mildly narcotic and sedative concoction. Today, this tends be more a show for tourists than a true and traditional form of welcome, but back in 1965, I experienced what was then the normal welcoming ceremony for strangers.

Following this, we walked back towards the boat for dinner. On the beach, the crew bent down on their knees to scrabble round like mad in the sand, before pulling crabs out into the open air. When they had enough, they cooked them over a fire for the first course. The main course was the mahi-mahi we had caught from the boat on the way over, roasted over the fire and served on palm leaves. And then came the final course.

A Yasawas marriage house nearly built in Fiji

The men armed themselves with sticks and stones, walked into the palm-tree jungle and threw their missiles at the flying foxes or fruit bats which flew amongst the palms. They knocked enough of them down to the ground to provide a meal, brought them back and roasted them over the fire for our dessert. It was the most memorable three-course dinner I have ever had.

The next day, we set off with a light wind back towards the Yasawas and, feeling thirsty, the skipper landed us on a small, uninhabited island. The youngest crew member quickly climbed the nearest palm tree and cut down half a dozen coconuts. The captain neatly took a slice off the top with his machete and handed one to each of us to drink the milk. It was delicious and cool, in spite of the heat. When we had all drunk our coconut milk, we handed them back to the captain, who sliced them in half. Using the original sliver cut from the coconuts, we spooned out the soft, unripe coconut flesh to eat. The skipper told me that the trees all belonged to somebody but any person was allowed to take and eat an immature coconut. It was only when they were fully mature and the white coconut flesh was hard that the owner came and collected them, stripping the fibre from the husks and selling the dried flesh, called copra. This was the islanders' main source of income.

I had thought I could simply sail over to the Yasawas and find a hotel, but tourism there in those days was non-existent and there were no hotels. In fact, I learnt that I was the first European to stay on the island who wasn't an anthropologist. Nevertheless, the villagers kindly let me stay, and I spent three happy days there, feeling as if I was back in the era of Captain Cook. I couldn't help thinking that, in England, buying a house when you were married was a major investment, as the mortgage took most of your money. But on this delightful tropical island, when a couple were married, the whole village came together and built a house for them from palm leaves and saplings in less than a week. All the people I met

Returning from Yasawa to Lautoka with islanders back to the mainland

seemed happy with their way of life. I was invited to a special dinner as the guest of honour. They served a varied selection of the fruit and vegetables they could grow on the island. This was only my second dinner in a third-world country and I was their first tourist guest. Many of them had relatives who lived on the main island, Viti Levu, in the town of Lautoka where they had become used to living in a western, monetised society, and where everything had a price. When the relatives came back to this island, they much preferred the cash-free life.

After sailing away from the Yasawas once again, in the same boat filled with their produce to sell in Lautoka, I went to a village where there was a luxury resort which I couldn't afford. I managed to watch the famous fire-walking ceremony – where the local Fijians walked across a bed of burning embers without damaging themselves. It was an amazing feat, and I didn't fully understand how they were able to do it. I couldn't return that night so had to stay unofficially in the grounds of the hotel where I could enjoy the spectacular sunrise in beautiful surroundings.

I took a bus round the north coast of Viti Levu to explore the capital, Suva, and, as usual, went down to the harbour. It was full of local sailing boats that had brought in the produce from all the small outlying islands of Fiji.

I then flew to Tahiti, where the artist Paul Gauguin had spent much of his time. At the time, it was still totally undeveloped, but there were plans to modernise it with money from the French, who intended to compensate the islanders for the nuclear testing they carried out on the neighbouring atoll of Mururoa. On the plane there, I met two fellow tourists and we

Watching the fire dancing at a luxury hotel in Fiji

began to discuss which hotel to stay in. We each went our different ways to our hotels, none of which were great. We met the following day and the subject of the hotels soon came up again as none of us had had a good night. I learnt that one was a brothel, one had bed-bugs, and in my own hotel a rat had run over my sheet. None of us decided it was worth changing hotels but we could see why the town needed improving.

I took a trip round the island to see the Gauguin Museum. I was also able to see the beautiful Tahitian women who mesmerised Captain Bligh's crew so much that they mutinied on the *Bounty*. Bastille Day was a few days later and, since Tahiti is the main island of French Polynesia, the celebrations in its capital Papeete, were spectacular. The competitions were impressive – one involved Polynesian islanders competing to show how quickly they could split a coconut and strip the white meat out of it. Another competition required pinpoint accuracy as men hurled spears at coconuts; yet another was a canoe race. I was in awe of the sheer strength on display as sixteen huge Tahitian men per boat powered their way through the water, trying to inch themselves ahead of the other boats.

I island-hopped to walk on Moorea's magical deserted beaches and then took a seaplane to Bora Bora, reputed to be one of the most beautiful islands on earth, and certainly the most beautiful I had ever seen, as well as the only one on which I've ever slept out on the beach. I came to understand the expression 'throwing the anchor out' when I watched the pilot open the door of the seaplane and throw a bucket over the side – it acted as a brake. After a memorable night on the beach and a day on Bora Bora, I flew back to Tahiti.

Racing catamarans on Bastille Day, Tahiti

One of the most beautiful islands in the world, Bora Bora Island, Tahiti.

Then I flew on to Mexico. In those days, the flight from Tahiti to Acapulco was the longest non-stop flight in the world. For me, it was also one of the most nerve-wracking. The 707 was only capable of flying that distance with seventy passengers, half its normal load. Before we started, the pilot parked at the very end of the runway and revved up the military engines to the limit, which really screamed with the brakes still on. He then released the brakes and we set off down the runway and, instead of taking off at a steep incline, the plane just flew straight off the end of the

Our Polynesian flying boat

Xochimilao floating market in Mexico

runway. By the time we passed Papeete, a full four miles away from the airport, we were still at rooftop height – which is no height at all when the tallest house in the village is only two storeys. We did not climb above 15 feet until we were well clear of the island.

Acapulco may be spoilt now, but back then it was one of the most popular tourist towns in Mexico. Its cliffs were spectacular, and I enjoyed watching divers diving right out into the shallow water, just missing the rocks. On the other side of the peninsula, I found a quiet little bay called Caleta Beach, a name that was to be significant to me a few years later. After a night enjoying the nightlife, it was time to take a flight to Guatemala.

Guatemala City in those days was a fairly dangerous place, as the civil war which was to ravage the country until 1996 had just begun. A group of us from the plane went to the same hotel for the first night and, while we stood in the lobby checking in, there was a sudden bang from outside. I rushed to the window to see what it was and while I did so the Germans in the group lay down on the floor and hid. I could not see what had caused the bang.

From Guatemala City, I took a bus to Chichicastenango. There, in the midst of an extensive indigenous market, was the Church of Santo Tomás, shared by all the locals regardless of religion. At times, it was used by those who still practised the native animist beliefs; at others, the Catholics would use it for their own sacraments and ceremonies. In the evening, there was an amazing firework display with Catherine wheels attached to a metal frame and swivelling on homemade metal spindles. I had watched it being assembled just before it was lit.

Not far from Chichicastenango were ancient Mayan pyramids, which I climbed at night. I remember looking out over the large expanse of scrub-covered land below me and noticing a group of men digging something nearby under floodlights. For a brief moment, I wondered if they were there illegally or if, in fact, it was only I who was the illegal one. Then, finally, just south of the city, I hiked up the Volcán Pacaya, an active volcano which has been erupting continually since 1961. Luckily for me, it was then just smouldering.

Bordering Guatemala is Belize, which used to be called British Honduras. My memories of it are as a basic and impoverished place, a real West Indian jungle of a country. If the atmosphere in Guatemala was tense, in Belize it felt more so, especially for an Englishman. Pro-independence activists were everywhere, as only one year before, in 1964, Britain had granted British Honduras self-government. I stayed in Belize City, and was forbidden to travel into the jungle, where the real danger existed. People passing on the streets complained to each other about 'guats' – a derogatory term for the Guatemalan soldiers who had their eyes on Belize and were thinking of taking it over. It was the first place that Harrier jump jets were used as they could take off from small jungle clearings. I stayed there just long enough to enjoy my first warm swims in the Caribbean.

A plane took me from Central America to Miami. I checked into my hotel, pleased to be free from the ever-present danger bubbling under the surface in Belize. But a few hours later all hell broke loose. That night,

View from bus tour of the Atitlan Volcano, Guatemala

Hurricane Betsy, one of the most destructive tropical cyclones to hit Florida in recent history, blasted its way through Miami. I spent the night standing in the doorway of the hotel, watching as the hurricane did its work. Sheets of corrugated iron, 20 feet up in the air, flew down the high street; road signs were ripped out of the ground; cars looked as if they might be blown over at any second. The hotel staff told me not to venture outside; seeing corrugated iron flying down the streets made sure I took their advice, and I did not leave the hotel until the hurricane had passed the following morning. When I did finally leave, I wore a pair of shorts, for walking along the streets towards the beach involved wading through knee-deep water. Debris and destruction were everywhere.

My next destination was the Bahamas and there I could see how the poor housing had suffered so much more than the concrete of Miami. Many more trees were blown over or had lost their palm-leaved crowns. The shanty houses were now just heaps of rusty corrugated iron. The flat sandy islands felt the full force of the hurricane. Nassau itself, being well built, suffered only slightly. I then island-hopped north to my last tropical island, Grand Bahama, where a British developer called Jack Hayward – dubbed 'Union' Jack Hayward thanks to his well-known patriotism – was investing heavily, building and developing the island into a free port. Adjacent to it, Hayward was developing a new Florida-style waterfront housing project. I was tempted by a plot of this land and, as the price had been reduced since it was the last plot, I decided to buy it with the last of my holiday money so as to keep my sunshine dream alive.

I flew to my last stop in Bermuda, a sophisticated and modern island-city with no apparent poverty and luxury everywhere. It was not a place where I wanted to stay, so I finally headed home.

My time away had flown by. The truth was, I didn't particularly want to go home. Up to this point, I had been secretly hoping that my farm in Suffolk would fall through somehow – perhaps the tenant farmer would want to stay on for another three years – so that I could remain out here in the world and continue living this marvellous life. That was why I had kept the soil engineer job in Australia open, just in case I was able to return. But it was not to be. The farm was ready, and my two years abroad had come to an end. It was time to stop playing and start earning my living.

CHAPTER SEVEN
A FARMER'S LIFE

In my grandfather's time between the wars, farming was not profitable. As a result, much of the family land was left bare for shooting or let to tenants because it was only worth about £5 an acre, the equivalent of one and a half weeks of the agricultural wage. My grandfather was able to let some of the farms at ten shillings an acre to tenants who could then sub-let the warrening rights to the gamekeeper for the same ten shillings an acre – so that on these farms, the rabbits paid the rent.

When the war came, some of the tenants were growing old and the rest of the land was in hand just for shooting and so was not considered to be helping the war effort. The country was short of food, so the government put out the famous 'Dig for Victory' advertisements and took back farms that were not being farmed efficiently. This happened to my grandfather, who was seventy-four years old at the time, and the government gave his tenancies to farmers of their choice to be farmed more efficiently. The Ministry of Agriculture employed a civil servant to do all this – to dispossess my grandfather and put their tenants in – and he later moved on to be the head of the Royal Agricultural College when I was a student there. I had no respect for him as he was not a good tutor, and about a third of what he taught me was wrong.

When I returned from Australia in 1965, my father had arranged for the old tenant to retire and, in the five years following that, all the other tenants had retired, having farmed the land for about twenty-five years. One of the last farmers to go died with his boots and hat on. He was found by one of his workers still driving his tractor round and round his field, slumped over the wheel. A 150-acre farm joined up with the existing 350-acre farm I was about to take over. The tenant, who had not lived on the farm himself, died when I was in Mexico and his foreman lived in the farmhouse. There was also a good tractor driver and an odd-job man. This meant that, at the age of twenty-five, I was suddenly the farmer of 500 acres with three members of staff but little money. I was very lucky to have the farm but after two years working 12,000 miles away and travelling, and with no real certainty of being able to take over the tenancy, I was not fully prepared. My parents could not help with money either, so I went to their banks to request an overdraft of £10,000. Both banks refused but each offered me £5,000, which I gladly accepted, hoping that neither bank would find out about the other.

It is traditional for tenancies to end on the 11th of October, which equates to Michaelmas Day in the old calendar – hence the name 'Michaelmas tenancy'. In early October, the outgoing tenant had his farm sale, selling off all his cattle and equipment. As he had run the place as a mixed dairy farm, I was allowed to start work as soon as the harvest was over. The first thing I did was buy two tractors. We had a demonstration in the field opposite and I bought the most suitable one, a Massey-Ferguson 185 with a canvas cab. I borrowed my father's Land Rover and bought a corn drill from Gloucestershire and then I bought a plough and a cultivator locally.

The previous tenant had been a proper old boy; he used to go to the pub on his little grey Fergie. Under his watch, the farm had not done terribly well and the farmhouse was a wreck, the floor having collapsed in one of the rooms. The water was heated by a small log-burning stove which never gave out any heat; there was one light bulb in the kitchen and everything was painted brown. All the south-facing windows needed replacing and much of the brickwork needed repointing. Nothing had

The Red House Suffolk - home of the author

been done since my grandfather had bought it in 1916. As such, I had my hands full not just running the farm but making my house as habitable as possible. I bought cheap carpets and second-hand furniture and whatever I could find locally to improve the state of the house. Whenever I heard about a sale, I attended it. I remember buying a fantastic wardrobe for £10. A plumber installed central heating and a builder repointed the brickwork and changed the windows. Finally, in December 1965, the house was habitable, so my stepmother evicted me from Cockfield because I was putting my farming before coming back in time for meals, and I moved into it. I have lived there ever since, apart from a five-year period when I divorced when I rented a nearby house.

Soon after moving into the semi-furnished house with a small fridge I suddenly saw a large rat run behind it. I didn't want to chase it out and have it running round my house, so I picked up my .22 revolver, which was luckily loaded with small buckshot, and shot it dead with no damage to the fridge. A few weeks later, another even larger rat ran behind my new radiator and was shot in the same way. I had a licence for my revolver for target practice and often used to shoot rabbits from my Land Rover. Also it was a very effective way to control pigeons, which liked to eat my newly planted oilseed rape seedlings. The first shot made them fly and the last five shots while they were flying made them stay away, except for a

Steiger tractor planting corn in Suffolk

few which I killed with very lucky shots. This was before the massacre of Dunblane in 1996, when the government banned revolvers.

I was helped by having good men working for me. The foreman and the tractor driver were reliable workers and good with machinery. The odd-job man was less reliable and didn't last long. But I and my two remaining staff worked well together and were able to make a success of the farm. We built a grain dryer and six 100-ton silos to store the corn. The system was to plough the fields through the autumn and winter. I would start the men in the morning and as I was the only welder, I did any welding needed on the plough. Then I would often go out shooting. At the end of the shooting season on the 1st of February we would start to plant spring barley for malting in February and March. I carted out the seed corn and did the relief drilling and cultivating at lunchtime. We had to use all the dry days available in the spring so that the crops could be planted early to avoid drought. In those days my staff were very loyal and would help me in many ways. George, my foreman, had a wonderful wife who would clean and do my washing and then ask if I would be so kind as to take the clean washing back in my Land Rover instead of risking it on her bicycle. As a landlord and employer, I tried to treat all my employees well; they all had rent-free cottages while they worked for me and kept them after they retired until they died. George's house recently sold for over £650,000, well after I had sold it.

Case tractor and 12-furrow plough in springtime Suffolk

In 1967 we had to work hard to build another six silos. We finished on Wednesday night, took the scaffolding down on Thursday and took it back to the hirer. On Friday we loaded my sailing boat onto the same trailer I got bathed and changed and drove my Land Rover and boat down to near my fiancé's house to be ready for our wedding the next day.

After the celebrations we drove away in a hire car with all the decorations to get into the Land Rover to take the yacht to the South of France for our honeymoon. We had chosen this to enjoy the riviera on our own and decide how we could manage with an open cockpit. We could not and we covered ourselves wiith towels when not swimming. We left the yacht in a marina for my sister to have it for two weeks. When returning we visited our chosen boat yard and ordered *Caleta* with a covered cockpit.

When I got home I immediately went to the farm to see the men were all ready to start combining, so with no more ado they started and I drove the trailer to collect the corn from the combine and bring it back to the farm. Celia brought some sandwiches on a plate and left them by the silos. I eventually found them somewhat curled up. Celia was quick to learn and was soon driving grain trailers. When we had two combines Leslie, my main tractor driver, always did the first round of the field so that George could do the second. This was because George's main hobby was catching rabbits so when the rabbits heard his combine coming, they ran out in front and hid under the straw from Leslie's combine. George then stopped, climbed down and pounced where he had seen the rabbits hide and usually caught them. He often had several free meals to take home at night. When he retired his great pleasure on moonless nights was to silently lay long nets next to the hedge and then frighten the rabbits, who ran towards their burrows and into his nets. On a good night he could get up to 30. He was one of the last of the old countrymen from between the wars who had the skills to be able to make money from their hobby. That is what he did in his retirement.

In the late 1970s, spring cropping was not profitable on the light land as it suffered strong winds from the west. One of these lasted a week, taking the top two inches off the field and leaving the seed grains one inch above the soil, just attached by their roots. It was similar to the dust bowl in America in the 1930s. That was when I went over to winter cropping, which became more profitable and was less at risk from strong winds and spring drought. This change happened when my old foreman retired and I appointed a new manager called John Short. Likewise, the machinery changed, becoming much bigger. We had to start immediately after the combining to burn the straw and plough the fields. The tractors got much bigger too, and the best one we had was a 14-litre Cummings-powered 330-horsepower Case Steiger with eight large wheels pulling a twelve-furrow plough that would cover the ground quickly but was difficult to drive. Instead of an accelerator, the right-hand pedal was a decelerator. When you put your foot down it would slow the tractor down, so it was just used when turning. I only drove it occasionally, and it took a lot of getting used to with three gear levers. Silencing was minimal and, even though half-deaf, I have heard its deep roar a mile away. Some of the London weekenders here soon realised country life was not their nineteenth-century dream. The tractor was a pure American prairie tractor.

At harvest time everybody was busy and I had to relief-drive the combines at lunch time as well as being the only driver of the farm lorry, which I used for grain carting. We began with an ex-military Bedford RL and ended with an 8x4 wheel tipper in which I once had to haul sugar beet to the factory on Christmas Day. I also had to run the grain dryer, checking each load was correctly dried and making sure that the drier was set to dry that day's grain overnight before they started the combining after the dew had gone in the morning. As the farm grew, the crop yield increased and the dryer started to become too small, so I frequently had to spend the night beside it in my campervan to ensure it kept going all night and was ready for the next day's crop. After one season of this, I knew it was time I bought a bigger dryer. I finished at about 11 p.m. most nights. Nobody wanted rain but when it did come, harvesting stopped and we could all enjoy an early night. The men could put the fertiliser, spray and plant the sugar beet when there was less pressure in the spring. My income was totally dependent on getting a good harvest and making sure all the crops were planted before the heavy winter rains started. I normally managed to finish planting by the 1st of October. After the harvest, we saved our own seed corn, dressed and cleaned it and carted it out to the corn drill.

Over the years I settled into this routine. It was most important for me to be at the farm for the harvest and the winter drilling, for that is what I built my life and income around. After the harvest I could enjoy the shooting season with friends before going to the Caribbean for sailing.

CHAPTER EIGHT
SHOOTING

Shooting is a tradition which has been in my family for generations. For my father, it was his life, as it was for *his* father too. My grandfather, Sir Ralph Blois, one of the finest shots in England, was really only interested in partridge shooting. He recorded all the birds he shot in his life in his game books and specifically noted every time he reached 1,000 partridges. The final recorded total in his game books was 68,000: an astonishing feat.

These game books date back to 1829, when Sir Charles Blois, the 7th Baronet and my great-great-grandfather, began keeping them at the Cockfield estate. In my grandfather's days, cars were mainly slow and open, so transport to shoots was often by the more comfortable train. In the last century the Cockfield estate extended to more than 7,000 acres. My father told me a story about a local landowner who decided towards the end of a season that he had too many grey partridges left and asked my grandfather to come and shoot some of them. The partridges were driven over him fast and he shot well. When the gamekeeper came to pick up, he asked my grandfather how many he had shot – to which he replied: 'I don't know, but count the cartridges. I only missed one.' The gamekeeper picked up forty-five cartridges after that drive; the landowner may well have regretted inviting my grandfather.

My grandfather's guns were bought from James Purdey & Sons, who have been making guns since 1814, the year before the Battle of Waterloo. They have been at Audley House since 1883, and it is not only where my grandfather purchased his guns but also where I visited to see their records. Their gunroom manager, Dr Nicholas Harlow, was kind enough to show me both the records of my grandfather's guns and his accounts as well. His first pair was purchased in April 1889, the year after he became the 9th Baronet. These were 12-bore hammer guns and cost £139 13s. including their case. I was told that these were already somewhat out of fashion, as most of the company's production had turned to hammerless guns by that date.

OPPOSITE:
Sir Ralph Blois with Percy Muttitt's father as loader in 1912

51

Sir Ralph Blois' pair of hammerless guns purchased from James Purdey in 1895

My grandfather appears to have been convinced to make the change after being loaned an example to try in the summer of 1894. His new pair of hammerless ejector guns was delivered in July 1895, at a cost of £178 10s., part of which was funded by returning his original pair for £40 in credit against his invoice. He bought a third gun in October 1897 for £84 5s., and a fourth gun in June 1907 for the same amount. He reconfigured the guns to operate as two pairs – the original pair being refitted with true-cylinder barrels, and the two later guns having fully choked barrels. True-cylinder guns give a wider shot spread best for closer birds, leaving fully choked barrels for higher or more distant birds. This was done so that he could shoot the *Tir aux Pigeons* – a forerunner of modern clay-pigeon shooting when reared pigeons had many feathers plucked out, so they would fly irregularly, would be let out of traps and therefore be extremely hard to shoot. To make the shooting harder and to increase the size of the wager the distances from the guns to the traps were increased. I inherited Numbers 1 and 4 of this set, and they served me throughout my shooting career. The only downside was that my grandfather was right-handed, and his guns had extremely light triggers, which meant that, when I first used them, both barrels fired together! As this was uncomfortable for a young man with his first shots, I had them suitably adjusted.

Purdey's accounts also show the number of cartridges my grandfather bought. Although at times the quantities were relatively small, he purchased 16,500 cartridges in the 1912/1913 season, and nearly a quarter of a million over the course of his shooting career. Even so, Dr Harlow believes that he probably supplemented his Purdey cartridges with others bought locally, or was being provided with them when he shot on other estates. When he was at home, my grandfather appears to have preferred to shoot alone, or with only one other gun, and at the close of each season he would tally up the game together with his personal thoughts on the season at the end of that year's game book. His comments often complained how the June and July storms killed all the young partridges, a fact repeated by my own gamekeeper Percy Muttitt fifty years later, who jokingly said the only solution was to give each covey an umbrella.

It's no surprise that shooting became part of my life too – my twenty-first birthday present from my father was four days' consecutive shooting after Christmas with some friends from Dublin, Charles Dewhurst and David Cant. I took up shooting in earnest when I began farming in 1965. My father was running the shoot then, when it was all very different from the shoots you find today. One noticeable difference were the birds. The game in this part of Suffolk used to be composed entirely of wild birds and, in particular, grey partridges. In 1959, 450 grey partridges were shot off 450 acres on my farm alone, an incredible number. Today, however, there are no grey partridges left, and all the game are reared birds. This is not solely down to humans, as marsh harriers are also to blame. Because partridges feed over a small area, the marsh harriers were easily able to fly back day after day to pick off their chicks. In my grandfather's time, the avian predators were 'taken away' by the keepers. In reality they were killed, but the euphemism was used because it was illegal.

Sir Gervase Blois after a shoot with keepers Muttitt, Dade, Smith and List, with the game

Early morning duck shooting with all my father's gamekeepers Suffolk 1960. (Mr Brown, Percy Muttitt, Charles Blois, Percy Smith, Monty Dade, Jack List)

When my father died in 1968, the shoot passed to me, and it became an important part of my social life. In the 1970s and 1980s, I was sometimes shooting five or six times a week on private shoots. I had a part-syndicate, some of which I took over from my father, of paying guns to ease the cost of the shoot, and would then have three or four guests to join me to make a full team of eight guns. It was an enjoyable time, and as the season neared each year, I would find myself eagerly looking forward to it.

Fifty years ago, when you ran a shoot on your land, you needed a good wild-bird gamekeeper. His main job in the spring was to kill all the vermin – stoats, weasels, hedgehogs, rats, crows and magpies that would eat all the eggs from the ground-nesting game birds which laid in the hedgerows. These were left to grow thick and wide to give cover from avian predators such as magpies and crows. Now all the birds are hatched in an incubator by a game farm and reared in pens. The hedges are cut neatly back so the wild birds have no way of breeding successfully. In the late 1950s there were a lot of wild partridges and, as a consequence, there were also a lot of poachers. Nowadays, a pheasant is worth barely 50p and the average agricultural wage is about £200 per week. Then, the average agricultural wage was £10 a week, and a brace of pheasants was worth £2.50. Hence, there was a considerable incentive for poaching, and a pressing need to keep poachers at bay.

Gamekeepers have worked for my family since the mid-nineteenth century and two generations of the Muttitt family were keepers for me,

With gamekeeper Percy Muttitt collecting birds after a day's shoot in Suffolk

my father and my grandfather for almost a hundred years. I was fortunate to have employed Percy Muttitt for fifteen years of traditional wild bird shooting, when I learnt much about wildlife from him.

Percy Muttitt was something of a local legend. Indeed, he was even the subject of an Anglia Television documentary called *The Keeper*, filmed and broadcast in 1975. You can still watch it today as it can be found on YouTube. The documentary captures Muttitt perfectly, as he rides his bicycle through country-lane puddles with a brace of plump pheasants dangling from its handlebars, or as he strides purposefully through the Suffolk fields, gun in hand and faithful dogs never far from his side. I had been given a veto on all aspects of the film to counteract a biased and distorted BBC anti-shooting film. In the end, I only asked for one part to be removed, to which they agreed.

I still have the programme on VHS, and I like to watch it sometimes, to remind myself of Muttitt and his wonderful ways. He was at least thirty years older than me, but we spent a lot of time together and developed a close friendship. He had that particular Suffolk accent which you don't hear much now. I remember that I could understand Muttitt, but there were friends of his who, when they spoke in their broad Suffolk accent, I couldn't understand at all. He was a gentle and considerate man with an innate understanding of the natural world. He spent his entire life in this tiny part of Suffolk. It was a life which he was perfectly content with.

The Muttitt family have a remarkable Second World War story. They lived in a cottage on the estate, about a mile from my house, and one morning Percy's son, Mickey, a ten-year-old aircraft enthusiast, rushed outside his house on hearing the familiar whirr of an aeroplane. It was late in the war – August 1943. Mickey looked upwards to see an American B-24 Liberator pass overhead. He watched as it made its way towards the coast, seeing flames coming out of its tail until, suddenly, the plane exploded in a deafening fireball. The plane was loaded with over 21,000 pounds of Torpex high explosive and blew up in mid-air over New Delight Covert, Blythburgh Fen, near his grandfather's house on the heath. It was the largest explosion ever recorded over Britain, damaging 147 houses. Mickey immediately cycled over to see if his grandfather was all right. He was, thankfully, but for the loss of a few windows. Mickey and his brother and their families still use the house at weekends.

The memory of the disaster stayed with Mickey for a long time. 'It happened more than a mile and a half away, but it still knocked the plaster off our ceiling,' he later said. Almost two decades after the explosion, Mickey learnt that one of the most famous men in the world had secretly visited the crash site: John F. Kennedy. It turned out that the pilot of the plane had been none other than his older brother, Joe Kennedy Jr, who had been piloting a 'flying bomb'. The plane was supposed to have been set to autopilot and Kennedy should have bailed out before reaching the coast, but with flames coming out of the tail, the plane exploded while he was still inside. If he hadn't died that day over our farmland, it's likely he would later have become president of the United States of America.

When Percy Muttitt retired, I was lucky to find Stanley Kerslake to replace him. Stanley was my keeper from 1985 until his retirement in 2000. He was a great character, a great friend and the last good keeper we had. After him, we tried a few others, but none ever matched Stanley's expertise, so we gradually wound down the shooting operation. He knew my land intimately – indeed, as a child he had lived in the Dairy Cottage at Cockfield Hall. He once told me about a particular night during the war when he had gone to bed and fallen asleep. That was the night Cockfield was bombed by the Germans. The roof of Stanley's bedroom fell in and, if Stanley had been lying the other way round in bed, it would have fallen on him and killed him.

Stanley was very skilled at his job. He had a special way with animals, and he also had an interesting way with people. Once, when he found a man looking for game, he escorted him to the road, but the man ran back on to the land. Stanley escorted him to the road once more, and again the man ran back on to the land. So, what did Stanley do to put an end to this little game? He threw the man face-first into a gorse bush; the man did not come back again.

There is a part of my land colloquially known as Toby's Walks, named after 'Black Toby', a black drummer boy hanged in chains for the rape and murder of a local girl in 1750, and whose ghost is still said to haunt these parts. Much of Toby's Walks was bracken and heathland, and people would regularly park their caravans and dump their old pianos and other rubbish there. Stanley had some most effective tricks for dealing with this kind of thing. If someone refused to leave, he'd say: 'Right then, I'll set you on fire.' After which, he would proceed to spray a can of water round the caravan, pretending that it was petrol. Or he would tell the gypsies that there was anthrax in the fields which would kill their horses. Few remained there for long after a talking to from Stanley.

Once, I decided to approach one of the caravans myself. I knocked and, within seconds, the door was filled by a very large man.

'You can't stay here,' I said. 'Do you mind moving?'

'I'm a chief inspector in the Metropolitan Police,' the man shouted at me. 'What are you going to do about it?'

I didn't know if he was telling the truth, but he was a big, aggressive fellow and he probably could have been a chief inspector. I chose not to ask any more questions because, in my experience, you just don't question a large policeman. I mumbled a few words and then, later, decided to deal with the problem once and for all. The following year, we tore up all the bracken and planted rye in its place, which is best grown on poor land. Now that it was working farmland, the caravans, pianos and chiefs of police stopped coming.

A rare opportunity meeting another yacht in the Atlantic who took a photograph of Caleta II sailing.

PART III:
SAILING AWAY

CHAPTER NINE
VIVACITY

It was not long before I began to miss the boat I had owned in Sydney, and I soon decided that I wanted to buy a sailing boat in England. I started to look for one while I was courting Celia Pritchett, and she happily joined me. Indeed, we even became engaged while we were looking for a boat together. We had travelled to Holland to view one and, during that visit, I proposed to her. Our engagement dinner was paid for by the boat seller: an exotic and delicious *rijsttafel* consisting of eight or nine different Indonesian dishes. *Rijsttafel* literally means 'rice table'. I was glad that Celia shared my love of sailing. In the past, I had been with other girls who, when a problem occurred with my boat, just sat in the car and waited while I resolved the issue by myself. But Celia was always willing to help and to become fully involved. She was very good crew. We went together on many voyages and sailing was our hobby.

Celia's parents organised our wedding in Mayfield, East Sussex, and we were married in the local church in 1967. Our honeymoon was a trip to the south of France on the small boat I had temporarily bought for coastal sailing: a 20-foot day sailor we called *Vivacity*. We towed *Vivacity* behind my father's Land Rover down to the Mediterranean. We launched it opposite the Porquerolles and then sailed over to them to enjoy a car-free island. The holiday was not without its difficulties but, overall, we had a good time: cruising along the French Mediterranean coast, stopping at Cannes, circumnavigating the islands, drinking good wine and soaking up the culture. Once, finding a secluded and private cove, we took a dip in the sea without our swimming clothes, and just managed to make it back on board and get dressed before a French gunboat turned up and told us we shouldn't have been there. We also learnt first-hand about the importance of cover. Sitting out on deck with nothing to protect us from the Mediterranean sun except for towels draped over our legs, we realised the necessity of shade, and decided that we definitely wanted a boat with a covered cockpit. At the end of our honeymoon, we flew back from the south of France, leaving *Vivacity* in the marina. My sister Gillian then took it with a friend for a fortnight's cruise before trailing it back to England.

One year later, in 1968, my father died. He was the 10th Baronet and, as such, after his death I became the 11th Baronet. Suddenly, at the age of twenty-eight, I was a Sir. There is an important distinction between knights, who are also Sirs, and baronets in that knights are created, but baronets are all hereditary. When a knight dies, his title dies with him. When a baronet dies, his title passes on to the next rightful male heir in the family. And in that case, it was me. Thus, I was never knighted, never had the Queen tap me on my shoulders with a sword and never had a ceremony to commemorate the occasion. One day, my father was the Sir of the family; the next day, it was me.

Celia, my brother Rodney and I were sitting down to dinner when the telephone rang and it was my stepmother calling to tell us that our father had died. As my father had stomach cancer it was fully expected. It was a subdued meal until Rodney congratulated me on being a Sir, although we both knew that he wished the title was his. Then Rodney asked me how long he should wait before getting married, to which I replied about three months. He agreed. About a month later, after courting two girls at the same time, he decided on the daughter of a lord and so a lady in her own right who, as the owner of a stately home, would suit his position. What I never knew until later was that before our father's death he had booked a grand suite on the last voyage of the liner *Queen Elizabeth*. My suggestion that he wait three months fortunately coincided with the start of the voyage, which became his honeymoon cruise. The cruise was absolutely made for him; when the selected guests went to the captain's table, his wife's name, Lady Caroline Blois, was formally called and then the master of ceremonies paused for a moments before saying: 'And, er… Lord Blois.' It was the icing on his wedding and his honeymoon.

There is not much that comes with a baronetcy, as one might expect. There are always problems with inheriting and maintaining a war-damaged stately home and its many estate cottages on controlled rents of six shillings a week, especially when it has only very limited farm rent income. There are many large stately homes which can only be managed by opening them to the public as a major tourist attraction. Luckily for me, we all knew, before our father died, that Rodney desperately wanted to live in the big house. I had no desire to, being happy restoring my farmhouse and having all the land to farm. Our father knew that Rodney would have trouble maintaining it so it was left to him on condition that he lived in it. He and Caroline had to paint all the windows to keep up appearances. As they could not afford to repair the roof, they had to live with permanent leaks and rotting timber. It was only when Cockfield was sold that I saw my grandfather's plans for a modern four-bedroom house within the old undamaged part of the building. The drawing dismissed the wing that my father and brother lived in as staff quarters. My father had chosen to live that way and use the war-damage money to build two flats instead for income. I was glad not to have the nightmare of maintaining this enormous house with its grand three-storeyed hall. I once went to a big lunch that Rodney gave which took a 50-kilogram gas cylinder to heat the hall just for that meal.

There are, regrettably, some disadvantages to a baronetcy. Once, the local police sergeant came into my office with an assistant and declared: 'You have deliberately damaged a car and threatened the owner. I am now charging you and, because of who you are, we are going to make this stick.' There was a long discussion, all written down by the assistant and taped by me. Two days later the sergeant returned and admitted that all the 'facts' had turned out to be totally untrue when he went back to investigate them properly. It sometimes seems hard to find an honest policeman in Suffolk.

The advantages of a baronetcy are, of course, the title, an interesting history and a fascinating family tree going all the way back to St Arnulf, Bishop of Metz (AD 582–640), and King Ealhmund of Kent (r. 784), down through William the Conqueror and to his grandson, King Stephen. Other than that, it has had little impact on my life. Perhaps the most significant thing to come with it is the fact that I have the living of two parishes, Blythburgh and Walberswick, and with that the power to appoint the vicar. I've done this only once, in the late 1960s, when the two parishes were combined as one. The bishop and I disagreed over who it should be. I chose the new vicar because he was the least pious and hand-rubbing of the candidates, and he turned out to be very successful indeed. He was popular with the locals and stayed for eighteen years before being promoted to the Newmarket diocese. It always felt slightly odd that it should be me, an atheist who described the Bible as just another fairy tale, who appointed a vicar, but I was happy to fulfil it as that was my role as patron of the combined living.

CHAPTER TEN
CALETA

The small plot of land I had bought in Grand Bahama had appreciated considerably over only three years and, when I sold it, I was able to use the money to buy a new sailing boat, a Salar 40, which we decided to call *Caleta* after the lovely little quiet beach I had discovered in Acapulco in 1965 (*caleta* is a Spanish noun meaning cove or small bay). We had to choose a name that was not duplicated on the British Register of Ships and that was easy to say over the radio.

At the time, our 40-foot *Caleta* was the second-biggest fibreglass boat built in England. I had it built in Essex to a design from Laurent Giles, who was best known for designing some marvellous large cruising yachts and the sloop *Wanderer III*, which Eric Hiscock – the author of the books I had read on my crossing to Australia five years earlier – had sailed round the world. In addition, I commissioned a beautiful teak interior for *Caleta* from Essex Yacht Builders. They wanted to build the best boat they could as they planned to show *Caleta* at the 1968 Earl's Court boat show. Unfortunately, this meant that many of the buyers at the show began to order the same interior for their boats, rather than the builders' standard kind. They weren't particularly pleased with me about that, but at least they didn't sell many more of their mass-produced 'kitchen interiors'.

Once it was ours, we sailed with *Caleta* across the North Sea and up and down the east coast and then, in 1969, set off on a test cruise from Lowestoft to Cork. In total, we spent three weeks on the journey, sailing to Cork in stages, around to the south-west of Ireland, and then making our way back via the same route. Celia and I were joined by David Cant on the way out and Peter King on the return.

Sailing then was different from sailing today. Nowadays, you just set up the GPS and it'll tell you your course, distance to travel and speed and will show you your current position. But there were no such things as GPS in the 1960s. We used a hand-bearing compass to take bearings of prominent landmarks such as lighthouses and land promontories.

On the way out, David and I argued more than once when headlands were misidentified. He came from Cork and thought he knew the lights, but I often disagreed with him, so we tended to sail between them until we decided which of us was right. On the way back with Peter, I asked him to keep watch one night while I was asleep, giving him instructions to wake me if he saw any lights which might be approaching ships. The next morning, Peter admitted to me that he had nearly woken me up when he had seen a large bright light coming closer and had begun to panic. He had stopped himself just in time when he realised that the light wasn't a ship at all but the moon.

We dropped Peter off at Falmouth and then headed for the Solent as we had heard that Alec Rose, a greengrocer from Southsea, was returning from his single-handed round-the-world trip on his yacht *Lively Lady*. This was two years after Sir Francis Chichester completed the first single-handed trip, on his yacht *Gypsy Moth V*. Since we were so close, we thought it would be fun to join the parade of boats escorting him to Portsmouth. Soon after, an aerial photograph of the parade was published in the papers, and we were delighted to see *Caleta* included in it.

CHAPTER ELEVEN
TO THE MEDITERRANEAN

The Ireland trip had been a success, so, in 1970, we decided to sail *Caleta* away from England for the final time, and set off for the Mediterranean.

The last time I had taken a boat out on the Mediterranean had been on our honeymoon; the time before that it had been the long-ago trip to Spain with my friends after graduating from the Royal Agricultural College. On both those occasions, I had towed the boats down through the continent. This time, we sailed there.

Before we set out, we made sure to stock up with whisky and gin at 50p a bottle from Yarmouth, taking advantage of the fact that a yacht leaving the country could buy cheap duty-free alcohol. We sailed down from Lowestoft to Calais in rough conditions and my friends, Charles and Jane Dewhurst with their young son Sam, were seasick on the crossing. They were relieved to reach Calais, where they chose to return by ferry as they'd had enough of *Caleta's* violent motion. Another crew joined us in Calais, but he was also sick as we sailed back to Newhaven, so we left him there and continued on our own.

Once we reached the Solent, we went to the Isle of Wight and visited Beken of Cowes, the well-known marine photographer. We asked him to take photographs of *Caleta*, which he did from his powered launch. They were not as good as he had hoped because I was afraid to sail as close to the buoy as he would have liked. After that, we continued our Channel crossing to Guernsey for a final stock-up of English food, and then headed along the rocky Brittany coast. Luckily, there are good lighthouses there, so we knew where we were all the time, and were easily able to find the port of L'Aber-Wrac'h: a long, deep channel running to a calm bay.

The next day, we headed out again, somewhat nervous about the passage through the Raz de Sein, with its fast current. We timed it right, so had the wind and the current behind us. We were able to go through at about 10 knots. Then we went into the little town of Bénodet for a nice French evening meal, before sailing on to Saint-Nazaire, where we anchored and went to meet my friend Peter and his French friend François de Dufort, at François's house on the Loire.

The next day, Peter and François joined us for the sail down the French coast to Spain. We stopped on the way in La Rochelle to see the city and then sailed overnight down to San Sebastián. As we approached the city, we had a great deal of trouble identifying the port, and mistook the red traffic lights for navigation lights, so we had to watch them at length to find out which they were and what was their frequency. Each navigation light has a different light frequency enabling it to be identified by the number of flashes and the number of seconds it is on and off.

Peter had a brother in San Sebastián called Andrew, with whom we stayed. We were treated very hospitably, but we had great difficulty with the Spanish hours – such as having dinner at 11.30 p.m. to midnight. The two brothers helped us obtain our papers for Spain before we set off again. It was still the Franco era and obtaining documentation was difficult.

We headed along the north coast of Spain to Bilbao, then to Cedeira, past A Coruña, and then from Cabo Vilano to Camariñas. The north-west coast is one of the most rugged coastal areas of Spain, which we much enjoyed as we sailed round Finisterre to Arousa. Then we headed down the coast of Portugal to Cascais. We experienced our strongest winds when sailing down the Portuguese coast at over 7 knots with no sails up. We left the boat for a few days to explore Lisbon and the surrounding countryside in comfort after a local yachtsman offered us free use of his car. Time was then running out, so we had to continue down the west coast, which was without any harbours, until we rounded Cape St Vincent. From there we sailed east along the Algarve and the Andalusian coasts down to Cádiz, where we stopped and went ashore to see the impressive forts of old Spain from where their navy had left to fight the Battle of Trafalgar. We set off for Gibraltar, but the Levanter wind blowing through the straits was far too strong. This was the first time we turned *Caleta* round because of the strength of the wind, and we waited in a little harbour in Tarifa. We had to enter Spain again from Portugal in Tarifa, and were much amused when the customs officers took down all our details in metres when we had given them in feet – making our boat seem enormous.

The next morning the wind dropped and we sailed to Gibraltar, where we left *Caleta* so that we could return home for the harvest. We came back again in October for a two-week cruise. Our first stop in the

Celia posing on Caleta *at anchor*

Mediterranean was Fuengirola, which I remembered fondly from my holiday there in 1963: the little village with its fishing boats, its dusty streets and its welcoming locals. Just seven years later, in 1970, I returned to a completely changed place. It was not a good time to be living under Franco's regime. The previous year, in 1969, Franco had tried to force the British to negotiate over Gibraltar, which resulted in a border closure between Gibraltar and Spain, one that was to last until 1985. The student revolts in Spanish universities were being repressed by armed police, causing widespread violence. Spain was not free from Franco's regime until his death in 1975. This was obvious the moment Celia and I arrived in Fuengirola. There was no harbour, no marina nor breakwater, so we anchored off the beach and took the dinghy into shore. A member of the Guardia Civil strode up to confront us. We presented the papers we had acquired in San Sebastián to him, but he wasn't pleased with them. We were, he said, not allowed ashore because we hadn't got the correct papers. We managed to explain that we needed to buy food and only wanted to visit the local supermarket. Eventually, after much discussion, he agreed, but only on condition that he escort us the entire way there, stand outside the door while we shopped, and then escort us the entire way back again. If we didn't agree to this, the only options were our immediate departure or our immediate arrest. We agreed and allowed him to escort us.

After visiting a few harbours and ports along the coast without further trouble, we sailed back to Gibraltar, took all the sails off *Caleta*, laid it up with extra mooring lines for safety, and flew home in a Monarch aeroplane from which we had to disembark because of a bomb scare. In those days, flights out of Gibraltar were often a problem because of having to stay out of Spanish airspace, which meant turning very quickly after taking off. We were told that air traffic control was extremely vigilant before arrivals to make sure there were no Spanish planes or military aircraft in the air. Furthermore, the main road from Gibraltar to Spain ran across the runway so had to be kept clear for the planes. The Spaniards regularly made the border as awkward as possible for the British by deliberately delaying crossings, even though most of the workforce in Gibraltar were Spanish.

CHAPTER TWELVE
THE GOOD OLD DAYS

I like to think of 1971 to 1976 as the good old days. As each year passed, Celia and I sailed all the way round the Mediterranean coast in a clockwise direction, taking in, amongst other places, Italy and Greece, the Adriatic and the Ionian Seas, Turkey and Tunisia. A pattern began to develop: we would sail during four to six weeks in the latter half of each spring, moor *Caleta* in the water wherever we ended up, and return home for the harvest. Then we would go out again for a shorter sail in October before the shooting season started. Finally, we would take *Caleta* out of the water to keep it safe throughout the winter, and then begin the cycle all over again the following spring.

In 1971, we returned to Gibraltar, where we had left *Caleta* the previous year. We sailed along the south-east coast of Spain, a little nervous when we went into port in case we received the same aggressive treatment afforded us in Fuengirola. Fortunately, that had been a one-off, and we encountered no problems whatsoever. We sailed up the east coast and then headed for the Balearics to avoid the Costa Brava. We had some great sailing around the small creeks and islands of Ibiza and Mallorca where we could tie up in little towns and enjoy Spanish meals. We started going out late at night as everything in Spain was lively until well after midnight and then remained quiet in the morning. We continued on to Menorca, where we met up with Peter and François once more. We relied on François to pick up the weather forecast towards Corsica where he said it was good, so we set off with our full crew. Soon, however, the weather deteriorated and became rough, with a strong northerly wind. Peter ceased to be a good crew, and was once seen with his feet on the bunk and his head in the lavatory, muttering: 'Why can't the bloody boat stay still?'

We eventually reached Ajaccio, where everybody started to feel better. We hired a car and had a scenic drive round the mountains of Corsica. Peter and François flew home shortly afterwards, having decided that sailing was not their sport.

From Ajaccio, we headed south and anchored off a little island with several other boats. The wind became very strong, which was not a problem for us as *Caleta* had a good anchor, about 50 per cent bigger than recommended, because we liked to stay put when we were anchored. But the boat in front was not as well equipped, and started to drift down towards us with its dinghy. I quickly shouted to Celia to get the breadknife. I cut the dinghy line and let the dinghy go to one side and the yacht to the other, otherwise we would have had the weight of two boats on our anchor bouncing against the side of us. Luckily, the yacht stopped in shallower water and they managed to pick the dinghy up on the shore in the morning.

We continued on south to Porto Cervo in Sardinia, which, by that time, was just turning into the millionaire's playground it is known as today, and then on to Malta. For two days, we motored down the east coast of Sardinia to Sicily in totally flat conditions: 150 miles a day with no wind at all. It became extremely hot, and my method of cooling off was, every four hours, to stop the engine, dive overboard, and then swim until I caught up with the boat as it slowly came to a stop. Sometimes, when *Caleta* was sailing at less than 2 knots, I would dive off the bow and then swim until the boat caught up with me. It was both a relief from the heat and good exercise. Celia was not confident enough for this, so she stayed on the boat. We were glad we had the covered cockpit to keep us out of the direct sun, and to have a breeze through the window.

We left *Caleta* in a marina in Malta to go back for harvest, and then returned again in October for our autumn break, sailing up to Sicily, where we climbed Mount Etna. We took a bus to the cable car station and then rode to the summit, where we looked down into the active volcano and then round at the glorious panoramic views from the rim of its caldera. It was a wonderful day, and very different from the next time we went to Mount Etna five years later. Then, the cable car was knocked down by an eruption, forcing us to walk up and find that, once we reached the top, the volcano was so smoky that we could barely see a thing.

We returned to Malta to find Dom Mintoff had become prime minister. It was a repressive time and everything was unnecessarily difficult, so we were glad to leave and return home. We left the boat inside a large hangar which had once been used by the military as a flying-boat base.

The next year, we did the long sail across southern Italy to the Adriatic Sea. I was a little nervous about this as Albania was totally out of bounds to yachts and tourists. My nautical charts listed a number of minefields off its coast, so I made sure to give them a wide berth. Once we passed them, we came to the mountainous coast of Yugoslavia, anchoring in the Bay of Kotor, in present-day Montenegro. It was a beautiful place. Back then, there were no cruise ships, just two or three yachts and nothing more. We climbed up the high walls of the old town built into the mountain and looked down from its fortifications, which were in near-perfect condition.

We cruised up the islands of Yugoslavia, which were totally deserted. In the mornings, we would wait in the bays, swimming until the wind picked up, and then would sail with the day breeze with no other yachts in sight to another deserted anchorage. It was ideal stress-free cruising. However, as we sailed north, the weather began to deteriorate. There was clearly a gale coming. It was the bora: a gale-force wind blowing down from the mountains. We went up into a bay which we thought would be sheltered, but the wind somehow turned and came into the bay, putting us on a lee shore and leaving our stern only about 50 yards from the beach. It was a frightening time, and we kept the engine running continuously so that, if the anchor did drag, we could motor into it and try and keep control. Having spent the day like this, we suddenly saw a coal-burning ship with smoke coming out of its stacks crossing the end of the bay, and we realised that beyond the bay we would be safe, the wind would be favourable and we could find a safer anchorage. As we sailed out and downwind in thunderous conditions we heard a loud bang. The instruments went dead, and we realised we had been struck by lightning. Luckily, that was the only damage. We then found a small bay out of the wind until the bora finished. Eventually, we sailed up to Monfalcone in Italy where we found a yard that would look after *Caleta*.

Or, at least, we hoped they would look after *Caleta*. We left the batteries to be charged while we were away but, when we returned, they were still sitting on the deck where we had left them. This was Italy, after all.

We sailed back down the Adriatic past the same beautiful islands and went to Dubrovnik, anchoring outside and taking the dinghy into the harbour to visit the city, which we were able to see as an old Yugoslavian town – before modernisation, the war and restoration changed it.

We stopped at Kotor because we had enjoyed it so much before and wanted to see it again. We were able to moor the boat right in the town. Then, in the south of Yugoslavia, we went inland until we found a little river where we could take the dinghy up and see a fresh waterfall. After the dry offlying islands, it was nice to see so much greenery.

The Adriatic Sea flows into the Ionian Sea between the west coast of Greece and the south-east coast of Italy and Sicily. We decided to spend some time exploring the Ionian Islands, and then sailed into the Gulf of Corinth, where we stopped at Delphi. We entered its harbour and took a taxi to the ruins. They were extremely well restored and completely free of tourists. We then went through the Corinth Canal, an amazing structure which, at sea level, has no locks. Coming out of the canal into the Saronic Gulf, we sailed on to Piraeus, but it was absolutely filthy and there was no possibility of swimming anywhere near it. The town was just a dirty Greek harbour. Finally, we made our way to Lavrion, where we knew there was a good boatyard, and where we knew we could lay *Caleta* up for the winter again.

◉ ◉ ◉

We returned via our Dormobile, which we had left at Lavrion for our return trip. We sailed up through the Dardanelles, the Sea of Marmara and the Bosporus to reach the Black Sea. It was not one of our best ideas as we were nearly killed. We found a quiet anchorage to the north-east of Istanbul where I felt safe enough to sleep. Suddenly, I was woken by the sound of shouting. I jumped up into the cockpit to find a 100-foot Turkish gunboat heading straight for us. The shouts were being yelled through a megaphone. I could not speak Turkish, but I knew what they were screaming. If we didn't move, they were going to ram us. I started the engine and went full astern with the anchor still in to move out of the way just in time for the gunboat to miss us by no more than ten feet. Had I not moved, it would have ploughed straight into us, and it is unlikely that Celia and I would have survived.

This was our introduction to the Black Sea, although back then it should have been called the Red Sea, for it was effectively the Soviet Ocean, and no foreign boats were allowed in there at all even though it was technically Turkish territory. After being ordered to tie up to the gunboat, we complied and let the ship's officers on board. They asked us what we were doing there, and our answers must have been unsatisfactory, because we were then told to follow the gunboat back down the Bosporus – not an easy task in the middle of the night when its minimum speed was 7 knots and *Caleta's* maximum speed was just below 7 knots. Nevertheless, we somehow managed to keep up, following as they led us out of the Black Sea and back down the Bosporus to a spot where we could anchor safely, and where nobody would trouble us anymore.

On our return to Greece, we sailed back and forth between the Greek islands and the Turkish mainland without clearing customs in either country as they are only a couple of miles apart. We were eating dinner one evening when we saw a flotilla of rough-looking little boats steam past. We wondered briefly what they were doing, and I turned on the radio to see if there was anything on the news. Unfortunately, in those days the only radio you could listen to was American forces' radio and all they talked about was Vietnam, so I stopped listening. After supper we set sail for Lavrion and, exhausted at about 4 a.m., I started looking for the lights to identify the coast as Greece has many islands and many lights. When we finally reached Lavrion in the morning, I was rather tired, and when we threw our lines ashore, they were thrown back at me by angry Greeks. I tried again but the lines were once more thrown back. Becoming increasingly irritated, I managed to go ashore and tie the lines up myself. At that moment a fat little man approached me shouting: 'Get out! Get out!' By now, I was close to losing my temper. I looked at the man, then I looked down at the water, tempted to push him in. It must have been obvious what I was thinking, for that was when the man played his ace card. 'I'm the captain of a Greek gunboat,' he explained. 'You're not allowed here. We've taken over the yard.'

'But why?' I asked.

'Because Turkey has invaded Cyprus and Greece is in a state of war.'

Suddenly, it all made sense. What we had seen the night before was the Turkish invasion fleet on its way down to Cyprus. It was also clear that we had to leave the marina, and possibly the country. Malta was too far away to be feasible, and for a few panicked moments we wondered what on earth we were going to do. Fortunately, as well as its marina, Lavrion has a commercial port, so we motored round to that, and then returned to the marina where our Dormobile was parked. We drove to the British embassy in Athens to find out what was happening and what our options were. We were the last people allowed into the embassy – the gates were shut behind us and a table placed in front of them. They told us in no uncertain terms that we needed to leave, and that the best option would be to drive out of Greece through Yugoslavia.

We agreed it was time for us to depart the country, and we were all ready to leave the embassy when two young women, no older than twenty or twenty-one, approached us. They were British and also needed to return home, but had no way of doing so. They asked if they could join us and have a lift in our Dormobile back to England. There was just one problem. The older of the two was employed by the Foreign Office and one of her conditions of employment was that she was forbidden from travelling to a communist country. Bordering Greece were Yugoslavia to the north-west and Bulgaria to the north-east, both of which, in 1974, were communist countries. If you wanted to travel overland to western Europe, you had to pass through one of them.

Nevertheless, the girls had no other choice, so we agreed to take them with us. But first we had to sort out *Caleta*, for it was still tied up in the commercial port and would not be allowed to remain there for much longer. We drove back to Lavrion. Luckily, the initial panic of the invasion had calmed down, and we talked to the marina staff instead of the captain of the gunboat. They said they were working normally and that *Caleta* could be left with them as it had been before. It turned out that the gunboat was being repaired and was not fit to go back in the water – it was hanging in the slings because that was what the government had negotiated with the marina.

After safely mooring *Caleta*, we began our drive north. Luckily, we had had the foresight to fill the Dormobile with fuel in Athens, because after that every other petrol station in the rest of Greece had long, stationary queues.

I am not a soldier; I never have been. But I learnt a lot about military tactics on that drive. The interior of mainland Greece is very bare. Therefore, whenever we saw some trees in the distance, we knew exactly what was in them: tanks. There were so few trees that any clusters of them were always used to hide tanks. Three or four times we spotted a group of trees ahead, guessed that there were probably tanks in them, and were proved right every time.

Eventually, we made it to the Yugoslav border. The Foreign Office girl sitting in the back of the Dormobile became extremely nervous. We tried to calm her as we entered the country, but without success. Further along the road north, we got stuck in some mud and couldn't move; she burst into tears, convinced the police would come and arrest her. Passing drivers stopped and offered their help, but since we couldn't speak the local language and they couldn't speak English, Celia resorted to making the noise of a tractor to indicate what we needed. I thought she mimicked the sound rather well, but the only reaction it produced from the locals was laughter. Finally, a bus stopped and was able to tow us out. We offered the driver some money but he refused. The bus was a government bus and he was using it illegally to take his friends to a party – as long as we didn't tell anyone about this he was happy. Not that we would have told anyone anyway, but such is the widespread fear and distrust which people fall victim to when living under a severe communist regime.

About 400 miles after becoming stuck, we passed a tractor, and it suddenly dawned on me that it was the first tractor I had seen during the whole trip. There had been acres and acres of maize just left out in trailers in the rain to rot. Nobody was responsible, they were just government crops which didn't matter to the locals. I understood then why those Yugoslavs had laughed at us when Celia mimicked the sound of a tractor. It was because they didn't know what one was.

Once we crossed the border from Yugoslavia into Austria, the girl stopped crying and was able to relax and enjoy the journey. Our drive reached its end at Calais, where we boarded the ferry back to England. We had driven almost 2,000 miles through Greece, Yugoslavia, Austria, Germany and France. The Dormobile had done us proud, but I longed to return to *Caleta* and the Aegean next year.

◎ ◎ ◎

So far, we hadn't had a good experience of Turkey, but we wanted to give it another chance, so we returned there the following year. Nowadays, the Turkish coast is packed with tourists, but then there were no recreational crafts around at all, and *Caleta* was the only civilian, non-fishing boat in Turkish waters. I like to think that we saw the Mediterranean before it became ruined by flotilla marinas.

I had seen hundreds of advertisements for a place called Ölüdeniz, where there was a beautiful lagoon entered by a narrow channel. Over the years, Ölüdeniz has become so popular that yachts have been banned from sailing up the channel to the lagoon, but then the rules seemed unclear, so we took *Caleta* in and anchored. A policeman came out to the boat. He asked what we were doing and demanded to see our passports. He didn't speak any English, and just repeated the word 'Passports'. We gave them to him and he looked at them thoroughly, turning all the pages over one by one. He handed them back politely and thanked us. He had never even held them the right way up. He must have just been told to look the part of an official police officer and act as if he knew what he was doing. When we went off to explore the local town, the customs officer insisted on escorting us and, as we walked from shop to shop, he developed a catchphrase.

'Buy this flag!' he would shout, pointing at the displayed red flags with their white star and crescent. They were large national flags, the size of an ensign, and far too big to be the standard courtesy flag, which is flown from the rigging of a yacht as a courtesy to a foreign country. But they were all that was available, and the only way we were going rid ourselves of the customs officer was to buy one. So we bought one, flew it from the spreaders and finally enjoyed the town.

We sailed back from Turkey past all the Greek islands in a meltemi – a strong near-gale-force wind from the north – which made the sailing hard and wet. When we moored at night, the whole boat – the deck and the ropes – was covered in dried salt. We enjoyed dinners in the main towns of all the islands after sailing into their circular harbours, mooring to the quay, enjoying the ancient architecture and being part of maritime Greece, and then walking to look at all the restaurants nearby. Nowadays, private boats have to go to characterless out-of-town marinas. The Greek meals were delicious. We knew we didn't even have to look at the menus, but could just go into the kitchens and peer into the various pots to decide what looked most tempting.

We left the boat in Lavrion again. When we returned, it was with a crew. By this point, we had decided that we were going to cross the Atlantic that year. It had been our long-held dream, and we were finally going to do it.

With Celia Blois and Judith Cargin on Caleta *in Greece*

We had seen the best of the Mediterranean, which was now being spoilt, and it was time to take on the Atlantic challenge. Celia and I agreed that we'd like to have one extra crew, and we decided that a girl would be best so that she could take the workload off Celia in the galley. We still had *Vivacity* in England, and used it to try out the three girls who applied. The best two would come out and sail with us in the Mediterranean that summer.

Judith Cargin was the first. She joined us in Greece, having caught a bus from Athens to the port, and then walked from there to the marina. She was a very pretty girl, so much so that, while she walked through the town, she caused a collision between two cars when their drivers, instead of looking at the road, had been looking at her.

Judith joined us and helped us get *Caleta* ready to sail to Santorini. After a day on the island, where I climbed the mountain on a donkey who had so little regard for me that he tried to crush me against any wall we happened to pass. We then walked down to the boat at night. We had to let go of the moorings – the bow was tied to a buoy – and Judith offered to jump in to swim and untie us. She dived into the sea naked and, to our surprise, suddenly lots of headlights from the nearby cars turned as their drivers watched her climb the buoy and untie the rope. Luckily, she did not have to go back ashore, and we were able to set off.

We had a long sail to Tunisia, where Judith quickly learnt the ropes and how to sail.

'Do you mind if I sunbathe topless?' she asked as soon as the sun came up in the morning.

'Fine,' I said. 'As long as you're always ready for crewing jobs.'

When we reached Tunisia and moored at the port of Nabeul near Tunis, a local man called Youssef offered to take Judith out for dinner.

'I'm not going out alone with you,' she told him. 'Charles, will you come with me?'

'You're not going out with Judith and leaving me here,' Celia said. 'I'm coming too.'

'Fine!' the Tunisian declared, determined to have his date with Judith no matter what the cost. 'I'll take you all out!'

My son Andrew, who was five years old, was with us for a holiday and, after discussing the matter, we decided we would have to take him to the restaurant with us. Youssef was happy with that. After what seemed like a long drive, we stopped at a street café belonging to a friend of Youssef's; all Arabs seem to have friends somewhere who will help them and give them a free meal. We sat down to order, and Andrew began to attract lots of attention from the locals. Like many young English boys, he was blond, and those around us were fascinated by his light-coloured hair, which at that time in Tunisia was still a rarity. Also, like many young boys, he found it impossible to sit still, so spent much of the meal running around the café to the delight of the locals, who absolutely adored him, and spoilt him with lots of things to eat, which he kept bringing back to us. After dinner, Youssef wanted more fun so drove us to a nearby disco where he also had friends, and we danced until midnight with Andrew on my shoulders.

Our main reason for stopping in Tunis had not been to eat, drink and party, but to see the desert. For this, we needed to hire a car. We found one at a reasonable price, but the owner refused to take our credit cards and would only take cash. Our money was extremely limited but, back at the boat, we were able to cobble together enough to pay. Unfortunately, by the time we returned the next day the owner had changed his mind; he only wanted the car to be used in the city. So, we went to Avis instead, hired a car using the cash as a deposit, and drove out towards the desert with me at the wheel, Celia beside me, and Judith and Andrew in the back.

After we left the city, we reached a village and stopped to ask at the tourist office the way to the desert. 'Go up that road,' he said, 'turn left and you'll see the fort. That's the desert.' It was as simple as that. We shouldn't have been allowed to go at all, of course, but we didn't know that. We were just following the tourist officer's instructions.

The problems soon began. We hit a wind-blown sand bar on the road and the car spluttered in protest. The further we travelled, the more difficult the terrain became. It was clear the car didn't like it, but we were determined to reach the fort, and were relieved when we arrived. We went to see the fort commander who was delighted to meet Andrew and gave him just what all little boys need: a half-empty bottle of warm Coke. But it kept Andrew happy. We knew we'd have trouble going back, so we asked the fort commander if he had any rope. He gave us a short length of blue polypropylene camel rope.

Having obtained our ropes and Andrew's Coke, we saw two Club Med Land Rovers arrive at the fort and decided we should leave before them. That way, if we did get stuck, there was a chance they would pull us out. It did not take long. We were soon stuck in a sand dune, which was too deep to drive through. Luckily, our forward thinking paid off, and one of the Land Rovers arrived and towed us out. We carried on while they returned to their car. As it was only a single-track road, they followed us for a while to the next sand dune, where we got stuck again. They then drove past and tried to tow us out once more, but this time it was not successful as the camel rope, which had seen better days, broke. And, in true Club Med style, they then drove off and left us.

It was clear that we were now in serious trouble, stuck in the sand with no tow rope and no way of freeing ourselves. It was time to take drastic measures, and the only solution seemed to be to cut the seat belts out and make a strong tow rope, which we did just as a private jeep arrived. It towed us out of the sand dune and stayed in front of us until we were clear of the dunes. The engine did not sound happy, so we didn't dare stop until we reached a hill. At the top, the car came to a halt and then would not restart. But by freewheeling down the hill we managed to bump-start it, and were able to keep going towards Tunis until the worst of the sand was cleared out of the engine and it would start in the ordinary way.

Feeling more confident again, we checked the oil, which was nearly empty, so we stopped at the next garage to buy some. We managed to return to Tunis, somewhat relieved. Fortunately, the Avis office was closed – with all our cash spent on the deposit, we knew we didn't have enough left over to pay for all the damages. So we behaved somewhat dishonestly, leaving the car key in the Avis box and disappearing. It wasn't the right thing to do, but it was the only way we were going to solve the problem. The engine was ruined and the seat belts were torn out. It would have cost us a fortune, a fortune we didn't have. And, once Avis discovered that we had ruined the car but couldn't afford to pay for it, there was no telling what might have happened to us. We were very relieved we had paid cash as a deposit. We took the bus back to *Caleta* and sailed away that night with me the only one without an Arab tummy.

From Tunis, we sailed up to Sardinia and Port Mahon: a calm crossing with light winds. I was able to practise my sextant sights, which was important as this was going to be our sole method of navigation crossing the Atlantic.

The sextant is a handheld device which is used to measure the angular distance between objects such as, for example, the horizon and the sun. Measuring this angle enables the sailor to calculate a position line on a nautical chart. To find a position with a sextant, you start by taking a morning sight, where you use the sextant to measure the angle from the horizon to the lower edge of the sun. You take the time to the nearest second, and then calculate your position line using astronomical tables and complex calculations involving your height of eye when taking the sight. At the same time, you take a reading of the distance log so you have a start distance. Then, at around noon, you take another sight of the sun and keep adjusting the sextant so that you find the highest angle the sun reaches, and then measure that angle. This is true noon and will give you the ship's latitude, and you can then draw a horizontal line on the chart along the latitude you have discovered. Finally, you do the afternoon sight and take the angle of the sun again. You take the log reading again at that time. From these log readings you calculate the distance travelled between morning and afternoon sights along your latitude line. From these sights you can calculate your exact afternoon position. Using a sextant is the old-fashioned method of navigation used by Captain Cook to chart the world's oceans. The new satellite-based navigation systems of today are far more reliable and user-friendly, but one downside of them is that they have taken much of the skill, adventure and uncertainty out of sailing.

By 4 p.m. we had our position. The wind was dying, so we started the engine and set a course for Port Mahon. We set the autopilot on the desired course so that we could relax as we motored towards the harbour, and Celia could concentrate on dinner instead of watching the clock. After dinner, we could see the lights of Port Mahon and were totally surprised because, after 40 miles from our calculated position, we arrived between the buoys at the mouth of Port Mahon harbour without changing course at all. Our navigation was perfect and absolutely accurate. It was final proof that I could navigate across the Atlantic accurately.

We picked up Judith's boyfriend Bob in Port Mahon. He joined us throughout the Balearics, and we all got on well. He was a Pan Am pilot and regaled us with aircraft horror stories. We dropped him off in Spain, carried on to Gibraltar, laid up *Caleta*, and then flew home in something of a panic as it was the hottest year I had known and the harvest was ready and waiting. Unfortunately, during the summer Judith and Bob split up. She decided that she no longer wanted to crew for us across the Atlantic, her reason being that spending any more time on *Caleta* would remind her of her boyfriend, and she didn't want such painful memories. It was a shame because she had been a good crew and had helped me with the navigation, learning along the way how it worked. In fact, I learnt later that before she left, she had taken copies of my crib-sheet and calculations. She used these when she joined another boat to cross the Atlantic – it was likely that her knowledge, along with my crib-sheet and calculations, enabled them to cross safely.

CHAPTER THIRTEEN
ATLANTIC CROSSING

Since we no longer had Judith, we decided to try and find a new crew when we returned to Gibraltar. This was, after all, the best place for it. Most boats leaving or entering the Mediterranean will stop in Gibraltar, and anybody wanting to cross the Atlantic will congregate there looking for boats. It is a hub for nautical travellers.

After meeting a few candidates, we settled on a young English couple who seemed pleasant enough. They gathered their belongings and moved on to the boat and, now with a complete team, we were ready to set off. We stocked up with plenty of fresh food, enough for four people and to fill the fridge. We reckoned that 30 gallons of water would be sufficient, as long as we only used it for drinking and cooking – it had to be made to last. All the washing up would be done in saltwater.

We left for the Canaries. The conditions were perfect: the weather was warm and summery and, with the wind behind us, we made it in five days. Our timing was perfect too. October was still enjoying the last of the summer northerlies coming down the coast of Portugal and on to the coast of Morocco, and we didn't want to reach the Caribbean before December, because the hurricane season there officially ends in November, after which major storms become extremely unlikely. Generally, the best time to set out on an east-to-west Atlantic crossing is to leave the Canaries in late November and arrive in the Caribbean just before Christmas.

Unfortunately, though the conditions and the timing were perfect, our new crew were not. They stole all the best food and generally made nuisances of themselves. They just wanted to be together and couldn't seem to keep their hands off each other. At night, when it was their turn to take watch, I was nervous of going down to wake them, for it was dark and they were always so intertwined that I never knew which one of them I was touching, nor which part. Celia and I sat down and talked it over one evening. The voyage we had ahead of us was, we knew, going to be one of the most ambitious things we had ever done, and we didn't want that ruined by two people we were finding increasingly unpleasant. But could we do it alone? Regardless of how little we enjoyed our crew's company, we had to put our safety first, and if we couldn't manage with just two pairs of hands then we would have to swallow our pride and take them. We talked long into the night. Finally, we reached our decision. Our workload would be doubled and our rest time halved, but we knew that we could do it. We had been sailing together for seven years and knew the boat extremely well. We could rely completely on each other.

So, the following day, we sat down with our crew and told them the bad news. They were disappointed, but took it in good heart, agreeing to leave *Caleta* in the Canaries. This, however, turned out to be easier said than done. When you enter a port in a foreign country, you enter with a crew list, which is stamped by customs. It is then your responsibility to take your crew away with you again when you leave. As much as you might want to, you can't just dump them there. This is one of the measures introduced to curb illegal immigration. Your crew either leaves with you, or they join another boat. So, as we waited in the Canaries, we looked for another boat. Convincing other sailors that the couple were good crew took some careful mishandling of the truth, but we eventually succeeded, and were relieved when they left *Caleta* for good.

Once we had rid ourselves of the couple, we were able to start readying ourselves and set a departure date. We washed all our clothes and sheets, and cleaned everything on the boat. We bought as much food as the fridge would hold and some extra food in tins. We also filled up the two freshwater tanks. We knew that when we finished one, we would have to be extremely careful, but we were used to using saltwater for everything other than cooking and drinking. When planning to cross the Atlantic, you should budget for approximately three weeks. If you end up at sea for longer than four weeks, things can become difficult; six weeks and you're in serious trouble. We kept these facts in mind while planning our supplies.

Finally, it was time to go. These days, there are organisations which take large convoys of boats, sometimes 300 of them at once, together across the Atlantic. Back then, there was no such thing, and an independent crossing such as ours was a rare thing; rare and possibly dangerous. I relied entirely on sun-sights and the distance log for navigation. This latter was essential when there was no sun. As we progressed across the Atlantic, using the daily sun-sights and the distance log we could work out how strong the current was. We were completely alone on the ocean.

After two days out, I became unhappy with eating dinner at 6 p.m. and getting up at 6 a.m. It all seemed too much of a strain from our usual shore-time life, so we decided to go back to our relaxed shore routine of 8 a.m. breakfasts and 8 p.m. dinners. This we did by moving the ship's clocks forward two hours so that the sun rose at 8 a.m. and set at 8 p.m. and we could use all the daylight and live by the times that we were used to.

For some people, crossing the Atlantic Ocean unsupported would have been too much, but Celia handled it all well. There was just one thing she couldn't bear. Often, I would not wear a harness at night, and this worried her. She began to fixate on the idea that I might fall overboard when she wasn't looking. It even affected her ability to sleep. When she would go to bed and hear me up on the deck, instead of sleeping, she would lie awake, waiting to see if I left the cockpit and went on deck. Then she would start worrying when she didn't hear me return. Once, she was on watch while I was sleeping. When I woke up naturally, instead of being woken by her, I walked up on deck and found her there, fast asleep at her post. She was, it seemed, unable to sleep when she was supposed to, and unable to stay awake when she needed to. To enable her to sleep peacefully I agreed to wear a harness so that, if I fell overboard, I would still be attached to the boat and be able to call Celia.

The weather helped us to keep comfortable. The trade winds were light, harnessed effectively by our twin running sails, which meant that with the wind behind us we were never at risk of gybing and could take wind 35–40 degrees either side of dead astern. We had gentle following seas too. All in all, it was perfect sailing.

As we grew more confident, we began to fish from the boat, and learnt that it was easier than we thought, perhaps thanks to our good fishing gear. During a previous early morning duck shoot at home, two of our friends had accidentally shot a swan which I then had to chase and kill. If you've ever seen *Swan Lake*, I can confirm that the representation of the dying swan in that ballet is absolutely perfect. After plucking it, another keen sailing friend told me that a swan's feathers are excellent for fishing, so I saved them long enough to use on the Atlantic. My friend was right: they were wonderful. We caught so many mahi-mahi, or dorado, with them that we had to stop fishing, because our catch was taking up too much room in the fridge and we couldn't eat them fast enough before they went off.

While we were good at catching the fish, killing them was not so easy. We had to bang their heads against the aft deck, gut them and cut them into pieces small enough to fit into meal-sized containers, and it all became rather gory. Fortunately, cleaning the deck was easy – we just put a bucket in the water and swilled all the mess back into the ocean. Often, one fish would provide three meals. It reached a point where it felt a luxury to eat something from a tin rather than the constant supply of fish, fish and more fish.

Towards the end of the trip, we lost the sun and the wind picked up considerably. We had near-continuous rain, and I had to steer much of the time. It was not looking at all pleasant. I thought we were in a tropical depression, and I started worrying about the risk worsening to a hurricane. Eventually, I decided that I had to ask Celia to look up preparations for a hurricane, not something I really wanted to do. It put frightening thoughts in our minds. She looked in the pilot book and found that there was little we could do except watch and wait. Luckily, it never happened as we were outside the hurricane season. Soon the sun came out again and we could revert to the relaxed trade wind sailing that we had dreamt of for so long. Occasionally, a storm cloud would appear, and if we found ourselves heading for it, we could just tack and head away to avoid the squalls. A change of direction for a few hours didn't make much difference to our final course.

On what we anticipated to be our final day, I took the sextant sights with the utmost care and precision, because I knew that everything depended on our position being as exact as possible. By 4.00 p.m. I had the final sight and the final position and did not need to change course. We had about two hours of daylight remaining, and I left it to Celia to watch out for Green Island, just off the easternmost point of Antigua. If we didn't see the island by sunset, we would have to think seriously about what to do. Celia, whose eyesight was better than mine, positioned herself at the front of the boat and watched. When she saw land at the right time and the right place, she whooped with joy. We were on a perfect course, heading to pass along the south coast of Antigua directly for English Harbour.

As we reached English Harbour and saw the lights, we took the sails down and started the engine, looking for the leading lights that would guide us into the harbour. We looked hard but couldn't find them. We finally realised that they were just symbols on a chart – as West Indians had little respect for charts. This meant we had to enter the harbour without lights, but luckily we had a good moon. The harbour has a narrow entrance, only about 70 yards wide with a rocky headland on the left-hand side, and a dangerous shallow reef to the right, which we had to make sure to avoid.

With Celia's good eyesight and the light from the moon, it was possible to see the shallow sand and coral, which enabled us to go round it and anchor in its lee. I felt relieved, not just from the fact that we had made it into the harbour safe and in one piece, but from the fact that we had made it after twenty-three days on our boat, without support or crew, having finally sailed across the Atlantic Ocean.

After we anchored, I checked the ship's clock. It was 11 p.m. Now, however, we could go back to land time, so we altered the clocks back to 9 p.m. in accordance with the time in Antigua. We hoped to have a good night's sleep and have a civilised breakfast at sunrise the following morning. But, as it happened, we were woken early by a fisherman beside *Caleta*. Not that we minded. We had woken in paradise, with perfect weather beside this idyllic Caribbean island. It felt as if we were in heaven. When we arrived home, we were asked to give talks about the Atlantic crossing to both the Cruising Association, of which I was a member, and the Little Ship Club. It indicated how unusual the crossing was.

CHAPTER FOURTEEN
SAILING THE CARIBBEAN

Before anything else, the first thing I needed to do in Antigua was go ashore, visit the police station to complete my entry, and then go to the customs to enter the boat. It didn't take long, and as soon as it was done, we were free to go and explore Nelson's Dockyard. When we went shopping, we were impressed by the large variety of fruit and vegetables, many of which were new to us. We had to ask the stallholders how best to prepare them – some needed cooking, some were only used to make drinks and there were others such as breadfruit. This was originally brought to the Caribbean to feed slaves but the first shipment, on the *Bounty*, failed to arrive after Fletcher Christian mutinied. When we went to the meat market, as we picked out the best-looking beef and started to order we were horrified to see the butcher spray all the meat with insecticide. We clearly realised that we had to think differently from shopping in England.

Super-yacht tender for a J-Class yacht

Nelson's Dockyard is both a major tourist attraction in Antigua and a working boatyard – indeed, it is the only Georgian working dockyard in the world. It had been left derelict for many years until Commander V. E. B. Nicholson arrived in 1948 with his yacht *Mollyhawk* to find this perfect dockyard which the English fleet had used centuries before. All the buildings were made of stone and coral, well built and extremely substantial, and he decided that he had found paradise. The few people who visited there were attracted by his yacht, so he offered it for charter and began to make his living chartering it to guests from America to cruise around the Caribbean islands. Cutting short his round-the-world trip, he formed Nicholson Yacht Charters – the first and best yacht charter company in the Caribbean. The continued interest and use of the dockyard for an increasing number of sailors encouraged the Antiguan government to invest in it – it had great potential as a yacht haven and tourist destination with an interesting naval history connected with Nelson. Much of the restoration was done by naval crews based in the Caribbean.

We enjoyed walking through Nelson's Dockyard, passing the officers' quarters, now used as tourist offices with the best natural air conditioning in the world. The doors are high up and the wind just blows straight through the buildings. Next to it are the copper and lumber store, now

English Harbour from Shirley Heights at sunset

converted into a luxury hotel, the sailmakers' loft, the sawpits, the pursers' office and the guardhouse. Pride of place is taken by the capstans, which were recently restored by the Royal Navy. These are three large drums with ten square holes at the top into which long wooden poles can be inserted, with six men on each pole – meaning sixty men per capstan. The three capstans could haul any ship down with a rope to its masthead until the underside was clear of the water and the men could then scrub it clean. This was why the British thrashed the French at the Battle of the Saintes in 1782, because the French ships' bottoms were covered in barnacles and weeds and the British navy easily outmanoeuvred them. These days, the capstans are the focal point for parties held in English Harbour. The first one we went to was a Christmas party hosted by the Nicholson children. It was a wonderful gathering of yachts from all over the world, and we celebrated Christmas under the hot Caribbean sun with bottles of Antigua rum.

English Harbour used to be protected by a small battlement, Fort Shirley, which was high up on the hill above the reef on the entrance, and which gave a superb view over the surrounding sea. It is now used for the main Sunday night party on the island, where a colourful steel band performs in the late afternoon before being taken over by a rock band for dancing in the evening. Fresh barbecued chicken is served all night. Fort Shirley gives a superb view over English Harbour and Falmouth Harbour, and in good weather you can see as far as Montserrat where, if you're lucky, you can watch the ash rising from its volcano.

Stunning sea sunset in Antigua

After a few days enjoying the dockyard and the sunshine, we decided to go for a short sail up the coast to a nearby creek. We had to tack against the wind. When Celia came to take the sails down, she noticed a massive crack on the deck at the foot of the mast. Immediately, we took the sails down, turned round and headed back to Antigua Slipway, relieved that we didn't have to go into the wind at any time during the crossing.

We took *Caleta* to the yard to see the yard manager, who was an experienced English marine surveyor. He arranged for the mast to be taken out so that he could inspect it further. They cut the mast step out and realised that the problem was the builder who, instead of using a solid 4-inch block of hardwood, had used pieces of plywood, including one which was just offcuts. It was a disastrous example of building, and all disguised under fibreglass. The manager produced a carpenter and found a good piece of greenheart. They cut it to shape and then fibreglassed it back into place. The carpenter was quite skilled and during the mornings his work was exceptional. However, he enjoyed good lunches, and he enjoyed having a little too much to drink during them, and as such he rarely did much during the afternoons. But this is life in the Caribbean and, rather than complain, we took this element of the local culture in our stride.

The work took five or six weeks to complete, so we spent that Christmas at English Harbour, living on *Caleta* at the slipway while the repairs were being done. Everyone was friendly and kind. Once, Desmond Nicholson, one of Commander Nicholson's sons, took us to an old Arawak village to show us the remains of some of the earliest known inhabitants of Antigua and the nearby islands.

Once the work was completed, we were able to start exploring the Caribbean. Antigua's west coast is flat and calm, but we soon learnt that the east coast has to be navigated with care. Behind the outlying reef there are lots of small reefs and islands – to be able to see them, you need the sun to be high in the sky. One of the largest islands is Great Bird Island, an islet which serves as a warning for ships coming from the east: it is halfway up Antigua with a reef six or seven miles out either side of it. Hundreds of boats have been wrecked on these reefs because they are so difficult to see, all but invisible until you are only 500 yards or so off them and being blown down on to them. Difficult in full sun, and deadly after dark.

Barbuda, which is about 25 miles north of Antigua, is much smaller and flatter and therefore harder to see and has an even more treacherous reef. Because it is so flat it attracts very little rainfall and has little soil, so it was

Male Frigate bird displaying its chest as part of a mating show

not suitable for growing sugar cane. It was once owned by Admiral Codrington, who was the governor of Barbados and in charge of all the British island colonies. As he could not grow anything of value there, he was reputed to use it as a slave stud farm. There are well over a hundred wrecks on Barbuda's windward reefs. About the only thing for tourists to see there is a rather unusual colony of frigate birds, often displaying their inflated bright-red chests in the nesting season, on a strip of mangrove-covered land between the lagoon and the sea. It is possible in the dinghy to approach to within 20 or 30 yards of their nests, and an ever-present flock of birds continually circles overhead, never seeming to stop, to eat, or to catch fish, just circling on the thermal currents above.

When we visited Barbuda we went to the island's only town, Codrington, which, in all honesty, was dreadful. It was quite an adventure to get there. There are two ways. For the first, we deflated the dinghy and carried it together with the outboard over a sand bar, then reinflated it and motored across a very choppy lagoon to the town. This needed four adults. The second way only needed two of us and with a bigger engine we could motor some four miles up the west coast and into the lagoon before crossing it to Codrington. We stopped there to buy some food. There was little on offer: tins of 'meat product' imported specially for Barbuda, frozen packets of stripped backs and necks of chicken, about as basic a foodstuff as you can find anywhere, and unsurprisingly awful.

We also needed some petrol for the dinghy, so I asked a passing islander where the petrol station was.

'At the crossroads,' he said, pointing towards the end of the town, which lay a few hundred yards away.

I walked to the crossroads, but there was no petrol station there. I stopped another local and asked him the same question.

'There, there,' the man said. '*That* is the petrol station.' He was pointing at a small building which looked like nothing more than a derelict house. 'Just go in the gate and ask,' he said, ushering me towards it.

I followed his instructions and walked inside. There, a man sitting on a single chair under a canopy in a junkyard stared at me, half-curious and half-hostile.

'I'm looking for petrol,' I said.

The man's demeanour changed in an instant. He jumped to his feet and smiled. 'Petrol! Yes! Come this way!'

I followed him to the back of the yard and there, I discovered, was the 'petrol station' – a 40-gallon drum, from which the 'attendant' siphoned my fuel.

Codrington nestles on the edge of Barbuda's enormous lagoon, which extends down much of the west coast of the island. In 1994, this lagoon was the setting for four horrific murders. Yachts tend to anchor behind the sandbank which marks the western aspect of the lagoon. Two Britons and two Americans were on their 65-foot ketch when, in the middle of the night, three Caribbean men crossed the lagoon, dragged their boat across the sandbank to the ocean side, and boarded the yacht. They bound and gagged the four sailors, stole thousands of dollars from them, and then shot each of them at point-blank range. Scotland Yard were called as it had become an international incident and beyond the scope of the Antiguan police. The killers were identified and, two years later, sentenced to death. Newspaper reports from the time state that one of them smiled broadly as the sentence was passed.

If this was not enough to keep people away from Barbuda, in 2017 Hurricane Irma devastated the island, destroying most of the property there, and making the place virtually uninhabitable. Almost all the 1,800 residents were evacuated to Antigua. The Antiguan government asked if anybody knew of any vacant houses where they could house the unfortunate Barbudans, and many were found for them. Sadly, they were not used to such modern conditions and took in many of their friends, quickly trashing the buildings, making them more like the shacks they had lived in on Barbuda. They knew they didn't belong on Antigua, and only wanted to return to their old Barbudan ways.

◖ ◖ ◖

From Antigua and Barbuda, we sailed to Montserrat, anchoring in the main harbour, which was still an old-fashioned jetty and unsuitable for modern ships. We explored the antiquated town where we did not see many tourists. The island itself was beautiful. We hired a guide to walk through the forest to a high, narrow waterfall where we had a swim. On the way back, the guide pointed out a fumarole, an opening in the ground which emits volcanic gases, up on the hill. We didn't know it at the time, but that fumarole may well have been the precursor for the devastating eruption which was to happen in 1995.

Dominica, local houses before the hurricane

It is a shame that such a beautiful island has suffered so much destruction. A few years after our first visit, we went back to see the devastation caused by Hurricane Hugo. The roofs of the churches were ripped off and the main town was almost totally destroyed. The football pitch was piled eight feet high with debris that had been cleared from the town. And then, a few years after the hurricane, the 1995 eruption covered the whole southern half of the island in volcanic ash. We went to see the observatory at the north end of the island, which was protected from the ash flow by another small mountain range. The guide failed to show up to meet us, but a scientist offered to show us round. In the half-hour we were with him, his bleeper went off three times, indicating that an interesting movement had occurred in the volcano. He was daily measuring the height of the volcanic plug, which was still growing by the day. We then drove down to the side of the volcano to see where houses had been destroyed and where hundreds of tons of lava had flowed down the hillside and into the sea. The volcano carried on erupting for three or four years and, once during this time when *Caleta* was laid up in Antigua, our yacht had an inch of volcanic ash on its deck even though it was 20 miles upwind of the island.

Leaving Montserrat, we sailed east towards Guadeloupe. This was the first time we had sailed into the trade winds instead of downwind. We soon realised the winds strengthened as we neared land, since they blew round the edge of the islands. There was a warning at the time to keep clear of southern Guadeloupe as, a little earlier, in August of 1976, a large amount of seismic activity had caused the evacuation of all 72,000 of Basse-Terre's residents. There were no warnings for northern Guadeloupe, however, and we headed for Deshaies, a quaint French town with one road through it and one road off it, disappearing into the jungle after 100 yards. It was signposted Ruelle No. 1. There were many nice little village shops and restaurants which catered for passing yachtsmen, as well as a small fishing harbour in the lee of the island.

We then sailed down in the lee of the island with calm seas and variable light winds until we reached the southern end of Guadeloupe, where we sailed outside the danger zone of the volcano. South of the island the wind massively strengthened, and we headed into it towards Îles des Saintes. This part of the Caribbean was the site of the 1792 Battle of the Saintes, the battle which the French lost because they had not harnessed the technology of capstans to clean the undersides of their ships, when the British scored their famous naval victory. Despite this victory, islands such as Les Saintes and Guadeloupe, unlike the sovereign state of Antigua and Barbuda or the British overseas territory of Montserrat, are French departments, and have remained full and non-autonomous regions of France. Today, they are officially part of the European Union, using the euro as their currency.

Since there have never been any sugar cane plantations on Les Saintes, there were likewise never any slaves there either. As such, what we found on Les Saintes in the late 1970s was something of a Caribbean curiosity, islands which were almost entirely white. They had an elite atmosphere to them, as if they were just for holidays and parties. There were plenty of eccentrics there too, and one of them had built a house which looked like the bow of a ship sticking out of the mountain. It now exists as a major tourist destination for residents of Guadeloupe, who visit it on numerous ferries during the day.

We continued south on to Dominica. Portsmouth, its second-largest town, is located at its north-western point. It has a lovely natural harbour where we anchored. Above Portsmouth is the Cabrits National Park peninsula, and it is here that you can find the remains of another Fort Shirley, this one a Georgian military outpost dating back to 1765 which, at its peak, could house 600 men. The garrison is famous for being the site of an 1802 revolt of African slave soldiers, causing all the slave soldiers to be freed five years later. Always tempted by things historical, I visited Fort Shirley, and was interested to find genuine grapeshot in the armoury, which I kept as a souvenir.

Portsmouth has changed little in the last twenty years with just a few more beach bars for yachtspeople. But back then it was a very basic town with a major part of its industry being bananas. The bananas were brought by truck to the Portsmouth packing station, where they were loaded into lighters and towed out to the Geest banana boats anchored in the bay. While we were there, one of the trucks broke down and missed the boat. The truck was stacked with bananas on which the farmers' livelihood depended, but which would soon spoil in the heat. We bought a 'leg' of bananas, the whole stalk, delighting the farmer, who was pleased to sell them to us cheaply as there was no other market. We ate the bananas as they ripened. Later, when they were fully ripe and starting to go off, Celia made banana bread and some delicious flambéed bananas for supper.

There was a small river next to where we bought the bananas which went into the jungle. It looked so beautiful that we took the dinghy up it, entering the jungle, just the two of us, with no one else around. This little river was a well-known spot where sailing ships used to replenish their freshwater supplies in the past. They would load their barrels into their rowing boats and row up the river to the freshwater. As a result, it became one of the most well-known freshwater rivers in the Caribbean, even marked on Admiralty charts. Now private dinghies are prohibited and visitors must use local guides. The peaceful river is no more.

We sailed down the coast from Portsmouth to Roseau, Dominica's capital, an old-fashioned town which hadn't changed much since the 1930s. Dominica has the largest population of pure indigenous Caribs in the West Indies. Like the Arawak, who historically populated the Greater Antilles, the Caribs are an American Indian tribe. They are descended from the mainland Caribs of South America, and migrated from the Orinoco Delta about 800 years ago. Their numbers were depleted heavily when European invaders brought diseases to the islands against which the Caribs had no resistance. The islands themselves have also been cruel to the Caribs and between 1812 and 1902 eruptions from a St Vincent volcano wiped out entire tribes. We came across a Carib man one afternoon, on a trip to a wild waterfall inland. He was fashioning a dugout from a single log with a chainsaw. His skill was exceptional and I really admired it. I thought about how, in the future, he would launch his dugout off a rocky beach into the Atlantic waves.

◑ ◑ ◑

Some of the remaining Caribs building a traditional dug out. Their ancestors migrated from South America and killed off the original indigenous Arawaks.

Sailing south from Roseau, you reach Scott's Head, the southernmost point of Dominica. The wind whistles round the headland and becomes near gale force for the first few miles into the passageway, and then reverts to regular trade winds before accelerating as you approach the north coast of Martinique. It strengthens again but reefing can be avoided because after years of experience I knew that in a short while it will become a flat calm, remaining so until the port town of Saint-Pierre is reached.

We anchored in a wide bay in the north of Martinique below Saint-Pierre. For many years, this was the cultural capital of Martinique, earning it the nickname 'the Paris of the Caribbean', until, in 1902, the town was destroyed by the worst volcanic disaster of the twentieth century. Just above Saint-Pierre, Mount Pelée erupted. The town had been waiting for elections, and the mayor wanted all the people to stay in Saint-Pierre to vote, so he told them to ignore the volcano's rumblings. The result was a tragedy. The eruption killed all but three of the town's 28,000 inhabitants. The survivors were a young girl who managed to escape on a small boat, a 30-year-old man who was in the town at the time of the explosion and yet somehow evaded the pyroclastic flow, perhaps by jumping into the ocean, where he was burnt by the rapidly boiling water, and Ludger Sylbaris, whose survival became the stuff of legend.

The night before the eruption, Sylbaris got into a bar fight. He was arrested for assault and thrown into jail. The cell he was locked in was a windowless, subterranean dungeon with poor ventilation, and it was this cell which protected him and saved his life while the superheated gases and debris razed the town above. He was pulled from the rubble of the prison four days after the eruption, badly burnt but conscious. Hearing his story, P. T. Barnum invited Sylbaris to join his circus, and for the next twenty years he toured America, showing off his scars, telling his story of survival, and gaining fame as 'The Man Who Lived Through Doomsday'.

It is still possible to visit Sylbaris's dungeon, and we did just that, wandering amongst the tombs, remains and ruins of the 1902 disaster. It is not as well preserved as Pompeii, as a shanty town has been built over much of old Saint-Pierre, but it was nevertheless interesting. So too was the volcanological museum and the ruined theatre: a classical, Roman-style amphitheatre.

The destruction of Saint-Pierre caused Fort-de-France, a town in the centre of the island, to become the capital of Martinique and one of the most important cities in the Caribbean. Much like Guadeloupe, we had been warned about Fort-de-France before arriving. There were no issues with volcanoes there, but political problems bubbled under the surface and there was a distinct threat of trouble.

We stopped there anyway, because we had to enter the country and we needed gas. We anchored and I made my way into the town, asking anyone I could find if they knew a place where I could get my cylinder of gas refilled. I was told there was none available owing to a general strike. Walking back into Fort-de-France, I passed one street that was closed. I looked down it to see a lot of military vehicles and huge numbers of skinheads: they were riot police from Marseille.

I walked back to the boat but, as I was having supper, I heard a few explosions and decided to go back into the town with my pockets empty to see what was happening. I found the main street where the trouble had been. There were relatively few people about, and I was the only white person. The locals were dispersing to the side streets, until all that was left in the main street was a solid rank of the French riot police standing shoulder to shoulder with their shields in front of them. They were being controlled with special collars held by their white colleagues which enabled them to defend themselves from the all-black rioters. I was within two feet of them, so I could see them clearly. The Martiniquais had all gone. I saw another group of about fourteen riot police retreating back along a wall in full defence mode with their shields up. Nobody approached them, but even at a distance I could see the look of total fear on their faces.

An ornate palace in St Pierre, Guadalupe, before the 1902 Mount Pelée eruption, the deadliest eruption in the 20th century with 29,000 deaths.

I guessed it was probably the only place in the world where the entire riot was by black people and the entire police force was white. The rioters were claiming, quite legitimately, that the French government was taking all their wealth back to France, as it had been doing for 300 years. I then saw the police climb into their off-road vehicles and drive back to their camp. This apparently continued for about a month. It had clearly been well planned, as the French had flown in several hundred of their riot police for this specific purpose.

Just south of Martinique lies a tiny, steep-sided coral island known as Diamond Rock. It has no beaches and is uninhabitable, with sheer coral cliffs on all sides. Nevertheless, Diamond Rock has played an important part in military history. In 1803, the British navy managed to hoist two 18-pounder cannons up the steep sides of the island, which was French, to its summit. Following that, they fortified the island and supplied enough food and water to support 122 men. Commodore Sir Samuel Hood commissioned the island as a British sloop, a word typically reserved for warships, naming it HMS *Diamond Rock*. It became the world's first stone frigate, and enjoyed seventeen months as a superb vantage point from which to harass the French and make it difficult for their ships to enter Fort-de-France.

Sailing around Diamond Rock, formally HMS Diamond Rock

Over 150 years later, and just a decade before Celia and I sailed round it, Diamond Rock was once more taken from the French, although this time it was by a civilian force, or 'motley crew'. Under the cover of night, a group of rather drunken British yachtsmen sailed out to the rock, anchored at its base, disembarked, climbed up its cliffs, and planted a large Union Jack at the top. The French, angered by the fact that there was a British flag on their land, sent in the commandos to take it down, but the commandos found it impossible to climb the rock. The Martinique authorities began to panic. The following day, the French navy was due to arrive for a state visit, and the prospect of them sailing past the sight of a Union Jack on top of their own island was an insufferable insult to French national pride. As a result, the French naval fleet was diverted all the way around the north end of Martinique, to obviate them seeing a Union Jack on their Diamond Rock. Not long afterwards, a helicopter from the fleet was sent to remove the flag.

CHAPTER FIFTEEN
WINDWARD

We sailed south from Martinique to St Lucia, crossing from the northern Leeward Islands to the southern Windward Islands. There is a peninsula stretching out of the north-west of St Lucia known as Pigeon Island. It was indeed once an island, separated from St Lucia by a shallow part of the Caribbean Sea, until an artificial causeway was built to link them. It was a big project, but then the 1973 oil crisis caused the development to stop, and nothing developed further, greatly disappointing the locals. Nevertheless, the artificial causeway created a beautiful bay that made a perfect anchorage outside the lagoon, and which became Rodney Bay marina and the finishing point for transatlantic rallies.

We used this as our base to explore St Lucia with its excellent network of minibuses. This type of service exists across much of the Caribbean: hundreds of minibuses which run far more cheaply and efficiently than our bus service in Britain. Then we went down the coast and into Marigot Bay, a little inlet south of Castries, where we could anchor in the outer bay and go by dinghy into the central lagoon. It was a well-known pirate haven where the palm trees hid the masts and the boats could not be seen by passing naval ships out at sea.

Below St Lucia lies St Vincent, a wild island whose northern half is out of bounds to tourists, thanks to the many drug farms spread across it and the likely reception should anyone enter. The Windward Highway follows the eastern coast but, apart from that, there are no other roads in the north. There are a few anchorages in the north which are so steep that it's only possible to anchor with a line to the shore, so that the anchor pulls uphill. This means that you are reliant on the locals to help you, who will want money, and they have easy access to boats because of the lines to the shore. This is the only contact these inland people have with the rich white people, who are regarded as a sort of goldmine. We went to one of the anchorages to see what it was like, finding it was all right, but we decided we wouldn't go back there again. Instead, we sailed to the south of

St Vincent, anchored off the town and went on to the island for a day trip. There was a general atmosphere of illicit behaviour and bad intentions, so we left fairly quickly, agreeing that we had no desire whatsoever to return.

Putting it all behind us, we continued south to Bequia, less than five miles away from St Vincent, yet feeling like another world. A quaint and picturesque fishing island, Bequia still had its dangers, although they were of a different kind to St Vincent's, coming not from the people who lived there but from the winds. The bay itself at Port Elizabeth was rather quiet, and the wind blew straight over the top. But during the night, any yachtsmen having had a few drinks needed to be extremely careful. Getting back to where the yachts were anchored, they had to be constantly aware of the strengthening wind the further they progressed out of the bay. Should their dinghy's engine have failed, or the oarsmen not been proficient, then the wind would have easily carried them straight out to sea. In the past, boats have been known to suffer this fate and to have been taken, as the saying goes, 'off to Panama'.

We enjoyed several drinks at the small hotels and bars that surrounded Bequia. The whole town was built for tourists, and little scooters, which could be hired by the hour or the day, seemed to be the main means of transport. We were lucky enough to see the old sailing schooner The Friendship Rose, which did the daily run to St Vincent, bringing all the fresh produce to the market and all the tourists to the hotels. This was before the airport had been built, when it became just another tourist island.

Sailing on, we went downwind to the westernmost point of Bequia and then beat against the trade wind to reach Mustique, taking care to avoid the big reef lying to the west of it, which has caught many yachts. We anchored offshore and dinghied in to Basil's Bar, a well-known beach bar on the shore of Britannia Bay. Run by a friendly man called Basil Charles, it has become an important part of Mustique nightlife over the years.

Mustique is one of the most exclusive of all the Caribbean islands. It has been privately owned since 1763, when it was bought by two British farmers. Its most famous owner, Colin Tennant, purchased the island almost 200 years later, in 1958, for £45,000. Two years after buying it, Tennant gave a ten-acre plot of Mustique's land to his friend Princess Margaret as a wedding present, and the villa Les Jolies Eaux was built on it. This was more than just an act of generosity: now that Princess Margaret owned land on Mustique, it raised the value of the rest of the island significantly, and she became its star attraction. Tennant, or Lord Glenconner as he later became, formed the Mustique Company which then owned the island, and set about dividing the land up into five- to ten-acre plots to sell off to the rich and famous. His enterprise was so successful that, over the years, landowners on Mustique have included people such as Mick Jagger, David Bowie, Tommy Hilfiger and Shania Twain, who have used their villas there, villas with exotic names such as Moongate, Fort Shandy, Mandalay and Sheherezade, to escape the world, and to relax in complete privacy.

These days some of the villas can be rented out, but apart from that there are few places for the casual visitor to stay in Mustique. In fact, back then there was only one hotel: the Cotton House. Not that we stayed there. We had *Caleta*, which we moored up and slept on at night, using our days to explore the island and enjoy its unique culture. Once, we took a car around the island and admired the large and elegant villas.

I enjoyed snorkelling over Mustique's reefs – even if the trip back from them was against the wind and into the steep waves. The dinghy only had a small Seagull engine, and I had to hold a flipper over the air intake to stop the water from being sucked into the carburettor. Rowing was not an option. The late 1970s was a good time to swim over these reefs, as it was for many of the reefs around the Grenadine islands. Before this, the French had almost destroyed all the aquatic life. They used to fly in tourists from the French islands in small charter planes. While the tourists were enjoying their lunch and swimming, they would strip out all the seats and load up the plane with fish and crustaceans which they paid the locals to catch by squirting Clorox into all the holes, thereby killing the fish and destroying the marine life. This had been outlawed by the time we were there, and most of the damaged areas had started to regenerate. Since then, however, circumstances have worsened again, as the area grows more and more overfished and overpopulated with divers every passing year.

We were lucky to have snorkelled Mustique's reef and the Tobago Keys reef when we did. Sometimes, I would take my speargun with me to catch our dinner, although I never caught more than Celia and I could eat. At other times, I would simply enjoy the snorkelling itself, swimming through the sparkling waters and amongst the coral, watching the parrotfish, four-eyed butterfly fish, surgeonfish with needle-like spears beside their tail, angelfish and the occasional pufferfish which, if frightened, inflates itself like a spiked football.

A chain of small islands stretches south-west from Mustique to Grenada. We hopped from one to the other, stopping at Union Island to exit St Vincent and the Grenadines and to buy some more supplies, and then going to Palm Island, which was once called Prune Island, until it became a regular routine for charter yacht skippers to collect sprouting coconuts and carry them down on their boats to plant them on Prune Island. Now it houses a large collection of young palms and is a major tourist resort. Clients fly into Union Island and take the short boat ride across to Palm Island.

From there, we visited Mopion Island and Punaise Island, whose names translate as 'Louse' and 'Bedbug', for some excellent diving. These two islands are little more than tiny sandbanks surrounded by shallow coral reefs, and the only structure on Mopion is a single coconut-leaf parasol. On Punaise there is nothing at all. Then it was on to Carriacou, a little fishing island with a boat repair business to look after the local fishing fleets. There was a lagoon north of that, accessible by dinghy and surrounded by mangrove trees.

After Carriacou, we sailed to Grenada, where there was a distinct sense of unease. A few years earlier, in 1974, Britain had granted it independence. Grenada remained as part of the Commonwealth with the Queen as head of state, but politically the country began to lean further and further to the left. In 1979, a Marxist-Leninist movement overthrew the existing government and began to form closer ties to both Cuba and Russia. When Cuban construction workers started to build an airstrip on the island, America became anxious that Grenada might become the next Soviet state, and invaded it, giving the British some notice out of respect for Grenada's membership of the Commonwealth. All this happened after our first visit in Caleta, but we could feel the atmosphere of mistrust across the island.

Nevertheless, we were lucky enough to enjoy our time there, before it all descended into coups and invasions. There is a beautiful natural harbour in the south-west of Grenada which is too small for many boats, but in which we were able to anchor *Caleta*. This is the harbour of St George's, the capital, a lovely town built on the hillside of the crater of a dormant volcano. In this harbour, sometime in the 1960s, the marina was virtually destroyed when a yacht's skipper lost his temper with the marina manager, revved up his engines full speed ahead and tore out half the marina.

It was about this time that something unusual happened. An old university friend of mine, Charles Dewhurst, had joined us for a sail with his wife and children. Since my children, Andrew and Helen, were also there, it meant that there were eight of us all living on the boat together, which was rather cramped. Nonetheless, it was nice to have them with us. In Bequia, we had bought some vegetables and spices off *The Friendship Rose*. Charles decided he would use them to make ginger beer while we were sailing the Grenadines. When we did the crossing to Grenada, the weather got rougher and I hadn't realised that Charles had corked the ginger beer jar to stop it spilling. He had also put it in the lavatory to keep it safe. But when we hit a bad wave, the pressure built up from the fermentation and blew out not only the jar but the lavatory bowl with it. They both exploded into a thousand pieces, spreading all over the cabin. Charles, Jane and Celia had to clean it all up while I sailed, and the children had to stay in the cockpit – because children and glass shards don't go together.

Since the lavatory bowl was entirely destroyed, we had to have another one shipped out the following year. We had the documentation that showed it had arrived and we went to collect it, but they said there was no sign of it. We later found ourselves chatting to the local priest when we told him our story and he said he would try to help. So we gave him the documents and off he went to the post office, where he had a long argument with the postman, who kept saying it wasn't there. But he was persistent, and asked if he could inspect the store for himself. Being a local priest, he was given permission to look in the store. Luckily for us, he found the lavatory bowl and brought it back to us.

'Well,' he said with a chuckle as he handed it over, 'that's the first time I've ever seen a black man blush.'

◯ ◯ ◯

We left *Caleta* in Grenada that year to return home in time for the harvest. On the way back, flying from Grenada to Barbados to Luxembourg to England, I took a calculated risk.

Whether they will admit it or not, a lot of people carry a gun on their boat because it can often be used to protect them. That said, simply carrying a gun is not in itself protection enough. You must also know how to use it properly. The story of Sir Peter Blake is proof of that.

Sir Peter Blake was a professional yachtsman from New Zealand who gained international renown for winning the Whitbread Round the World Race and leading Team New Zealand to victory in the America's Cup. His career was so distinguished that he was awarded an MBE in 1983 and then knighted in 1995 for his services to yachting. After he retired from racing, he started to lead nautical expeditions to places like Antarctica and the Amazon. It was at the mouth of the latter that, during an environmental exploration trip for the United Nations in 2001, Blake's boat was boarded by pirates: between six and eight armed and masked robbers. Blake, who was in the cabin when the pirates boarded, grabbed his rifle, jumped out on to the deck and fired. Unfortunately, though he was a great yachtsman he was not a firearms expert. He shot one of the assailants in the hand and was about to fire again, when his rifle jammed. As soon as the pirates knew the crew were armed, they had no option but to shoot to kill. Blake was fatally shot in the back.

I have always ensured that any of my guns, especially those I travel with, are well maintained, as I am used to shooting with them. After we left *Caleta* in Grenada, it seemed to me that the right thing to do was to take home one of the guns, a .22 revolver, which I kept onboard. I'd regularly used it in England before and shot several rabbits with it, and even one unlucky pigeon which I shot flying at 100 yards. When I arrived in Grenada, I declared the gun to the customs and said I wanted to take it home. The customs officer arranged for the gun to be taken to the airport and given to the captain of the plane, who showed it to me before he took it. At Barbados, we changed flights, and the gun changed with us, being handed from one captain to the other with me watching. This transatlantic flight was with Laker Airways – unknown now since they ceased operations in 1983, but at the time one of the first low-cost airlines and, as such, widely used – and it took us from Barbados to Luxembourg.

It was in Luxembourg airport, in the transit lounge, that a member of staff, holding a tray out in front of him as if it contained the Crown Jewels, approached me.

'I think this is yours,' he said.

'Oh,' I replied, a little surprised to be offered a revolver in the middle of an international airport, even if it was mine. 'Yes. That belongs to me. Thank you very much.'

He handed it to me and I took it, stuffing it into my hand luggage. Now, it seems obvious to say that you really shouldn't come through an airport with a revolver, but this was all long before 9/11 and Lockerbie, and the dos and don'ts of flying were not as strict as they are today. Still, before I had left the Caribbean, I had written to my local police, who knew about my firearm certificate, to say I was bringing the gun through Gatwick airport. I knew that without the firearms certificate the gun would be confiscated. But the police never did anything about it, which was how I ended up walking through Gatwick airport with a revolver in my hand luggage.

CHAPTER SIXTEEN
CARNIVAL

Time passed and, before we knew it, we were reunited with *Caleta* again, refitting it in Grenada and sailing off on the next leg of our Caribbean adventure.

There's a strong current between Grenada and Trinidad, and as it is 70 miles between the two, it was too far for *Caleta* to sail in a day. So, we sailed in the evening, staying up-current to the east as far as we could to make certain we made the Bocas del Dragón ('Mouths of the Dragon'): two narrow channels which pass down either side of Monos Island, a rocky outcropping just off Trinidad's north-western peninsula. The Atlantic trade wind current is accelerated with the Amazon and Orinoco waters coming up the coast of South America and joining it, some going up between Trinidad and Venezuela, and the rest going round the top of Trinidad, and both meeting at the Bocas del Dragón. This tends to make for turbulent seas at the entrance and is why we wanted to be running down the current and downwind there, rather than beating against it. This is also why we went as far east as we could at night.

All went well and we saw the Chacachacare lights, one of the brightest lights in the Caribbean, slightly to the east of where we expected. This meant we were well up-current and could now ease off and head for the lighthouse. The sailing became much easier and we soon neared Monos Island and passed into the calm at the entrance to the Gulf of Paria. We then had a gentle sail amongst a lot of cargo boats anchored out waiting to unload. Trinidad had an inefficient port and ships had to wait a long time before they could unload. One in particular, which we thought was anchored, was in fact moving slowly towards the port. We let it go first.

Now that we had arrived, we needed to enter. Trinidad was once a British island and, as such, it has inherited our innate love of bureaucracy. We had become used to the various systems of immigration and customs and health checks throughout all the different countries we had visited so far, but in Trinidad they went one further. They required a certificate of 'deratisation'. This was the job I had done in Australia many years before, so I knew all about it. It is the assurance that any rats on your vessel have been exterminated. It's an old-fashioned policy and rarely if ever applies to yachts, but in the capital, Port of Spain, they still demanded it. After all, yachts only came to Trinidad for the Carnival, so they saw no need to modify their immigration policy for these sailing boats which were there for just two weeks a year. This was, and still is, principally a commercial port.

Trinidad is a busy and prosperous country, due to its large oil fields in the south. A lot of this wealth finds its way into the Carnival: a colourful and exuberant festival which takes place in the period just before Lent. Filled with parades, dancers, wild costumes and endless calypso music, the Carnival transforms Port of Spain into one enormous party, and we had arrived there just in time for it.

We had the children with us and walked with them from the port towards a park at the top of the city. Helen, who was only three years old at the time, hated being carried and always insisted on walking. As she tottered along, often falling behind because she was so slow, she attracted plenty of attention from the passing locals, and women approached us every few minutes asking if they could look after our daughter. It was so safe in Trinidad back then that we were happy to nod and say yes, and Helen, delighted by all the attention, had no problem with taking their hands and letting them guide her along beside us. Now, with the rise in gun crime in Trinidad, I would not be so confident to allow a stranger to take my infant daughter's hand.

From the park at the top of the city, we were able to experience the spectacle of the Carnival in all its glory. It begins with calypso competitions, where various calypso kings sing in preliminaries to find the King of the Carnival. Each calypso singer has a home-built theatre, where he performs his traditional songs and creates new ones especially for the event.

The next day, in the evening, is the parade of steel bands. The numbers are limited to 100 members per band, but with many of the drummers playing five or six drums the total number of drums can be as many as 600. They are all mounted on wheels so they can be wheeled along the roadway and then up on the stage. When they started playing, I found it one of the loudest and most amazing sounds I had ever heard. Of all the bands of Trinidad, there are only about three or four who are really good, sponsored by big companies with a vested interest in Trinidad. Texaco, for example, always sponsored one. My favourite, however, was sponsored by the West Indian Tobacco Company (WITCO), and was formerly named the WITCO Gay Desperadoes, but now called just the WITCO Desperadoes. Much of the success depends on the tuners, and there are few good tuners in the country, so often two bands have to share one tuner. It's difficult to imagine how one person can tune 1,200 drums all ready for the same night. But the sound they created is one I will never forget.

In the early morning, before dawn, there is a competition called Jouvert, where the poorer people dress up in colourful simple costumes and have their own small dances through the stadium and out on to the main street. This enables the drinking to start early in the morning, but it is a wonderful spectacle of people making the best with so little.

The next night is for fancy dress, where each band has an extremely elaborate king and queen, who are judged separately. Some of the fancy dress costumes can be up to 12 feet tall and can take hours to put on. It is amazing how they can dance with such huge headdresses and costumes.

On the final day all the bands follow the king and queen in their specially made costumes. Some of the bands can be up to 500-strong, all dancing with one or two trucks or lorries with the musicians and all the amplifiers mounted on the back. When they finish going through the show to be judged, they carry on dancing round the streets of Trinidad with all the locals. This goes on all day. It can be quite difficult to obtain tickets for the good shows in the shade.

We ended up returning to the Carnival in Trinidad three more times. Once, with our friends Pat Roberts and Kate Bracken, we joined in. Pat had a friend who was the managing director of a business in Trinidad, and he arranged for us to join a band and be dressed in the band's costumes, which were *Pirates of the Caribbean* themed. As all the costumes had to be hand-made, we sent our measurements out to them, including shoe measurements so they could make a suitable pair of pirate shoes. When we arrived, a few days before the carnival, we went to the dressmakers to check that everything fitted, and we wondered how a small town could make 2,000 costumes individually for all the band members. This was effectively a year-round business. When one carnival finished, the band organiser immediately thought up the theme for the next year so that production of the costumes could begin again. Only the best seamstresses could make the elaborate kings' and queens' costumes. It was all a huge amount of work for perhaps just two days of use.

Visiting a local colourful waterfall.

On the day of the Carnival, Pat, Kate, Celia and I fitted into our allotted place and walked through the town park. We started to dance as we approached the stand and then danced our way in front of the judges carrying our sail wings on our backs with our music truck playing at full blast right beside us. Once we'd left the stand and been judged, we then carried on dancing on a pre-arranged route around Port of Spain with Pat and me keeping ourselves fortified with rum, drinking it straight from the bottle. All the villagers cheered from their houses and from the side of the road. Many of them had a hose running, so we could have a drink of fresh water to dilute the rum and a hose-down if we became too hot. I don't drink much, but Pat and I managed to drink a whole bottle of rum during the day, and yet were still completely sober at the end of it. We must have sweated it all out quite quickly.

Finally, after about four or five hours, we were totally exhausted. The music truck had by then stopped and the band dispersed. It was a wonderful experience to be not just a part of Trinidadian music, but a part of the festival itself.

CHAPTER SEVENTEEN
THE END OF AN ERA

After our first visit to the stage of the Carnival, we returned to *Caleta* to find it swinging wildly around, in spite of there being no wind. We looked about and suddenly realised a big tug was sitting with its bows against the dock and its engines on full bore, just trying to make life difficult for the yachts. We eventually had to go to the harbourmaster to explain that we had paid to be here for the Carnival and ask if they could stop the tug. They eventually did, and we went back to our nice, calm anchorage with all the yachts tied peacefully together.

Once, on a trip in the dinghy to the shore, we passed a ship's lifeboat drifting. The crew waved to us, signalling that they wanted help. Our little dinghy only had a 2-horsepower Seagull on the back, but I agreed to try. The man in command of the lifeboat was a shamefully embarrassed ship's chief engineer. His engine had broken down and he asked if we could tow him into the dock. I wondered why some of these derelict ships were anchored off Trinidad – if the ships' chief engineers couldn't keep the tenders going to take the crew to the shore and back, how did they manage to keep the ship's main engines going to cross the oceans?

We sailed down the coast of Trinidad to explore. We could see that there was a harbour down there so we went to check it out. We discovered that it was privately owned by Texaco. We were welcomed by one of the oil company's employees who lived on the harbour and liked meeting the yachts. He looked after us well and we could see it was safe, so we decided we could leave *Caleta* there and take a quick tour round South America.

It was a bus-and-hitchhiking tour when Venezuela was calm and prosperous, but Colombia was at the peak of Pablo Escobar's notoriety. Bogotá had a very bad reputation for pickpockets and in those days we carried money in travellers' cheques. This meant that we had to go to a bank to cash them. It was well known that white men coming out of a bank would have lots of cash, and so the pickpockets would all be watching. We had to cross the road and, even though I was fully aware of the situation and watched my pockets intently, they were still picked without me seeing by whom. Fortunately, the pickpockets got nothing as Celia was carrying all the money. We walked as fast as possible on the edge of the pavement for safety. We managed to stay safe, but the stress at high altitude made Celia sick.

She soon recovered and we took a local flight to Leticia on the banks of the Amazon River. We were met by a local guide who offered to take us and three Americans – Richard, Pat and David – from the plane for a 'jungle tour', which we accepted. We were met next day and taken to the river to board a large outboard-powered dugout canoe and motored swiftly downriver before entering a small tributary and being put ashore for what we were told was a one-hour jungle walk. Immediately we got into the jungle we realised our newfound American companions knew far more about the plants than our guide. We saw so many new orchids and other rarities that they wanted to collect that the walk took three hours. One of the men, Richard, was very tall, and his wife, Pat, got on his shoulders to cut down the rare orchids to take back to the US. We got back on the river with all the plants we could carry and, on the next stop, we were shown a 25-foot anaconda big enough to swallow people. On a later trip we saw a photograph of a big anaconda with just the legs of a man in blue jeans sticking out of his mouth. One night we were taken in a small dugout to paddle close to the shore and with torches we could see fish near the surface and watch our Indian guide spear them from the bow – a practice handed down through the centuries. Celia and I took a ride ourselves in a dugout where I spent a lot of the time sticking clay into holes to stop the craft filling with water.

A dugout which was kept watertight by putting a soft clay putty in the holes, Amazon River, Colombia

*Practising with a local
blow pipe, a traditional
method used to hunt
prey, Colombia.*

When we finally got back to our hotel, Celia and I sat and watched Richard, Pat and David strip all the leaves off the plants and put the roots into the hotel bath, which they had filled with formaldehyde to kill any pests so they could carry them through US customs. They were no ordinary tourists but very knowledgeable botanists who were taking all the plants to the Fairchild Botanical Garden in Coral Gables to get help in identifying them. Four were found to be new to science and kept by the museum, and Richard and Pat took the rest home to add to their tropical jungle home in Miami. Richard took cuttings and cross-bred some of them, which he sold on to gardeners. He said he'd made $500,000 from our jungle hike. He sadly died a few years later as a result of having played under DDT tobacco crop spray as a child in old Southern Rhodesia.

*Local Macaw playing
with and destroying
a pen, Colombia.*

Charter yacht in the Galapagos

We decided to visit the Galapagos and chartered a small boat with some friends to see the amazing wildlife which Charles Darwin had made famous as a young man when he visited the islands in the *Beagle* in 1835. By going on a yacht, we could visit the small islands as a complete crew and walk within a few feet of blue-footed boobies and frigate birds displaying their inflated bright red chests. We also saw 4-foot-long iguanas and the famous giant turtles, some of which live to be 150 years old. I also enjoyed diving and watching all the colourful reef fish and being startled by sea lions swimming straight at my mask before turning away at the very last minute.

Giant turtles on Galapagos

Following that, we greatly enjoyed the arid coast of Peru and the perfectly preserved sprawling mud-walled city of Chan Chan, with its intricate mud moulding over 400 years old. We were very lucky to see it when we did – since then, heavy rains have destroyed all the most delicate work. We took the mountain railway with its shunting corner all the way to Cuzco. The Inca remains were even more impressive than we had imagined and we enjoyed their magic. Unfortunately, Peru was suffering from multiple strike action and the Machu Picchu train was only running every other day. We got our tickets and made the 4.30 a.m. train for the fabled ride through the jungle and mountains to the foot of the historic site. We left our luggage at the hotel and climbed up to the ruins long before the days of souvenir sellers and their stalls. The ruins were far more impressive than the pictures showed and we were glad we had an extra day. We climbed back the next day in pouring rain, and when we reached the top were welcomed by a kind American hotel guest who let us dry out. He informed us that he had studied these Inca ruins in detail and realised that their use of concave and convex stones on top of each other made them survive earthquakes. He had used this discovery to help write the California building codes so that skyscrapers could be built. The site was nearly empty that day but we still had the morning of the next day before our train back. This gave us a unique and most memorable morning, having the whole of Machu Picchu to ourselves with no one else to spoil the experience.

When we got down the mountain and on to the train, we realised there was a price for our special morning. The train was overloaded and, although I had got a seat, all passageways were packed with standing travellers. Not surprisingly, the man next to me suggested that he share my seat. I could hardly object as we started the very slow ride back to Cuzco. After a few changes and frustration at the crawling speed, I was fast asleep when I was woken by the train stopping and everybody getting out. Of course, I followed to find out what the problem was. We had been

Machu Pichu with no tourists due to the rail strike.

derailed by the Maoists only 20 yards before a bridge over a canyon. We knew then why we had been travelling so slowly. We were very lucky one of our passengers was an American who understood trains and, with his instructions, the crew and passengers placed stones in strategic places under the wheels and the driver inched the engine backwards on to the track at the first attempt. Fully awake, we endured the rest of the eight-hour ride, thankful that we had been saved from the ravine.

There were no trains running at all to our next country, Brazil, so we had to squash into a taxi for a late afternoon drive to the border. The road was little used and very South American with lots of potholes. One was too deep for a timber lorry, which rolled over, spilling its entire load on to the road. It was nearly dusk and they decided to wait until morning to clear it. We spent a long, cold, cramped night with the snowline only 1,600 feet or so above us. In contrast, the hot Brazilian jungle next day was idyllic. We then went to the Rio beaches with their beautiful girls, then on to Brasilia with its vast empty spaces, and finally back via Suriname to Trinidad. It had been a wonderful trip and a complete change from sailing.

Once we were back, we cruised along the Venezuelan coast to the island of Margarita, where my passport was stolen. I was trying to obtain my clearance but, in the immigration office, a man purporting to help me was actually just trying to sell me tickets. 'Fifteen dollars,' he said. 'Give me fifteen dollars and I will arrange it all for you.'

With a sigh, for I suspected I was being ripped off, I handed over the money, and he gave me a piece of paper. I looked at it. It was a ticket for a dance.

'This isn't what I want,' I said, growing angry now. 'I want to pay for my clearance.'

'No, no, no,' he replied, shaking his head at me as if I didn't know what I wanted. Our conversation turned into an argument before my money was returned and I was told I had to pay for the clearance at the customs office.

I didn't realise I had left my passport behind until I was a few yards down the road, at which point I turned and ran back to the immigration office. Travelling teaches you that many of your possessions are inessential. Your passport is most assuredly not one of them. In fact, it is the most important possession of all when you're travelling.

I returned to where I had left it. The same man was there, but my passport was not. 'Where is it?' I demanded.

He looked at me blankly. 'Where is what?'

'My passport. I left it here.'

The man shrugged. 'I don't know. Maybe the Frenchman took it.'

'What Frenchman?' I asked.

'He was here when we were talking. Maybe he took your passport.'

I vaguely recalled seeing this man, standing to one side of us during our argument. 'Where is he?'

The man shrugged again. 'Maybe at the other office.'

I set off for the customs office, and there was the Frenchman.

I approached him and bluntly asked: 'Do you have my passport?'

'No,' he said. 'No, of course not. Why should I have your passport?'

I stared hard at him. He seemed shocked by what I had asked him, and I suspected he was probably telling the truth. I decided that it must have been the man in the immigration office who had taken my passport.

I went back there, burst through the doorway, spoke to the man at the desk loudly, and demanded the return of my passport. He said he would go and see his boss. And that was when the boss came in with a sword. He slammed it down on the table three times, and screamed: 'Get out!'

As you can imagine, I left very quickly.

Feeling stressed, I went back to the local restaurant and explained what had happened to the man in charge, who was a decent Venezuelan who had been living in America for a few years and then returned. He understood the situation and explained to me that it was unlikely the customs man would have taken my passport because I was clearly an Englishman and could not be mistaken for a South American. The strong probability was that the Frenchman had taken it, after all. He could sell it to a South African for about $4,000, because South Africans were not allowed into the Caribbean during the time of Apartheid. Nevertheless, the man said that, quite clearly, the officer had behaved appallingly. He went to see his superior about the case, and the man who slammed the sword down had his holiday stopped for a month as a punishment for his behaviour. As I'd obtained my clearance, he advised me that I could now leave.

However, my problem was not solved as I still had no passport. The British embassy was in Caracas. I was unable to hire a car or to travel on public transport without a passport. Discussing our options, Celia and I decided that the best plan would be to sail due north to Aves Island.

Aves Island is only a tiny sandspit, but it has been the subject of a number of territorial disputes, most notably between Venezuela, the Netherlands and Dominica. It seems logical that, of them all, Dominica should have the strongest claim, as it's the closest to Aves and both lie on a similar latitude. However, not long before our arrival there, in 1978 the Venezuelans built a huge scientific naval base at its southern tip, which they declared helped keep the island hurricane-proof, and meant they could also claim it as theirs. We saw the lights of the naval base as we approached Aves Island: a welcome relief after a difficult crossing. The landing in the dinghy was similarly rough, but once we arrived, we were delighted to find that everyone was friendly to us, happily showing us the local turtle population and welcoming us into their huge concrete building, built to withstand a hurricane.

With so few resources, there was, of course, no passport control on Aves Island, and we left it without difficulties. However, our next destination, St Thomas Island, would not be so easy. A part of the US Virgin Islands, it shares America's strict system of immigration control. Entering and leaving St Thomas without a passport was going to be a challenge. But we had no choice. Our children, Andrew and Helen, were flying out to meet us and were due to land there.

Somehow, we managed it. We anchored just off the coast, went ashore in the dinghy, walked to the airport, picked the children up after they had cleared customs, waved goodbye to their escorts for they were too young to travel alone, and brought them back to the dinghy without our clearing customs. It was all completely illegal, but the four of us ended up back on *Caleta* safe and sound. The only problem we experienced was that the children's luggage had been lost. We arranged for it to be taken to the Holiday Inn the following morning.

Back on the boat we sailed the few miles to the capital, Charlotte Amalie, and went to the Holiday Inn and there was the luggage, which had arrived that morning. We were now free to leave St Thomas and head eastwards to Tortola in the British Virgin Islands. We went to the governor's office to see how they could help. As we were on a boat, we had crew lists, so we had all our passport numbers and our various entry documents. This made it easier to check our details and, after two days, we could come back and collect a one-year temporary passport to enable us to carry on with our holiday.

We then set off to the west to the Passage Islands next to Puerto Rico and were coming round the eastern edge of Vieques when a polite voice on the radio called out: 'Yacht sailing round the western edge of Vieques.'

Celia and I looked at each other. 'It can't be us,' I said. 'We're sailing round the eastern end.'

We continued on and, a few moments later, the same voice called out: 'Yacht sailing round the eastern edge of Vieques.'

That was clearly us, and the man had obviously muddled up his east and west. Then, in an extremely polite voice, he asked if we would mind sailing round the stern of the American warships because they were firing live rounds at the island. We were happy to oblige, and were surprised we could sail so close to naval ships firing live ammunition.

On we went to the Dutch ABC Islands – the initials of their individual names, Aruba, Bonaire and Curaçao – which were back down south, near the border of Venezuela and Colombia. This meant another long crossing of the Caribbean Sea. It was a difficult sail, perhaps worse than our earlier trip north from Venezuela to the Virgin Islands via Aves, but it was nothing compared to what we were about to contend with, as we set off west from the ABC Islands to Panama.

We had been told in Curaçao that, recently, a yacht had rolled while on the same journey as we were about to undertake. I had shrugged my shoulders at the information, thinking: *Well, it's not going to happen to us.* I should have paid more attention.

The rough conditions of the journey ahead became immediately apparent, so much so that we could not even lift the dinghy up on deck. Clouds raced across the sky, and for the next six days we did not see the sun once. I felt tremendously relieved that I had recently invested in a new-fangled transit satnav system – one of the first ever satnavs, which came complete with its own 12-inch cathode-ray-tubed television screen – since my earlier technique of navigating by sun sights would have been impossible in these conditions. There was no sun visible whatsoever.

As we progressed, the weather gradually worsened. The seas grew enormous. It was the first time we had ever used washboards to stop water coming into the cockpit, and Andrew had to pump the bilge to keep the fridge going. We rose up and down with giant waves continually sweeping the aft deck. Ahead of us lay a mile-wide entrance to the anchorage. Thanks to the satnav giving two positions in twenty minutes after six hours with nothing, we were absolutely certain of our position: we were right where we needed to be, everything was correct, and it looked like we were going to make it. I started to relax. Until Celia screamed.

'Breakers ahead!'

I looked ahead. Sure enough, there was nothing but white water across where we needed to enter. With conditions like this, and these breakers, the entrance to the anchorage would be impassable. Our only other option was to head into the enormous seas straight to Panama. I knew instinctively that, if we attempted that, it would be a horrendous sail into a Force 8 gale.

I looked out towards the entrance again and, this time, spotted a few traces of green amongst the white. That was when I realised that it wasn't a reef at all: the green revealed that they were huge breaking waves. I rechecked the chart and saw three patches of shallow water, each at a depth of 42 feet. I had never considered that depth as any danger. It meant that the waves were 42 feet high, the rule of thumb being that waves break in water at the same height as the water's depth. That meant we had a good chance of sailing between the shallow patches and making a safe entrance. I decided to go for it, and headed towards the gaps, navigating with the towering breakers driven by the same Force 8 winds. Sea spray washed over us, terrifying and yet deeply thrilling. When we came through it all and made it in one piece to the calm behind the shallows, I felt a tremendous sense of achievement.

Beyond the entrance, in contrast to the rough seas behind us, lay the beautiful San Blas Islands, occupied by an Indian tribe called the Kuna, and a part of Panama. It was the perfect place to relax, and we made our way round the islands, stopping when and where the fancy took us. It was a tropical paradise. We experienced sizeable islands for the first time that were completely free of vehicles or roads, just sand tracks kept perfectly clean, with palm trees, native thatched huts and some of the most welcoming people we'd ever met. There were lots of children running free, and the adults delighted in selling us their delicious food and their appliqué quilts, which was their speciality, one of which we bought to frame and hang in *Caleta*.

Navigating around the San Blas Islands had become a little tricky because it was now rainy and stormy. The rivers from the mountainous Panamanian mainland, where they grew all their crops and did their work, were infested with mosquitos, unlike these dry little islands that were bug-free. They also spewed millions of gallons of muddy water into the sea, discolouring it and obscuring the colourful reefs from view.

We spent most of the holidays snorkelling after the mud flows stopped and meeting more kind families. Then we sailed on to a small harbour overlooked by a fort that Francis Drake had occupied for a few years, and finally to the port of Colón at the entrance to the Panama Canal. There, yachts awaited their transit to the Pacific, arranging all their line handlers for the journey along the canal, and being organised into a group so that they could go through together with one pilot. We decided to take the train beside the canal so that we and the children could see Panama City, Gatún Lake in the middle of the canal, and, of course, the Pacific Ocean.

◯ ◯ ◯

Celia and the children flew home from Panama, and I picked up a crew to sail up to America. We stopped at two isolated Panamanian Corn Islands with no facilities but just lots of palm trees. We then went to Honduras and the bay islands of Roatan. The most popular attraction was a 30-foot shark, but I couldn't see it as I had no diving certificate, even though I had been diving for ten years without one. We joined a convoy of four yachts and, cruising together, we all made our way north. We wanted the security of numbers when dealing with Central American customs. This proved very advisable as once one skipper forgot some of his papers and had to get another office to retype them, for which he was charged at great cost. As there were no witnesses, he had no one to prove his case. However, the four of us cleared customs at no cost.

I had some trouble at Belize customs. I mistakenly said that I had come from Guatemala, but I didn't have the necessary exit papers. After being threatened with jail, I quickly remembered my papers were from Honduras, having just stopped briefly in Guatemala but not having formally entered. Once that was dealt with, I was pleased to be back in Belize. The last time I had been there, fifteen years earlier on my way home from Australia, it was still called British Honduras.

After clearing customs, we hired a pilot to navigate inside the Belize reef. This part of the sail, 50 miles in no more than six or seven feet of water, was exciting: a unique experience for me, since there was no possibility that I could have done it by myself. It was a masterclass in precision eyeball sailing, judging the depth of water by its colour, and needed to be undertaken so carefully that even the pilot in the leading yacht got stuck on the sand several times. Thankfully, because the boat in front drew more water than my boat, I was able to tail him and use him as a warning system. My boat had a shallower draft, and I knew that if the boat ahead could make it through then I definitely could too. I had the pleasure of sailing over the clear, sandy bottom with no navigational worries. It didn't even look 6 feet deep.

On we went, up to Cancún via Isla Mujeres, named after women of the past, through the Yucatán Channel between Mexico and Cuba. Then we sailed long the southern edge of the Gulf of Mexico to the Dry Tortugas, an American national park consisting of a small archipelago about 70 miles out from Key West. I anchored under a big fort overlooking a spectacular shallow bay, one which looked perfect for snorkelling. Not far out from the anchorage was the wreck of a plane, which had evidently crashed on to the reef. The body was still intact and I thought it would be interesting to snorkel around it. Unfortunately, while talking to one of the customs officers, I was warned off.

'That', he said to me in a severe voice, 'is a drug-smuggling plane. Keep clear of it.'

I am firmly of the opinion that if an American official tells you to keep clear of something, and it involves drugs, you do as you're told. It's a good rule, and I stand by it.

As a result, I never went snorkelling that day. Instead, I continued on up to Tampa Bay on the west coast of Florida to enter America officially. That was where I left the convoy, and where my crew left me, and I was again alone with *Caleta* to myself. My time that year was coming to an end, the harvest was drawing closer, so I decided to leave *Caleta* in Florida and return home.

I looked for a marina and found one in St Petersburg, a twin city with Tampa. It seemed suitable so I was given a contract to leave the boat for a year. I read through it and was ready to sign, when one particular clause caught my eye:

> *In the event of a hurricane warning, you must immediately remove your boat from the marina. If you fail to remove your boat, it will be sunk in the marina.*

I handed the unsigned contract back to the man and, just managing to stop myself from sticking two fingers up at him, walked away to get *Caleta* dry-docked elsewhere.

◎ ◎ ◎

The following year turned out to be our last in *Caleta*. At home, I had been studying the Intracoastal Waterway (ICW), and was keen to begin sailing it. The ICW is a magnificent feat of engineering: a 3,000-mile inland waterway which stretches all the way along the Atlantic seaboard to Florida and then round the Gulf of Mexico to Texas and Mexico. It is a unique vantage point from which to travel through America, with no risk of dangerous ocean storms. Boats can enjoy the Great Lakes in the American summer and leave by the Erie Canal to join the Intra Coastal Waterway towards the Atlantic Ocean. They can then cruise down to Florida and the Bahamas in the winter. As well as linking the extreme north to the extreme south via many natural coastal waterways connected by canals, it also allows large numbers of Americans to have waterfront houses.

We started by heading south from St Petersburg to Miami and Key West. Before we got there we found a quiet bay with an inlet to an enormous mangrove swamp – the Everglades National Park. On the way in, we passed a yacht anchored there, but we didn't want to stay so far out, so we continued on deeper into the interior. We then spent a whole day exploring the mangrove-lined waterways by dinghy, even seeing the remains of an old steam boiler rusting in the mangroves. On the way back, the same yacht was still there, with the man gesturing at us to stop from his deck. We tied up beside them. It turned out that the man had grown nervous when we hadn't immediately returned, and he had called the coastguard, thinking that we must have run into trouble. He was told that if we looked experienced then we probably were and, thankfully, the coastguard never came out looking for us. We talked a little longer and he admitted he was new to sailing. He had bought a house in the right place at the right time: a motorway junction was built near to it, and he had been given a considerable amount of money in compensation. But, instead of buying another house, he had bought this yacht, despite having no proper idea of how to cruise it.

We left him to sail round the outside of Key West and into the marina to explore Hemingway's old haunts and its old-fashioned buildings. To our surprise, we then found ourselves next to our friend from the mangroves again. In need of help, he waved us down.

His batteries were completely flat. He had drained them overnight by leaving all his electrics on, thinking it was all much the same as the virtually limitless mains electricity at his house. He had no idea that leisure batteries could be drained and, worse still, he had no idea how to make them work again. He had connected them to the mains but they were too low to start the engine. I guessed a few more minutes would enable us to get it going, so I suggested that Celia should have a shower while I waited for the batteries to charge. It worked and the man was extremely grateful; he assured me that he had learnt his lesson. I can only take his word for it, as we sailed away soon after and never saw him again. I doubt if he kept cruising for much longer.

We spent some time sailing outside the Keys, and then rejoined the ICW at Miami. It was only then that we realised that navigation by day was easy as all the water towers had the towns' names on them. It was very helpful as it is easy to underestimate the speed of the Gulf Stream. We went up to Port Canaveral and anchored in a bay to the west of the Kennedy Space Center. We had timed it perfectly to watch a Space Shuttle launch. To keep Andrew occupied, I taught him how to use the sextant to measure the angle to the top of the shuttle. Since we knew the height, he could work out how far away we were. We watched the launch and could hear the tremendous roar the rocket engines made. Not surprisingly, it was the highlight of his and our holiday; reality is so much better than television.

Then we sailed on to St Augustine in the north of Florida. And it was there that something momentous happened: we felt cold. This was, we realised, the furthest north we had been in *Caleta* since leaving the Mediterranean seven years earlier, and it was the coldest we had been since we left England. If we wanted to keep going and not repeat ourselves, the only way from there was even further north, where it would get colder and colder as we sailed.

We were, you see, tropical sailors avoiding the British winter. North of Florida was continental America, and the only time it was warm enough to sail there was the summer, when we were occupied by farm work. The Bahamas were relatively close, but neither of us were particularly interested in sailing to them. There was also the issue of the boat itself, which was getting old by that time, and beginning to require a lot of work to maintain.

Celia and I talked about it for some time. We had, we realised, gone as far as we were going to go. It was the end of an era, but we knew it was the right thing to do. We turned around, headed back for Miami, found a waterside house with space to moor *Caleta*, and then put it up for sale.

We commissioned an agent to sell the boat for us while we returned to England. It didn't take long. Soon after, we received notification that *Caleta* had been sold, just like that. Our second home of fourteen years was gone. But our time on it had been wonderful; we had made full use of *Caleta* and realised all our dreams.

CHAPTER EIGHTEEN
LIFE AFTER CALETA

After selling *Caleta*, we began to think about what to do in the future. We met a former neighbour who farmed, Pat Roberts, and his partner, Kate Bracken, at a cocktail party. We got on well, and they asked us to join them sailing their yacht *Aurlyn II* down the east coast of America. Everything went well and we enjoyed the sail and they later asked us to accompany them to Mexico in a campervan to give them more confidence, which we also enjoyed. We were lucky that our only problem, which occurred when Pat was driving, was that we hit a rock and nearly tore the back axle off the campervan.

Their boat, *Aurlyn II*, had an interesting history. Its previous owners were Maurice and Maralyn Bailey. In 1973, they set out on a grand voyage from England to New Zealand in their first boat, the original *Aurlyn*, a conflation of their names. After crossing the Atlantic, they passed through the Panama Canal and sailed into the Pacific Ocean. It was there that their boat was struck by a whale. Maurice and Maralyn had just enough time to transfer some vital supplies to their inflatable life raft before Aurlyn sank. For the next four months, they drifted in the Pacific, managing to survive by catching fish and sea turtles and drinking rainwater. They were finally rescued by a South Korean fishing boat about 1,500 miles from where *Aurlyn* had sunk. Their book about the experience, *117 Days Adrift*, became a bestseller amongst the sailing community. The Baileys, who hadn't been put off by the disaster, soon bought a new boat, having spent the time while drifting on the raft designing it. They called it *Aurlyn II* and hoped to be able to pay for it with another successful book. But they weren't particularly good writers: it was the amazing experience which had sold their book, not the quality of their writing. After a time, they gave up the idea, and Pat and Kate bought *Aurlyn II* from them ten years later.

We made a number of trips across the South Pacific with Pat and Kate on *Aurlyn II*. They invited us under the guise of companionship and experience, but both Celia and I suspected ulterior motives. Pat was never the best sailor, and I'm sure my presence and support gave him much-needed confidence. Meanwhile, Celia was convinced that Kate was after me, something I was oblivious to at the time. Celia was eventually proved right when, on a skiing holiday a few years later, Kate made a pass at me. Nevertheless, they were easy to travel with and, overall, we enjoyed their company, enjoyed sailing with them, and travelled to some exotic places.

For all his failings as a skipper, Pat was pretty tough. Unlike me, his idea of boat security was not a gun, but a machete. Once, in the Caribbean, while he and Kate slept in their cabin, a man swam out to their boat under the cover of night, boarded, and began to loot their money and belongings, leaning over them as they slept. The noise woke Pat, who proceeded to chase the man back to shore in his dinghy and then beat him over the head with his machete. He did not kill the man, which was lucky for both of them, but I am sure the looter never looked the same again. As the machete was a local weapon, Pat escaped a charge of assault from the police.

We joined them again in the Marquesas Islands after a somewhat unusual flight whose last section was on a small cabin craft. After exploring a mountainous island in the Marquesas that few non-sailing people visit, we cruised with one of Pat and Kate's friends, called Maggie, who had a larger, more comfortable boat. One calm night, Maggie and her husband invited us all for dinner. We left the navigation and mast lights on, climbed into the dinghy, and went over to their yacht, leaving *Aurlyn II* adrift on its own. Maggie had cooked a wonderful dinner which we all greatly enjoyed, accompanied by excellent wines that had travelled well. When we came up on deck some hours later, we were grateful that Pat could still see *Aurlyn II* about half a mile away. After thanking our hosts, we climbed back into the dinghy in the middle of the Pacific, motored back to rehoist the sails and carried on gently westwards.

We were soon approaching the Tuamotus, a chain of islands and atolls in French Polynesia also known as the 'Dangerous Archipelago'. They were so named because they are all low coral islands with strong and unpredictable currents round them, so difficult that even inter-island steamers run aground. I was having to concentrate hard on the navigation and hoped the satnav positions came close together to reduce the errors caused by variable currents. We had two on watch at night so one could concentrate on looking for land and listening for breakers. Luckily, we saw land about a quarter of a mile away. We then sailed along the edge of the island until we reached the entrance channel. This was about 60 feet wide and we had to motor into it as the current was coming out at about 5 knots. All the inhabited Pacific atolls have the same system of a sandspit with the village beside the entrance channel on the downwind side of the atoll. The windward side is usually a full coral reef which the trade wind-driven seas break over to keep filling the lagoon with clean seawater, and the excess streams out of the village channel, giving a constant outgoing current.

We went to the island's village to meet the chief, where we soon noticed something peculiar. Many of the village's younger boys, who ran, chased and laughed around us, had strange marks and scars across their bare legs. I looked closer, and suddenly realised that they were shark bites.

I took Pat to one side and told him. We agreed it was best to say nothing to Celia and Kate. If they knew, they would never go snorkelling, and would probably forbid us from doing so too. But the water was so clear and the reef so colourful that I wasn't going to let a few sharks stop me, and I was pleased when Pat said that he felt the same. Sometimes it's good to have someone tough by your side.

In the end, Kate decided not to join us anyway because she knew about the sharks. Pat, Celia and I swam out towards the reef and began our snorkel. I had been right: the conditions there were wonderful, with sun-kissed waters, vibrant brain coral, fire coral and stag coral, and hundreds of colourful tropical fish swimming everywhere.

Suddenly, a flash of something caught my eye. I turned round to look to my right and there, edging its way through the deeper waters, was the unmistakeable sight of a blacktip shark. About five feet long, it was still some distance from us, but closing the gap with quick, darting turns. I watched it as it swam; it was clear that it was circling us.

A scream sounded from behind me; it was Celia. She had seen the shark and was desperately swimming away from it. I managed to grab her and told her to keep calm as the worst thing we could do was panic. Pat had also noticed the shark and, together, the three of us slowly backed towards the tallest part of the reef protruding from the surface of the water. Without taking our eyes off the shark, which was getting closer to us with every second, we clambered backwards up on to the reef and huddled on its peak. The shark continued to swim round us and, even though we were out of the water, it could obviously still see us.

Celia pulled her mask off. 'Can sharks … *jump*?' she muttered.

'We're safe now,' I said. 'It can't get us up here.' The words helped reassure Celia, but I was not so sure I believed them myself. Sharks most certainly could propel themselves out of the water, and this one seemed big enough and agile enough to take one of us by the leg and drag us off the reef and out to sea.

The three of us perched on top of that length of coral for the next few minutes, mesmerised by the shark as it swam to and fro, its black skin flashing in the sunlight, its beady eyes staring up at us. When it finally gave up and swam off, we remained where we were, only daring to re-enter the water when we were certain the shark had gone. Coaxing Celia back into the water was the hardest part of all.

◎ ◎ ◎

Pat and Kate sailed down to New Zealand for the hurricane season, and we were then invited back to sail north the following year with them to the tropics, but during the dangerous time between the hurricane season and the southern winter. It is quite a long sail and, as the winter approaches, so does the likelihood of bad weather.

We were heading for Tonga but, with the Kermadec Islands on our route, we hoped for a break there. After a rough start, the southerly winds behind us gave us an easy ride into warmer weather. The wind steadily eased as we approached Raoul Island and it seemed as if it would be calm enough to stop. We were observed coming in and given a welcome hand to moor as, without help, we couldn't have managed it. We threw out ropes to them where they had places to tie them. Then we had to climb into our dinghy with the yacht tied well away from the rocks. We neared the shore and each of us was finally hoisted on a crane to take us ashore. The dinghy was pulled up after us.

Raoul Island was a weather station in name, but was really kept inhabited to extend New Zealand's maritime territory some 300 miles out from its coastline. The meteorological people lived an isolated but happy life with the whole island to enjoy. The weekly postman came in style, flying low over the island and dropping mail and supplies from the open door of a Naval Patrol Orion aircraft. We stayed three nights. Because the anchorage was so dangerous if the weather turned bad, I spent one of the nights on the boat and Pat spent the other two. My night alone was somewhat nerve-wracking, as I wondered how bad the weather would have to be to force me to leave. I also wondered how I would be able to return in a yacht I didn't know much about. Fortunately, I stayed calm, and so did the weather.

There was another New Zealand yacht there and the owners kindly offered to take me on a dive with them. This was the reason they had come to Raoul Island. It was one of the most amazing dives I have ever done. One of the divers was a Maori and he seemed to have magical powers with fish. He found a large wild grouper, three or more feet long, which he could hold under his arm, and it remained totally calm throughout the dive. It just seemed to want to stay with him. I was sad to leave such an isolated place with such friendly people. We managed to board safely and had an easy passage to Tonga and a few weeks enjoying Pacific island hospitality – including a visit to a small community where the men dressed in their traditional costume of nothing but penis sheaths – as well as some reef swimming with, most importantly, no sharks.

CHAPTER NINETEEN
CALETA II

In 1984, we decided we wanted to own another sailing boat, so we began work on designing and building the 50-foot *Caleta II* from scratch. We had specific requirements for a similar covered cockpit to the one on *Caleta* and, in order for the boat to look right and not be too high, we spent a long time designing it. We even did a mock-up at home. The boat was to be built of aluminium by Whisstocks of Woodbridge to fit our exact requirements. We saw it cut from aluminium sheets and watched it slowly take shape upside down, until the hull was finished. Then with the aid of two cranes it was turned the correct way up, and the builders started fitting it out. We went down every week to ensure the drawings agreed with what we wanted. The boat was extremely well built, but like everything else it took longer than was intended. We had set a launch date well in advance, to which the builders agreed, but when the date came, it was a long way from being finished. Nevertheless, we launched it as scheduled.

The builders moored it against the quay, but it was a mud berth and at low tide the boat heeled to about 45 degrees. The boatbuilders had to work in extremely difficult conditions. We should have put the launch date back, but they wanted to carry on as planned. While it was waiting, they tried to haul up another yacht, but they failed to locate it on the slip, and it tipped over towards us, only missing us by two feet.

Caleta II was finished by Whisstocks in the autumn of 1985, and we did a few test runs up and down the coast in September. Then we left it in the marina with the sails on all winter and we spent a nervous season worrying in case Customs discovered we were still in England, as our plan was to sail to the Caribbean in the autumn to save the VAT. The boat had to be ready to leave at short notice if Customs demanded we left. It was finally fully ready the following spring and looked terrific. We were delighted with it, and even more delighted that Customs had not found us, as its launch had been long delayed.

*Having built the hull,
Caleta II is turned over
to fit out the interior.
Woodbridge, Suffolk*

Caleta II *launched in
Woodbridge, Suffolk.*
(LEFT TO RIGHT*: Andrew,
Helen, family member,
Celia, Charles, Celia's
mother)*

We began our journey in the Easter holidays with the children, who were teenagers by now. To remove any stress of Customs forcing us to go or charging us VAT, we sailed straight from Suffolk, past Dover to the Channel Islands when, about 50 miles away from our destination of Jersey, the steering suddenly broke. It was not an impossible obstacle to overcome, as this had been planned in the design. We had an emergency tiller which we fitted in place. It was extremely heavy, so I used it to steer, and shouted to Celia to operate the engine controls. As we reached the marina, Andrew and Helen jumped ashore with the lines and tied us up safely and without accident. We were relieved to be in a safe harbour at Cherbourg.

As we didn't want to remain in Cherbourg, I bought some wire to replace the broken wire and rebuilt the steering. When that was fixed, we set sail for Jersey. We arrived with proper steering control and left the boat in a safe marina where we asked the builders to repair the steering. This they grudgingly did, after admitting they had used stainless steel wire when it should have been galvanised.

With the problems finally fixed, we continued along the French coast without the children, who had gone back to school, and across the Bay of Biscay to Finisterre. Then we sailed down to Cascais to enjoy Portuguese wine and life and to restock with food. From Cascais, we sailed straight to Madeira for two days, and then finally down to the Canaries.

We left *Caleta II* in Tenerife for the harvest and to plant the following year's crops. We should have had time for good shooting, but Michael Fish, a well-known BBC reporter, forecast the weather totally wrong and we had unexpected hurricane-force winds of over 100 miles an hour, which shook our solid brick house. The winds brought down hundreds of trees, even felling the whole centre of the large woods and leaving the outer trees still standing. Two old timber barns were also blown down. I was lucky to have good men who spent the winter clearing up the tons of fallen timber, which was mostly used for pit props.

We decided to wait until the Christmas holidays in 1987 so that we could take the children out to experience an Atlantic crossing. As soon as school was finished, we all flew out to Tenerife together.

We had installed a generator on *Caleta II*, mainly to save us having to find gas and to avoid the danger of it leaking. With the generator we could charge the batteries twice daily, simultaneously cool the fridge and deep freeze and, most importantly, power our electric cooker. It was good to think that the noise made during cooking was keeping the rest of the boat going, enabling us to have croissants and coffee each morning. It was also good to avoid running the main engine just for charging the battery.

We stocked up with food in Tenerife, knowing we would not have to rely so heavily on fishing as we had during our previous crossing ten years before. When everything was ready, we set off. It soon became obvious to us that *Caleta II* was a far superior boat to the first *Caleta*. On the second night out, we had a yacht on the port side – we kept our eye on it by watching its mast lights. Suddenly, I realised I could not see it, so I looked out of the cockpit and was horrified to find it was only ten feet from us. We did a quick course alteration and averted disaster. Otherwise, the voyage was smooth and passed without incident. By now, Celia and I knew exactly what we were doing with all the confidence of long-term sailors. Andrew and Helen helped out when they could, and we were especially grateful to be able to divide the watch between three rather than just two (Helen was too young to take a watch alone).

Caleta II *sailing*

One evening, when both Andrew and Helen were on watch together, the first watch after supper, I went up on deck to take over. They were huddled up and engrossed in conversation. I had a quick look round at the seas, and then turned to my children. 'Is everything all right?' I asked.

Surprised by my question, for they had not even noticed me appear, they recoiled from each other in shock. 'Everything's fine,' they both said.

'Good,' I said, and then turned to my son. 'Andrew, could you please do me a favour? Go up to the bow and just have a look round. Check the sky and the sea. Then come back and tell me what's going through your mind.'

Andrew walked up to the bow and looked round, before returning moments later, looking rather abashed as he did so.

A rare opportunity – meeting another yacht in the Atlantic who took a photograph of Caleta II *sailing*

'What's the problem?' I asked.

'There's a ship out there.'

'Where is it heading?'

'Towards us.'

'So why didn't you tell me that when I asked if everything was all right?'

'I didn't see it then.'

'And why didn't you see it?'

Andrew looked down at his shoes. 'Because I was talking to Helen.'

'Were you watching for shipping?'

'No.'

They went below, feeling sheepish that they had put *Caleta II* and the family at risk. I then took over for the first night watch. We controlled the speed of *Caleta* as the wind strength changed by reefing one of our twin sails or letting more sail out if it dropped. We had twin headsails up so there was never any risk of gybing.

The crossing went smoothly. One day we saw a small yacht with a red sail ahead which we soon caught up with. We slowed down, waved to each other and took mid-ocean photographs. By chance we met again in the Grenadines, exchanged contact details and, on returning home, sent each other the photographs we had taken. We did have one sudden strong unseen squall, during which both booms holding the sails bent. This was a design failure as the designer had made them too long and too thin. We thus had to use less sail to take the strain off the booms. The weather stayed fine for the rest of the crossing, and we reached English Harbour in daylight, feeling surprisingly fresh. In total, the crossing took us 17 days, much faster than our first, which had taken 23.

◗ ◗ ◗

Andrew and I did a lot of diving from *Caleta II*. By the following year, he had qualified as a diver, so he was technically more qualified than me. We often went off together, and once he swam into a cave in quite turbulent conditions, which he later admitted he should never have done. During one particular sail, we neared the British Virgin Islands, and I told him about a dive site I was keen to try.

Just off the coast of Salt Island lies the wreck of RMS *Rhone*. Its sinking in 1867 is a tragic story. Anchored off Peter Island, the Rhone was loaded with its usual consignment of mail and cargo. It also carried passengers and, this time, took on more than usual. Nobody questioned the overloading because the *Rhone* was considered to be an unsinkable ship. This was proved completely wrong when the San Narciso Hurricane drove the *Rhone* into Salt Island's Black Rock Point, causing the ship to break in two, the boilers to explode, and 123 of the 145 crew and passengers to drown. Since then, the Rhone has become a popular wreck dive site. Andrew agreed that it sounded fascinating, and we made our way out there to dive on it.

As we were swimming towards the wreck, a diving boat came over us and its skipper stupidly dropped his anchor. The boat was directly overhead and, as such, the anchor itself missed me by about five yards, which is too close by any standards. Had it been any closer, I would have been seriously injured.

I was enraged by such stupidity, but I wasn't going to stop that letting us enjoy this world-class dive site. Andrew had swum ahead by this point and I was following him. We approached the wreck and swam up and down through parts of it, including inside the old boiler. I was having trouble with my ears and tried to clear them. If I had been on my own, I would have stopped and swallowed to clear them, but because I was trying to keep up with Andrew, I continued swimming while I did so. And that was when, in an instant, I overpressurised. I didn't know what was wrong – all I knew was that, suddenly, I could no longer hear. We carried on with the dive, then returned in the dinghy to *Caleta II*. I tried to clear my ears, but nothing changed. This sometimes happens after diving: the hearing takes a while to return to normal. But it persisted for the rest of the holiday. As soon as we returned to England, I visited my doctor, who gave me some medicine which had no effect. Eventually, he referred me to a specialist, who told me that I had burst my inner ear drum. There was nothing that he could do to restore my hearing, except to perform an emergency operation to prevent it becoming infected, which would have destroyed my balance forever. I have been deaf in that ear ever since.

I continued to sail *Caleta II* with Celia and later on my own until 2019, when I sold it to an Antiguan yacht skipper.

PART IV:
THE UNIMOG

Unimog beside the Caspian Sea

CHAPTER TWENTY
A NEW WAY TO TRAVEL

In the autumn of 1987, Celia took her mother to New Zealand when her father died. With this unexpected free time on my hands, I decided to do something different, and took a fortnight's trip through the game parks of Kenya and Tanzania in a big safari vehicle. Overlanding was a refreshing change from sailing. I enjoyed seeing the wildlife close up, enjoyed the vast plains of the Serengeti and the Ngorongoro Crater, and enjoyed being driven as a passenger in an overland truck.

On my return home, Andrew asked me how my holiday had been. I told him all about it, and he listened with fascination. The following Easter, he came out to join us on *Caleta II* in the Caribbean for his holidays. He had brought with him a book by Chris Scott called *Sahara Overland*, which he had already read several times. He dreamt of overlanding and wanted to try it himself. Inspired by my recent journey through Africa, he asked if it was something we could do together, which seemed a good idea.

We spent the rest of the holiday discussing the pros and cons of an African overland journey: where we could go; for how long; what provisions we would need beforehand and what we could buy on the way; costs and requirements; borders and red tape. Perhaps the most important issue was *how* to travel and, more specifically, which vehicle would be best suited to our wants and needs. Andrew's book, *Sahara Overland*, featured something called a Unimog, a kind of all-terrain German military vehicle hardy enough to withstand any journey, no matter how extreme. We decided that it was the perfect vehicle for us.

When we returned home, we booked an appointment at the Unimog factory in Germany. There, we were given a demonstration over their test track, and were much impressed by the vehicle. We discussed with the engineers the various options we wanted and what they suggested for us. The book for Unimog options is as thick as a telephone directory. It must be the only vehicle of which you can buy half. If, for example, you just want the front half, you can have it.

We made our decisions in the factory and ordered a Unimog to my specification. We chose, amongst other things, a six-cylinder 6-litre turbo-diesel engine developing 155 horsepower, air-operated differential locks, air-over-oil-operated disc brakes and an air-operated exhaust brake. This latter closes the exhaust pipe to give engine braking. We also decided on 14.50×20 Michelin XL(C) tyres. The manufacturers worked most efficiently, completing our bespoke vehicle in just four months. They made one mistake, fitting springs that were far too soft. But once they had checked the specification and saw that we had ordered the strongest springs available, they admitted their mistake and replaced the springs without hesitation.

When it was delivered to England, both Andrew and I undertook an off-road trial in a pit on the farm near Blythburgh. Due to the unique design of the Unimog, it took Andrew a little while to become used to it. Driving a Unimog is rather like driving an old tractor, and most people wouldn't understand how to operate it. With its hand throttle, also used to stop the engine, its clutch safety switch start and its 16-speed shuttle gearbox, later modified to 32 speeds of which 16 are just for reverse, it is rather different to driving an average car or even a truck. For me, with my decades of farm experience and tractor driving, it was all fairly easy to master as it was in fact a big farm tractor, but one which needed an HGV licence. Fortunately, I had one due to 'grandfathers' rights', which allowed people with years of experience to avoid the newly required test.

Now that we had this enormous, portal-axled cross-country behemoth, we began the next stage of the build: the body. Andrew had studied technical drawing at college and, now his A levels were complete, he had both the time and the ability to draw the interior design. We found Belle Coachworks, a local truck builder in Lowestoft, who agreed to build a commercial insulated body.

At the same time, I began to think about the Unimog's front. I bought a 10,000-pound Pierce electric winch – an absolute necessity if we were ever stuck in the sand or mud. In addition, I also had the idea of using this part of the vehicle for motorbike storage. It seemed to me that this would help balance the Unimog far more effectively than if it was on the back, where bike carriers are usually kept. I bought a small forklift frame and employed my farm mechanic to fit it on to the front, where it worked perfectly as a carrier. It could be raised and lowered with the front winch cable. I invested in a Kawasaki KLR250: the type of run-around bike which is ideal for both off-roading and busy city streets. While others considered this a luxury, for me having a bike with us was a necessity. I thought of it in the same way as I thought of a yacht's dinghy: if we ran into trouble with the Unimog, we could use the bike to escape and find help. It would also enable us to explore small villages and make more personal contact with the local people – aided by the fact that I never used a helmet for those kinds of local trips.

Down on the south coast, we found a small company which was able to build the interior, turning the Unimog into a fully habitable campervan. Based on our designs, they installed one double bed and two single beds, a stove, twin refrigerators, a lavatory and shower, and plenty of storage space accessible from the outside for easy access and to keep the vehicle's weight low down. We also fitted three extra fuel tanks to give us the maximum range in Africa. It turned out that these held enough for us to reach Gibraltar without refuelling.

Finally, we were ready to go. Rather than begin with a major expedition, Andrew and I decided to take things easy for our first trip. We still wanted to go to Africa, but we agreed that a three-week journey to Morocco and back would be enough for the maiden voyage. It would be a good trial run.

In 1989, we took the ferry to Calais and then drove down through France and Spain, sharing the driving between us. At Gibraltar we flew a Union Jack from the front of the Unimog, until the police told us to take it down because it was far too big and obstructed our view through the windscreen.

We drove on from Gibraltar to Algeciras, and then caught the ferry to Ceuta. There we experienced our first foreign customs post, with lots of Arabs wanting to offer their services for bribes and telling us all sorts of stories about who was dangerous and what might happen to us. After about three hours, with the Unimog details entered on to my passport, we were free to explore Morocco.

Good roads run south from Ceuta to Tetouan, so we stopped there for a break. Sadly, there seemed to be more hassle than beauty in Tetouan, so we didn't stay long. Instead, we travelled on further south towards the larger towns and cities, Fez and Marrakesh, where the souks were extensive and exotic. We wandered through these bazaars for hours, enjoying the tiny passageways filled with people, donkeys, piles of spices, and intricate bowls and lanterns. It was all bright and colourful. I especially liked the white-painted roofs, where the dyed cloths were hung at head height to dry in the light winds.

The next stop was Marrakesh, further south still, away from the coast and into the mountains on the fringe of the desert. The Unimog was holding up well, although we still hadn't tested it properly. Conditions so far had been good, with roads suitable for any kind of campervan. That said, we had driven almost 2,000 miles between Calais and Marrakesh, and the Unimog had covered the whole distance with ease, continually drawing stares from the locals wherever we went. They were fascinated by our giant truck, and especially so by the motorbike on the front, which was a rare sight. Every young man wanted to ride it and buy it, or mostly to be given it.

An evening with a Berber family in Algeria

It was now time to be adventurous, to leave the good roads behind us and venture into more challenging territory. We turned east, towards the High Atlas Mountains, where we found the beautiful Todra and Dadès gorges. The Unimog tackled the canyons and climbs wonderfully, and we never felt ill at ease or out of our depth.

We camped wild in the Todra Gorge, backing off a road and stopping on a dry river bed. It seemed safe enough at the time – we were at a fairly high altitude and facing in the right direction. If it were to rain and the river were to fill, we were bound to hear the water coming down, and the Unimog's three feet of clearance would have given us ample opportunity to drive clear. It was only ten yards to get back on the road. Nevertheless, when I look back on it now, I realise that camping on the river bed was a foolish thing to do, regardless of what we considered

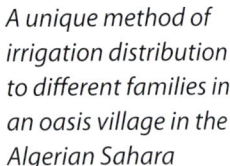

A unique method of irrigation distribution to different families in an oasis village in the Algerian Sahara

to be our safeguards. Avoiding camping on any river bed anywhere is a good general rule to follow, and especially so in the Moroccan desert, where the water can quickly come down from heavy rain in the mountains while you are relaxing in the desert sunshine. Flash floods are not uncommon out there, and when they happen people, and their vehicles, are easily swept away.

The strange and beautiful landscape of the mountains was hypnotic, and we continued across them. Everywhere we stopped there were children around who immediately flocked to us. At first, we thought they might want to sell us things, but in fact they just wanted to know if we had anything to give them. The two most common words shouted at us were '*Bonbons!*' and '*Bics!*', sweets and pens. We had loaded up with both in England because we knew this was going to happen.

After coming down from the mountains, we ventured further into the desert, but never attempted the sand dunes, which the Unimog couldn't climb. You need about 500 horsepower to go up sand dunes, and we only had 155 horsepower and 8 tons. Nevertheless, as long as the ground remained solid, our progress was good and as we drove, we passed fellow off-roaders: Berbers, some with camels and others with four-wheel-drive trucks.

Our three weeks were drawing to an end, so we began to make our way back up north, in the direction of Europe. It had been a wonderful expedition, completely different to all the sailing adventures of the last twenty years. I couldn't wait to try testing the Unimog even further, to see how far into Africa I could penetrate.

CHAPTER TWENTY-ONE
SAHARAN FRONTIERS

Andrew was unable to join me in 1991 for the next adventure, but I preferred the idea of travelling with a companion who could speak French to help with customs and to talk with locals. I had been a fellow of the Royal Geographical Society for many years, so I looked through its list of people who wanted to join adventures.

My requirements were few: a companion needed to be healthy and strong-minded enough for the expedition which, although not expected to be extreme, was not going to be easy. I needed someone who could cook and who had a good knowledge of French. I've never had much of a talent for languages and, for the countries I was aiming to travel through, I knew that I wouldn't be able to manage with English alone. I contacted a few possible people and found Hélène: a young and pretty French woman who was living in England and was keen for an adventure. She was confident that she could handle all French matters.

On our way down through France, we stopped at Hélène's hometown north of the Pyrenees, and then carried on south through Spain, for a change of scenery, and took a different route from the one I had taken two years earlier with Andrew. The ferry took us to Morocco and the same Ceuta checkpoint to enter the country. We drove the Unimog east and headed for the Algerian border.

Once there, I joined the queue at customs; there were only four other cars in front of us. I handed Hélène our passports and then sat back and let her take over. Although Algeria's official language is Arabic, thanks to its colonial history French is spoken everywhere and by everyone. From here on, Hélène would do all the talking for me. I was glad that I had had the foresight to bring a French speaker with me.

The four cars in front passed through the border without difficulty, and we came to the final barrier. Hélène opened her door and climbed down from the cab. Unfortunately, despite her ability to speak French with the guard, there seemed to be a problem. We were missing a particular police stamp and, to obtain it, we had to go back to the office to collect and complete the necessary forms. We did as we were told, but this queue was much longer than the first, and by the time we reached the front we were told that we needed a special permit to proceed, and that special permit could only be applied for in the nearby town of Tlemcen. Worse still, the office there had closed for the day and we would have to spend the night camping in the customs compound.

With no alternative, we bedded down for the night, grateful that the height of the Unimog's windows meant that passing border guards were unable to peer inside. The next day, I took the KLR down from the carrier and, with Hélène on the back, set off for Tlemcen. It took us two hours to travel there and, once we arrived, we were given a form and told to go to another office to have it stamped, and then to bring it back to have it finally counterstamped by the immigration police. We then headed back to the border, by which time the customs had closed for the night. We tried again in the morning and were finally allowed through, having wasted three days.

As I drove into Algeria, I felt relieved. The ordeal was over and the adventure could begin. Hélène, on the other hand, was rather subdued. She had turned her head away from me to stare out of her window.

'Is everything all right?' I asked.

She slowly turned round to face me. 'I'm sorry,' she said. 'That was all my fault.'

'No, it was their fault,' I said. 'With their ridiculous rules. They could have let us through but they just wanted to be pig-headed about it all.'

'Exactly. They *were* pig-headed, but it was because of my saying something I shouldn't have.'

'What?'

'When I first spoke with the border guard, he was taking so long that I lost my temper. I called him a rude word in French. That's why we had the delay; it was his revenge.'

I thought back to that first day at the border, when Hélène had climbed down from the cab with our passports. I had heard their conversation, but my French is so poor that, even if I had been listening closely, I still wouldn't have picked up what she had said. Nevertheless, she had said it, and rather than being let straight through, we had been forced to suffer three days of interminable bureaucracy, and were now well behind schedule.

I asked Hélène what word she had used but she wouldn't tell me. Whatever it was, I guessed that it must have been pretty offensive.

◎ ◎ ◎

With the desert before us, our priority was to stock up with fuel. This turned out to be as much of a challenge as crossing the border. The first fuel station had an annoyingly long queue. The second one was a little shorter, with only eight vehicles, but the fuel had not even arrived at the station. The third queue seemed perfect until the fuel ran out. The same happened at the fourth. It was becoming increasingly frustrating. The only way to solve the problem was to return to Tlemcen. It was in completely the wrong direction, but we knew that there was fuel there, which was all that mattered. At least it only cost seven pence a gallon. That helped make up for all the frustrations.

Finally, it was time to make a start and we set off south. Around us, the land became open scrub plains, scattered with sheep and goats. We drove off the road through the tufted grass, which slowed the Unimog to a crawl, to look for a campsite away from the tents. We were so slow that a local man was able to catch us up on foot.

I stopped. The man introduced himself as Ahmed and invited us to his tent for a drink. We were delighted to accept and parked the Unimog outside his tent and, on Ahmed's recommendation, locked it. His lovely wife welcomed us into their home, and Ahmed showed us how the tufted grass which had slowed us was in fact an incredibly useful material. It was used in many ways: to feed his animals; to make raffia-style baskets; even his tent was woven from tufted grass.

Ahmed invited us to sit down while he began to prepare the drink for which he had invited us. In the middle of the tent, a small fire burnt, its smoke drifting up and out through the chimney: a square hole in the roof which also served as a skylight. The fire seemed to be built from a local root, which wasn't the most flammable material in the world, for Ahmed often had to drench it in diesel to stoke up the flames. I assumed he would cook on the fire, but instead he lit a small gas stove and boiled some water on it, pouring in liquids from two different pots and mixing them together. When it was finally time to drink, the concoction turned out to be a milky kind of coffee, and was absolutely delicious.

We thanked our hosts, exchanged names and addresses with them, and then set off again, warmed by the drink and the kind welcome we had received. It was, we soon came to understand, characteristic of this area. Our next stop was in a village further south, where we took a short break to buy some bread. Sure enough, the baker invited us to his home while we waited for him to bake the next fresh batch. Of all the legacies the French left behind, a fondness for freshly baked bread is surely one of the best. In his house, we were not only served drinks but lunch too: couscous soup with bread, which we ate sitting cross-legged on the floor with the baker, his father and his uncle. Conversation was free-flowing and friendly. As is often the case in these situations, it soon turned to travel. The father proudly revealed that he had been to Mecca six times.

'We're on our way south,' Hélène said. 'We've already covered 140 kilometres this morning.'

'More like 150,' the father said, and then named the exact place we had camped the previous night.

'How did you know that?' Hélène asked.

'I was there this morning!' the father said, winking at her. 'I always know the gossip.'

Our first proper desert town was Aïn Séfra, in the north-west of Algeria close to the Moroccan border. Astonishingly for this arid land, it rained so hard that we had to use the double-speed setting on the windscreen wipers. A couple of hundred miles south at Taghit, we began to search for a place to camp – finding a good spot where it was flat and just out of view from the road. In the morning, we woke and gazed out the window at the valley, noticing the fresh camel tracks in the nearby sand.

Taghit, an oasis town fed by the underground Oued Zouzfana, is best observed from high up. We drove to the edge of the escarpment and looked down. From there, Taghit appeared as a little mud village nestled into the 300-foot-tall dunes of the Grand Erg Occidental, stretching into the horizon. We decided to drive down into the town to explore the covered passageways, abandoned buildings and fortified parapets. In the foothills of the dunes, we met two fellow travellers, Americans called Robert and Jan. They were heading in the same direction as us so we invited them to join us in the Unimog, an invitation which benefitted us all. They were given free transport and accommodation; we had two extra pairs of hands to help us if stuck in the sand.

The night passed in friendly conversation, and then the next morning we set off for Béni Abbès, driving along the periphery of the Erg to reach it. Ramadan had just begun, and we wondered if perhaps this Muslim month of fasting might affect the opening hours of all the places we hoped to visit. Fortunately, it seemed to have no effect whatsoever, and we spent that afternoon visiting the town's museum.

So far, we had stayed in Algeria's west, close to the Moroccan border. Now it was time to penetrate deeper into the interior, and we drove east to Timimoun, a mud-walled, ochre-red town with domed buildings. An oasis served as Timimoun's centre, where date palms and vegetables grew, and where old men sat and passed their days together. To the south-west of the town is Sebkha de Timimoun, a salt lake surrounded by small villages. An off-road tour of these villages seemed a good idea, so we set off in the Unimog to do a circuit of the lake.

With nothing to follow except the basic map in my guidebook, the off-road tour was far more ambitious than we had anticipated. The first turning was non-existent. We tried the opposite direction and found a tarmac turning, making a GPS waypoint as we left the road, to find that the distance just didn't agree with our map. Undeterred, we continued, following the tarmac down to a village where, before we knew it, we were suddenly driving through streets only a foot or two wider than the Unimog itself, with fragile-looking mud walls rising six feet high on either side of us. Thankfully, the local children came out to guide us through these impossibly narrow streets. When we came to a dead end in the next village, it was another local who showed us how to find our way through the network of field tracks, tracks we never would have found on our own. Along the way, we continued to plot the GPS track of our route and soon came to the conclusion that all the roads we were using were not as old as our map, which was clearly obsolete by this point. We camped that night in a village where people lived in caves and tunnels hewn into the ochre-coloured rock. It felt as if we had stepped back in time to a primitive civilisation until night fell and lights lit up the caves and tunnels. These people were not that primitive as, after all, they did have electricity.

The next morning, we felt that, with our guidebook and the map we had been drawing ourselves, we now had a better sense of where we were and decided to complete our circuit of the lake. The road led us round enormous boulders to a dry river bed. I climbed out of the Unimog to find the best point to cross, ensuring that the surface was hard, and then climbed back in. We drove over the river bed and then, a mile or so later, began our ascent up a rocky slope. At the top, we found the track and rejoined the tarmac to drive back to Timimoun. As we arrived, I felt proud of the Unimog. It had completed a tough journey without a single problem.

Travelling on further south in the direction of the Malian border, we stopped at Reggane, with its centre of old red-walled buildings and sandy streets. This was in sharp contrast to the outskirts of unfinished and abandoned buildings. My map indicated that the town of In Salah could be reached from Reggane via a small and probably unused track. The distance, 150 miles, seemed too much for the Unimog but we soon found out that, once again, the map was out of date. The first 60 miles were brand-new tarmac which we cruised over in comfort.

For the remaining 90 miles, conditions worsened, but never became intolerable. The road widened where vehicles had made new tracks to avoid the corrugations of the older ones. Usually, the surface was hard enough for easy driving, but it could suddenly change to soft sand, or *fesh fesh*. Then I would have to change down two gears as quickly as possible to find enough power to drive through the fesh fesh. Few other vehicles passed us in either direction, and the desert stretched untouched into the distance, except for the irregular concrete marker posts or burst and abandoned tyres. Once, when we stopped at a small oasis for a rest, a Tuareg man and his camel approached us. We asked where he was going and he told us that his destination was the same as ours: In Salah. It was still over 60 miles away and would take him three days to walk there. I would have given him a lift, but there was no room for his camel in the Unimog, and the man wouldn't hear of leaving the animal behind. So, as a compromise, I offered him my spare pair of shoes. He was thrilled with the gift and eagerly took the shoes. I have a photograph of him sitting in the sand by his camel, beaming as he fitted the new shoes to his feet. It remains one of my very favourite photographs.

◎ ◎ ◎

The road to In Salah was so rough that the Unimog's diesel tank strap broke. This was the only time that the Unimog suffered any damage. I tied on a Span Set strap to hold it in place until we reached In Salah. Once there, I was able to find a mechanic to weld it for me. As we waited, we walked round the town. This was a place where the battle against the desert was perpetual: sand settled on the streets like snowdrifts, piling against the walls of buildings, blanketing the walkways, and burying the trunks of the palm trees.

Once the welding was complete, we set out towards our next destination: Tamanrasset, some 400 miles to the south, nestled in a crook of the Ahaggar National Park close to the Niger border. Sand continued to drift in, swirling in the wind and filling every available opening. That night, when we stopped to camp in a spot overlooking a valley with dark and towering mountains behind it, I tried to take the KLR out for a ride. But the winds intensified and, realising I was riding into a sandstorm, I was forced to turn round. On the way back to the Unimog, I was able to measure the speed of the storm, 35 miles an hour, by reaching the same speed on my bike and clocking it.

About halfway between In Salah and Tamanrasset are the Arak Gorges, a series of desert canyons with walls, in some places, as tall as 1,600 feet. The view through the gorges by the side of the dry river bed was breathtaking as we gazed round us.

I was excited when we finally reached Tamanrasset. I had always dreamt of visiting it, the centre of the Sahara, and an ancient hub of trade routes from Nigeria, Chad, Mali and Niger. For a city situated so deep in the desert, it is surprising how much life exists in Tamanrasset: fruit trees, cereals and nuts are all plentiful, grown from the oasis which forms the heart of the city. Back then, in 1991, the tourist industry which today characterises Tamanrasset was already growing, and most of the vehicles were Nissan Patrols or Toyotas used by tour companies or the police. These 4x4s were in varying states of roadworthiness, but they all had one thing in common. Strapped to their sides, with legs and neck still attached, were goatskin water bags.

We agreed that we wanted to make a tour into the Hoggar Mountains. But, before we did so, we needed fuel. Finding a fuel station, we joined the queue, with twelve or so vehicles in front of us. We watched as each driver filled the tank of his car, and then began to fill the 20-litre barrels they kept in their boots and on their back seats. I couldn't help thinking back to our first day in Algeria, when we had driven from one fuel station to another desperately looking for diesel. I started to panic that all the fuel would be gone by the time our turn came. If that happened, our options were somewhat limited. The nearest sizeable town, Abalessa, was almost 60 miles away, and there was no guarantee they would have any fuel either. After that was Idlès, over 130 miles away, and I was unsure whether we had enough diesel left to go that far. As each vehicle filled, paid and left the forecourt, we edged forward expectantly.

Admiring the moon rise at dusk from the Hoggar Mountain Monastery

Fortunately, our luck, and the diesel reserves, held out. I bought as much fuel as the Unimog could hold, and then found a campsite for the night to plan our trip to the Hoggar mountains. Robert and Jan, who I had picked up on the way, were keen to leave first thing in the morning, but I was cautious. Before leaving England, I had heard from the Foreign Office that, earlier in the year, a truck overlanding through the Hoggar Mountains had been robbed and had its tyres slashed. To add to the danger, a fellow camper told us that something similar had happened just five days before, when a group of French tourists had set out into the mountains in five Toyotas. They were stopped by Kalashnikov-wielding Tuaregs, who robbed the tourists and stole the best of the Toyotas. I was dubious about us driving the Unimog into that region. It was too conspicuous and, if it was stolen, our entire trip would be ruined. It would be better for us to hire a local vehicle, which was not so conspicuous, and to leave the Unimog safely at the campsite until we returned. We also agreed not to take any of our own possessions with us in case we were robbed. Even the bedding we took was borrowed.

The vehicle we settled on was a Series II Land Rover. It was so battered and damaged that nobody would want to steal it. It was a classic vehicle, but I felt confident it was capable of doing the 100-mile round trip. I was right: it may have broken down six times, but we made it.

We drove out to Assekrem, a 9,000-foot-high plateau, to see the hermitage where Charles de Foucauld spent his final years. Foucauld was a French explorer, geographer and Catholic priest who lived as a hermit amongst the Tuareg until his assassination in 1916. The Land Rover broke down half a mile away from the hermitage, but we didn't mind, for it meant we could walk the final portion of the road. We watched the sun set behind the volcanic lava peaks in a fiery display of different reds. That night, we slept on rubber mattresses in the mountain hostel, rising at 5.30 a.m. to watch a sunrise which was even more spectacular than the sunset the night before. Feeling pleased with our achievement, we walked back to the Land Rover and returned to Tamanrasset, albeit arriving without brakes.

Back at the campsite, we were relieved to discover the Unimog was still there. The campsite was filled with overlanders like us, some in cars, others in 4x4s, and others in ex-NATO service trucks. We talked to many of them and learnt that most were on their way to Niger, where they planned to sell their vehicles and fly home. But there was a problem. Algeria's border with Niger had been closed for six weeks, ruining many people's plans. Some considered driving north; others talked about heading east to Djanet and trying to cross from there. But that was a difficult route, suitable only for the toughest vehicles. Most decided to stay put and wait patiently for the border to reopen. It was the easiest option, but also the most frustrating.

I met Ian, who had an overland truck which he was driving to east Africa, but his plans had been scuppered by the Niger border closure, forcing him to fly his passengers to Nigeria to pick up another truck. As a result, he needed to drive up the Amguid desert track to Algiers, a difficult and dangerous route. My guidebook described it as 'for experienced Sahara travellers, only in convoy'. I had dismissed the route, but now I had met Ian and heard his plans, I wondered if we could tackle it together by forming a convoy amongst ourselves. The opportunity was too good to turn down.

Knowing that the journey would take five or six days, we stocked up with everything we could: food, water and, most importantly, fuel. The track was corrugated but straightforward enough to navigate, until a series of sudden and deep holes broke the bike frame safety chain, so we decided to stay put that night. While I replaced the chain with a variety of shackles, Hélène made herself useful by plucking and dressing the chickens we had brought with us.

All seemed well the following morning, when Ian discovered he had a far worse problem. His main fuel tank had split on the track, and 100 gallons of it could be lost by continuing. We considered sharing my fuel, but it was too risky, leaving us both unlikely to make it to the next fuel station. Ian decided to return to In Eker to have the tank welded.

Without Ian, we were no longer a convoy. This was precisely the kind of situation which had put me off attempting this route. Hélène, Robert, Jan and I had a serious discussion about turning back, but it seemed a shame to give up. They deferred to my judgement as I had the most experience of long-distance, self-sufficient journeys. I didn't know if we would make it, but I was determined to try.

The best option seemed to be a shortcut across the open desert. As long as we drove slowly to minimise potential damage, being continually careful and cautious, I thought we would be all right. We took cross-bearings on two of the nearby mountains so that, if the desert crossing proved too difficult for us, we could at least return to our starting point. I took a GPS position of the mountain to the north which gave us a course to steer. We were heading across open desert with no tracks for 60 miles where we would meet neither people nor vehicles. Our only map was an old French air navigational map which showed it as flat land, so in theory our only obstacles should be dry river beds or oueds where it would be possible to find somewhere to cross. Our GPS would continue to show a course to the mountain. We passed a small hill which we decided to climb and were surprised to notice on the way up that the surface showed signs of little rivulets flowing into dry streams, a clear indication of heavy rain in the distant past. We carried on crossing oueds until we sighted the mountain, giving us confidence that we would complete my first totally off-road adventure. This saved us 150 miles of officially mapped desert. Six miles from the mountain we crossed the first track of a desert road at right angles then carried on until we reached the last track and were astonished to find the desert road was 6 miles wide, the amazing width being caused by numerous vehicles choosing to drive on virgin desert. We turned left on to the mapped road. I was thrilled that the Unimog had enabled me to complete 60 miles of off-road driving across the Sahara desert.

◎ ◎ ◎

To begin with, the ground near Amguid remained fairly flat and even, rocky and with little sand, a type of terrain known as *hamada*. We came across a pick-up truck full of Algerians looking rather forlorn with a flat tyre who asked us for help. Luckily, as we had an air compressor and a hose, we could inflate their tyre. They were extremely happy, thanking us profusely. We wondered how they would have managed with a flat tyre in the middle of the desert under the baking sun with nobody around.

Unmarked mountains rose on either side of us as we drove on. The oueds we crossed were, thankfully, all dry. I was able to cruise in sixth gear at a speed of 20–30 miles an hour, and we remained on target to reach Amguid, the following day. We wanted to top up our water supply, but were told that, before anything else, we needed to check in at the police station. Hélène did so while I studied the map to find our route out of the village.

All tracks leading from the village were at best ambiguous, so we decided to trust our instincts and follow the mountains towering over us on our right, hoping we might find a pass at the northern end. We drove on a good track out of the village until being confronted by a forbidding-looking sand dune which seemed impassable. We found another track leading to the left which we followed over a smaller sand dune which came to an abrupt end. Penetrating virgin dunes was far too risky so our only option was to turn back. Our first attempt failed as the sand too looked as if it had been driven over before. I then looked for a new route with a less steep gradient on virgin sand. I drove at it as fast as I could, hoping that my choice of gear was correct and would enable me to climb the hill. Stalling on it would have meant churning up the sand, making subsequent attempts impossible. Luckily, we made it to the top and back on to the *hamada*.

The most sensible thing to do was return to Amguid and seek advice from the local police. Again, Hélène did all the talking in French, and this time succeeded in not upsetting anyone. The policeman assured us that we had wandered off on the wrong track and that he knew precisely where the right one was. In fact, he said, if we followed him, he would lead us straight to it. I looked out of the window of the police station; it was 7.00 p.m. and getting dark. The prospect of driving through the night and tackling sand dunes which had tested us in daylight did not seem a good idea.

However, it was now or never. We needed a guide if we were to ever leave Amguid and here was a policeman offering to lead us out.

As a precaution, I lowered the Unimog's tyre pressure from 60 pounds per square inch to 40. Then we followed the police car's flashing blue lights into the dunes. Hélène was growing nervous as we drove into the nothingness. In the back, Robert and Jan wondered if we had done the right thing. We didn't know the area and we didn't know the policeman. Might it all be a trap to steal the Unimog and leave us for dead in the middle of nowhere? Although our spotlights lit up all the sand around us, we had no idea where we were.

Suddenly, beneath the tyres, I felt we were on solid ground and our floodlights showed no sand. We were out of the sand and on to the track. It had taken just a short while. The police car drove away into the distance and, now that we were finally on terra firma, we stopped to camp for the night.

The next morning, feeling relaxed and refreshed, we drove back over the sand dunes to see where we had driven during the night and then turned back north. Later that day, we found the flat, black stone-covered track which, according to the guidebook, would take us the full 120 miles back to civilisation. The four of us agreed that we had never been so pleased to see such a track before.

◐ ◐ ◐

Fuel stations in the Algerian desert are few and far between and, when we saw one in the distance, we decided to stop and refuel. Hélène spoke to the attendant, who asked us if we would do him a favour. Further up the road, a truck had broken down, and the attendant needed a pair of tyre levers sent there. Since we were heading that way, would we mind taking them, he asked?

We agreed and set off, keeping a lookout for the truck as we drove north. About 50 miles later, we found the truck, which had driven off the road and become stuck in the soft sand. I stopped and climbed out of the Unimog to assess the situation. It was a 6×4 artic and its wheels had dug deep into the sand. The two drivers had neither ropes nor sand mats, or even a shovel, and had given up. However, I thought the truck could be possibly be dug out and that it was worth a try.

I gave the drivers our shovel and, with Hélène acting as interpreter, instructed them to dig as much as they could around the truck's eight wheels. They started digging, but weren't happy about it, sometimes digging with just one hand, and complaining that they were drivers, not manual labourers. I hooked up the artic to the Unimog with my 50-foot nylon tow rope. I told Hélène to instruct the drivers to start the engine and put it into reverse gear and, when I sounded the horn, to let the clutch in on full power. Then I climbed into the cab of the Unimog and drove off at full speed with my hand on the horn. When the rope took up the strain

Pumping the tyre up for a Bedouin truck in Algeria

with the Unimog pulling it, its strength and stretch were enough, together with the truck's own power, to drag it out of the sand. The drivers were delighted that their problem had been solved, and even happier at not having to dig anymore. They thanked us, promising to take the tyre levers back to the fuel station so that we could continue on our way.

Since it was growing late, we decided to camp for the night and we slept like logs. We were in the arid desert of Algeria, and far from the green fringes along its Mediterranean coast. Pockets of civilisation began to appear as we proceeded north. The next was the town of Hassi Messaoud, the centre of Algeria's oil industry, where we saw numerous oil pipelines littering the ground like snakes, and which we needed to take care not to drive over. After that came Beni Isguen, where the Islamic laws are so strict that visitors are only allowed to come to the town between 4.30 p.m. and 6.30 p.m., and then only with a guide. Next was Ghardaïa, a large hilltop city in the M'Zab valley, with its stunning pyramid-style mosque and terraces of pink clay houses.

Travelling on to El Oued, the tarmac suddenly came to an end, forcing us to tackle sand tracks again. Then the track became a delta of smaller tracks within a network of cultivated plots of land fed by a nearby oasis. We would surely have become lost had it not been for a friendly donkey driver, who guided us back to the right track. Beyond the oasis, we faced more sand dunes, covering the track. Some we could drive over, but most needed

Enjoying a meeting with another Unimog in Algeria

to be driven round, slowing our progress. It wasn't long before the track disappeared altogether, under deep sand. I followed the path of the electric pylon line, my one directional marker, and paid particular attention to the solid 18-inch mounds of sand and tussock grass rising from the ground. It would be a bad idea to drive over them, but the Unimog's ground clearance did mean they could pass easily between the wheels.

When El Oued appeared on the horizon, we were pleased to be leaving the desert. It was the first time that we had seen brick-made buildings, and we wandered around this 'City of a Thousand Domes' taking everything in with great interest, including the members of the strict local Muslim sect, who demanded that all women wore white gowns with disorientating veils which rendered only one eye visible. We gorged ourselves with fresh food and cold drinks, and even the 45-degree heat was, somehow, more tolerable.

The following day, with El Oued behind us, we realised that we were nearing the end of our journey. We had overcome all the difficulties of the Sahara and emerged with some unforgettable and wonderful memories.

Like all good adventures, this one ended with an unexpected surprise. Just ten miles from our last palm tree, we awoke to, of all things, a swirling snowstorm.

CHAPTER TWENTY-TWO

WEST AFRICAN ODYSSEY
PART I: MOROCCO-BURKINA-FASO

By the time I returned home from the Sahara, I had already started to plan my next adventure. The intention had always been to go to east Africa and use the Unimog as a safari vehicle. The seating was set up for four people to face forward, and for them to be able to stand up on their seats with the hatch above to watch the wildlife. The plan was to go through Algeria to west Africa and then cross to east Africa. That failed to materialise when the Algerian border was closed, so the next option was west Africa. In 1991, I set off, this time with a new pair of travelling companions, Josie and Francis. Since there is little to write about them that is actually printable, perhaps I shall just leave it at the mention of their names.

We went to Paris first to obtain our Malian visas. This found us camped on the side of the road outside the Malian embassy in Paris, attracting a lot of attention, as the Unimog had been built for wild country camping, and was not suitable for a capital city. We had no grey water tank for washing up and for shower water, so it was embarrassing to see it drain on to the streets of Paris. Thankfully, nobody complained. We went to the embassy and obtained the visas.

Once more, we entered the African continent through Morocco, driving down to Rabat so that we could visit the Mauritanian embassy and acquire a visa. Unfortunately, the border had been closed for the previous two weeks and the embassy wasn't issuing visas to anyone. We contacted the British consul, who confirmed the closure, informing us that political tensions in Mauritania were such that waiting for the border to reopen would be a waste of time.

Following the consul's advice, we drove down to Casablanca to explore a different option. Perhaps we could bypass Mauritania altogether and ship the Unimog directly to Dakar in Senegal. This plan turned out to be entirely possible. We met with a friendly employee of the Comarine shipping agency called Mr Charidi, who bent over backwards to ensure that all our requirements were met. He could, he promised us, guarantee deck cargo space for the Unimog on a Delmas ship called the *St Francis of Assisi* in just ten days.

We booked the space and, while we waited, decided to pass the ten days with a trip through Morocco, down to Marrakesh and the southern Atlas Mountains, and then to Agadir, the endpoint for those who like to escape the European winter in their campers and caravans. Back in Casablanca once more, we were delayed by the bureaucracy involved in shipping a vehicle from one African country to another. The paperwork seemed never-ending, and completing it required countless trips between Mr Charidi's office and the docks. The first time, he took me on the back of his moped. But one hair-rising ride along Casablanca's roads weaving between the hurtling trucks and lorries was one too many for me, and I decided to walk after that.

Finally, everything was in order, and I drove the Unimog down to the docks. I expected there to be a ramp to drive up on to the ship, or perhaps a platform which could be lifted up. Instead, I was asked to roll forward carefully on to two rough steel nets, one for the front wheels and one for the back wheels, which, when hoisted up, wrapped round the Unimog and lifted it from the dock. I watched, my heart in my mouth, as all eight tons of my pride and joy were swung up into the air, over the containers, and then down into the one remaining space on top of the highest container. As the Unimog was securely chained down, I approached the captain, offering him a small backhander to ensure nothing happened to it while at sea. It seemed a wise thing to do.

With the Unimog safely on the ship to Senegal, we needed to book a flight to Dakar. I was looking forward to the bird's-eye view of the desert, but a severe sandstorm at 35,000 feet meant we were diverted over the Atlantic. I was, however, able to catch a glimpse of the Canary Islands as we flew over them, which brought back vivid memories of setting off from there on my first ocean crossing in *Caleta*. It was difficult to believe that fifteen years had elapsed since then.

Dakar was said to be one of west Africa's most sophisticated cities, but to me it felt like one enormous suburb with all forms of modernity packed into its minuscule centre. We could not walk anywhere without being trailed by Wolof tribesmen who demanded we buy whatever they were selling. The city's claim to fame at the time was its role as the finishing line for the Paris–Dakar rally, a role the locals had gladly taken on and promoted, for it covered up Dakar's more insalubrious past.

Ancient cannons on Gorée Island, Senegal

While we waited for the *St Francis of Assisi* to arrive, we took a boat over to Gorée Island and visited its House of Slaves Museum, where we were told that this tiny island, no bigger than 40 acres, had once been a major departure point for some 500,000 ships on the slave trade route, carrying their millions of Africans on the 5,000-mile journey across the Atlantic to the Americas and the Caribbean. Also on Gorée Island we saw a pair of ancient cannons, a historic relic of the French colonial age, which reminded us of the film *The Guns of Navarone,* which was partly shot on the island.

A memorial to the thousands of slaves shipped from Gorée Island, Senegal

LEFT: *Waiting at the port for* St Francis of Assisi *to dock to unload the Unimog from Morocco. Dakar, Senegal*

RIGHT: *Unloading the Unimog at Dakar Port*

Determined that no Senegalese would have access to the Unimog while I wasn't there, I sat on a mooring bollard and watched the *St Francis of Assisi* sail into the harbour. I saw it being tied up and waited to be one of the first allowed on the ship before the dockers. The Unimog was safely unloaded by crane without problems as it was at the top of the ship. I was soon able to drive it off the strops to the gate of the dock, hoping to be out of the port that afternoon. Unfortunately, the Senegalese customs were unusually complicated, and we were forced to camp on the dock while I went through the rigmarole of paperwork, taxi rides into the town and back, with lots of hangers-on all wanting their taxi fares and, of course, bribes. We had assured the customs that the bike would not come off the front, in order to save paying road tax for it. In the end, it took two days and ten forms before we cleared all the necessary formalities. After we left, it was growing late, and we were only able to make it as far as Dakar's pink salt flats at the Lac Rose – the famous finishing point of the Dakar Rally, where we parked for the night amidst the men and women who bagged up the salt to sell.

The following day, determined to put the city behind us, we set off south along a poorly maintained dirt road. As we progressed, a smooth track appeared beside the road and, naturally, I crossed over and on to it. From the road, it had seemed a good idea as the track had the appearance of a hard surface. But once we were on it, I realised my mistake as the hard surface was just a veneer. Beneath it was a layer of soft mud which quickly began to suck down the Unimog's left side. We were completely

Digging and utilising sand mats to unstick the Unimog in Morocco

stuck. I tried every available option, laying out the sand mats, attaching a single-line winch wire to ground anchors, but nothing worked. The wheels had sunk into the mud by fully two feet, causing the Unimog to lean at a 20-degree angle.

Locals had been gathering round us since the start of the ordeal, with many pitching in and offering to help. One said that a friend of his in a nearby village owned a truck which might be able to pull us out. It seemed our only remaining option, so I lowered the bike frame, removed the KLR, and rode off to the village with the man on the back. The village was eight miles away and, sure enough, there was the truck: a battered 6-ton vehicle which looked as if it would either rescue us or fall to pieces in the attempt. With the help of my new friend, I negotiated a deal with the owner. He was not going to take on such a job for free, nor was he going to do it quickly. He would come to help us, with his truck, the following morning.

That meant a night spent trying to sleep in our awkwardly angled, half-sunk Unimog. The thought of that didn't appeal to me, so I decided to try one last idea. With the light now fading round us, I set to work quickly, doubling the 12,000-pound winch pull by fixing a pulley beneath the winch to enable a rear pull, and rigging an extra length of wire with a turning block. With all this in place, I attached it and the 506 Tirfor 5-ton manual winch to a 1¼-inch nylon rope to provide some elasticity. The ground anchors I had driven in earlier were still in place, and I shackled the rope to them. It was time to test my last idea.

The winches began to strain and, to my delight, the ground anchors remained in place. Sadly, so too did the Unimog, refusing to budge an inch. It was now 9.00 p.m. and, though darkness had fallen long ago, the locals still clustered around us, enjoying the evening's entertainment. One of them, an old man with a donkey and cart, must have had an idea, for he hurried off and returned a little later with his cart full of tree roots. Together, we used them to fill the two-feet-deep holes of soft mud around the wheels, giving the sand ladders a much firmer base from which to work. I tried the winches again and, to a chorus of cheers from the crowd, the Unimog slowly began to move, finally wrenched free from the mud and back on firm ground once more.

By now it was 11.00 p.m. We knew we would be camping there for the night anyway, but at least the Unimog was now level. Before I went to sleep, however, I had one last job. I needed to return to the truck driver in the nearby village and tell him his services were no longer required. I climbed back on the KLR and set off into the night, winding my way in the pitch black through herds of cattle lying in the road in a village with no people and no lights, and then into the next small town, where the lights were on and hordes of people filled the streets. Everybody was outside and even the street sellers and small shops were open to sell their wares. It soon dawned on me why. Ramadan was in full swing, and the locals were offsetting their daytimes of abstinence with night-time merriment. I found the truck driver and offered him both my thanks and apologies. He took it with good grace and wished me luck for the rest of my journey.

Back on the road again the following day, we set a course for Niokolo-Koba, a national park in the south-east of Senegal. It was to be our first game park, and I was excited about going on a safari through it. To begin with, we hired a guide, but his ineptitude soon made itself clear when, after following some tracks for a morning, he stopped at noon and insisted he needed a three-hour break. We got rid of him to continue on alone, spotting plenty of small game as we drove through the park, but sadly nothing of a decent size. I had been hoping to see elephants, but we didn't see any and, that night in the park campsite, instead of coming face to face with elephants, we met two Americans.

One worked for the Peace Corps and, while the other poured us out some delicious Texan wine, she explained why we had found nothing in the park. Her job was to track and study elephants and, for the two years she had worked in the park, she had not seen one single live elephant.

They lived in the park, but they were extremely elusive, and even the local guides had trouble locating them.

With this knowledge, we left the park the next day. We knew we wouldn't see any elephants there, and instead enjoyed a few glimpses of monkeys and antelopes on the way out. The map showed a direct road out, but when we reached it, we found that, as with so many African maps, it was totally incorrect as the road was overgrown and impassable. We followed a potholed track east until we reached the border post which was little more than a tent, a couple of chairs, a table, and a number of dozing guards. A pile of forms lay on the table before us, one of which I completed, put a bribe on, and handed to the guard.

He smiled, taking the bribe and tucking it into his pocket. 'Welcome to Mali,' he said.

◎ ◎ ◎

Situated on the banks of the Senegal River and ringed by mountains, Kayes was sweltering. It is from this heat that it has derived the nickname 'The Pressure Cooker of Africa'. There is little to no rain for seven months, with the surrounding mountains creating an area of inescapable suffocating heat.

Washerwomen in Senegal

The locals were used to the conditions, thronging the market in their brightly coloured kaftans, haggling and laughing and calling to each other. We stocked up with fresh local river fish, and then made our way to the police station to have our passports stamped. They asked us where we were planning to go after Kayes.

'Bamako,' I said.

'Of course.' They nodded, as if this was a good decision. 'You must see our capital.'

Although Bamako was only 400 miles away, it was to take us seven days to get there. Leaving Kayes via a scenic route along the lip of a dramatic bluff, we set up camp for the night. In the Unimog's interior, I unfolded my map across the table and began to plot my position from the GPS. If the map was correct, we were a long way from the road we needed. At that stage, I was not too concerned. We could find the road tomorrow, and from there it would be a straightforward drive.

The next day, confident with the direction we had decided on, we set off. Soon, the main road was only five or ten miles away from the track along which we were driving, and both met at the town of Bafoulabé. However, to reach there it was necessary to cross the Bafing River. The one bridge was exclusively for the use of trains; all road vehicles needed to cross by ferry. Despite the ferry's rather random approach to both fares and departure times, we managed to board it and cross the river.

Local ferry crossing on the Niger River, Mali

Happy that we were now definitely on the main Bamako road, we continued but, once more, conditions deteriorated. The road became a trail, and then the trail became a donkey track, and then the donkey track became a narrow lane through a village. Convinced that, somehow, we had mistakenly come off the road, I stopped and asked one of the locals if we needed to turn round. No, he assured us, we were on the right road, the correct way to Bamako. We just needed to continue on through the village and round the next mountain. We followed his advice, but we did so as slowly as possible, for on either side of the Unimog there was less than three inches' clearance between the wing mirrors and the walls of the houses.

As we drove round the mountain, we were forced to go slowly. The track cut a narrow path between the steep slope of the mountain on the right and the even steeper 100-foot drop down to a rocky river bed on the left. I stayed in first gear throughout, taking care to stick to the track as centrally as I could. It wasn't easy, for boulders and debris were strewn over its surface, and I had to try to keep the tilt of the Unimog at an angle no greater than 20 degrees. There was no space to turn round and go back. It was one of the most terrifying drives I have ever had to tackle, and I did so in absolute silence, focusing on the road. The fact that monkeys further up the mountain decided to fling rocks at us did not help.

Locals crossing the Niger River in Mali

I had one thing for which to be grateful: it was the dry season. Although this made it hotter, it also meant that the many steep gulleys we needed to cross were hard and dry. Once, a gulley was so steep that, making our way across it, both the rear and the front bumpers, which are more than three feet high, touched the ground simultaneously, and we were close to being stuck, surely one of the worst places in the world for this to happen. Beside us, cyclists passed easily, grinning as they cruised past our windows and disappeared into the distance. We could only watch them with envy, and continue on at our snail's pace. In the space of one day, after driving for nine hours, we managed to cover only 60 miles.

The next day, Mali provided an even more nerve-wracking challenge. The road surface improved beyond the mountain, running beside the railway and often crossing it. To begin with, all seemed well. The terrain was relatively hard and flat and, when we did need to cross the railway, it was simple enough until we came to a river.

There was only one bridge.

The rail bridge.

We stopped the Unimog, climbed out and studied everything around us, looking for any possible alternative, but there wasn't one. We couldn't drive down through the river and we couldn't turn round and head back. We had to go forward, and the only way to do that was to drive over the rail bridge.

We tried to recall when and how often trains had passed us throughout the day, but we couldn't. For all we knew, the next train could have been due in two minutes, two hours, or two days. Perhaps we could wait for the next train to cross and then follow that, but even that gave us no guarantee of safety. Given the randomness of timetables in this part of the world, another train could be following right behind.

We just had to go for it as there was no other alternative. So, I drove up on to the rail track and made my way towards the bridge. I looked at how far we had to go before we could drive off the rail track: it seemed to be about half a mile. My instinct was to put my foot down, to speed up and cross the bridge as quickly as possible. I decided to keep my speed slow and steady as increasing our speed would only heighten the risk of making a wrong move and falling off the bridge.

As we drove, I kept looking from windscreen to wing mirror, checking for any trains coming from either in front or behind. Not that it would have made any difference even if I had seen one. We wouldn't have been

Utilising a local rail bridge to cross in the Unimog whilst hoping a train does not come the other way

able to avoid a train in time; the collision would have been swift and fatal. All I could do was keep calm and keep driving.

Finally, we made it across, giving me a great sense of relief as we drove off the rail track and back on to the road that has rarely been matched in my life. From there, conditions improved, and I was even able to change up to sixth gear and drive at 25 miles an hour. We stopped in villages along the way to fill our water tanks. Few of the villages had any food to sell, but they always had a well, and the villagers were always happy to help us.

When we arrived in Bamako, it felt as if we had driven across the entire continent, and, as a reward, we booked ourselves into the International Amity Hotel, a five-star hotel with a gourmet restaurant, air-conditioned rooms, a tennis court and a swimming pool; we felt we deserved it. Sadly, the hotel was full of mosquitos, and we were mercilessly attacked. As we nursed our bites and tried not to scratch them, we missed the secure bug-free interior of the Unimog as we realised it had all the luxury we needed.

We explored Bamako, a large, ancient and bustling African city, more a working town than a tourist attraction. We walked through the streets without being hassled, no one bothering us to buy their goods, nor trailing us for miles and insisting that we give them money. Instead, all the local people were friendly and kind and generally getting on with their lives. It was quite surprising, given that Mali's position is near the bottom of the global wealth league and that the average daily income at the time was $1.50, that there was nonetheless a sense of prosperity and contentment.

The markets were filled with both buyers and sellers. In one, further out towards the city's limits, we found stalls where all manner of animal parts were sold, possibly for medicine or rituals, including lion skins, monkey paws, bird wings, and a variety of skulls, horns and bones.

Our next stop was Djenné, 250 miles away, a shorter distance than our route from Kayes to Bamako. But the roads were good and we arrived at our destination in a single day.

Children surrounded us as we parked. They wanted to look after the Unimog while we went for a walk. Since we were new to Djenné and didn't want to risk anything, I chose the most distinctive-looking child, hoping I would recognise him in the dark when we returned. As it happened, I didn't and, a few hours later, ended up putting coins into at least twenty outstretched hands.

◎ ◎ ◎

I had heard a lot about Djenné and was keen to see it. Just four years earlier, in 1988, it and its neighbouring site Djenné-Djenno, which translates as 'ancient Djenné', had been designated a UNESCO World Heritage Site. This was thanks in part to the famous Great Mosque with its triple minarets, which is built from sun-baked mud and requires constant maintenance. Every year, the locals come together to shore up the mosque's walls in the annual mud-plastering festival.

We wandered through Djenné's streets, looking at the adobe architecture. Despite its terrible roads, Mali is a pleasant country, and its

The Great Mosque of Djenné, a World Heritage site in Mali

people are welcoming and kind. Unlike other countries I have visited both before and after Mali, I rarely felt uncomfortable or out of place there, and I was glad that I had taken the time and the effort to travel through this landlocked Saharan nation which so few bother to visit.

The city was on the edge of a flat sand plain and I took the bike across it to another small village which appeared to have no road connection. I rode through the streets, which were so narrow that not even a trail bike could turn round the corners from one street to another without damaging itself or the adobe houses. The village was pedestrian only, and about as far from civilisation as I'd ever been.

Our next Malian town was Mopti, also known as 'the Venice of Mali' because of its situation at the confluence of the Niger and the Bani rivers. We had previously met a Malian man in Bamako who had offered to take us on a short trip on the Niger River from Mopti. At the time, we hadn't wanted to commit to anything and had said to the man that if we saw him in Mopti, we would discuss it there. We thought that was the end of the discussion, but then, because the Unimog was so obvious, he soon found us in Mopti and agreed a good price for a trip down the river with a night of camping. We were also approached by other locals offering similar trips, mostly at ridiculous prices, such as one two-hour trip which would cost the same as our guide's two-day trip. Our guide and the locals came close to fighting when we chose him to take us. We felt lucky to have found him as he was a kind man compared with all the cowboys on the riverbank.

We left the Unimog for the night and took the trip down the Niger in a pirogue, a traditional type of dugout canoe. Our pirogue was just one of many, and we soon became lost amongst the people of Mopti as they fished or transported their cargo up and down the river.

As we motored down the river, the locals we saw belonged to two distinct tribes: the Fulani, a traditionally nomadic and pastoralist people; and the Bozo, a far smaller group composed largely of fishermen. One of the latter approached us in his boat and sold us some fish, which we cooked and ate that night while camping on a sand spit. With full stomachs, we fell asleep, to be woken repeatedly throughout the night by the calls of hippos, which sounded too close for comfort. When we woke up the following morning, I realised how lucky we had been to escape an attack by the hippos, for it turned out that we had camped right on a track which could have been recently made. Josie and Francis set off 300 yards away to attend to a call of nature, finding it extremely difficult to look nonchalant on the flat sand bar. They were totally visible, but fortunately there were no people around to see them except the camp crew.

Our guide down the river had been good, both entertaining and educational, so when we returned to Mopti and he offered to take us on another trip to the Bandiagara Escarpment, we gladly accepted. The escarpment is a chain of sandstone cliffs which rise from the sandy flats by as much as 300 feet, and which are the home of the Dogon people. As we approached one of

A boat trip on the river

their villages, the guide explained how their society was organised.

'Each village has a headman called the *ogon*,' he said. 'The *ogon* does not live with the other villagers, but in caves in the cliffs made by people in ancient times. The Dogon call these people the *tellem*, which means "those who were before us". The *ogon* is usually the oldest man in the village, and tradition has it that when his wife reaches sixty, he must change her for a younger wife in her twenties. The *ogon* doesn't usually live much longer after the arrival of his new wife.'

'At least he dies with a smile on his face,' I said.

When we reached the first village, we found out that, sadly, the *ogon* had died a month earlier. He had lived beyond the ripe old age of ninety and we found out that he had fought in the trenches during the First World War. Our guide showed us round, introducing us to the villagers. Some

A Dogon coronation ceremony on the Dogon Escarpment in Mali

Visiting a local Animist shop displaying traditional wood carvings in Senegal

of them were Muslim and others Christian, though most were animists. Rituals were still held to cure infertility and animals were still sacrificed to ensure good fortune. We went to a small Christian church, the smallest I have ever seen, which only had space for two people.

We climbed up one of the escarpment's 300-foot-high cliff faces. At the summit, we were invited to spend the night in a village where a new *ogon* had just been initiated in a ceremony which had lasted several days and ended the day before our arrival; we were sorry to have missed it. To our delight, some of the dancers put their costumes back on and performed a fertility dance with their long, well-decorated spears.

We finally left Mopti, which meant leaving Mali too. Our next destination was Burkina Faso, some 150 miles to the south-east. At its border, the welcome sign still read 'Haute Volta', the name the country had taken on after freeing itself from French rule, and which it then changed just eight years before our arrival to Burkina Faso, which means 'The Land of Incorruptible People'.

Whether they were incorruptible or not, the Burkinabé certainly knew how to build roads. After the tracks and trails of Mali, Burkina Faso's modern tarmac highways were a pleasure to drive on, because they were financed by tolls. We reached the capital, Ouagadougou, without difficulty and continued, exploring the markets and monuments as we went. For something different, we visited a sacred crocodile pond. Unfortunately, there was little sacred about the pond, which was clearly just an attempt at a tourist attraction. After watching one poor crocodile being dragged from the filthy pool by its tail to be fed a scrawny chicken, we made our excuses and left.

Burkina Faso is a relatively small country, just one-fifth the size of Mali and only one-tenth the size of Algeria. With its small size and its good roads, it did not take long to cross. As we drove south-west from the capital to Bobo-Dioulasso, the landscape changed from the yellows and oranges of the desert to the bright greens of the tropics. Soon, we were on our way to the border with Ivory Coast.

I have one final memory of Burkina Faso. Between Bobo-Dioulasso and the border, a distance of just 40 miles, we were stopped no less than four times for police checks. The first policeman asked if he could buy my motorbike. The next three simply asked if I would give it to them. When we finally got to the border, I was not sorry to leave the country behind.

CHAPTER TWENTY-THREE
WEST AFRICAN ODYSSEY
PART II: IVORY COAST-CAMEROON

Crossing from Burkina Faso to Ivory Coast took three hours while the police communicated with their compatriots in Abidjan. When it was finally confirmed that we didn't need a visa, a fact we had been trying to explain to them for several hours, we were allowed across.

We had intended to drive through the Comoé National Park, but heavy rains the previous night had left it too wet to cross safely, so we drove round it along an old and little-used road. Every few miles, bridges made from steel and timber connected the road over rivers and gulleys. They were narrow and basic, but they supported the Unimog as we crossed each one. That is, until we reached a bridge which, as we climbed out to inspect it, we soon realised had far too little timber to be safe. I took measurements, and saw that the bridge was only wide enough to take three-quarters of the tyre width, so attempting to cross it would have been foolish. Our only other option was to drive down and cross the dry river bed. Making a track down one bank and up the other meant hacking down trees and branches. It was difficult to work out which trees to cut down, as some branches, which were ten feet off the ground, had to be cut from the top of the vehicle because we could not climb the trees. By the time we were finally able to manage the crossing, it was night.

We continued further south through thick jungles towards Yamoussoukro, Ivory Coast's capital. It replaced Abidjan, which had been the capital until a decade before our arrival. Yamoussukro had grown so fast that its days as a small, mud-built agricultural village could still be remembered. In 1950 it had a population of only 500 people. By the time we arrived, its transformation had slowed, disappointingly, with only three cars per mile on a giant six-lane highway. The enormous presidential palace was surrounded by a 14-foot wall. The flagship conference centre was complete with 20 large conference rooms, although not many meetings were held there in a year. The Basilica of Our Lady of Peace, a $600 million replica of Rome's Basilica of St Peter, was officially the largest

*A tight squeeze round
a tree in the Ivory Coast*

church in the world, and it had an adjacent mansion built purely for the two-night visit of Pope John Paul II in 1990 so that it could receive a papal consecration. The Pope had agreed to consecrate the basilica on condition that the president build a hospital for the poor, but this had just been a form of bribery to tempt John Paul to come. The whole city was for the vainglory of the president. His spending had been so lavish that it had doubled the national debt and impoverished the citizens.

From Yamoussoukro, we continued on to Ivory Coast's former capital, Abidjan. Although it had lost its title in 1983, it was still a large and important economic hub, with a busy port and roughly one-fifth of the country's entire population. Built over a huge lagoon, with its land connected by a network of bridges, we found Abidjan a divided city: a thoroughly modern centre full of innovation with its surroundings being poverty-filled shanty towns. We made the most of the city, but decided that it would be safer for us to stay in the Unimog at night.

It was in Abidjan that I decided to part company with Josie and Francis. Their company had proved to be more of a hindrance than a help, and we were beginning to irritate each other. When I set out alone from Abidjan, having enjoyed this extremely civilised and modern city, I took the highway out and then turned off on a flyover to drive suddenly into the middle of the slums and a police roadblock. It was something of a shock to the system. The two parts were so close together, and were a wake-up call to return to African culture. Things were made more difficult when the police wanted to see my motorcycle insurance and I had to convince them that my English insurance was valid. Luckily, they accepted it and I could return to the civilised road. I found the slums in the cities intimidating.

I drove along the coast and through coconut plantations to the border with Ghana, the first English-speaking country so far on my expedition through west Africa. Once I crossed the border, I stopped for fuel. As well as a change in language, there was a change in currency. In Ghana, rather than the CFA franc, the currency tied to the French franc which was used in all France's former sub-Saharan African colonies, I was now using the cedi, a currency which had suffered a number of recent devaluations. Half a tank of diesel required 480 cedi notes, which took the pump attendant longer to count than it did to fill my tank.

I made my way along the coast road to Elmina, an old fort town which, like Gorée in Senegal, had once been another of west Africa's principal slave-trading posts. The old fort of Elmina, which was originally built by the Portuguese for the gold trade before being taken by the Dutch for slave trading and soon after captured by the English, was designed for protection against European armies. Back then, Africans could not possibly have captured it. The African chiefs brought in their slaves to trade with the fort commander and with ships' captains from European countries. When the Dutch built the fort, they were more religious than the English and had built a small church and, as with all churches, it had a pulpit. When the English captured Elmina, they enclosed this pulpit to create a small private

Fort Elmina was built by the Portuguese as a gold fort then conquered by the Dutch before being taken by the British as a slave trading fort.

room from which the rest of the church could be secretly observed through a spy hole. This gave the slave buyers the opportunity to choose and inspect the slaves while keeping their identities secret from them. Once the trading had been completed, the slaves were put into holding dungeons in the fort. They were then led down an underground passageway, on to the beach and out to the waiting ships. They were sold by the Africans, who only chose the strongest ones to sell as they knew that buyers would not choose any small or weak slaves. During my visit, there was a large tour group of black Americans who had come to see where their forebears had originally come from and how they had left Africa.

After Fort Elmina, I decided to make another tour, this time of the Ashanti gold fields, away from the coast and deep into Ghana's interior. It was an amazing sight to see, where towering mountains had been destroyed by huge dumper trucks transporting the bare rock to have the gold extracted. Plenty of it was unearthed, for Ghana, previously known as the Gold Coast, used to have one of the world's largest gold deposits. It brought huge riches to Britain, then Africa after independence.

Not far from the gold fields was the city of Kumasi, the capital of the historical Ashanti Empire, an indigenous kingdom which stretched across much of modern-day Ghana. There still existed in Kumasi an Ashanti king and court, although it had little authority, and was more of a token nod to the ancient kingdom than anything with real power. I stopped there to obtain the necessary immigration stamps, realising as I did so that I would need to spend the night in or near the town, which left me feeling a little uneasy. I have never liked camping in spaces where there are lots of people around and, after politely seeking permission from the inspector, I was allowed to park in the police compound for the night.

Before settling down for the night, I decided to look for one of Kumasi's larger hotels, where I hoped to find a telephone from which to call home. Unfortunately, I took a wrong turn and, before I could do anything about it, a policeman appeared on the road before me and waved me down. I stopped beside him. Brandishing an AK47 machine gun, he climbed into the Unimog, banging his gun against the windscreen, worrying me that he would break it, and began to shout at me.

'You are under arrest! You are driving a large vehicle after dark! This is forbidden! You are under arrest!'

It took all my composure to ignore the gun he was waving about, and I calmly dropped the inspector's name into our conversation as many times as possible. It had a softening effect on the policeman, who eventually agreed to drop the potential arrest, and his gun, as long as I drove directly back to the police compound. To ensure I would do as I was told, he would come with me. When we arrived at the police station, the friendly inspector was luckily still there, remembered me and welcomed me back. He told the policeman everything was all right and he could go away.

The policeman turned to me. 'Now,' he said, 'you must give me money.'

'Why?' I asked.

'I must get a taxi back to my post.'

I sighed. It was a blatant bribe he was after, but rather that than a jail cell for the night. I asked him how much he needed.

'50p,' he said.

I gave it to him before he could change his mind and increase the amount.

◑ ◑ ◑

The night in the police compound passed without further problems, and the following day I drove north to the Mole National Park, hoping that I might finally see some elephants there. Along the way, the sides of the road were strewn with broken-down trucks, not abandoned, but in the process of being repaired, for in Ghana all vehicle repairs were done on the roadside where they had broken down.

At the Mole National Park, I was surprised to learn that they offered walking tours with armed guides. This is extremely rare in game parks, so I booked one. We walked through the park in search of the wildlife, tracking antelopes and baboons at less than 50 yards, and then, to my absolute delight, we came upon three elephants. We followed them for what felt like hours, so close that we could hear their immense stomachs rumbling. I was fascinated by their silent footsteps, and the skill with which their trunks picked up large mouthfuls of vegetation, which still seemed relatively small compared to their great size. They seemed to care little about our being so close. I could have watched them longer, but it was becoming dark and I had to leave the park.

From Mole, I turned east towards Togo, the next on this long strip of countries that reach from the coast to the Sahel. The roads of northern Ghana were crumbling to dust and often had better tracks beside them, which I used whenever possible. I didn't want to cross the border at night so I camped close to a village – too close, in fact, for after darkness fell a large group of the villagers came out towards me. I was somewhat nervous so shone my searchlight from the roof, which made them stop at a safe distance so we could negotiate my stay in the village. In general, they were friendly and not aggressive. They just wanted to see the Unimog. I was glad I was behind my searchlight and not on the ground, surrounded by large numbers of strange people at night.

The next day, I crossed over into Togo, back in French-speaking territory once more. Children were everywhere. The older boys charged up and down the streets on their Chinese bicycles; the younger boys were hot on my heels with constant demands for *cadeaux, cadeaux*, 'gifts'. Togo is a long, thin country and, rather than make my way down it to the Gulf of Guinea coast, I chose instead to cut across the north in the direction of Benin. Between the two borders of Ghana and Benin, I found a small national park and decided to stop off and visit it. My fascination with game parks had grown with each one I had visited and I was keen to see what Togo had to offer.

At the entrance, an uninterested local man greeted me with a nod and a few desultory words. I asked if I could continue and he waved me on without even demanding a fee. I took his disregard as encouragement and drove the Unimog into the park, only to be greeted, a few hundred yards later, by an army truck filled with soldiers. They poured out of the truck like ants, surrounding me and insisting that I would have to accompany them back to their camp, where I would be detained until they could decide what to do with me. I asked them what I had done wrong and if the park was closed. Was entry forbidden? But they merely repeated their demands, and I had no choice but to follow them back to their camp. Once there, I parked and waited while they found an officer to deal with me. The soldiers retreated to their campfire, gathering around the remains of a half-cooked antelope and eyeing me suspiciously. I looked at them equally suspiciously, wondering how game park officers could be living off the game they were supposed to be protecting.

Eventually, an officer arrived; he apologised for what had happened. This was not, he explained, a good time for Togo. The one-party system of President Eyadéma Gnassingbé was creating a great deal of civil unrest across the country, and the soldiers had been sent in to guard the park. I let the officer show me to the main gate and bade him farewell. He had told me that there were likely to be police checks every four miles on the main road to Benin, so I chose to follow a narrow and dilapidated dirt track, which zigzagged through a string of villages where traditional ways of life had been preserved. All the houses were approximately 15 yards apart, built as a cone with a single entrance and a spiral staircase going round the living space and upwards to the rooftop terrace with walls round the edges. These were fully modern and busy villages. When I asked why the houses were built like that, they explained that this was a design to protect them from slave raiders. If one house was attacked, all the neighbours could climb on to their roofs, where they kept piles of stones, and hurl them at the slavers raiding the next house. The owner of that house would defend the staircase in much the same way as Scottish barons used to defend themselves. The difference was that the Scots knew they were going to be killed, whereas the Africans knew they were going to be taken into slavery. It raised the question of why this method of construction and living was still their choice today. Were they still in fear of slavers? I could not find out.

Disheartened by the dead end I had experienced in the Togolese game park, I made straight for the Pendjari National Park as soon as I entered Benin. It is well known for its abundance of lions, elephants, hippos and buffalos. On my first afternoon there, I parked beside a watering hole. While I was watching, a game ranger's truck came past and I was advised to leave the park before dark. It was the only vehicle I had seen in the park all day. Just after it left, I watched in awe as ten lions came down to drink from the watering hole. It was such an amazing sight that I continued watching as it became dark and took the view that I could risk staying there a bit later. Nobody came and I was able to enjoy the entire evening looking through the hatch at the top of the truck with my one-million-candlepower searchlight to watch all the lions coming to drink. When they left, the smaller animals took the opportunity to take their place. Luckily for me, either the same or another pride of lions came to the watering hole, and I had the never-to-be-forgotten view of six lions all close together, all drinking together, completely oblivious to my searchlight. It was one of the most amazing evenings of my life.

Eventually, it was now time to have some sleep, so I took the risk and drove into some scrub out of sight of the lake, where I could not be seen by a passing ranger. I went back in the morning and was able to park within a few yards of a kill that the lions had made the night before, and to stand on top of the Unimog with only its height to protect me. The lions were not interested in me; all their concentration was on having their fill from the buffalo they had killed. I spent the whole morning there, and still nobody appeared. I felt this must have been a unique experience, to have all this wildlife to see with nobody else around. It fully justified my choice of the Unimog, which was the perfect vehicle from which to watch game.

I would have liked to have spent more time in Benin, but my Nigerian entry visa was running out, with three days left before it was due to expire. I had to go to the border, and go there quickly. Racing across the north of Benin, I arrived at the Nigerian border with only a day to spare, so I counted myself lucky.

Crossing into Nigeria was problematic enough, and I could not imagine how difficult it would have been with an expired visa. Eight immigration officers accosted me from the moment I arrived, firing off questions which I found difficult to answer. 'Why have you come to Nigeria?' 'Do you know how difficult it is for me to go to London? Why should I make it easy for you to come here?' 'You should not be allowed to enter. You should turn back.' 'Where will you go after Nigeria? How quickly can you get there?' 'Why should we let you in?' 'If we open the gates to you, how long will you spend here? When will you leave?'

Despite the interrogation, I kept calm throughout, and was eventually allowed a two-week stay. Relieved to be through and that everything was officially legal and above board, I was nevertheless stopped once more in Kaduna. In fact, I was not technically stopped, for the Unimog was stationary at a crossroads at the time, while I waited for the traffic policeman to wave me across. And yet he still ordered me to 'stop' and to 'park'. Then, without invitation, he climbed inside and began to demand that I pay a fine of 1,800 naira, the equivalent of about £50.

'What for?' I protested.

'I do not like the way you were driving.'

I tried to tell him that, actually, I had not been driving at all. But the truth seemed only to make him angrier. He continued to demand the money, even threatening to put me in handcuffs and arrest me if I kept disobeying him. When he finally realised that I was not going to give him his £50, we agreed to £6 for his boss and £3 for himself. For that, he would let me go free. It still seemed too much to me, but he had a gun and time and I wanted to move on, so I agreed, handing over the money. That was the price for driving in Africa. They live off bribes to keep the local economy going, whereas in England they do it much more formally and for much larger sums.

Despite being a major producer and exporter of fuel, the locals regularly had shortages because they didn't have a refinery and thus had to import refined fuel.

Though I had a fair amount of diesel remaining, I kept an eye out for a fuel station as I continued through Nigeria, which is a major oil producer but still suffers from massive fuel shortages. Every station I passed was closed. In Zaria, after I stopped beside a station, a fuel truck drove up and a queue started to form. The road was too narrow to turn round, so I had to back up into the queue, facing in the wrong direction. Once there, I was in the queue for two and a half hours, while the fuel truck driver emptied his tank and the locals who had walked and driven their trucks to the station were served first. Many of them had 200-litre drums on handcarts which they were going to take away and sell at a profit as soon as the tankerload of fuel had gone. Finally, I was able to turn round, approach the pumps correctly, and fill all my tanks. The fuel cost just twenty-two pence per gallon, and I was glad that I filled up with it, for this turned out to be the only open fuel station I encountered in my entire two weeks in Nigeria.

◑ ◑ ◑

Lake Chad covers an area where four countries meet: Cameroon, Niger, Nigeria and, of course, Chad. Before making my way down through Cameroon, I wondered if I might be able to visit the Nigerian portion of the lake, and made my way towards it. Unfortunately, it was perhaps the worst time in recorded history to visit Lake Chad. From 1963 until 1998, the lake shrank by a staggering 95 per cent and in 1992, the year of my west African odyssey, the Nigerian shoreline had receded by over 50 miles. As such, there were no routes or tracks safe enough or stable

A large cargo boat being sailed down the Niger

enough for me to reach the water, so I turned the Unimog round and made for Cameroon.

Flowing north into Lake Chad, the Logone River forms part of the border between Cameroon and Chad, one of the many countries I only saw from across the border but never visited, and I followed it upstream via a sand track which cut through dusty villages where time seemed to stand still. The tribespeople watched as I passed: not with hostility, but with curiosity. I met their gazes with a smile and a wave. Many had traditional scarification markings across their faces and upper bodies: intentional and carefully applied knife-wounds denoting rites of passage and milestones such as puberty and marriage. Some of the men and women had decorated their scars with patterns painted across their faces. There was plenty of life in these villages, with adults and children around every corner, but they seemed slow and quiet, exhausted perhaps by the encroaching desert and the receding waters and the relentless, scorching heat that characterised this part of the world.

Soon, I found a turning which led away from the river. I checked the GPS, which confirmed that this was the track I had been looking for: the road to the Waza National Park. There was no gate or official entrance to the park as it was a rarely used road. I drove into the park, where I came upon a water truck stuck and deeply embedded in the mud. A Cameroonian came up to me. He said he was a guide and asked if I would help pull out the truck. I agreed and chose my big nylon tow rope to pull him out. Slowly but steadily, I pulled, and the water truck slid from the mud and back on to the track. The guide climbed into my truck and said that, as thanks, he would guide me round the huge park.

There followed a long drive around the park, seeing nothing but three giraffes and two dead elephants with their tusks removed, proving they had been killed by ivory poachers. I was almost ready to leave and accept that there was no live game in the park, when the guide persuaded me to try just one more spot, a watering hole he knew of which sometimes served as a gathering place for wildlife. Although luck had not been on my side that day, it was nevertheless worth a try, so I agreed, following his directions along a narrow and dusty track.

To this day, I'm still grateful that I followed the guide's advice. If I hadn't, I never would have seen a truly wonderful natural spectacle. When we arrived at the watering hole, there was a herd of about thirty elephants there and a local family having a picnic. The elephants were playing around in the water, drinking and washing. Then, another large herd of more than fifty elephants came running out of the forest in a cloud of dust to quench their thirst and play in the watering hole, completely oblivious to us sitting and watching. A third herd soon joined. Between them, they covered the whole range of ages: the babies walking between the legs of the adults; the bulls presiding over their herds; and even the older adults, which joined in with the play but did so in a slower, more cautious manner, and quite understandably too, for some African elephants can live for as long as seventy years.

The guide told me to follow him out of the Unimog. We walked around the elephants and, if they noticed us, they did not show it. They simply continued with their washing, drinking and playing. We stayed there for hours, and I could have stayed longer, but the guide was becoming restless and keen for us to move. Finally, we did so and, on the way back, were treated to an even more glorious sight. Sheltering under a grove of thorn trees, several hundred elephants gathered together, keeping cool by shading themselves from the setting sun. And then, to cap it all, came the perfect end to the day. We found a small pride of lions asleep under a thicket of bushes. Edging as close to them as we could without causing a disturbance, they seemed perfectly content with our proximity, and we watched them with a kind of mutual curiosity. Annoyingly, a group of uncivilised Frenchmen on safari in three Toyotas did not share our quiet caution. With noisy engines and the wrong attitude, they drove far too close, causing the lions to run away in fright.

Bidding farewell to my guide, I left the Waza National Park and carried on south down through Cameroon. There are few large towns in the north of the country. Instead, the hills are peppered with small villages, where large, extended families live in their huts with patches of land behind fences and walls. Subsistence living dominates this area and, as I drove through, the villagers were preparing for the start of the rainy season. Millet and maize were being planted, and across the fields I could see the villagers bent double, using short-handled mattocks to plant the seeds by hand. Those who were lucky enough to own chickens placed them into baskets on their heads and then carried them out to the fields to feed. There were few other animals around. In one particular village, I was invited to watch the rituals of a witch doctor who, for reasons I cannot fathom, cured problems by letting a crab run around a sandpit.

The rainy season affected not just the farming but the roads too. As I drove further south, heavy storms left the clay roads slippery and dangerous. Twice, the Unimog slid into the bank before I could stop it. Fearing further accidents, I reduced the tyre pressures to enable better self-cleaning of the treads and maximise the grip. It worked well and the Unimog stayed firmly on the road from then on.

Now that the sliding-on-the-road problem had been dealt with, I had to contend with a new issue. The gulleys and beds which had been bone dry a few weeks earlier had now become deep rivers. I approached one crossing to find the waters were so high that a barrier had been put in place. This could only mean one thing. This part of the road was now too dangerous to cross, and I would have to make a detour which would add three full days to my journey.

Noticing my frustration, two villagers approached the Unimog. They told me they had laid down stones along the crossing, that it was perfectly passable, but that I would need a guide to help me across, and for this there would be a fee. Although I felt some trepidation about plunging into the river, it was well worth the risk as the villagers knew about the condition of the river bottom. I agreed to pay them to guide me across. One jumped into the passenger seat and the other, just a teenager, walked into the river. Within seconds, the river was up to his chest.

'Go!' the man beside me said. 'Quickly. Follow him.'

I looked at the boy again, making quick calculations in my head. Judging by his height, the water at its deepest rose to about four or five feet. As the Unimog's exhaust and air intake were eight feet up in the air, I could make it.

'Go now!' the man persisted. 'Quickly!'

I took a deep breath, and drove forward, following the boy as precisely as I could. The water quickly rose around us, but the bow wave stayed below the bonnet. I could feel the bottom under the Unimog's tyres; it was rough but solid so I ploughed on. To slow down or stop would have been a grave mistake. When we made it to the other side and crawled back on to dry land, I felt relieved. I would never have attempted it without a guide.

I continued on, further and further south. Thick tropical jungle rose round me on either side of the road, and the few villages which existed here were in clearings hacked out of it. With just the road and these villages and then nothing else but the impenetrable jungle, locating quiet and private camping spots became almost impossible. I eventually managed to find a suitable place near a series of waterfalls, and one of the villagers, acting as my guide, took me up to walk across them. The views from the top were sensational and, when I returned to the Unimog, I was a little disheartened when I was given an unexpected note. I had, it seemed, been extremely rude by failing to secure permission from the king to visit the falls. Should I not wish to displease him further, I must immediately go and see him. It occurred to me that I could quite easily return to the Unimog and drive off into the distance and never hear of this king again. But that would have been discourteous, and possibly dangerous. I did not want to cause offence to the king, so I was shown the way to his house.

Compared to the standard huts of the villagers, the king's house was enormous. Two storeys high and made of stone, it had been built by his grandfather when Cameroon was the German colony of Kamerun. The king himself was dressed in everyday attire and was surprisingly friendly. He accepted that the incident was nothing but an innocent misunderstanding. Nevertheless, it was important that I showed repentance for my ignorance, and if I simply honoured him with a small gift, then all would be well. A sum of money was suggested, and I gladly offered it, although I had to give it to the translator as the king did not personally handle money.

Now that the potential diplomatic crisis had been averted, I returned to the road, making my way as far south as it is possible to drive in Cameroon, where the Ntem River forms the border with Equatorial Guinea. On its banks, I watched the boats as they came in and out, all sailed by local fishermen. One boat in particular caught my eye: a large, outboard-powered open boat, looking like an oversized dugout, which was anchored in the river. I waited for a while, taking it all in, and then suddenly realised that the village people were doing the same, watching me and wondering what I was doing. They must have decided that I didn't intend any harm to them, for a large group of men came out of the largest house and walked down to the beach. About thirty of them climbed onboard the big dugout, sitting tightly together so that none of their heads were visible above the top of the gunwales. When they were all onboard and invisible, the skipper started the engine and motored down the river and out to sea. The men were illegal immigrants, on their way around Equatorial Guinea to Gabon in search of work. Others would go even further down the coast to Angola and its diamond mines, an eighteen-hour open-sea crossing with a night landing at its conclusion.

Like these men, my time in Cameroon was coming to an end, as was my time in west Africa. A few hundred miles up the coast was my final destination, Douala, not Cameroon's capital but its largest city and port, where the Unimog was booked on to a ship bound for home. I set off towards it, crossing myriad rivers as I drove north; some were small as streams, some grand and spectacular. One in particular, the Lobé, culminated in a stunning waterfall which plunged directly into the sea. I allowed myself one final adventure, taking a small dugout upstream along the deep, dark waters of the Lobé into pristine jungle. I was taken to a small and otherwise hidden clearing, to visit a Baka family, the indigenous tribespeople of this region who were once known as Pygmies, and who lived in the village as hunter-gatherers.

Finally, I came to Douala, where I had to go to the shipping office to complete the usual paperwork to make the return journey, and to complete the customs documentation. Luckily, this time it was a drive-on ship, so there were no problems. I parked the Unimog in the waiting area for the dockers to drive it on to the ship when it arrived.

I turned my back on the docks and headed away to the airport, thinking about the journey I had just completed. Ten countries, 12,000 miles, through deserts and jungles, across mountains and valleys. It had been a great adventure with few problems and, more importantly, the Unimog had behaved perfectly. I hadn't reached east Africa, but that didn't matter. If I had tried, I would have missed all the best of west Africa.

It was time to get back to harvest.

CHAPTER TWENTY-FOUR
THREE THOUSAND CAMELS

In 1995 I met some friends who were planning to drive down to southern Africa. It sounded like great fun so I decided to join them. A lovely young traveller called Sarah Fowkes agreed to come with me in the Unimog. The plan was for us to follow my friends' route, fit in with their sponsors and generally to help them out, but just as we were making our arrangements the Egypt–Sudan border closed. It seemed that the Egyptians believed the Sudanese were planning a coup. As a result, my friends cancelled their trip. Nevertheless, I was still keen to go, and so was Sarah, so we agreed that we would do the journey without my friends.

I picked Sarah up in London and we caught the ferry over the Channel and then drove fairly speedily down through the Balkans to Istanbul. We spent a few days visiting the Blue Mosque, Hagia Sophia and the Grand Bazaar: a gigantic covered souk with all its varied spice stalls and carpet shops. We both tried a hammam, a Turkish bath … separately, of course. On our final evening, we ate at a restaurant on the top of a tower next to the Galatea Bridge and, since the Turks liked Sarah, we were allowed to watch the belly-dancing show for free. By the time we left the show, it had grown late. Fortunately, we found an empty building site not far from the Blue Mosque which was too rough for ordinary cars and therefore a perfect campsite for us.

The next morning, we left Europe for Asia, crossing the Bosporus on the Fatih Sultan Mehmet suspension bridge, which at that time was still only seven years old. Driving down the west coast of Turkey, we took in some extraordinary sights, such as the Pamukkale salt ridges, where the thermal spring waters deposit carbonate mineral, which over the centuries has built up into a mountainside of white travertine terraces and turquoise pools. We then continued on to Cappadocia to explore the underground city of Kaymaklı. I revisited this extraordinary place later on an overland trip to Beijing and describe it more fully in Chapter 46.

Flying high in a balloon over Cappadocia

There is another town in the area, Çannakale on the Dardanelles, where the ancient Turks used to live in caves in the side of the hills, but unfortunately, they have become extremely overdeveloped for tourists. The inhabitants moved out and now the caves have been smartened up into boutique hotels complete with swimming pools. So instead, we moved on to Göreme, where thousands of years ago volcanic ash settled, hardening into rock. Where the surface of the rock was weak, all the ash was washed away, leaving behind a series of pillars known as 'fairy chimneys' with their characteristic stone weatherproof hats. We took a balloon flight over all the fairy chimneys, even landing on one. The flight ended with our skilled pilot and ground crew managing to land the basket directly on its trailer before deflating the balloon.

We headed towards Syria, deciding to go to one of the lesser-used border points which, we hoped, would be free from problems. When we arrived, it was quiet and the border was closed. We had set our hearts on getting into Syria that night, so we turned around and headed to the main border post. By now it was 11.00 p.m. so we kept our fingers crossed. Customs were fairly easy, but there was an unexpected tax we needed to pay. We explained to the officers that we didn't have the money for it.

'No problem!' one of them said. He banged on a door and opened it. There, inside the room, was the banker; he was in bed. Grumbling something I couldn't understand, he got up, dressed in his full robes, walked to his desk, changed enough dollars for us to pay the tax, and then went back to bed.

With everything taken care of, we entered Syria. It was late by now, so we found the first olive grove to park in so that we could be well away from the road. By the time we parked and were ready to settle, it was already one o'clock in the morning. The next day, we drove down to Aleppo, one of the oldest continuously inhabited cities in the world. These days, it has been largely bombed out of existence, but in 1995 it was still a thriving, functioning city, Syria's biggest, in fact, set on a hill with a fortified wall around it. There were no suitable and safe places to park, so we drove east to camp on the bank of the Euphrates River where, in the surrounding floodplains, superb crops of sugar beet were being grown. Waking up the following morning, we decided to set off for Palmyra, one of the most beautiful of ancient Roman cities with very few tourists. Palmyra has, sadly, since been destroyed by ISIS. Our night there was very peaceful with the Roman columns looking even more beautiful by moonlight.

Since we were actually on the Road to Damascus, we made our way there the next day. Another of the oldest continuously lived-in cities in the world, Damascus was first settled in the second millennium BC and even features in the Bible. We visited the House of Saint Ananias, where Paul the Apostle was baptised, then walked the road he walked as told in the Bible. We then went from the Old Town of Damascus to the new city which, with all its modern facilities, was strikingly different.

Jordan was our next country. Since this was before the days of internet cafes, we had arranged to pick up our post at the Poste Restante in the capital, Amman. It was a lovely city and everyone was friendly. We decided to visit the Dead Sea, the lowest point on earth at 1,400 feet below sea level and 1,000 feet deep. As we were crossing a bridge on our way there we were waved down by a distinguished-looking Arab. He asked us if we would kindly tow his son out of the river, where he had been washing the family car. I agreed and, after we got his son out, the father, as a token of his gratitude, invited us to lunch: a delicious traditional Arab picnic. His children, on the other hand, were not invited.

We talked throughout the meal and the man told us about himself. He was a retired general, a Bedouin, and he was happy to revert to wearing his traditional dress. After we had eaten, he placed an empty beer bottle on a pile of stones and then produced a revolver from under his robe.

'We should have some sport!' he said, before firing two shots at the bottle. Both missed.

He invited Sarah to try. She took careful aim, squeezed the trigger, and the bottle shattered.

It was my turn next. I was a little nervous after Sarah had hit the first bottle, but I was lucky enough to break the second bottle. It was then that I realised the Bedouin general had deliberately missed. Letting us shoot at the bottles showed how kind he was. I found the whole experience an interesting insight into Arab culture.

◎ ◎ ◎

Leaving the Bedouin general to deal with his son, we said a fond farewell, and carried on to the Dead Sea, determined to have our swim in the salty waters. We both struck the classic pose of lying back and holding a book above the water. We had a lot of fun playing in the Dead Sea, but when we came out, we needed a freshwater shower to get our skin clean from all the salt and the mud.

By now, it was Easter weekend. We made our way to Petra to see the rock carvings. Parking on a slope we walked down the steep gorge and round a corner to see before us the incredible Treasury building in full sunlight. We wandered round, visiting the other temples, which were perfectly preserved, and where we could even climb up on to the roofs of the largest. Since the next day was Easter Sunday, we thought it would be appropriate to go to church, so we found the foundations of an ancient church and stood amongst them.

Leaving Petra, we drove to Wadi Rum with its series of vertical rocky pinnacles in the sandy desert. This was where *Lawrence of Arabia* was filmed, and I wanted to explore it, so, with Sarah on the back, I took the motorbike out and set off. Unfortunately, I was not good enough to ride in sand with a pillion, and we fell over many times. Fortunately, it always was on sand, so we remained without injuries.

While we sat and watched the sun set behind the rocks, we were astonished suddenly to see the figure of a European running towards us. We were in the middle of the desert, and yet he seemed to be running surprisingly effortlessly. When he reached us, he introduced himself, and I could tell from his accent that he was from New Zealand.

'A guide took me to see Wadi Rum,' he explained, 'but then our vehicle got stuck. He said he didn't know the area and he couldn't walk well anyway. That's when I remembered I'd seen you guys and this.' He pointed to the Unimog. 'Any chance you could come and pull us out?'

The New Zealander seemed a decent man, so I agreed to help him. We followed his directions to his car and managed to pull it out of the sand without too much trouble. Once we were sure he was all right, we headed back to where we had been earlier, which we had marked by leaving our table there. It took us a long time to find the table, but when we eventually did so, we were still early enough to enjoy a drink and watch the sun go down behind the rocky escarpment.

After a peaceful night, we woke in time to watch the sun rise again, which is always a special sight in the desert. Since we had seen all Jordan's sights, we drove to the town of Aqaba where we had to deal with the problems of another border crossing. This time, we had to board a ferry, and I backed the Unimog on to the ship with a guide standing on the step and telling me which way to turn the steering wheel. It was highly stressful.

We set sail across the Gulf of Aqaba, with Saudi Arabia passing on our port side, to dock in Egypt. The Egyptian customs were reasonably straightforward: with just a small fee to pay, we were able to disembark from the ferry and drive across the Sinai Peninsula. We headed straight for Saint Catherine's Monastery, built in the sixth century BC on what was believed to have been the site of Moses' Burning Bush.

Following the coast road along the Gulf of Aqaba, we crossed the Suez Canal at Port Said and then had the nightmare of entering Cairo, with its millions of people and vehicles, without a decent map. Fortunately, someone asked us where we were going and then jumped into the cab and guided us to the tourist area in the west of the city, where it was much quieter. We went to Tahrir Square to visit the Museum of Egyptian Antiquities and to look at all the ancient monuments, including the Mask of Tutankhamun, the gold artefacts and 'the wonderful things' which

A local camel herder in Egypt

Howard Carter discovered in the tomb in 1922. As ever, Sarah proved to be very popular with the local men, and one in particular kindly offered me 3,000 camels for her.

'Sorry,' I said. 'She's not for sale. And what on earth would I do with 3,000 camels?'

Driving south from Cairo, we visited the pyramids and saw the *son et lumière* around the Sphinx, the night-time sound and light show which tells the history of ancient Egypt in a series of audio recordings and illuminations. We then headed out of the city towards the Mediterranean and joined the coast road to El-Alamein, where we stopped so I could visit the war memorial to the battle which my father had fought in over fifty years earlier.

Making our way inland, we set out into the desert, passing through several checkpoints. We stopped at one to realise that there was no one there. Since the Unimog wasn't fast enough to get away from any pursuing guards, I thought I should announce our presence, which I did with the air horn. There was a short pause, and then the door of the hut was thrown open. A soldier stumbled out, carrying a rifle in one hand and doing up his trousers with the other. Four more soldiers followed him, all in a similar state of undress. They approached the Unimog, took a cursory look at our papers, and then let us go. I couldn't see what they did after we left.

That night, we camped in the desert near a borehole, and decided to take advantage of the water to do some washing. Sarah washed everything in the small kitchen sink and then I rinsed it all under the tap from the borehole and hung it from the roof to dry. By the time the second set of sheets and clothes were washed, the first set had already dried in the desert wind.

Satisfied with our clean sheets and clothes, we headed across the desert to Aswan, where we went out on the River Nile in a *felucca*, a wooden sailing boat traditional to the area. Unfortunately, the skipper was a

Abu Simbal from Lake Nasser

terrible sailor, and I had to take over to return us safely back to the shore. Aswan sits at the lower end of Lake Nasser, from where we set off early in the morning for the long drive through the desert to Abu Simbel, located much further south on the banks of the same lake. Abu Simbel was cut into pieces with saws and rebuilt above the water level after the Aswan High Dam was constructed and Lower Nubia flooded. Despite their relocation, the famous Abu Simbel temples still look perfect on the outside and everything appears original, but when you look at the back of the temples you can see the concrete structure built to support them. We arrived there in the early morning, having the whole site to ourselves. The tourist buses soon arrived, spilling out visitors who spoilt the tranquillity of the area, but after they left in the late afternoon it was ours once more, and we saw the best of it at both sunrise and sunset.

We had travelled as far south as we could before the border between Egypt and Sudan, so we turned and started to make our way back down beside the Nile. We were having a good lunch high up in the Unimog, with our eye level ten feet off the ground, when we looked out of the windows and saw six armed men standing there staring at us. They were all in uniform and we realised they were police and not terrorists. They told us it was not safe to stop on the roads. Rather distressed by this encounter, we decided to take their word for it, and drove on to Hurghada, a beach resort where I hoped to have a dive in the Red Sea. I knew they weren't strict there and that they let people dive without a certificate, and they did. I didn't have all the equipment I was used to, but it was still a wonderful dive, and amazing to see all those tropical fish just a few hundred yards from the desert.

Back on the road, we continued north, driving along the main road with the intention of finding the camel market. I missed the turning but, since there wasn't much traffic, I reversed on the motorway, changing from third to sixth gear in reverse and trying to keep my eye on the mirror to make sure that there was nothing I could hit. All went well, but I am unlikely ever to attempt such a manoeuvre again. We turned off the main road and found the camel market. Several hundred camels had made the long trek up from the markets of Sudan where they were being sold. I briefly wondered if Sarah really was worth as little as 3,000 camels; I knew she was worth much more!

Soon, it was time to retrace our route through Jordan to Syria. We stopped at the city of Hama, famous for its historic norias, the enormous waterwheels powered by the Orontes River. Hama is also famous as the site of the 1982 Hama Uprising and then the Hama Massacre, when a Muslim Brotherhood revolt against President Hafez al-Assad was mercilessly put down.

Following Syria's Mediterranean coast, we looked for a campsite and found a beautiful spot on the shoreline. It was too rocky to swim there, but we had a wonderful al fresco supper listening to the sound of the waves. There was a nearby heap of rubbish, which we decided to burn to make a large campfire to sit around and enjoy the sea and the stars. It was a memorable evening and we went to sleep feeling deeply content.

However, the next morning things turned distinctly nasty. While Sarah showered and I was checking the engine, I suddenly noticed that we were being approached by a small patrol of Syrian army troops. They became aggressive, unsheathing their bayonets and pointing them at me while I desperately tried to hurry Sarah up to finish her shower. This she did and the presence of a pretty girl worked wonders, quickly quietening them down. Now that things were calmer, I asked them what they wanted and they told us to follow them; we had no alternative but to do as we were told. We drove after them to their camp, where we were taken to the commander. After lengthy discussions, we finally realised what the problem was. The army unit was there to protect Syria's shores against an Israeli attack. The commander was enraged to find a vehicle, especially one with the military look of the Unimog, camped out overnight. It could have been an Israeli invasion force which they hadn't noticed. When we eventually managed to convince them that we weren't a risk to them, one of the soldiers with a bayonet was so relieved that he insisted on kissing me goodbye.

After being allowed to leave, we drove on to an easy border crossing into Turkey and then to an even easier one into Greece, where we spent the night at our last campsite beside an idyllic little river. It was perfect to bodysurf down, although walking back to the Unimog without my glasses was rather more difficult. Driving through the north of Greece, we came to the big ferry port of Igoumenitsa and, the next day, caught the ferry to Italy. We then drove through the lovely countryside along narrow lanes. Branches of ripe cherries sprang back into the Unimog's open window after hitting my mirror, and I couldn't resist the temptation to pick lots of them for breakfast. Finally, the road took us through the Apennine Mountains to northern Italy and into France, where we caught the ferry home.

CHAPTER TWENTY-FIVE
TO BHUTAN
AND KAZAKHSTAN

I first met Kinley Tshering at the NEC Bike Show in 2010. He was manning a stand which offered an off-road bike trip from China into Nepal and Bhutan. The expedition looked fascinating and to a unique part of the world, so I signed up for it. Unfortunately, a few months later he discovered that the Chinese were not issuing permits for motorcycles to cross the border. I was still eager for an adventure, so I managed to persuade Kinley, who was a Bhutanese national, to take me and his half-English cousin, who was his agent in Britain, on a two-week tour of Bhutan.

I flew out to the capital, Thimphu, where I was met and taken to a good hotel. We spent the first two days in the city and Kinley showed me all the ancient and traditional religious sights. So that I looked the part, he even gave me a traditional coat and scarf.

Kinley was well connected. His father was a senior government minister, with access to permits from his ministry. When he was unable to obtain a visa stamp for a tour, it did not deter him. He entered the ministry at night and stamped all the documents himself so that he would be ready to leave the following morning. One day, he took me to meet another of his cousins, which gave me the opportunity to see the inside of a local house; it was beautifully furnished. Inside the house, his cousin kept two golden retrievers, which looked very healthy and well looked after. She kept referring to the dogs as 'His Majesty's', and I soon understood why they looked so good. She was taking care of them for His Majesty the King, to whom they belonged.

Local school children playing on the bike, Bhutan

LEFT: *Monastery displaying prayer flags in Bhutan*
RIGHT: *Thimphu temple stopping point in Bhutan*

Kinley was slightly nervous of my riding around Bhutan, so we had a trial ride through Thimphu. When he considered that I had 'passed', we set off into the mountains together. Bhutan is an extremely mountainous country. They have a saying there: 'You know when you reach the border. If you throw a stone down the mountain, when it stops rolling – that is India.' We rode for six days through the mountains, climbing right up into the clouds. My bike, a KTM 640 Adventure, was perfect for the steep, narrow and twisting roads. There were frequently 2,000-foot drops beside the roads and endless tight corners. Throughout the entire six days, I was never able to change above third gear. The small trucks we passed needed all their power, so they never slowed down to go around corners. The drivers simply kept their foot down and hoped that nothing was coming the other way.

We spent our nights in small rural hotels, eating traditional Bhutanese food, and then went back out on the roads again each morning. It was some of the most beautiful country I have ever seen, with many rivers crossed by old-fashioned bridges often leading to temples. We rode towards one of these, known as the Tiger's Nest: a spectacular eyrie temple perched on top of a mountain. It was too high for me to climb, but even from below it looked magnificent. I could only imagine how incredible its views over the valley must have been. Only the most dedicated monks lived and meditated there.

One of the difficulties with biking in Bhutan was the numerous landslides we had to ride through. At one, which was especially long and

A gnarly road with regular landslides in Bhutan

A river crossing in Bhutan

Charles with his KTM 640 Adventure by a field of prayer flags in Bhutan

Arriving at the highest point on the Dantak Road, Chelela in Bhutan

muddy, I was forced to stop behind a car. On either side of me was nothing but deep mud, and when I lowered a foot to the ground it sank into the mud and I fell over. Luckily, the helpful driver behind us picked up both me and the bike, and I was able to continue. On our last day, I used my GPS for the first time – until then, I had been following a guide, so the GPS was purely for amusement – and was amazed to discover that we had covered only 35 miles as the crow flies, and yet had ridden 175 miles.

Carrying freshly picked tea leaves to be weighed at the factory in Assam

It was time to head into India. We rode downwards until the road flattened out and the stones stopped rolling. The weather became wet and overcast, reminding me of England. We were told that we needed a guide for the crossing to India and had to be there at 7.30 a.m. However, when we arrived, Kinley discovered that, in fact, we should have been there at 7.00 a.m. After much persuasion, and Kinley's threat of calling his father in the ministry, we were eventually allowed to cross into India for our final day.

We were now on the flat plains of Assam, and rode on towards and through the tea plantations, which we stopped to admire. We watched the women picking the young leaves off the top of the tea plants, which were rather short bushes, so that the ground under the plants received no light and therefore competing vegetation was unable to grow. At our next stop, our guide explained that local bandits used the tea plantations to attack vehicles on the road. They would creep under the bushes, hiding undetected, and then stand up suddenly to shoot at the vehicles on the road. They could then escape through the plantations, using the bushes as cover. The tea bushes were so tightly packed that soldiers found it almost impossible to pursue bandits. This was why we should have had an armed escort with us, but the escorts only went every other day, and we had missed the escort for that day. When we learnt this, we realised that we probably shouldn't have stopped at the plantations to admire them. Fortunately, we had been all right, and nothing had happened.

We then had to ride back across the flat plains of northern India. The road was rough and wide. Under construction was a 200-yard-wide superhighway, as yet unfinished, but chaotic and filled with traffic. We had been told to ride this section as quickly as possible. If we didn't make the border by closing time, we would be forced to stay in a nasty little Indian hotel rather than a luxurious Bhutanese one. I rode as fast as I could, hitting bumps which were far too hard for comfort, knowing that I had to in order to keep up with my guide. Every now and then, I would look over at the beautiful sections of new road beside us, which were very tempting, but I stayed behind the guide. I soon realised why he wasn't using these sections of new road. They were perfect for the local Indian farmers to dry their crops, and they knew they would not be disturbed there. The road was so disorganised and wide that we often passed vehicles on completely the wrong side, but no one seemed to care. This was India, after all, where no road rules apply. You just go wherever you think you can.

Chatting with the tour guides outside of our support vehicle in Bhutan

Behind us was our support truck. It had disappeared for a while, but now was back behind us again. At our next stop, the support team explained to us that they had been stopped by local bandits, who had demanded money. The drivers told them that they didn't have any money and that, in fact, all the money was on the bikes in front. The bandits then confessed why they had not stopped us. They thought we were a rival gang and had been too frightened to stop us. That was when we realised just how lucky we had been.

We finally reached the border, despite our fairly late start. It had taken us the best part of a day, but somehow, we had managed to cover the same distance as we had over six days riding through Bhutan. At the side of the road, local sellers hawked tiny crafts they had made in their little workshops. We had no chance to buy anything, but it was interesting to see that everyone there had a job to do. Some worked on the crafts, others helped, and others went to fetch parts or deliver things. Needless to say, they were all men.

We crossed the border, leaving the chaos of India for the quiet civilisation of Bhutan. It had been a wonderful experience which I had enjoyed immensely. Not only had I got on well with Kinley, I also came to realise that he had good connections in Russia and Kazakhstan. He liked the idea of my Unimog, so we agreed to drive to Kazakhstan together the following year. He suggested that he could bring his friend and assistant along to drive, so that we could ride our bikes on the steppes of Russia and Kazakhstan while his friend drove the Unimog and did the cooking. I could keep my KTM on the front and put a small Suzuki up on the back for Kinley. It sounded like an excellent plan.

◎ ◎ ◎

Kinley and his friend flew to England, and from there we drove to Germany. It did not take long to realise that Kinley's friend could not drive the Unimog. Used to Indian trucks, where brute force is needed to change gears, he was doing damage to the Unimog's gearbox, so I had to do the driving.

Taking care to avoid all the main towns, we drove through the western German countryside and forests, before crossing the former border into eastern Germany, where there still existed huge lorry parks for the trucks which had had to wait at the border before reunification. Eastern Germany had modernised enormously since the fall of the Berlin Wall, but I could still see the poverty and the dereliction there in comparison to the west of the country.

We crossed the border into Poland, paying extra attention to the road signs, for they were all in Polish, and only the main towns had signs with an English translation. We stopped at Auschwitz, left the Unimog in the car park, and walked through the entrance gate beneath the *ARBEIT MACHT FREI* (Work Sets You Free) inscription. It was the original gate, so too were the guardhouses and two or three of the huts where the prisoners had lived. The railway lines which had brought the Jews into the camp were mostly intact, although those leading directly to the gas chambers had been partially destroyed before the Russians arrived. The chambers themselves were visible but access was restricted, so we were left to imagine the trainloads of Jews walking direct from the train into the gas chambers to be dispatched to their deaths, and how the guards might have disposed of the bodies after the gas had done its work. We all knew the horrors of what the Nazis had done, but seeing the actual site of so much merciless killing brought home the terrifying reality of it all. There was a large memorial wall filled with thousands of names, and nearby pictures of the emaciated bodies taken from the camp when it was finally liberated. Auschwitz was a truly sobering experience for us, and by seeing it we could now fully understand this tragic part of the past, but we were also glad to be able to leave it behind us.

Continuing with our Second World War theme, we went on to Kraków to see the devastation and almost entire destruction of the old city, with only a memorial standing to remind people of what was gone, and the new city all around it. Then it was Warsaw, which was much the same but on a bigger scale. I found it difficult to imagine the memories that people must retain of those times, of the Nazi occupation, of the wartime destruction, and then of the Soviet occupation and finally the liberation.

There is a kind of lake district in north-east Poland, a huge area of lakes and rivers. I had brought along a small dinghy on the roof of the Unimog, and I was able to spend the next three days exploring all the canals and waterways of the region. In contrast to Kraków and Warsaw, this was an extremely rural place and, since it was impossible terrain for tank warfare, the region suffered little from either Hitler's or Stalin's armies. The war had largely passed it by.

To reach Russia from Poland, you have to cross either Ukraine, Belarus or the Baltic countries of Lithuania and Latvia. We planned to take the northern route, but there was a problem. At the time, Lithuania was not part of the Schengen zone and had its own border controls.

Since my Bhutanese friends had entered Europe on a Schengen visa, it meant that, for the first time in my life, I would have to become a people smuggler. While we were still in Poland, I put Kinley and his friend in the clamshell sleeping quarters on the roof of the Unimog and closed it almost completely. With that done, I drove to the border. Although Lithuania was not part of the Schengen zone, it was still a part of the EU, and that meant that the old border structures with their high platforms from which guards could look into vehicles were no longer manned. I drove through without a problem and then, when we reached the first gateway on a quiet road, I opened the clamshell to let my friends out.

Now that we were in the country, it was unlikely we would be stopped and searched, but still we kept to the countryside and the forests where quiet camping sites were easy to find. From Lithuania, we continued on into and across Latvia, and then headed for the Russian border. There were long queues of trucks, which had clearly been expected, for every hundred yards or so there were portable lavatories beside the road. Feeling optimistic, we drove past the trucks straight to the front. The border guards asked for our documents, and it didn't take them long to deduce that my two Bhutanese friends must have crossed Lithuania illegally. Fortunately, Kinley knew exactly what to do. He understood that, like many border guards, their minds could be changed with a gift. It worked and we were allowed into Russia.

One of the beauties of having Kinley with me was that he was capable of this kind of 'persuasion'. He had various connections in Russia and promised that his security contacts were with people in high places and would be useful to us if ever we needed them. I later learnt that he was trying to raise finance to build a casino in Bhutan, and was pushing things through via his close contact with the king's brother. Unfortunately for Kinley, the king himself did not want gambling in his country, and in the end his will prevailed.

Once clear of the border, we continued on the road towards Moscow, which was extremely narrow. It was difficult to avoid having the wing mirrors hit by the Eastern European truck drivers who sped past us, racing to get to the capital. When we found a beautiful campsite that night in deserted farmland with nobody about, it was a great relief.

The following morning, we set off on the long drive to Moscow. Once we finally reached the city's outskirts, we found a good campsite on the edge of a village. We could see that the living conditions in the suburbs were extremely basic, but probably no worse than the suburbs of any other big city. The next day, after an early morning start, we headed with considerable trepidation towards the centre of Moscow, hoping to visit the Kremlin. We had chosen a Sunday – mostly by luck – and thankfully the streets were nearly empty. We had no trouble parking and were able to take an extensive tour of the Kremlin with its beautiful gold-plated dome structures, so familiar from television, but so much more impressive in real life. After that, we went to visit vast Red Square, where the Soviet army was displayed regularly. It was just as big as it looked on television and was surrounded by smart shops for wealthy Muscovites and tourists.

It was soon time to leave Moscow and, on the way out, I took advantage of the empty streets to perform a U-turn so as to face in the right direction. Unfortunately for me, the Unimog is large and conspicuous, especially on empty streets. The police pulled me over and I was ordered to walk back to their car some 200 yards across the street. There followed a long discussion, complicated by the fact that neither of us could speak the other's language. Eventually, we seemed to reach some sort of agreement, and I was waved on with no penalty and his wishing me a good journey. Based on that encounter, the Russian police rose considerably in my estimation.

We were able to head out of Moscow with no further trouble, and made our way towards Kazakhstan. We had one or two stops in the open steppes, where we were able to take the bikes off the Unimog and ride for miles over lovely grasslands, leaving Kinley's friend to look after the Unimog.

We drove on to Ufa and then, just after that, we were stopped by the police. Once more, I was asked to get out of the Unimog and sit in the police car.

'You are no longer in a Moscow district,' one of the officers said to me in the car. His English was sufficient enough for me to understand him. 'You are in our district, and you must pay us some money.'

I shook my head. 'I've paid my fees,' I said. 'I don't need to pay any more money.'

On and on we went like this for some time: the officer demanding money; me refusing. It was a stalemate but still I refused to give them any money.

Suddenly, Kinley appeared beside the police car. He had become bored of waiting. 'Here,' he said to the officers, producing a beautifully wrapped package of special Bhutanese tea. 'I would like to give this gift to the Russian police because this is such a beautiful country.' He was formal and polite, and the officers accepted the tea and placed it on their dashboard.

It did not take them much longer after that to realise that I was not going to give them any money, so they handed the tea back to Kinley, handed my passport back to me, and told us to carry on. It had been a tedious experience, but also an interesting demonstration of the eastern way of life.

○ ○ ○

A wide motorway took us out of the city. We passed through an unmanned checkpoint and, feeling hopeful, I drove straight through without stopping, but my hope was misplaced. A police car suddenly drove up beside us and stopped us. When the policeman got out of his car, he blew his whistle directly into my ear and then jumped into the Unimog.

The officer took us through an underpass back to his checkpoint. Kinley, his friend Briska and I stepped out of the Unimog to see if we could talk our way out of the situation. Kinley took the polite approach, telling the officer he was from Bhutan and, when the officer admitted he had never heard of the place, Kinley produced a map showing him exactly where it was. By now, more police had arrived, a big, fat sergeant and two young officers. Somehow, Kinley seemed to charm them all. He chatted away to them and invited them into the Unimog, and the young officers climbed into the back, delighted to explore this western camper van. Unfortunately, the sergeant was not so happy; he was too fat to climb up. Nevertheless, Kinley's approach worked, for they eventually agreed that there was nothing they could do and that they should let us go. In fact, they did better than that; they gave us a ceremonial send-off, which involved several police officers closing six lanes of traffic so that we could perform a U-turn and be on our way.

We headed to Astana, the then capital of Kazakhstan. It was an open city with lots of smart new buildings, yet there was no one around. We carried on across the desert landscape, past Lake Balkhash, one of the largest lakes in Asia, to Almaty, the old capital and still Kazakhstan's biggest city. Kinley had a friend in Almaty who would let us store the Unimog. We plugged in the hook-up to keep the fridge and freezer running and ensure our food stayed cool, or frozen, while Kinley tried to obtain a visa, leaving the rest of us to be entertained in the city's various bars. The place also gave Kinley, I'm sure, the opportunity for lots of behind-the-scenes discussions regarding casinos and new hotels in Bhutan.

Almaty is a very hot town right on the edge of the plain. Kinley's friend took us out of the town up to the Tian Shan mountains where we had a ride on a ski-lift. Incredibly, there was snow in the middle of summer. After being in arid desert just an hour and a half earlier, this was rather astonishing. Since it was the weekend, we all went out to one of their friends' villas which had a hot sauna and a cold pool. I put my head round the door of the sauna but I couldn't take the heat at all. I left them all to carry on with their naked beatings and their cold baths – all typical and traditional for the Kazakhs, and certainly one of their favourite pastimes.

Back in Almaty, Kinley faced further visa difficulties. He could not seem to obtain a visa for Ukraine, so we made the decision that he would continue travelling with me as far as the border, at which point he would have to make his own way home. We set out from Almaty back into the countryside, driving across the south of Kazakhstan to reach the cotton fields of Uzbekistan. We followed the Amu Darya, a large river some 300 yards wide which flows from the Tian Shan mountains to the Aral Sea. The Russians created a giant irrigation scheme here, making 150-yard-wide canals to irrigate all of Uzbekistan. This has enabled cotton and other plants to grow from the desert, sometimes giving as many as three crops a year. From this, Uzbekistan has been able to create a major agricultural industry dependent on water and semi-slave labour to farm and pick the cotton flowers but, sadly, it has destroyed the Aral Sea in the process. It used to be the fourth-largest lake in the world. Now just ten per cent of it remains.

The heat grew unbearable and, because of it, Kinley and I had our only row.

'It is too hot,' he said. 'We're going to die!'

'Nonsense,' I replied.

'It's true! I've queued up for visas in India when the heat was 45 degrees, and this is much worse.'

'If I can stand the heat,' I said, 'then I'm sure you can.'

'Well, I can't stand it. We should go to a hotel.'

I stood my ground. I had no intention of staying at a hotel. We had everything we needed in the Unimog, and I wanted to see the Aral Sea. In the end, I had my way, he lived, and we continued on.

The disappearance of the lake soon became clear. We passed towns which were once on the waterfront, where sizeable fishing boats now lay in dried-out sand. My invaluable GPS took me along the road well into the

Ural Bike beside the Caspian Sea in Kazakhstan

night and, according to it, five miles into where the lake used to be. I had to trust the GPS, for there was no water around, just dry, dusty, fine sand. It was strange driving where the lake had been, but overall, it was tragic to see what decimation the Russians had deliberately achieved by destroying the lake and the fishing town around it, just to produce cotton.

Leaving the Aral Sea behind us, I drove up through the south-west of Kazakhstan over the northern coast of the Caspian Sea to cross the border back into Russia. We went to Volgograd on the banks of the Volga River, a city with a rich and famous history. Once known as Stalingrad, it was the scene of one of the fiercest and longest battles of the Second World War, fought in the middle of an extremely cold winter, when the Russians eventually defeated the Germans and put an end to their advance, changing the course of the war. That winter was one of the coldest ever – the Volga froze over, and planes could not take off without the fuel being heated first. The city had been shelled relentlessly, and today one building has been left as it was to show visitors what the damage had been like. We went to see it for ourselves, and I couldn't help feeling that it seemed fairly minor compared to the effects of modern-day warfare in the Middle East. After that, we went to the Museum of the Battle of Stalingrad: one of the most impressive museums I have ever visited, which showed the fighting in truly realistic 3D.

The Unimog camped at the edge of the Caspian Sea showing the second motorbike mounted on the back

Kinley never managed to obtain his Ukraine visa, so he left me at Volgograd, and I drove on to the border without him. At the time of writing, the east of Ukraine is occupied by the Russians, but it was still free and friendly when I travelled through. I followed the Sea of Azov coast down to Crimea to see all the names made famous during the Crimean War, such as Balaklava and Sevastopol. The latter is an incredibly steep port city, and I had a few moments of panic when the Unimog's brakes overheated, and I found myself trying to control its 8 tons going down hills on the handbrake alone. I had to stop and rest for a while to let them cool down.

Once the brakes were working again, I drove to Yalta on the coast of the Black Sea, where Churchill, Roosevelt and Stalin met late in the Second World War in February 1945 to discuss the break-up and division of Europe. Roosevelt died soon after the conference. The city was an interesting historic site and I am glad I had the chance to visit it; unfortunately, it is now in a completely inaccessible part of Russia.

⊙ ⊙ ⊙

I left Ukraine by heading into Moldova; the border crossing was extremely difficult. I had been in Russian and Ukrainian territory for some time, and it took me a while to realise that a different language was

Churchill shaking hands with Stalin at the 1945 Yalta Summit which decided the future of Europe after World War II

being spoken at the border. I tried to speak English with them, and it was then that they explained to me that Ukraine wanted to join the EU. Because of that, there were Spanish and Italian customs officers at the border monitoring the behaviour of the Ukrainians and trying to stop them being totally corrupt. I had a leaking diesel can which they insisted on fining me for, even though I was about to leave the country. They then warned me, somewhat unusually, that I should not pay too much money when going through the Moldovan side of the border. Coming from a customs officer, and especially after the fine they had just made me pay, it all seemed rather strange.

When I approached the Moldovan side, it was with trepidation. How much money was I now going to have to pay? And for what? I duly entered immigration, and had nearly filled in all the paperwork, when I was told that they wanted a $50 payment. Like most travellers, I always carry dollars in various small denominations for exactly this kind of event. I pulled out two twenties and a ten to pay for this corruption. The officer looked at them with a sneer. They were well-used notes and one, a twenty, was obviously too scruffy for his liking, so he handed it back to me. We progressed to the next customs officer, who demanded a payment of $20. I gave him the old $20 note his colleague had returned to me, saying it was all I had. Finally, he accepted it and let me through.

I have travelled through many countries in my life, but at no other time have I entered one whose name I didn't know. I thought I was entering Moldova but, in fact, I was actually entering Transnistria: a breakaway state which is internationally recognised as part of Moldova but which claims independence from it. The dispute and ensuing civil war between Transnistria and Moldova continues to this day.

As I drove into Transnistria, I could see from my GPS that the road headed across a bridge. All the traffic had turned left but I, with total faith in my GPS, kept on course. I remained wary, keeping a lookout all around, and yet, despite this, I suddenly had to stop. About 30 yards in front of me, extremely well camouflaged, was a tank, with its gun pointing directly in my face. A dozen soldiers, also camouflaged, appeared and came towards me. It became immediately clear that I had taken the wrong route. The soldiers explained that I had to go through the town, so I backed up the road to return there, relieved as I did so.

Since this was not the way I was expecting to go, I took a wrong turning in the town and had to retrace my steps. When I found myself back at the point where I had made the error, I was stopped again, this time by the police. They told me I was in the wrong lane and demanded to see my international driving licence. When I produced this, they explained that I had violated traffic laws and would have to pay a fine. If I didn't, they would confiscate my licence. I was daunted at the prospect of continuing without my international driving licence, although I was nearly back in the EU and therefore wouldn't need it for much longer. Nevertheless, I decided that it would be better to pay the $50 fine, even though it was totally corrupt, and retain my driving licence. I was glad I did, for not long after I was stopped again. My papers were checked and, once more, they specifically asked to see my international driving licence. By then I clearly understood the system. If you did not pay the fine the first time, you would be sure to have to pay it the second time. As soon as the whole rigmarole was over, I made my way out into the countryside, where I felt much happier.

I finally found a deserted rural campsite in an apparently 19th-century village. The following day, I entered Moldova, leaving Transnistria behind, probably the most expensive country I have ever spent twenty-four hours in, but one which few people have ever heard of, let alone visited. Moldova was one of the least interesting former communist countries I have ever visited, with almost nothing to recommend it. I then journeyed into Romania, the start of my return home to complete my crossing of Europe to the Channel.

PART V:
RIBALETA

Navigating Ribaleta
in Providenciales

CHAPTER TWENTY-SIX
THE ROAD TO RIBALETA

In September 1996, Celia and I visited the Southampton Boat Show, where we went out for a test ride on a rigid inflatable boat, more commonly referred to by its acronym RIB, and discovered that it was extremely good fun. RIBs are seaworthy inflatable boats, with a rigid hull bottom and side-forming air tubes, inflated to a high pressure to retain buoyancy. They are incredibly robust and capable of reaching very high speeds. It's for these reasons that they are popular as lifeboats and military craft.

It occurred to me that, if we had our own RIB, it would replace our ageing Westerly Pageant sailing boat and could be launched quickly for use on the rivers and coasts of Suffolk where we lived in the summer. We still had *Caleta II* out in the Caribbean and returned to it each winter. But I liked the idea of a fast, easily trailed motor boat. It would not be something to sail from one tropical island to another, but a high-performance boat we could use for quick trips when, for example, we might have a day off during harvest. Celia agreed, so we bought our first ever RIB.

We made good use of it, but the more I drove it, the more I wanted to take it further afield. Our RIB was only 20 feet and not very seaworthy, and I liked the idea of something a bit bigger and more seaworthy. Searching for alternatives, I came across the Scorpion, a good-looking RIB often used for racing, something I had been thinking about doing. I visited the factory and was taken for a demonstration on their test boat. It was smooth and fast and, above all, fun. After the demonstration I walked round the boatyard and saw a beautiful Revenger RIB being driven into the yard. I had a chat with the owner, who told me it was for sale. We agreed a date for a test run, which was very successful, and I learnt more about RIBs as he raced them. I agreed to buy it. Revengers, often referred to as 'the Porsche of the sea', are superb high-speed RIBs, and this one, although it was second-hand, was in excellent condition.

As soon as I brought my new Revenger home, I learnt of a cruise round the Scottish islands with the British Inflatable Boat Owners Association (BIBOA), which I had recently joined. I drove the Revenger with Celia and our daughter Helen up to Oban in the Unimog, camping on the way. After launching the Revenger, I found a yellow Scorpion RIB cruising alongside, apparently looking for a race. I accepted and we raced out of the bay. To my delight, I discovered I could beat this race boat on my first attempt at full speed. This was clearly going to be a magnificent boat for us. With its manoeuvrability as a RIB, Douglas Crockett our Scottish guide was able to lead us into wonderful little bays and coves we never would have found otherwise. We stayed in a nice hotel and on the first night I met Jonathan again, who had demonstrated the Scorpion to me before I bought the Revenger and was now navigating the Scorpion I had just beaten. He and Helen were the only young people there; they got on well and were married a year later.

My next cruise was a BIBOA trip to Holland which I did on my own. It was great fun, and included a party given by our Dutch hosts at Ostend. The wind the next day had increased considerably and, when I set out, I had difficulty following the other club boats to Dover. I therefore headed directly towards the Thames Estuary. The waves were becoming much steeper and I felt I risked being capsized over backwards. I cut the power immediately to slow down, then opened the throttles up to 4,000rpm and waited for the propeller to grip the water and give sudden acceleration. This was the racing propeller fitted to the boat when I bought it, which was too fine a pitch for cruising. This happened many times, possibly submerging the engine. I had loose spare plastic petrol tanks in the boat but even so I was concerned about running out of fuel. While worrying about what to do, the engine suddenly stopped. Luckily, I had a spare 8-horsepower engine at the back which I could clamp on to the transom. Dipping the fuel line into a spare can enabled me to start the engine. In preparation for this emergency, I had adapted the throttle to be set at maximum. Now I was able to start the engine, engage the gear and give it full throttle. I could now return to the driving seat to see my GPS, balance the boat and see my way ahead; I could steer with the steering wheel connected to the main engine; and, using the GPS chart plotter, I could set a course back to Ostend which allowed for the current. As the spare engine only had 8 horsepower my speed was only 4 knots, which meant my having to drive 15 degrees off the direct route to allow for the current. Luckily, my engine kept going and I had enough fuel in my spare tanks to reach Ostend harbour. If I hadn't had the spare engine and fuel tanks rigged for remote control, I would have been at the mercy of the sea and dependent on being rescued by a lifeboat.

On the next BIBOA trip from Yarmouth on the Isle of Wight to Cherbourg, when I arrived on my own, I was asked to take two young girls because their father's boat was smaller and would be overloaded. Delighted to have a lovely young crew, we set off round the Needles following a bigger twin-engine cabin RIB called *Sea Hound*. When we cleared the island and were well out into the English Channel, the wind and seas increased so that it became difficult to see my instruments. I was relying mostly on watching the stern of *Sea Hound* to keep up with a heavier RIB with twice the power. I had to have a short stop as the girl at the back of the boat complained of a pain. I could do nothing to help her as investigating the reason for the pain would not have been appropriate, so she agreed that we carry on regardless. We kept in sight of *Sea Hound* until we reached Cherbourg. It was a very challenging trip and we were the only boats to complete it. We were well entertained with an oyster and champagne reception, albeit my never having eaten oysters before, as this was all that was available. The girls had only my clothes to wear at the reception as all theirs were wet, but they really had enjoyed the whole adventure and their achievement.

Both experiences made me realise something crucial: if I was going to continue driving a RIB then, for my own safety, I needed one with two engines. I've always been happiest when I have had my vehicles built for myself, so I decided to do the same for my next RIB. I found a builder near me who agreed to take on the job. After long and detailed conversations with the designers regarding exactly what I wanted, the builder started building the boat. I left him to it, confident that my RIB dream was soon to become reality.

I could not have been more wrong.

He built the fibreglass hull of the boat fairly quickly, but couldn't fit the engines, so I took it down to Dave Crawford, a great mechanic on the south coast who I know well, and he put the engines in. All seemed to be progressing in the right direction until I returned to the builder, who immediately started an argument with me about costs as there was still plenty of work to be done. At this point, the hull and side-forming tubes had been built, but only the engines had been installed and nothing more. I decided to have it surveyed, which revealed it already had some problems of which I was unaware. When the survey was discussed with the builder, it only made him angrier and even more argumentative.

I was beginning to dislike this man as I already knew that his principal job was to repair bullet holes in boats which had been used for drug runs in southern Spain. The drug connection and the way he was behaving over my RIB were making me uneasy. The arguments halted any further work. I towed the boat from Dave Crawford back to my farm and kept it in one of the barns until the situation was resolved. From then on, things got completely out of hand.

One evening, the builder sneaked into my barn and hid inside until it was locked up. Once everyone had gone, he poured petrol all around the boat and set fire to it, before escaping through one of the doors which could be opened from the inside. The fire was so intense that it bent the barn's thick metal beams and rafters 15 feet up in the air and destroyed the boat. By the time things were under control, all that was left was the diesel in the tank, quite astonishing considering the metal-warping heat of the fire and the destruction of my barn. The dishonest builder later went to jail.

It goes without saying that this incident ended all further business between me and that builder. I began to look around for alternatives, and it was at the RIBEX Power Boat Show that I found one. I saw a sketch of a RIB which met many of my specifications. At 33 feet long, it was the size I was looking for, and it was big enough to take the new twin Yanmar 300-horsepower 4.2-litre engines that had just been introduced. The hull was from a former J&B Whisky outboard offshore powerboat, well known to be sea-kindly.

I found out that the mould was with a company called Ocean and, when I contacted them and explained what I was after, they agreed to build a one-off RIB for me using the mould. It took some time, but I didn't mind, because their work was good, and I wanted them to follow the specifications which were drawn up with my naval architect. What I wanted was an offshore race boat produced for maximum speed and lightness with a hull that could keep the tubes clear of the water when loaded with 400 gallons of fuel – and building that is not an easy job.

Nevertheless, Ocean did it, and did it well. Once the hull was complete and the engines were installed, we started to create the 'interior'. The console was all made from aluminium with a locker at the back to access the instruments and provide space for an electric lavatory, possibly the only one on a race boat. I chose not to put in a windscreen, as windscreens are too fragile and always end up being covered in salt, obscuring visibility. Instead, we angled the top face of the console forward to deflect the wind over the crew while ensuring perfect visibility. It was an admirable solution, so that when I drive at 50 knots the wind only feels like 10 knots.

The front end, which a brochure would describe as a 'sun lounger', became, in fact, a fully functioning living space. A large locker was built to hold an 8-foot dinghy, a 2-horsepower outboard and basics such as stores of water. Over it, a bed could be laid out. Also kept in the locker was a tent which, when pulled out and put up, covered the whole front end, supported by the A-frame. With additional support in the middle, it also carried the lights. The tent gave six feet six inches of headroom, which was important given my height. On either side of it, two 4-foot-square panels could be opened to create windows. With an electric fridge for storing food and gas stoves for cooking, it was perfectly habitable. Each engine had its own starter battery and a 100 ampere-hour service battery for the fridge, lights and other equipment. All could be connected together in emergency.

One crucial aspect I needed to address was that the boat had to be trailable. I made sure that the tubes were built to give a maximum width of 9 feet 2 inches in order to keep it within the legal limit for trailing. It was probably the longest trailable and self-launching boat that has ever been built in England. As I began to use it, I trailed it behind the Unimog and, when we stopped at service stations, the combination of both truck and boat could often take up three HGV spaces.

Finally, it was finished. All that remained was to give the RIB a name. While thinking of something suitable, we had an idea. *Caleta* had become almost a family name for our boats, and by combining that with the word RIB we realised that we could make a great name for a great boat. *Ribaleta* was born, and with it came a whole new world of possibilities.

CHAPTER TWENTY-SEVEN
ROUND BRITAIN

Ribaleta was designed for me to cruise single-handed without any other boats in support across the Channel and the North Sea. When I first began using it, I never envisaged that one day I would take it across the Bay of Biscay at 40 knots or across the Mediterranean to Africa, and I certainly never dreamt I would use it to explore the Orinoco Delta. All I had in my mind at the time was a series of British cruises and races.

However, I still required a good navigation system, so I adapted the console to include a half Admiralty Chart table under Perspex and a B&G chart plotter. I also had a Navionics chart plotter as *Ribaleta's* main navigation instrument which had course and speed repeaters at eye level. There is also a Garmin GPS plotter; two B&G depth sounders, one forward and one aft; a radar with another chart plotter; and two compasses. Over the years, I have come to find it essential to see my position at all times on both an electronic and a real chart. Since I was brought up in the old school where it was unlucky to enter a destination in the log or a route on the chart, I rarely have a destination at the start of each day.

In 1999, *Ribaleta* was finished just in time to join the Round Britain cruise organised by BIBOA. It was not a race, but a supported cruise on which I could test my new boat. I had installed fully sprung racing bucket seats in *Ribaleta* so that I could push the hull nearer to its limits with less damage to my back.

Slightly later than I had intended, I launched on to the Lymington River and had to speed down it a little too fast to reach the starting line on time. Fortunately, I wasn't caught, and I made it to the Solent and headed east to Portsmouth, where the cruise was due to begin. I had made good time and was only five minutes late for the start.

The first leg of the cruise was along the south coast from Portsmouth to Plymouth. All began well until, coming around Berry Head between Torquay and Dartmouth, there was a severe electrical storm. It was violent and potentially dangerous, so I decided that the safest course of action was to stop and wait for it to pass. While the rest of the entrants found hotels for the night, I had no need. I still had the lifelong aversion to hotels developed during my post-graduation trip to Spain thirty-five years earlier, and *Ribaleta* had been built for self-contained living in the same way as the Unimog and both *Caletas*. I slept that night in the locker at the front end of the boat. Despite others calling it the 'little coffin', I found it quite comfortable.

Stopping and waiting for the storm to clear was a wise decision, as I found out when I arrived at Plymouth. One of the boats had attempted to weather the storm, but the conditions became so frightening that the driver had decided to give up, leaving his crew stranded in Plymouth. Since I was travelling alone, I agreed to take on his crew and he joined me as we began the next leg from Plymouth to Pwllheli.

We cruised up along the coast of the West Country and crossed the Bristol Channel to south Wales and then, somewhere in Carmarthen Bay, one of the engines suffered a fuel blockage. This gave me the opportunity to test my twin-engine system – one of the main reasons I had upgraded from the Revenger to *Ribaleta*, as I had not felt safe with only one engine. I continued on a single engine, never exceeding 8 knots, which meant that we arrived at Pwllheli late. But that didn't matter. What was important was that we made it and the next day I cleared the fuel blockage. Knowing I could run *Ribaleta* on just one engine if the other failed increased my confidence in the boat.

From Pwllheli, the next leg ended at Oban on the west coast of Scotland. Conditions had been better since the awful storm near Plymouth. But the next day when we approached Cape Wrath the seas became extremely rough. Sometimes it felt as if we were on top of a mountain of water, wondering how on earth we were going to drive down. One of the other boats in the convoy filled with water and, since it didn't have decent drainage, the batteries soon became submerged. The boat's crew no longer had to deal with simply being stuck in the middle of heavy seas, but also with being electrocuted.

Fearing for their safety, I wanted to stay close so as to keep them in view, but I soon began to encounter problems of my own. The fuel pipes were becoming blocked again so I headed direct to the north Scottish coast and found a quiet anchorage where I could clear the blockage. While I was anchored in the bay, I suddenly heard an urgent announcement coming over the radio: 'All RIBs get well out to sea! Live bombing runs overhead now! All RIBs get well out to sea!'

I looked up just in time to see military planes flying over the sea, but realised that we had nothing to fear. Living in Suffolk, where pilots often use the silos on my farm as a turning place, I was used to military planes overhead, and I could see that we were well out of the way of being bombed.

Conditions improved as we headed east to our overnight and refuelling stop at Thurso. Next day we rounded John O'Groats for the long quiet cruise down to Hull. With calm seas and both engines functioning, I was really able to open *Ribaleta* up and see what it could do. Its performance was most impressive, reaching 45 knots.

The next challenge was soon to come. Crossing the Wash, we struck a wave so hard that it broke the A-frame. This, in itself, was not a total disaster and it could have been repaired quite easily, but it affected the crew member I had picked up in Plymouth very badly.

'I'm going to die!' he screamed.

I turned to look at him. '*What?*' It was not easy to hear my passengers on *Ribaleta* at the best of times, and I hoped I had misheard.

'I'm going to die!' he repeated. 'Where's the nearest hospital?'

'Why?' I shouted back at him. 'What's wrong?'

'My heart! It's my heart! I'm going to die!'

'We're still three or four hours away from our destination,' I said.

'I won't make it! My heart's going to stop! I've got to go to a hospital!'

I turned round and looked at him closely. What was going on? Was he having some sort of panic attack? Or was he genuinely in trouble? Did he have some pre-existing condition he hadn't told me about when he joined my boat? It was impossible to tell.

'Is there anything I can do to help?' I asked.

'Nothing,' he said. 'It's a problem I have. My heart needs to be stopped and then restarted again. It's beyond first aid.'

I studied him once more, checking to see if he was beginning to talk nonsense, but he seemed in full possession of his senses.

'I should never have joined this cruise,' he continued. 'It was stupid of me. It's too much. I can't handle it anymore. Not in this condition. Please. I need to go to a hospital. I need to go there immediately.'

'OK,' I said. 'I'll see what I can do.'

'Thank you,' he breathed. 'Thank you.'

I put out a call on the VHF, declaring 'pan-pan', the international standard urgency signal, to Great Yarmouth Coastguard three times over, but no one answered. I then put a call out to 'All Stations' and was answered by a nearby ship. The operator asked if they could help, and I explained that I had someone who needed evacuating urgently. I gave our

GPS co-ordinates, direction of travel and the colour of the hull and tubes. Soon an RAF helicopter appeared from behind us. Hovering directly overhead, one of the crewmen dropped down on to *Ribaleta's* deck on a winch, strapped up my companion and carried him off. He was taken directly to Queen Elizabeth Hospital, King's Lynn, where they stopped his heart quite easily but were only able to restart it on the second attempt. Annoyingly, he ended up getting to the finishing line before I did.

Because my A-frame was broken, I had to motor slowly after the departure of my crew member. Walberswick was not too far away, so I put in there and called my farm manager, John Short, instructing him to cut out some triangular aluminium plates so that I could fix them to the frame with a rivet gun. He arrived with the necessary equipment soon after, and together we were able to fix the A-frame. By that time, it was late and I was so tired that I could not continue to Broadstairs that night, so Celia drove to Walberswick, picked me up and took me home.

At 4.00 the following morning, I was back on board *Ribaleta*, ready to continue a day late. I tested the A-frame and it still felt secure, so I set off towards Dover hoping to make Portsmouth that night. But the fuel problem reoccurred, causing my speed to drop dramatically as darkness fell, and so I decided to put into Brighton Marina for my final night. The next day only took a few hours to the finishing line, at Portsmouth. I was a day late, but I had completed my maiden 1,800-mile RIB trip round Britain. Many of my BIBOA friends had stayed on to welcome me, and we all celebrated together that evening.

CHAPTER TWENTY-EIGHT
THE COWES-TORQUAY RACE

The Cowes Powerboat Festival is a week of races. It has a generous sponsor who gives a wonderful buffet dinner at the Royal Yacht Squadron (RYS) in Cowes the night before, and I had signed up *Ribaleta* to act as a safety boat.

The main event of the festival is the Cowes–Torquay powerboat race. It was to be my first official race in *Ribaleta* and I was looking forward to it. Unfortunately, the wind was growing stronger all the time, so we had a meeting in a tent in the RYS to discuss it. The gale was so bad that it was shaking the marquee so the committee asked all the drivers what they wanted to do.

'Well, I've entered so we'll start,' I said. 'But we're not going to do any dangerous racing. We're not putting anyone's life at risk. I don't want to have to call the RNLI.' I remembered the 1979 Fastnet Race, a yachting race from Cowes to Fastnet Rock, just south of Cork, and to Plymouth via the Isles of Scilly. It has been held every two years since 1925, and the 1979 race ended in tragedy. Gale Force 11 winds hit the racers between Land's End and Fastnet Rock. Seventy-five boats capsized, five sank, and fifteen sailors died. Even one of the Dutch safety tug boats nearly sank when it turned over 90 degrees and water went down the funnel, stopping all the engines. The loss of life was terrible, and the organisers were heavily criticised.

The Cowes committee eventually decided that the conditions were too dangerous, and that the best idea would be to have a shortened course and make it a handicapped race.

Ribaleta was the second-from-last boat to start. The race was outside the Solent, but thankfully the wind had calmed down dramatically by the morning. As I set off past the Needles, I could see my competitors, way out in front of me, by their spray. I felt that I could probably beat them and, on the approach to the Solent, I passed between my two main competitors, both Scorpions, and into the lead. I never saw the scratch boat, but I won comfortably on handicap and a few seconds faster overall than the scratch boat.

After the race, the presentation was held at the RYS, and I realised how lucky I had been to win and equal the overall time. The scratch boat won an award for lifetime achievement for contribution to RIB design and racing. I was given the winner's laurel on the podium, which was not only a great honour, but was also the first and only time in my life I have ever received one.

I was proud of *Ribaleta*, and proud of myself. With a home-designed inboard diesel cruiser/racer RIB I had beaten the well-known Italian RIB builder and racer Fabio Buzzi. He had used his latest design with the same engines, and he had been devastated that he couldn't beat us even with a handicap. After this loss, he vowed that he would return the following year and win. This he did, with his 3,200-horsepower RIB against mine with a mere 600 horsepower.

CHAPTER TWENTY-NINE
CROSSING THE BAY OF BISCAY

I n 2000 I wanted to take *Ribaleta* out of England for my summer cruise. I knew the coastline of France well, having sailed along it in both *Caleta* and *Caleta II*, so I decided to go there first.

I went from Felixstowe across the Channel to St-Malo by way of the Channel Islands. On the north coast of Brittany, I battled with enormous swells and had also to contend with the huge tidal ranges of the region. I had to be especially careful where I anchored because it was easy to run aground or drag the anchor. The numerous rocks were frightening and had to be carefully avoided at RIB speeds of 35 knots.

As I came round the north-western peninsula of Brittany, I headed inside the island of Ushant. With the swells around me still high, I wanted to see the lighthouse of La Jument, depicted by Jean Guichard's world-famous series of photographs dating from 1989. In them, 100-foot-high waves engulf the granite lighthouse, nearly sweeping away the tiny figure of the lighthouse keeper, who stands in the doorway, dwarfed by the waves. As I neared the lighthouse, I could see that conditions were similar, and the gigantic waves which crashed against the lighthouse's walls could have been the same as in those in Guichard's photographs.

Motoring back towards the Breton mainland, I moored and spent the night in the beautiful little harbour of Bénodet where I could take *Ribaleta* right into the town. I had planned to follow the coast, but when I came out of the river the following morning it was a flat calm, perfect conditions for crossing the Bay of Biscay. The perfect conditions made the temptation too much to resist, so I decided to give the crossing a try.

I soon reached my cruising speed of 35 knots in the flat conditions and, although I could easily have gone faster, I didn't want to strain my engines yet. The Bay of Biscay is a large expanse of water and, although I knew from my cruise around Britain that *Ribaleta* could cope on one engine should the other fail, it was not a prospect I wanted to risk. Halfway across, I began to feel nervous. I was 140 miles away from the nearest coast, the furthest I had ever been in a RIB. If an engine failed, it would take me approximately twenty hours to reach land – not a pleasant thought in the middle of the Bay of Biscay.

I continued on and, as I began to near the north coast of Spain, the wind grew stronger and more exciting. So, I decided to speed up, and powered across the choppy waters as fast as I could. In the end, the crossing took just seven hours, which meant that I was averaging about 40 miles an hour.

I moored up in Santander, which I can only describe as a dreadful, godforsaken place. Perhaps the most disappointing city in the whole of Spain, it also seemed to be the least hospitable. I could find nowhere to cash any money nor a decent place to eat. The city was totally lifeless, and when I did find somewhere to eat, the food was no better than a boat meal. Needless to say, I didn't stay there long. I took pride in the fact that my crossing of the Bay of Biscay was probably the first ever solo RIB crossing.

It's not far from Santander to the French coast, about 130 miles by road. I had a lovely, gentle cruise along the north coast visiting many charming little harbours. It was wonderful seeing some old traditional Spanish life away from tourists, although the ports were often far too small, designed with little fishing boats in mind. Anything bigger than 20 feet or thereabouts was too large, making it impossible for *Ribaleta*, at 33 feet, to moor or turn round in those tiny Spanish ports.

Back in France again, I followed the west coast back up north. There wasn't much wind, and I could drive virtually on the backs of the waves, riding them up the coast some ten yards before they broke. It was great fun with the wind blowing the spray back out to sea. I came into the bay at Arcachon, past the enormous sand dunes, some of the tallest in Europe, went up the river into the French countryside for a change from the sea and then headed back out between the breaking waves over the sand bars at the mouth of the river.

Further north, I stopped at La Rochelle, passing the huge yacht harbours at the entrance and taking *Ribaleta* right into the fortified town with its medieval city centre. From there, I went back to L'Aber-Wrac'h, my favourite French anchorage, and had my last French meal before heading into a long ocean swell, across the Channel to Plymouth. Finally, I made my way along the south coast past Dartmouth, across Lyme Bay and into the Solent. Once there, I met some fellow BIBOA members and claimed my membership of the 'two thousand club', for *Ribaleta* had now done a cruise of more than 2,000 miles.

When I returned home, I was very satisfied with the cruise and felt confident with my boat. Only one issue remained: each night, when I had tried to put up the new tent, made to avoid sleeping in the 'little coffin', it leaked and didn't fit because of bad manufacturing and design. If I wanted to continue my adventures on *Ribaleta*, I needed a functioning and reliable tent. When I returned, I was able to give the problem my full attention, employing the same man who, as well as crafting covers for swimming pools and lorries, made pig tents for my farm. He parked *Ribaleta* in his yard so that he could make the tent fit over the front deck rather than relying on measurements. The result was heavier than I had expected, perhaps as much as 30 or 40 pounds, but he made a good job of it. So good, in fact, that the same tent still remains on *Ribaleta* today.

CHAPTER THIRTY
THE MEDITERRANEAN SEA

The following year, in 2001, I was ready to push *Ribaleta* even further. The original plan was to cruise back across the Bay of Biscay and then continue down the coast of Portugal, but by the time I put *Ribaleta* into the water at Felixstowe I realised it was far too cold. I checked the farm anemometer I had put on the truck: the wind chill factor was two degrees Centigrade. It was June; I've had better wind chill factors in November. The weather forecast indicated that conditions were not going to change for at least a fortnight. Rather than cruise in horrible weather, I decided on a complete change of plan. This is one of advantages of self-sufficient travelling – there are no hotels or flights to cancel; I can go wherever I like whenever I like.

I put *Ribaleta* back on the trailer, which was still connected to the Unimog, and dragged it out of the river. I called P&O, booked a passage on a ferry that afternoon and drove to Dover to meet it. Everything was simple and straightforward and that evening I found myself not motoring through cold rough French seas, but driving along French highways in the direction of the Mediterranean. I was there by five o'clock the following evening.

The weather was hot and sunny when I reached Narbonne, a small town on the French Mediterranean coast. I took the motorcycle off the front of the Unimog and rode down to the port to make sure I could go through, where I found a slipway large enough for me to launch the boat into the marina. I left the Unimog in the car park, confident that it wouldn't be stolen. If anyone did try, I was doubtful they would know how to drive it.

Once *Ribaleta* was on the open sea, I had to decide where to go. To the east was Monaco and then Italy; to the west Spain. I chose the latter, and began to cruise along the French coast to the Spanish Costa Brava. I soon realised how full of tourists the beaches and bays now were on Spain's eastern coast, so I headed off to the Balearic Islands. There I motored into the wonderful little coves of Ibiza and Mallorca before going to Fornells

Bay, a beautiful, little-used bay with few dinghies in it, on the north coast of Menorca.

From Menorca, I planned to head east, hoping to reach Sardinia. It would probably be a long and rough crossing, so I started early in the morning, intending to take advantage of lighter morning winds. These did not last long, changing into a buffeting headwind and a rough sea. It was the only time I have ever had to alter course for another boat. As I motored into the waves, a small fishing boat crossed in front of me, absolutely dead on course, and I had no choice but to veer off to avoid it. I kept hoping that I would soon be in the lee of Sardinia, but a relentless Force 5 or 6 wind prevented this happening. At the end of the day, I finally found some shelter and an anchorage at Sant'Antioco, an island off the south-west of Sardinia, where I was able to dry out and appreciate the Mediterranean sun and forget my English Channel plans.

Not far south from Sardinia is Tunisia, and I liked the idea of taking *Ribaleta* to Africa. I was not quite sure what I would find, or what reception I would meet when I arrived, but I wanted to find out. It was 25 years since I had last been to Tunisia, when I had arrived by sail. This time, I would be arriving by power. I headed south over a flat Mediterranean Sea until Africa came into sight.

Bizerte was quiet, with only three boats in the harbour and a few customs officials. I motored on to Tunis and spent the day there exploring Carthage, the archaeological site of the ancient city founded by the Phoenicians in the ninth century BC, destroyed and then rebuilt by the Romans in the second century BC, and finally razed by the Arabs in the seventh century AD. Near the archaeological site are the smart and modern embassy buildings, which I thought were an interesting contrast to the ruins.

From Tunis, I drove *Ribaleta* out to the small islands off the coast, expecting a quiet night, but they turned out to be military strongholds and I had to leave fairly quickly. Fortunately, *Ribaleta* was fast enough to take me away from their territorial waters before they could catch me. Midway between Tunisia and Sicily is Lampedusa, the southernmost of Italy's outlying islands. The town of Lampedusa was beautiful and quiet, and the island had not yet turned into what it is today: an illegal immigration hub. I hired a motorbike, hoping to explore the place, but the tracks soon deteriorated into rocky footpaths with nobody on them, far beyond my abilities as a biker, so I returned to the port.

I then headed up to Sicily. I arrived at Tràpani, a tiny port on the north-western coast of the island where there were no other foreign vessels. Luckily, my arrival coincided with the re-enactment of a religious ceremony. Across the water from me was a little boat full of people in religious fancy dress. When the villagers stepped ashore from their boat, they danced in procession through the streets, in and out of churches, to the local cathedral. I joined in and much enjoyed myself, even though I couldn't understand any of it. It was a beautiful, traditional event, free of tourists, in an isolated part of Sicily. The whole village was present, all of it in fancy dress.

That night it was so warm that, for the first time, I was able to sleep on deck without a cover. The next day, I set off around the north of Sicily, passing hundreds of other RIBs all being used for sunbathing, to the Aeolian Islands, a small archipelago in the Tyrrhenian Sea. The weather was still hot and sunny and I was so pleased to have to come to the Mediterranean.

But then disaster struck.

I was heading for the volcano of Stromboli, the most north-eastern of the Aeolian Islands, when I came upon a beautiful 70-foot J-class yacht, *Sovereign*, anchored by a deserted island, being worked on by its crew. I passed it slowly to have a good look at it and then, as I began to accelerate back to cruising speed, all of a sudden one of the drive shafts broke. On one engine, I had a tedious drive to a small port on the mainland called Tropea. It was difficult to keep awake at 8 knots. Once I'd arrived there, it was dusk and I saw there was a slipway where I could lift the boat out. I then

Ribaleta with the awning up making a tent for protection and camping.

realised that obtaining the necessary parts out there would be a nightmare and that, somehow, I needed to return *Ribaleta* back to England.

Leaving the boat in Tropea, I had to take three separate flights to the south of France, then two bus journeys to Narbonne and finally walk along the beach to the Unimog. Exhausted by the time I climbed inside, I had no time to rest, for one of the brakes on the trailer was seized. Fortunately, one of the French children playing nearby could speak some English, and he was able to tell me which wheel it was.

Driving along the French coast and down through Italy, eating in the Unimog and sleeping in lay-bys, after three days I grew bored of the journey along these highways so, at Naples, I decided to continue along the coast to see some of the countryside. In the centre of Naples, I came up against a road block. Signs pointed me towards a diversion, which I took. But I could soon see that it followed a small road winding up into the mountains at the back of a town, one which I knew the Unimog and trailer was incapable of traversing. All I could do was turn round and head back, not the easiest thing to do in the middle of a town at night, backing over two three-lane highways, with a 50-foot rig. I stayed on the motorways from then on.

Finally, I made it to Tropea, went down the steep track and loaded the RIB, but the way out was too tight and I split a tyre on a rock. After changing the wheel, it left me with only one spare for the entire journey back to England. The going was good throughout Italy, but when I reached Austria, passing Innsbruck, I noticed the car overtaking me had slowed to match my speed. I turned to look at the driver, who shouted to me that my wheels were on fire. I pulled over immediately and managed to put out the blaze with my fire extinguisher. I breathed a sigh of relief, but it only lasted for about two seconds or so, for the wheel quickly burst into flames again so I quickly had to get some water from the Unimog to put the fire out and cool it all down.

The one thing for which I could be grateful was that I was near Innsbruck, where there was a Mercedes garage. A mechanic came out to change the wheel and tyre and replace the hub bearings. I was then able to set off again, and to reach Calais and the ferry without any further troubles.

Back in England, I made the mistake at Dover of driving through the entrance for cars rather than the entrance for trucks, which meant that I couldn't go round the corners, so had to have the AA come out and manoeuvre the trailer. The AA were not the only ones to come to me; the police did too. They were concerned about my rig's size and wanted to inspect it, quickly finding out that the brakes, which had seized after the fire, were still not working properly.

'And that's not all,' one of the officers said to me. 'You're not allowed to tow a trailer with your vehicle.'

'Of course I'm allowed to tow a trailer with my vehicle,' I said. 'Why on earth wouldn't I be?'

The officer refused to let me leave, insisting instead that we go to a weighbridge. And that was how I ended up driving through Dover docks with a police escort front and back.

'What do you think it weighs?' the same officer asked me.

I shrugged. 'I don't know exactly. I've never weighed it. I'd guess about 14 to 15 tons.'

The whole process of weighing took close to two hours and, when it was finally weighed, the police were horrified to discover that the weight was 14½ tons. They then told me I had an 18-ton total weight limit, having called Mercedes to find the correct weight limit. Next, they said I was not allowed to tow my trailer home because of the fault with the brake. Worse still, they wouldn't even let me disconnect the trailer from the Unimog in the flat lorry park, so I had to stay there with it connected. All I could do at this point was call my farm lorry driver and ask for his help. He dropped his bulk trailer off, picked up a low loader I had hired, and then came down the next day to Dover. We then disconnected the Unimog and managed to winch my boat and trailer on to his low loader. We bent part of my trailer in the process, but it was soon lashed down. As he drove back, even with the trailer on board he was much faster than me, with him at his limit of 56 miles an hour and the Unimog at only 45. My journey home, with nine days continuously on the motorway, was one I never want to repeat, but it was better than the alternatives, and my cruise around the Mediterranean had been wonderful.

CHAPTER THIRTY-ONE
THE LONDON TRIPS

On my return from the Mediterranean, once the harvest was over that year, I began to take regular trips to London. Sometimes I went on the motorbike but, if there was an especially nice day, I preferred to take *Ribaleta*. I knew that, generally, any bad weather would come from the west, so I could certainly return home with the wind following without it becoming too rough.

Just up the River Orwell from Felixstowe is Levington, from where I launched *Ribaleta* from its marina and motored down the river, past Felixstowe Docks and then out to sea. Following the Essex coast from Walton to Clacton, I would then cross the first of the many sandbanks on the way to London. These sandbanks all run north-east to south-west, and you have to rely heavily on the buoys along the River Crouch. A deep-water channel comes out of the Crouch and goes round Maplin Sands, where there were once plans to build an airport. Now they are just a huge mudflat too shallow to sail over, where you can rarely see the shore, so I had to watch for the navigation buoys very closely before entering the main shipping channel of the Thames. Once there, I would follow the river to pass Southend pier and the commercial docks on the east, until the river narrows and passes under the Queen Elizabeth II Bridge. The channel then winds backwards and forwards, becoming narrower all the time, with new housing developments beginning to appear. Eventually, the Tate & Lyle factory, the last big factory on the Thames, comes into sight.

All boats going up or down the river are followed by radar to ensure they keep to the channel, as I found out: on one occasion when I approached the Thames Barrier, the harbourmaster put on the red lights, indicating that the barrier was closed. He had been watching me on radar cutting the corners of the empty river and was clearly unhappy about this. Unfortunately for him, a local ferry pulled out in front of me and, since there was no reason for the lights to be red, the harbourmaster immediately had to switch the lights back to green. As soon as the ferry passed through the barrier, the lights returned to red again, but I ignored them. Obviously, the red light was aimed at me, and I knew they could not close the gates quickly enough to stop me going through. I was later stopped by a police boat, and the officer said that I had cut corners and suggested I apologise to the harbourmaster, even though, the officer admitted, he was well known to be a difficult man.

Beyond the Thames Barrier, I would continue past the O2 Arena, at that time still called the Millennium Dome, and the Greenwich Naval Dockyard and Canary Wharf to turn, just downriver of Tower Bridge, into the Limehouse Yacht Basin. This is a marina which connects the sea to the inland waterways, so both canal boats coming from the canal system and sea-going boats heading out along the Thames are moored there.

This marina is where I would moor *Ribaleta*. The Cruising Association, of which I'm a member, has its headquarters at the entrance of the marina. There is accommodation available, but I always preferred to sleep on the boat. I kept my bags dry in the locker, so it was easy enough to change into my 'London clothes' so as to be presentable for city life. I always made sure to put up my tent while it was still daytime so that I didn't have to worry about doing so when I returned in the evening. I could walk the short distance to Limehouse station on the Docklands Light Railway, from where it was easy to connect to the Underground and go wherever I wanted in London. Overall, the marina was the perfect place for me to stay. I never encountered any problems there – although, once, when I tied up to the pontoon next to the Limehouse lock and waited for it to open, a police boat pulled up behind me. An outsized officer climbed off the boat, walked towards me, and then gave me the rare view of the bottom of both his size 12 boots just before his backside hit the deck with an almighty crash. At this moment, the gate opened and I could only conceal my smile as I pushed *Ribaleta* off the dock and into the lock.

I particularly enjoyed going to South Kensington and the Royal Geographical Society, of which I am a Fellow, to attend the Monday lectures. After the lectures, dinners were held and, since they were generally filled with distinguished people from the adventure world, I attended them regularly, taking advantage of the opportunity to trade travel stories. At one lecture in particular, standing outside because I hadn't booked, I began chatting to a nearby couple, David and Ali, who were also waiting to attend. By the time we were told that there was space and we could come in, it seemed only natural that we were put together in the only remaining seats.

'So how did you get to London?' David asked. 'Train?'

I shook my head. 'Boat. I've got a 10-metre RIB. I often drive that down and tie it up at Limehouse.'

David looked fascinated. 'A boat,' he said. 'I've always wanted a boat. Do you use it much?'

I told him about my adventures round Britain, across the Bay of Biscay and around the Mediterranean.

'So, where's the next big trip?' he said.

'I'd like to ship my boat across to the Caribbean and then to Venezuela and into the Orinoco. I don't think anyone's been in a boat like *Ribaleta* in the Orinoco before. But I need someone with me who can speak Spanish.'

At that, David's eyes lit up, and he turned to his girlfriend, who had not spoken to me so far. 'Ali, you speak Spanish, don't you?'

She blinked at him. 'Yes. Why?'

'Charles here is thinking of taking his RIB up the Orinoco River, and he wants someone who speaks Spanish to go with him.'

Ali turned to look at me. She smiled. 'I'll go,' she said.

Later, Ali admitted to me that she didn't even know what a RIB was. But the mention of the Orinoco and all the romance it conjured up was irresistible.

'But what will you do for accommodation?' David asked.

'I sleep on the boat,' I replied. 'There's room for two. Why don't you come down and have a look at it?'

We agreed they would come down to Limehouse the next day to see *Ribaleta*, just to see what it looked like. Ali was coming with me; she had already decided that. Although she and David were a couple, they seemed to find nothing unusual about the prospect of her venturing off to Venezuela with a strange man they had only just met. For me too, it wasn't unusual either. By this time, having travelled with various crews on *Caleta* and in the Unimog, I was used to teaming up with fairly random people. I had no reservations about taking Ali with me. She seemed very nice, obviously brave enough to do it, and I had the distinct impression that if she said she would do something, she would do it. And, of course, as she spoke Spanish, I needed her. I knew that in the Orinoco the only languages spoken were the native ones and Spanish; there would certainly not be any English spoken.

Ali and I were to become partners and enjoy many adventures and have a great life together. In 2002, after thirty-five years together, Celia and I were divorced. Sailing had been our hobby and together we had been on numerous trips and exciting journeys on *Caleta* and *Ribaleta*.

◦ ◦ ◦

Sometimes I would make my way home after mooring at Limehouse, but if I had the time and the weather was still good, I would continue further up the Thames. Beyond Tower Bridge I could drive at full speed up the river as there is no speed limit until Wandsworth Bridge. This part of the river would take me past the many houseboats moored there. Most of them appeared to be genuine and traditional, but there were plenty which had just been put inside concrete hulls so that the owners didn't need to worry about them leaking.

On one particular trip, as I was passing Putney where rowing teams trained and competed, it was quite a rough day and one of the rowing boats sank. I became involved in the effort of rescuing people and their oars from the water. The current was dragging us towards the boats moored opposite the slipway and we couldn't risk injuring the people in the water. Fortunately, we managed to save them all and transfer them into the rescue boats.

From there, I carried on past Kew Gardens and Eel Pie Island, where more houseboats were moored behind the island, well off the main river. Then I went through Teddington Lock, which marks the end of the tidal Thames and the beginning of a more rural and peaceful waterway. Here, there are clubs and pubs with tables right down to the river. Further up, luxury waterfront houses line the Thames as far as the M25, at which point the riverside changes, becoming fully rural and the river small and slow.

I turned to go back downriver, through Teddington Lock again and on to the tidal reaches. Passing the Houses of Parliament, I was surprised to discover that I could moor at the House of Commons terrace. If I had been so inclined, I could easily have let a full crew jump ashore with backpacks of explosives, and nobody would have stopped them. There seemed to be an astonishing lack of security; I could have followed the example of Guy Fawkes. I might even have got back through the barrage and out to sea!

Later, on a separate trip, as I was taking *Ribaleta* round the docks near Canary Wharf Dock at 40 knots, a small police boat zigzagged across the water, signalling me to stop. It came alongside and the policeman asked me to wait until his colleague had caught up. Eventually, a larger launch came alongside and another policeman jumped aboard, flashing his warrant card; he was from the anti-terrorism police. I told him about the complete lack of security at the House of Commons, but he just said that there were no special rules in place for Parliament.

Since there was no speed limit, I drove *Ribaleta* at 50 miles an hour under Tower Bridge, just for the fun of it. I had to take care to avoid the steel work boats, as boats going so fast were definitely not expected and, if I hit one of them, I knew that not only would *Ribaleta* be badly damaged, but that I would also end up with a prison sentence for reckless driving.

Finally, I drove back to Limehouse for the night. When I came out of the marina the following morning, I had been hoping for a quick trip home, so was rather disappointed to see a police boat outside on the river. Expecting to have to follow the police boat slowly down the river, things turned out otherwise. The police boat wasn't there for that reason. The driver sped his boat up to its maximum speed, which I knew was way below mine. So, having followed the police boat for about 30 seconds, I opened my throttles fully and shot past it at 50 miles an hour outside Canary Wharf, giving the policeman a friendly wave as I passed, which he returned with a smile. It was a unique experience for me in London's docklands.

CHAPTER THIRTY-TWO

THE ORINOCO RIVER WITH ALI

This book began with one of the most terrifying moments of my life: in 2002, when I stood at the helm of *Ribaleta*, high in the air, as it swung towards a collision with the hull of a freighter. As you already know, the collision was averted, not by the hand of God, but by the hand of a dockworker, and, for the first time, *Ribaleta* entered the waters of the Caribbean Sea.

The following morning, Ali and I set off out of Castries harbour and up to Rodney Bay, the main yacht marina in St Lucia, where we met the customs officer. Even though we were going to leave the port immediately, we still had to pay import duty on *Ribaleta* since the shipping company had entered us as arriving in St Lucia, rather than transiting St Lucia on the way to Grenada, which is what they should have done. This is one of the many problems of international shipping and of using little islands.

As we waited in the marina, I began to admire a yacht, the biggest in the harbour. The owner saw me and, noticing that my clothes were not particularly smart, looked at me strangely. 'Which yacht are you from?' he asked me. The implication was clear. He thought that *Ribaleta* was just a tender to some superyacht anchored out in the bay. When I explained that this was, in fact, our one and only boat, he looked amazed.

Rodney Bay was a good place to stock up with the supplies we needed for the journey ahead and Ali was delighted by the fact that the boat had a fridge. With two leisure batteries on board, each charged by a different engine, it meant we could keep the fridge running 24 hours a day. Our food would be kept fresh, and we could eat in a civilised manner.

We set off south down the west side of St Lucia to Marigot Bay, a delightful little inlet which in former years was used as a smuggling base. At the head of the bay there is a passage on the left which leads to a lagoon where sailing boats could hide their masts out of sight from the sea. As such, it was used as a pirates' lair for years. We tied up at the inner harbour and walked ashore on a boardwalk. It crossed a mangrove swamp filled with thousands of crabs and tangled roots coming out of the muddy water. The mangrove swamps help protect the land from heavy waves and so make it a safe hurricane hole, although you still have to be careful of one particular danger: the flying coconuts. Beyond the mangroves was a little restaurant, where we had the local drink, a delicious mixture of fruits, and planned the journey ahead.

Ali admitted that she was nervous. This was not only her first time in the Caribbean, but it was also the first time she had ever been in a small boat on a large expanse of water. I too felt nervous. I had never driven *Ribaleta* between the Caribbean islands with the full trade winds blowing across our course line.

To reassure Ali, I took things easy on the way down St Lucia, keeping to the calm waters in the lee of the island for as long as possible. She coped well and, when we stopped for lunch after our first ocean crossing in the lee of St Vincent, she had begun to relax a little. While we ate, I kept both engines running because, for safety, I never stop them when at sea. Unfortunately, when we finished lunch and were ready to head off, the port engine wouldn't go into gear. I lifted up the engine hatch and put it into gear manually, and we made our way down to Bequia where, luckily, we were able to find a mechanic. As we tied up to a wooden jetty and sat on plastic chairs beneath a torn parasol, the mechanic, a stern-faced man in an oil-stained shirt and flip-flops, welded the engine controls back together – so effectively, in fact, that it lasted for the whole trip.

Since we had made good time and overcome our first problem, we decided to treat ourselves to a day in Bequia: still as picturesque as I remembered it, and still with the same strong winds which could carry drunken sailors in their dinghy on their way back to their yacht out to sea and be lost before they reached Panama. This time, I was in a RIB rather than a yacht, so I could motor against the wind, which gave me greater flexibility to explore the island. Stretching out of the south-west of Bequia is a long and thin peninsula. *Caleta* would never have made it around and then back up this peninsula against the trade wind, but *Ribaleta* could do it quite easily, and it was wonderful to motor around parts of the island which I had never seen before. We found a secluded bay in the south, where we came on an enormous, freshly slaughtered whale, guts fully intact, floating near the shore. It could not have been there for long; the entrails spreading out from it indicated that it was a recent kill. This could only mean one thing. The tradition of small-boat

Signs of local whaling with the guts of a whale left in the water, Bequia

whaling, which I thought had long been abandoned in these parts, was still very much alive.

We continued on down to Tobago Cays, the heart of the Grenadines, where we anchored. Having a shallow draft meant we could anchor closer to the reef than I ever could have in *Caleta*. We swam in the shallow clear blue sea and enjoyed some perfect snorkelling over pristine staghorn coral. We then spent a lovely evening with the shallow reef in front of us, the deep water of the Atlantic behind, and the steady trade winds all the way from Africa.

The following day, we went south to Union Island, where we had to exit St Vincent and the Grenadines, before crossing to Carriacou. The marina there was modern and well equipped, but both Ali and I wanted something more remote, so I motored *Ribaleta* slowly round the coast until I found a tiny secluded cove too shallow for yachts and surrounded by mangroves. We put up the tent for the night. We could open the windows on either side to let the breeze through, and when it grew colder, we could shut a plastic curtain down, keeping the wind out but still allowing the light to come in. This meant that we could always perfectly control the light and temperature of our tent, and we were never too hot nor too cold. In the evening we inflated our little dinghy and slowly motored round the edge of the mangroves, seeing close up the herons and small crabs that make the area their home.

After a good night's sleep, we motored down to Grenada and moored in the harbour at St George's, a lovely, old-fashioned town built on a hill. The harbour used to take old sailing ships, and we had been able to moor

Caleta there when we were last there, but it had become too small and the yachts were now confined to the marina. We went ashore to buy our supply of spices – for which Grenada is famous – and look at all the handicrafts. Then we headed south to St James' Bay, a perfect, palm-fringed bay with a beautiful hotel where my parents-in-law had stayed when they brought the children out twenty-four years earlier. This was our last night in familiar surroundings before we headed off across the 80 miles of open ocean to the South American coast.

◎ ◎ ◎

I knew from experience that the long open water crossing ahead could be treacherous. I remembered sailing it in *Caleta* in the 1970s, remembered the strength of the currents which could drag you off course, remembered that, at the end of the crossing, things only worsened when you reached the Bocas del Dragón.

But this time it was different; I had the advantages of satnav and adequate power. Also, I did not have to worry about staying upwind. The power of my twin engines ensured I could ignore the currents and take the most direct route. As it happened, the sea conditions were fairly calm. I was glad that Ali would not have to endure a difficult crossing so early in our journey.

We were making good time when, suddenly, we hit a wave and all the electrics went off. I looked at Ali, who had turned white.

'Is everything all right?' she asked.

I checked the console but, with no power, I was unable to find my course from the satnav. I decided not to tell Ali that I had lost the satnav. 'The engines are still running,' I said. 'We'll be fine.'

I soon found out that the wave had turned off the battery isolator. From then on, I realised, I would have to start packing the locker better.

Soon, out of the mist, we saw land: it was South America. We entered the Bocas del Dragón and sped into the sheltered Gulf of Paria. There we turned west towards Venezuela and headed to Guiria: a military port and the port of entry, as well as the place where we had arranged to rendezvous with Karl.

My racing navigator friend, Paul Lemmer, had recommended Karl to us as a guide and fixer. A large German man well into his seventies, he had a colourful past. Until the age of sixteen, he had been a member of the Hitler Youth and had fought in the Second World War. However, he soon realised that if he ever tried to shoot at British or American troops, they would simply call air support and machine-gun him. It didn't take him long to understand that Germany was going to lose the war, so he emigrated to South America, where he remade his life. He spoke good Spanish and liked boats and began to earn his living from boat work, mostly by repairing propellers. He also acted as a guide and fixer for travellers who wanted to avail themselves of his intimate knowledge of the area, offering trips up and down the Orinoco River. He was excellent at this, having explored every navigable inch of the region. He could speak many of the local languages, and his driver had a knack of being able to spot rocks four feet under water.

Karl greeted us with a big smile and a firm handshake. We talked a little and I immediately liked him, which was lucky, because he was coming with us up the Orinoco. He prepared our customs and immigration papers, and also arranged a pick-up truck with two 200-litre barrels of fuel. After clearing us through customs, he drove his pick-up truck on to the dock. We connected our diesel pump to the barrels and started transferring the fuel to *Ribaleta*. Technically, we were not supposed to be doing this. Venezuela keeps its fuel cheap for its citizens but charges foreigners much more, but Karl managed to keep the port officers distracted with a prolonged conversation in Spanish, and we were able to fill *Ribaleta* up with the cheap fuel.

With the tanks full, Karl clambered onboard and we set off. At 22 stone, he was too big to fit into the seats, had difficulty walking and was happiest in the water and off the boat altogether. On the boat, he resigned himself to sitting on top of the hatch on the front deck. We headed down and out through the Boca de la Serpiente ('Mouth of the Serpent'), the southern entrance to the Gulf of Paria, until we found the entrance to the Orinoco River.

From there, I had to rely on Karl as our pilot, but I kept a close eye on the depth sounder too. The water soon became extremely shallow, far too shallow for us. Karl spotted some fishing boats amongst the mangroves and asked the men in Spanish where we should have been. They shouted back instructions and we moved a few hundred yards slowly across, where we found deep water. Inside the bar, we were into the river proper, which was about 300 yards wide and completely calm. Karl told me to keep well on the outside of the curves where there was about 40 feet of water, whereas on the inside there was only about two or three feet. I followed his advice, carrying on in the deep water until we came to the main deep-water channel, which is easily navigable by big ships.

We pulled into a dock, where I tied up while Karl and Ali went to find accommodation. Ali managed to find herself a cabin, and Karl slept on the deck of a ship. During the night, most of his belongings were stolen while he slept, but Karl knew what to do. After a few Spanish words in the right places, he soon had everything returned to him.

This was, we quickly learnt, par for the course when it came to Karl. He knew the area and he knew the locals. The Orinoco Delta is about the size of Wales, so it was extraordinary for someone to know it as intimately as Karl did. But he had connections there which most men did not have, and he understood the native Warao Indians perfectly.

The second night, after motoring further up the delta, he told us to moor to the banks of a little village where he knew he could stay ashore. Karl couldn't sleep on *Ribaleta* and always found his own places ashore. He found Ali a room in a little hut, and the two of them walked ashore while I stayed on the boat. It was nice to have the tent all to myself that night, and I stretched out and soon fell fast asleep, when suddenly I was woken by the violent rocking of *Ribaleta*. It was Ali, who had leapt on to the boat and came into my tent.

'What's the matter?' I said.

'Spiders!' she said. 'Horrible things. The hut's full of them. Can I sleep in here?'

From then on, Ali spent her nights on *Ribaleta*. It was far preferable to putting up with all the spiders in the local houses.

◎ ◎ ◎

Ribaleta *moored up on the riverbank of the Orinoco*

Navigating the Orinoco River

As we continued further down the Orinoco, Karl suggested we visit a village which could be found up one of the tributaries. There was not much water, so we went slowly. Finally, we found the village, and were greeted by a family and their pet, a carnivorous four-foot-long giant river otter, called *perro de agua* or 'water dog' in Spanish. Their vegetables were grown around the edge of an area of grass, away from the jungle and the mosquitos. Nearby, the skin of a jaguar had been stretched out over a frame to dry.

After saying our farewells, we motored back down the channel, driving at full speed because we knew there was plenty of water. Coming across a cattle boat moored to the bank, we went ashore to find some gauchos herding cattle on to the boat with traditional lassos. As I watched them work, I learnt for the first time what the horse's tail could be used for. The gauchos would tie the end of the lasso to the horses' tails and drag the cattle on to the boat. Since this was the dry season, the ranchers brought their herds down to graze on the large islands, which are eight or ten feet above the water level in the delta. When the rainy season approached, all the cattle were then rounded up on to these boats and taken back to the inland ranches before the whole delta flooded.

We needed more fuel, so we headed towards a fuel station. On arrival, we realised that the fuel pumps were about 30 feet up in the air and about 40 yards from the water, so the whole process was rather nerve-wracking. To make matters worse, a strong wind was blowing on to the shore, so we had to have the anchor ready. I told Ali when to throw it out so that, hopefully, I had enough rope to reach the shore and enough for the anchor to hold. We fixed the anchor when the bow reached the pump attendant, who was waiting for us waist deep in the water. We were then secure.

'*Petróleo o gasóleo*?' he asked.

'*Gasóleo*,' I replied, and the petrol attendant changed the hose, flushing the petrol out into the river. We had to put the hose quickly into the tank, and then watched the level rise until it reached 220 gallons.

'How much?' Ali asked in Spanish. Frightened of an enormous bill, I didn't want to hear the answer.

The man replied: 'Fifty dollars,' which I knew was totally illegal. Venezuela subsidises the price of fuel for its people and, in fact, subsidises the price for river people more than most. There were no other tourist or foreign boats anywhere near and so because they were unaware of the higher tourist prices, we had been given the local price.

Having refuelled, we made our way back down the river towards a little port which Karl knew. There, we drank some beers in a café while Karl introduced us to some of the locals. They were smugglers. This was the first time I had ever met smugglers, and they looked and acted just like anyone else. They smuggled fuel from Venezuela into Guyana and it was obvious that, given how cheap the fuel was here, they made a lot of money from their enterprise.

We tied up to a riverbank on a slightly higher island, where children played in the muddy water. There were small and impoverished shacks spread out all over this island and the neighbouring ones. Life here was clearly difficult enough when it was the dry season. But I couldn't help wondering what it must be like in the rainy season.

One of the largest villages in the Orinoco Delta is San Francisco de Guayo, an indigenous Warao village with a church whose pastor doubles up as the village chief. There are no roads in or out, and the only way to get there is by boat. Supplies are shipped in once a week from Ciudad Bolívar, once known as Angostura, and famed for its bitters, the essential ingredient of a 'pink gin'. Most of the houses are on stilts and there is a small factory where hearts of palm are canned using entirely hand-operated canning machines. Hearts of palm are vegetables found as the crown or fruit of certain palm trees, and it takes one 15-foot tree to produce enough hearts to fill a single can.

We found a nice hotel in San Francisco de Guayo, where we allowed ourselves the luxury of a room for a couple of nights, Karl being especially pleased with the comfort. While he rested, Ali and I took a guided tour on *Ribaleta* of some of the local plantations where spices are grown. The guide then took us further down towards the mouth of the delta, but unfortunately there wasn't enough water, so we had to take the unusual step of lifting up the front hatch to use as a sail to drift over the shallow water. It worked surprisingly well until there was enough depth for us to put the drives down to regain full power. It was the first time that *Ribaleta*, or I think any RIB, had been used as a sailing boat.

Thinking it might be wiser to take the dinghy out instead, Ali and I inflated it and put the 2-horsepower outboard on the back. It was perfect for exploring the tiny creeks and, while we were doing so, the heavens opened. We were in a 12-foot-wide channel as the rain began to pour down, and the sky was totally obscured by huge, dripping leaves. All of a sudden, there was a loud squawking nearby, and a large and ungainly bird, a guacharaca, similar to a pheasant and unique to the area, flew between the treetops. It was a magical experience, and we felt truly part of the tropical jungle.

We returned to San Francisco de Guayo. As Karl's time had run out, we had to take him back to the port of Guiria. We had a fast run up the smooth waters for about 200 miles of the delta to the mouth of the Orinoco and then into the Mouth of the Serpent. Karl's usual position on the hatch at the front deck must have been extremely uncomfortable for him as we bounced over the seas. But as he was too big for the seats he had no other choice.

When we reached the Mouth of the Serpent, we suddenly noticed that the water had become shallow, only showing three feet where the chart said there should have been three fathoms (18 feet). This caused me to panic as we were completely exposed to the Atlantic waves and we had to resort to once again sailing downwind with the drives lifted up as we drifted over the shallows until we were back in deep water. This was the only new chart I had bought for the trip, and it turned out to be totally inaccurate where it mattered most.

Across the Gulf of Paria, with the wind behind us, we made good progress with Karl not being too uncomfortable. We dropped him off at Guiria, thanking him for his help and his company. He had enjoyed himself immensely and kindly invited us to join him on his boat in the upper Orinoco on the Colombian border.

○ ○ ○

Karl's time may have run out, but ours had not. Feeling confident with the region, Ali and I decided to go back to the Orinoco on our own. Now that we knew the way, we took the same route back and found a little deserted creek for our first night. We slept well and, when we woke in the morning, Ali was the first up and looked outside. There, right next to us, was a dugout canoe which had come up beside us without our hearing it.

Ali turned to look at me. 'There's a man in a boat with a gun,' she said. The panic in her voice was audible.

I quickly thought about our available options. We could not make a sudden run for it as the tent was still up and all our bedding was out. We would have to stow it all before even thinking of lifting the anchor, and that would take too much time.

I peered out of our tent at the dugout where I could see the gun. I recognised it as an old 12-bore shotgun, just like those I used to shoot game at home. This gave me some relief. I knew that type of gun well and was confident that it was probably used for similar purposes here, to hunt game in the forest. Still, I was nonetheless aware that a shotgun is more deadly than a revolver and even more lethal than a rifle at close range, so we needed to be cautious. Ali began talking to the man in Spanish, keeping him occupied while I tidied up the inside of *Ribaleta* and took the tent down. I could then start the engines, which gave me a greater feeling of control over events. I began to pull away and, as I did so, Ali told me that the man in the dugout was not a threat. It was just another friendly encounter with the local Warao. When the fishing was not productive, they often went hunting for food, paddling along the river, coming ashore and then creeping through the jungle to shoot anything that moved.

We motored deeper into the delta and up another tributary, where we saw various people on the banks of the river. They all looked like rough bandits, so we decided it would be safer not to go ashore but to anchor in the middle of the river. The next day, we carried on even deeper into the jungle, and soon found ourselves being waved ashore by some of the local tribesmen. They didn't look like bandits and, in fact, turned out to be kind and friendly ranchers. One took us to a tin bath and showed us his prize catch, a skinned caiman, a South American crocodile. Another offered Ali a ride on his horse, which she happily accepted. Their friendliness changed our mind about

Ali washing up after cooking on Ribaleta *with the side curtains open for ventilation on the Orinoco River*

Trekking through the jungle with our tour guide

the locals of this region, although we were a little worried now that we knew nasty things such as caimans were lurking in the water.

Eager to explore further, we took *Ribaleta* up a narrow creek, where branches hit the A-frame and almost blocked our progress. It led us to some little-travelled waterways where the Warao we met wanted to show us around, and one in particular took us to a caiman's nest, explaining that they ate the eggs.

When we eventually returned to the main river, it became shallow, and we had trouble finding a route through it. We had no tide tables to help us, and I suspected that there were none available. Only the locals used the river and, even though it was tidal, the main influence on the current and depth was the amount of rain which fell on to the inland ranches before feeding into the river. A kind gaucho spotted us and jumped off his horse and ran into the river. He waded out to us and climbed on to the bow of *Ribaleta*, where he used a boat hook to find the deepest part of the channel. When he couldn't take us any further, he jumped back into the water, made his way to the bank and mounted his waiting horse.

Then a local boat appeared and, as it came past us, it also got stuck. The crew jumped overboard and started to push the boat. Ali and I had to make a quick decision. With the memory of those caimans still fresh in our mind, we were reluctant to enter the water, but we knew that the only way we were going to free ourselves would be to tie our boat to theirs and then help them to push. We agreed that a 75-horsepower outboard on full power should frighten any caiman away and, as long as we were careful of the propeller, we should be fine. Plus, once they were afloat, we could just follow the other boat and hopefully avoid becoming stuck again. Knowing it was our best option, we tied *Ribaleta* to our neighbouring boat and joined the effort to push it free. Finally, we were able to motor on down the river, with a great sense of relief.

By now, it was time to leave. We had our last lunch on the Orinoco beside some mangroves with a family of scarlet ibis, one of the most beautiful birds in the jungle, perched in the trees next to us. It was too late to go back to Guiria so we decided on one last night in our empty little creek. We spent the night listening to all the jungle sounds, the loudest of all coming from a large troupe of howler monkeys. We couldn't see them, but their screams were so loud that they drowned out all the other jungle noises. When we woke up the following morning, it was to the shrieks of the same monkeys.

Ali checked to see if there were any other boats nearby and, as the bay was empty, we could take the tent down and enjoy a leisurely final breakfast in the Orinoco jungle. However, just as we were finishing, we noticed a dugout in the middle of the creek's exit. This was worrying as we knew they would have guns, and we knew that the only way out was past them, well within killing range of a gun. The RIB would be a prize possession for a drug smuggler, and there were no police for miles in any direction. It was well known that the coast of Venezuela is so thick with drug boats that no one dares sail there.

I considered my options. It had been over a week since we were last in the bay; I felt that news of our boat might have spread amongst the drug smugglers. As the English police had boarded all my RIBs looking for drugs, I was well aware how attractive a big black RIB would be to a smuggler. If a smuggler was interested in the boat, the most obvious way to hijack it would be to have a powerful rifle in the dugout rather than a shotgun. Should we try to drive past them, they could easily shoot and kill us with an AK47.

I believed our best option was to head straight at them with the bow up so we would be protected by our Kevlar hull, made with the same material as a bulletproof vest. We headed slowly for them with my hands on the throttle, looking for any sign of the occupants aiming a gun at us. If they had done so, I would have had no option other than opening the throttles, cutting their boat in half and fleeing the country in less than an hour, obviously taking Ali with me. I had learnt this strategy from a friend who worked for the Gibraltar drug squad. Once, as they were pursuing and catching up with a drug-smuggling RIB, the RIB turned round 270 degrees and hit the Gibraltar drug squad boat on the side with its sharp hull. The Gibraltar drug boat was disabled and the crew terrified; this ended the Gibraltar drug patrols.

Both Ali and I watched the men carefully and, fortunately, the gun stayed at the bottom of the dugout. As *Ribaleta's* tubes drew level, we had a good chat with them, although we made sure to ask them to stay in their boat.

'That was terrifying,' Ali said as we left the creek, and the dugout, behind. Even though nothing had happened, we still knew we had been lucky. After all, firearms are designed to kill.

'I'm glad we had a solution,' I said. 'But I hope I never have to think like that again.'

○ ○ ○

We made our way out of the delta and over the shallows to Guiria, where we cleared customs. We then headed east across the Gulf of Paria and passed through the Bocas del Dragón. After 1,000 miles in the Orinoco Delta, reality hit us. We were back out at sea, in the midst of currents running north from the Mouth of the Serpent and east from the Atlantic. This, along with the tides, resulted in very confused seas. We were heading in the right direction and making 20 knots, and I knew it was going to be uncomfortable for the following five hours. Ali, however, had different ideas. She began to scream so loudly that, even though I am deaf, was wearing a motorcycle helmet and had a 600-horsepower open exhaust 6 feet away, my ears still hurt.

'I can't go on like this!' Ali screamed.

I tried to tell her that I didn't want to turn round, but she refused to listen.

'I'm going to die!'

In a rage, I turned *Ribaleta* round. Since we were out of sight of land, I had to look at the chart plotter to find out where we should be heading. We had left Venezuela heading north for Grenada and now had to find a course for Trinidad.

And that was why I did not see the wave.

Suddenly, we were eight feet under water. We had driven through a wave. Now we were out of sight of land and had a boat full of a few tons of water, but at least Ali's screaming had stopped.

I knew exactly what I had to do. In this situation, I needed to put on full power immediately, even before I could see, so that the bow would go up in the air, sending most of the water over the engine casing and back into the sea and letting the rest drain out. In just 15 seconds, I had emptied all the water out.

I turned to look at Ali. She was deathly white and wouldn't speak.

I quickly found a course for Trinidad and headed towards it at about 12 knots. The conditions were much rougher on the way back than they had been before Ali made me turn round, but Trinidad and dry land were not far away and wouldn't take us long to reach. As we drew near land, Ali and

A giant leatherback turtle comes ashore on a pitch black beach. Once she has started laying she goes into a trance at which point we were allowed to approach, watch and touch her, on the East Coast of Trinidad

I started to talk to each other again. Soon, all was quiet in bright sunshine, and we were back to normal once more.

We looked for something to do and found that we could go out that evening with guides to a beach on the east coast of Trinidad, where we could have a chance to watch sea turtles come out of the water to dig deep holes and deposit their eggs. We waited for them in complete darkness; if there are any lights, the turtles will not come ashore. Then the guides spotted two turtles coming out of the water and we were able to watch them. When sea turtles start to dig their holes in the sand, they go into a kind of trance, when nature compels them to complete their egg-laying process. It was at that stage that we were allowed to watch them at close range. We saw each egg as it was deposited and, when all had been laid, the turtles covered them with their back flippers until the beach was smooth again. Then it was time for them to make their last big effort to drag their enormous bodies back into the ocean to swim away.

Ali and I agreed that it had been an amazing end to a frightening afternoon. We had made up and were happy again and were grateful to have had such a magical experience. Unfortunately, Ali had to return to England. She would come back to rejoin me a month later, but we both agreed it was a shame she couldn't do the next part of the adventure with me. Her flight was departing from St Lucia and, even though I offered to take her there in *Ribaleta*, she did not have the stomach for another ocean crossing, and chose to fly instead.

CHAPTER THIRTY-THREE
TRINIDAD TO HISPANIOLA – SOLO

With Ali gone, I spent a quiet night just inside the Bocas del Dragón and then, the following morning, woke up to perfect conditions. I motored off to a calm and fast crossing with no sign whatsoever of big waves. Skirting around Grenada, I made straight for the Grenadines, stopping to rest at Mayreau. As the smallest inhabited island of the Grenadines, where less than 300 people live, I was keen to explore it. That year, a generator had been installed to give the island electricity for the first time. I hoped Mayreau would be untouched, but when I arrived it was to find that a small cruise ship had anchored just off its coast, and that all the passengers were ashore buying local handicrafts. It was horribly crowded so, rather than stay there, I quickly went round to the reefs, on the windward side of the island, just a quarter of an hour away.

As I anchored, a large black cloud filled the sky, and to avoid the thunderstorm I jumped into the water to snorkel. As I swam over the coral in the rain, I thought of the hundreds of cruise ship passengers standing in the heavy tropical downpour with their newly bought T-shirts as they waited to go back to the ship and dry off. I thought too of the poor locals, desperately trying to keep their merchandise dry or carry their soaking-wet goods back home to shelter. I did not envy either group. I had the perfect spot here, snorkelling in the rain on some of the best reefs in the Caribbean with no land to windward other than the west African coast 3,000 miles away.

I continued on north, passing Canouan, Mustique, Bequia, St Vincent, St Lucia and Martinique to reach Dominica. There, I anchored in Portsmouth Bay, which I remembered well from visiting it with Celia in *Caleta* 25 years before. I was surprised that, in the early twenty-first century, it was still such a primitive place, with the same small wooden shacks in which islanders sold their fruit and vegetables, grown on the hillside behind the town. Dominica is a mountainous, heavily forested island with a very rough east coast, the home of the last remaining Caribs, whose ancestors had migrated from the jungles of South America.

On I went, past Guadeloupe and Montserrat to Antigua. I was driving much more into the wind, and the seas became rougher and more unpleasant until, as if by a miracle, a pod of orcas, rare killer whales, appeared in the distance. I wanted to motor nearer, to observe them as closely as possible, but *Ribaleta's* twin diesel engines were far too noisy, and they moved away before I was able to see them properly.

Finally, I made it into English Harbour in Antigua – the harbour where Celia and I had moored *Caleta* after our first Atlantic crossing. English Harbour had continued to act as a kind of base for many of my sailing trips over the two and a half decades since then. As I entered, passing the Pillars of Hercules into Freeman's Bay and Nelson's Dockyard, it almost felt as if I were returning home.

I tied up and caught a bus into the capital, St John's. I had come to Antigua to obtain my American visa but annoyingly, when I arrived at the American embassy, it was closed. My only hope, I was told, of obtaining the visa was to return to Trinidad. Having just spent the last few days travelling from Trinidad, covering perhaps 600 miles in total, I wasn't keen to drive *Ribaleta* all the way back there. So instead, I caught a flight, hoping my stay there would be as short as possible. From the airport, I went directly to the American embassy and sat in the waiting room, the only white man amongst dozens of Trinidadians hoping to go to America. When it finally came to my turn to be seen, the officer I spoke to was most unhelpful, until I told him that my that my arrival in America would be by sea.

'If you're going to bring a boat in,' he laughed, 'then of course I'll give you a visa!'

With all in order, I flew back to Antigua and *Ribaleta*. Sadly, some yachtsman had taken advantage of my absence and, seeing the boat unattended, had stolen all my best food and tools.

I left Antigua early the next morning for the now calmer downwind legs to the British Virgin Islands, passing Richard Branson's beautiful Necker Island on the right. At Virgin Gorda, I anchored for breakfast after 120 miles. Then I crossed from the British to the US Virgin Islands, a popular yachting area with sailing boats, both owned and chartered, where I stopped at St Thomas for fuel. The US Virgin Islands are unique in America, for they are the only part of the country where they drive on the left. The reason for this is because, in 1917, they were sold to America by Denmark.

Once they came under American ownership, the governor changed the driving rules from left to right to conform with American standards. In those days most islanders used horses and carts, and habitually drank to excess. Men would become so drunk that they would simply trust their horses to take them home, which they did, but on the left-hand side of the road, for this was what the horses had always done. As you can't teach an old horse new tricks, the islanders simply avoided the horses in their cars by driving on the left and, as such, the Americans had to change the law back again to driving on the left.

Watching a seaplane take off right in front of us in the Virgin Islands

With *Ribaleta* full of fuel, I motored out of the marina and left all the virgins to Richard Branson. Just before the turbos caught, my little engines were drowned out by an almighty roar. I looked around and saw a little spray ahead of me and above it saw a petrolhead's dream of twin 750-horsepower radial engines on full power only 150 yards ahead of me as the seaplane started its take-off. The pilot would not have seen me as I was not on a plane so making no spray. I stopped and waited enjoying the spectacle. These seaplanes, which carry passengers between the islands, are flown by what could be described as the last fly-by-the-seat-of-your-pants pilots in the world. From the air, they need to find a clear landing space between the many yachts, as close to the port as possible, taxi through all the boats to the harbour, and then drive up a ramp so that the passengers can disembark on dry land. Once that's done, they have to do the whole process in reverse and find a gap amongst the yachts to take off again. It's an incredibly difficult thing to do and, as the number of yachts increases every year, it is becoming ever harder.

Leaving St Thomas, I drove *Ribaleta* round all the small Virgin Islands to the west and then along the north coast of Puerto Rico, avoiding San Juan as I searched for a small and safe-looking harbour. When I found one, I anchored and put up the tent. Soon, a small boat came out to me. The boatman only spoke Spanish, but when I showed him my papers, he seemed satisfied and left. During my supper, exactly the same thing happened again. Another small boat came out to me with a Spanish-speaking driver. Once again, I showed him my papers and he left. Thinking that this was surely the end of the matter, I returned to my supper, when I heard the noise of an approaching helicopter. I soon realised that the noise was different, and once outside my tent, I looked up and saw that it was hovering directly overhead. I stared up into its searchlight, smiled, waved, and then went back to finish eating.

Twenty minutes later, as I was washing up, another boat came alongside *Ribaleta*. Three policemen came on board and, when I came out of the tent to greet them, they demanded an official inspection ashore. With as much good grace as I could muster, I suggested that perhaps they might like to wait ashore while I finished my washing up and took the tent down, but they made it clear that they didn't want to let me out of their sight in case I drove off into the night. They would wait, they said, until I had finished, and then escort me ashore.

I packed everything away, took the tent down, lifted up the anchor and motored to the dock to tie up. There were nine police officers, five patrol vehicles and the helicopter, which still hovered overhead. As the officers came aboard, they brought with them a sniffer dog to check for drugs.

'Would you mind', I asked, 'keeping the dog out of my food locker? I wouldn't want him to eat anything.'

They agreed to my request and just let him search the other lockers. Then they took photographs of me and of *Ribaleta*.

'You know,' I said, 'what I've done is all perfectly legal. I didn't come ashore until you requested it. I anchored temporarily, and that is allowed under international law.'

'This is America,' one of them replied with a low growl. 'We make the rules.'

Whatever those rules were, they came to nothing, for neither the police nor the dog could find anything suspicious, and finally they were forced to let me go back to my anchorage for the rest of the night.

'Have a good trip,' one of the officers said as he disembarked. I found it impossible to tell whether or not he was being genuine.

◯ ◯ ◯

I left Puerto Rico early the next morning. After the harassment of the previous night, I wanted to make an early start, as the longest leg yet, 280 miles, lay ahead of me and I wanted to complete it in daylight. I had good reason for this: I knew that container ships do not fix down their top containers. This is because of the value of the ships themselves and their crews. When the seas are very rough, it is far better for the containers to slide off than for the ships to lose their stability and capsize. Knowing this, I wanted to ensure I had good visibility, so as to avoid hitting a container dropped in a hurricane at 35 knots and face certain death.

I didn't meet any containers, but I was glad I had chosen to undertake this leg in daylight, for the conditions were challenging. At one point, I found myself motoring up the back of an enormous wave and being slowed right down. The wave must have been travelling at close to 45 knots, the fastest I've ever seen. It felt less like a trade wind wave and more like a tsunami.

I managed to make it round to the north coast of Hispaniola, the large island which is sub-divided into the two countries of Haiti to the west and the Dominican Republic to the east, but the commercial harbour I had chosen for the night was far too busy. Driving a little further along the coast, I came across a small port which seemed perfect. With its sandy bay there was no risk of coral damage, and I was able to enter it safely in the fading light.

The following day, I headed along the north-western coast of the Dominican Republic, passing the Massacre River. This is the British-charted name for the Dajabón River, which forms the northernmost part of the border between the Dominican Republic and Haiti. The name dates from 1728, when Spanish settlers on the island killed thirty French buccaneers and dumped their bodies in the river. Far more gruesome, and much more recent, was the Parsley Massacre in 1937, when more than 12,000 Haitians were slaughtered by the Dominican army in a horrific act of genocide. Much like the killings 200 years earlier, many of the dead bodies were dumped in the Massacre River.

I have always felt sympathy for Haiti and the Haitians. They have had to contend with so much, from massacres to catastrophic earthquakes and unimaginable poverty. The poverty was almost certainly caused by the French who, when Haitian slaves overthrew their French owners and gained independence in 1804, demanded reparations, the equivalent of $21 billion in today's money, for all the potential slaves and plantations Haiti had supposedly 'stolen' by becoming free and independent. Haiti had to repay that debt until 1947 and has never recovered.

From Haiti's coast, I drove north, making my way to the Turks and Caicos Islands. The crossing was not particularly long, but I sped over the waters, determined to make it there by the early afternoon, knowing that the entrance to Providenciales Island was complex and twisting, with jagged reefs on both sides and impossible to navigate after 3 p.m. when the sun becomes too low and its glare is reflected off the water, making the shallow coral invisible.

There was another reason I did not want to be late: Ali was due to fly into Providenciales that evening. After mooring and cleaning up both myself and *Ribaleta*, I caught a taxi to the airport.

CHAPTER THIRTY-FOUR
THE BAHAMAS WITH ALI

Ali was delighted to be back in the tropics. I hoped that she had put the Bocas del Dragón fright behind her and, as we cruised the sheltered coral bays of Providenciales to swim and to snorkel, it seemed that all was forgotten. That is, until she spoke to some of the other yachtsmen, whose predictions about the incoming weather panicked her once more.

'They're sailing in the same direction as us,' she told me later that day, 'and they're nervous. They said they're dreading the conditions.'

I tried to calm her down. I needed her to regain her confidence or the whole trip would become a nightmare. 'Look,' I said, 'they need two or three days of good weather to allow their passage. But we can make it over there in just two or three hours. You don't need to be nervous.'

'Are you sure?'

'It's been easy for them so far, but now they're facing the heavy windward crossings with no safe harbours, so they've started frightening themselves. Don't let them frighten you too.'

Ali agreed to ignore the yachtsmen and to stay calm and confident. The following morning, with all looking clear, we decided to make a move, and the crossing to Acklins in the Bahamas was as wonderfully sunny and as flat calm as I could have hoped for. Ali relaxed, and we found a deep, sheltered bay surrounded by coral reefs which was perfect for snorkelling. By night, the waters lit up in a magical show of lights, with hundreds of luminous sea creatures rising from the depths around the hull of *Ribaleta*.

Days passed as we cruised from island to island – from Acklins to Crooked Island to Long Island – discovering deserted bays which we had all to ourselves. Where we happened to meet locals, they greeted us with amazement. 'Oh man, you guys came over the ocean in 'dat boat?' one said, pointing at *Ribaleta*. 'Didn't it dance around a bit?'

On Great Exuma we moored at George Town, colloquially known amongst sailors as 'Chicken Harbour'. This name comes from the fact that many yachtsmen stop there with the intention of continuing to the Virgin Islands and the Caribbean. There they hit the strong trade winds and the far rougher sailing and 'chicken out', turning back either to head up north or to remain forever in George Town. With all rough seas behind us, I knew we had easy conditions ahead as we cruised north. Unfortunately, one of the drive shafts broke, forcing us to continue with one engine.

Ribaleta picking up some knots in Turks and Caicos

Nevertheless, we were still able to do and see lots of things as we drove north through the Bahamas. The outer islands were primitive but attractive, with their quaintly painted houses, homes of the local fishermen. Shallow coral was everywhere, and we were even able to swim in the Thunderball Grotto – an underwater cave system between Staniel Cay and Pig Island, famous as a location for the James Bond film *Thunderball*. We had a new drive shaft fitted to *Ribaleta* and, once that was done, we were able to regain our old cruising speed to Nassau. Paradise Island has many famous casinos and luxury hotels: a winter playground for Americans wanting to escape the northern states for winter sunshine.

From Nassau, we cruised north to Grand Bahama, where we moored at Freeport. This was where, in 1965, I had bought the seafront plot of land that I later sold to fund the purchase of *Caleta*. We walked around the place and I was surprised to see that, although almost 40 years had passed, little had changed. I was glad I had sold the plot.

One of the engines had begun to sound unhealthy again, obviously with serious trouble. I decided that I didn't want to risk crossing the Gulf Stream and found a mechanic on the island, who confirmed that the engine needed a complete rebuild, with all the parts having to be flown over from Florida. I felt sorry for Ali as I had a couple of months left before I had to return to the farm, but her time was limited. Spending her remaining days stuck on Grand Bahama seemed rather unfair on her.

We agreed that, with all this free time at our disposal, we would make the most of it. Grand Bahama had the distinct advantage of having regular flights to Cuba, and as neither of us had been there before, we took a plane to Havana. We expected our fellow passengers to be Spanish speakers but almost all of them were American. They were not allowed to fly directly from the US to Cuba, so Grand Bahama was the best indirect route.

Cuba was wonderful and we both thoroughly enjoyed it. We wandered amongst the restored Spanish colonial buildings in Havana and others which were propped up awaiting restoration. At the end of the day, we had a drink in Floridita, the bar where Ernest Hemingway habitually drank an incredible number of daiquiris daily. A life-size bronze statue stands at the end of the bar as a permanent memorial to him.

We were keen to explore Havana's harbour, which we knew was rich in history. It was just as impressive as I'd imagined; it is still the country's main port, with Old Havana rising behind it. Once, this was the biggest fort in the New World, invaluable to the Spanish, being the port from which all their stolen gold and silver was shipped back to Spain. When the British under Lord Albemarle laid siege to the port for several months in 1762, the Spanish eventually capitulated and handed over the territory to Britain. Naturally, furious about such a loss of face, they insisted that the terms of the Treaty of Paris ensured that the Spanish regained Havana in return for giving Florida back to the British.

We hired a car to see more of the island and were amazed to discover virtually no traffic on the roads. During one excursion, we took pity on a hitchhiker and decided to pick him up. He turned out to be a government official and, after thanking us for stopping, he explained that he'd been walking for two and a half hours, owing to the lack of public transport. Ours was the first car he had seen all morning. We saw triangular huts where tobacco was hung on bars up into the roof to dry before being sent to the factories to be rolled into expensive cigars, and we went round the Cohiba factory to see how the best cigars were made in a cottage-industry network before buying a few of them on the black market.

Soon, our time in Cuba ended, and we returned to the airport for our flight. The airport was extremely crowded and some of the American passengers were not allowed to board, having arrived late. There were floods of tears from one girl when she realised that all tickets and passenger details were processed through a central computer, putting her visit to Cuba at risk of being discovered by the American authorities. She could have been fined as much as $70,000 just for being there.

Back in Grand Bahama, *Ribaleta* was almost finished. Unfortunately, so was Ali's time on this particular adventure. We went to the airport, from where she was due to fly back to England. I was sad to see her leave as we had enjoyed a truly wonderful journey together; but my journey was not yet over.

CHAPTER THIRTY-FIVE

GRAND BAHAMA TO BALTIMORE – SOLO

I walked slowly back from the airport feeling very sad at saying goodbye to Ali. The mechanic had finished his work and *Ribaleta* was ready, so I started up the engines, thanked the mechanic, and then realised that I didn't have enough money on me to pay him. It was growing late, and all the banks had closed for the day.

'Don't worry about it,' the mechanic said. 'Take the boat now and pay me in the morning. I trust you.'

Grateful for his easy-going manner, I promised I would see him the following morning, and took the boat out to find a quiet place to sleep for the night. When I returned the next morning with the cash, I wondered if the mechanic had considered that I might vanish into the night, never to reappear with his money. He had not asked for any kind of assurance, my passport for example, to guarantee his payment.

'I knew I could trust you,' he said when I handed him the money. It was not a small amount and would certainly go a long way in Grand Bahama, but it seemed that the prospect of my running off with it had never crossed his mind.

Now that the mechanic had been paid, all I had to do was fill my tanks and leave. Unfortunately, a new obstacle appeared: there was no electricity to power the fuel pumps. I dipped my tanks to measure my remaining diesel. My aim was to reach Port Canaveral as my entry point into America, about 100 miles away. After calculating that I had just enough fuel to make it, I set off. Even if the engines did stop on the crossing, I knew that there were always boats off the coast of Florida and I could call on the VHF radio for a tow to land. This was not good seamanship, but I would be passing through a busy cruising area and, as Port Canaveral is one of the busiest cruise ports in the world, I knew I could be picked up if needed.

Fortunately, all went well. My fuel reserves lasted to Port Canaveral but, as I soon found out, they would not have gone any further. Arriving at the fuel dock, I dipped the tanks and found nothing at all on the dipstick. I was very thankful for the precision of *Ribaleta's* instruments.

With my visa and passport in order, entering America was totally trouble-free. I found a little portacabin where a customs officer stamped all my documents and all that remained was to fill up with fuel. Returning to *Ribaleta*, I saw a beautiful 50-foot powerboat in the harbour. I envied the driver, whose job was to push the prototype engine almost to destruction, surely one of the best jobs in the world.

With a full tank, I then headed up the coast from Port Canaveral. The chart indicated that I should go a long way out, but I could see that there was plenty of water near the coast. A little further north, I came abeam of the Kennedy Space Center launch site. There, right before me, was the Space Shuttle, secured on its launch pad with its enormous orange fuel tank directly facing me, which I took a photograph of. In my picture, the Space Shuttle fills the whole frame of the camera. I have never seen another photograph like it – but this is because boats are not allowed within 5 miles of the coast at Cape Canaveral, so no professional photographer has ever been able to get as close to the site as I did.

At this point, I had no idea about the five-mile exclusion zone, so I continued on the same course until, all of a sudden, an 80-foot coastguard cutter appeared on my port side. From our positions I decided that we were probably on collision course, so I carried out the correct collision avoidance procedure, making a sharp turn to starboard. Instantaneously, the cutter turned hard to port at full speed, heeling over to about 45 degrees – a truly spectacular sight.

Watching the Space Shuttle in the restricted area just under a mile out to sea at Cape Canaveral in Florida

I considered making a run for it. I had speed on my side, but because the cutter was ahead of me, the only way I could escape was by heading straight out to sea. If they couldn't catch me, they knew how to stop me, as the cutter had a 4-inch gun on the bow, and I had no wish to tempt them to use it. Reluctantly, I slowed down and let the cutter approach. As it drew alongside, I was ordered to follow it into Ponce de Leon, where we tied up and where I was arrested and then taken into an office.

Six men stood round me. 'You've just come from Puerto Rico,' one said aggressively.

'No, I haven't,' I replied. 'I've come from Port Canaveral.'

'*You've come from Puerto Rico.*'

'No,' I said. 'I've come from Port Canaveral.'

'There's no point in lying. We've got all the photos.'

'What photos?'

'Your boat was stopped and searched in Puerto Rico. We know all about it, so don't lie to me.'

'I'm not lying. I was in Puerto Rico, over a month ago. Since then, I've been to lots of places. But the most recent place was Port Canaveral – look.' I took out my passport, showing each of the men the relevant stamps.

'No, that can't be right,' the first one said. 'You've come from Puerto Rico. We have it documented.'

'Then what's this?' I asked, pointing at the stamp I had received from the customs officer in Port Canaveral. 'Do you really think I can forge an American passport stamp?'

This made the man pause. 'Hmm. No. You probably can't.' He turned to his colleagues. Between them, they decided the best course of action would be to call the customs officer at Port Canaveral. I could hear the dialling tone clearly as the man held the receiver to his ear. The phone at the other end was picked up after a couple of rings. 'Hello?'

The officer introduced himself and then gave a description of me and of *Ribaleta*. 'Has this guy been in to clear?' he asked.

There was a brief pause, and then: 'Oh yeah! He did! But I haven't got round to putting it on the computer yet. Sorry.'

That was enough for them. Now that they knew I was legal, the six men escorted me back to *Ribaleta* and let me leave. Ahead of me lay the entire American Eastern Seaboard. It would be good to stay in one country for a while, I thought. I was getting tired of border-zone bureaucracy.

๏ ๏ ๏

With Florida behind me, I joined the Intracoastal Waterway (ICW) in Georgia, motoring through swamps of wild mangroves, stopping here and there in the little bays and lagoons to enjoy the wildlife. At Georgia's border with South Carolina, I came to Savannah, the oldest city in the state. It seemed appropriate that I should stop where General Sherman's 'March to the Sea' stopped in 1864, a defining campaign battle of the American Civil War.

The following morning, I passed Hilton Head Island, famous for its gated communities, which comprise 70 per cent of the island. Many well-known nineteenth- and twentieth-century millionaires, such as the Rockefellers and the Fords, had holiday mansions on Hilton Head. Amongst their luxury houses they built a large communal dining room to share between them, ensuring that they could socialise with each other and avoid any possible competition about dinner parties and poaching each other's staff.

From there, I spent the rest of the day sailing on up the ICW through its network of mangrove swamps and waterside villages to Charleston. I entered late at night, and found travelling down the river and searching for an anchorage in this big city a nerve-wracking experience. This was a world away from the forgotten backwaters of the Orinoco, where sometimes it seemed as if Ali and I were the last people on earth.

Fortunately, I was able to find the Marriott, a five-star hotel where they allowed me to tie up for free if I had dinner, even though it was past 11.00 p.m. After my best three-course meal of the trip I left to find a quiet anchorage for the night.

The ICW seemed to grow wilder the further north I progressed, its lagoons spreading over larger and larger areas. South Carolina became North Carolina and North Carolina became Virginia. On the southern end of Chesapeake Bay, I stopped at Norfolk to tour the battleship USS *Wisconsin*, a sister ship of the USS *Missouri*, on which Japan formally surrendered in 1945. It had served in the Second World War, the Korean War and Operation Desert Storm, and now functioned as a museum ship. I walked over its deck: 4½ acres of teak, and home to nine 16-inch guns. I would have liked to have gone down below decks, but that was out of bounds. At the time, the *Wisconsin* was still in full reserve as a serviceable warship. Four years later, in 2006, it was finally struck off from the Naval Vessel Register and assigned permanent museum-ship status.

After the ICW, entering the wide expanse of Chesapeake Bay felt like re-entering the ocean. I kept heading north, passing Hampton, Newport

News and Mobjack Bay to the west, then Jamesville, Hacksneck and Tangier Island to the east. Finally, I reached the mouth of the Potomac, that wide and deep river which leads directly to the nation's capital, Washington. I was not, however, allowed too far along it. Coming into a military zone, I soon realised that I was being chased by another boat. Made wary by the aggression of the officers in Cape Canaveral, I decided it would be easier if I fully opened the throttles and left my pursuers behind me.

Back in Chesapeake Bay, I continued as far north as I could, up the Delaware Canal to New Jersey, before it was time to return to Baltimore. There, I hoped a freighter awaited me, on which I had booked passage to England for *Ribaleta*.

I arrived in Baltimore with 24 hours to spare. To ensure I was prepared for the following day, I drove into the docks area to look for my designated haul-out place. I had the dock number on me, but once there I found it to be deserted, with little more than a sheer steel wall and nowhere for me to tie up and investigate. The emptiness of the place made me nervous and I wondered if there would be anyone there the following morning to haul *Ribaleta* out of the water. Fortunately, when I returned the next day, a docker was waiting for me on the wall.

'Sir Charles Blois?' he shouted down at me.

I nodded in relief.

'Come back in half an hour,' he said. 'I'll be ready for you then.'

I did as I was instructed, fitting the slings in place while I waited; when I returned half an hour later, a crane was in position. The hook was lowered and I connected the slings, before riding up and being lowered on to a wooden platform; it was all over in a matter of minutes.

Leaving the workers to finish the loading job, I walked to the office to have my papers stamped. There were no difficulties with customs and soon all the formalities were completed. I was out of the dock after just an hour and a half of motoring up to it. It was, I thought, a surprisingly quick end to such a unique and thrilling journey. After 5,500 miles in five and a half months, mine and Ali's Americas adventures were over.

CHAPTER THIRTY-SIX
THE BALKANS

In 2004, two years after our Americas adventures, Ali and I embarked on another epic journey in *Ribaleta*. This time, we planned to travel from Passau in Germany down the Danube to its delta on the Black Sea, through the Bosporus and amongst the islands of Greece, and then up the Adriatic to our finishing line, Venice – in total a 3,800-mile circumnavigation of the Balkans.

To reach Passau, we drove the Unimog, towing the boat behind on its custom-made 33-foot trailer. Our crossing of France and Germany was slow, with hills reducing our speed to as little as 20 miles an hour in places, and with constant rain hampering us even further. The cold weather didn't help either, as although it was May it was only seven degrees. Finally, we reached the small town of Obernzell, where we launched *Ribaleta* into the wide and fast-flowing Blue Danube. There were 1,500 miles of river between us and the Black Sea.

The Danube has been a well-used waterway for centuries. These days, it has many more locks, dams and hydroelectric plants than formerly. We reached the first lock after being on the river for just five minutes. Coming alongside an enormous barge which dwarfed *Ribaleta*, we waited as the water level dropped. 60-feet-high concrete walls rose on either side of us, covered in slime and algae. Halfway down, we suddenly ran out of rope and had to attach another line. Later, we discovered that these locks had bollards set into the concrete every six feet, and we soon became used to the process of 'bollard hopping' with the line.

We stopped for our first night in a shipyard, where we tied up to a pontoon. It was a rather miserable place with nothing but smoking chimneys along the waterfront, and the temperature still hadn't risen above seven degrees. We began to put up the tent.

'The bedding's damp,' Ali said as she took it out of the locker.

'Everything is always damp on a boat when it's raining outside,' I replied.

Despite the cold, we slept well, and the next morning treated ourselves to breakfast at the Strandcafe, a riverside café with its own pontoon. We ate delicious wiener schnitzel and apple strudel and chatted with the owner, who was so impressed by our itinerary that she asked us to write in her guest book. When it was time to leave, she gathered all the staff together on the balcony to bid us farewell. With them looking on, it was embarrassing when one engine wouldn't start, but eventually I managed to start it and we were on our way.

About 50 miles from Vienna, we tied up in a small marina when a back eddy swept *Ribaleta* on to a sharp aluminium corner, puncturing a tube. After inspecting the damage, I predicted that, as long as we kept the tubes clear of the water, we would be able to make it to Vienna. Luckily, we did, and found a brand-new marina where we could moor and I could speak to the manager of an inflatable company. His fitter came to look at the tube and agreed that he could repair it, and *Ribaleta* was lifted out of the water. The repairs were going to take a full twenty-four hours, so we decided to make the most of our unexpected free time and visit Vienna. We had a lovely afternoon and evening strolling through the old Habsburg city centre and visiting the Spanish Riding School, where we saw the white Lippizaner horses being trained.

Ribaleta was ready the next day, as promised, and we set off along the Danube for Bratislava. There were only two hours of daylight left, but I felt confident that, as long as we maintained a good speed, we could make it. And we would have, if it had not been for the unexpected lock which blocked our passage. It had only recently been built and was not on the chart or in our guidebook. As we entered, we failed to get the stern line on the bollard the first time, so I engaged astern, only to hear a horrible crunching sound. The drives had lifted on their own and the prop had hit the trim tab. With no other choice, we turned round and made our way back to Vienna, where we were greeted by the workshop manager who laughed: 'You again!'

Once more, *Ribaleta* was lifted out of the water, this time revealing a bent propshaft, needing a whole new lower unit. I made some calls to England, only to be told by the manufacturer that it would take six weeks for a new unit to be made. It seemed that perhaps our adventure was over before it had barely started, until the Austrian fitter succeeded in tracking down a local manufacturer who agreed to look at it. The job took them only two days to fit and test, which was rather better than six weeks, and we were pleased to be on our way again.

When we finally made it to Bratislava, we found it to be a vibrant city. Both Ali and I had been expecting a dismal relic of the Eastern bloc, but in fact it was a lot of fun, with its beautifully restored old town, its streets full of cafés and its river full of hydrofoils. We walked along the old, cobbled streets up to the castle, which had a magnificent view of the terracotta roofs of the old town.

On the far side of Bratislava, the Danube grows wider and its currents faster. The wind increased as we motored towards the Hungarian border, whipping up waves which, as turbulent as they were, were no match for the ones Ali and I had experienced on the seas of the Caribbean. Eventually, we reached Esztergom, the old capital of Hungary, where we tied up in a marina with just one other boat. We talked to our neighbours, two young Hungarians called Marcel and Attila. 'Attila, like the Hun,' he said. They were heading in the opposite direction to us, up the Danube towards Regensburg in Germany.

The focal point of Esztergom is the magnificent basilica. We walked up to it to visit the famous treasury, home to a vast collection of jewels, gold-wrought masterpieces and ornate chalices. From the basilica, we had a wonderful view of the river as it made its way east. Beyond the horizon lay the famous Danube Bend, a U-shaped loop which changes the trajectory of the river south towards what was once Yugoslavia. This was where we were heading and, once we rounded it the following day, winding between the Transdanubia Mountains on one bank and the North Hungarian Mountains on the other, we continued on downstream for another 40 miles to reach Budapest. The marina there was a cluttered and noisy shipyard. We didn't stay for long, but just long enough to climb the Fisherman's Bastion in Buda and look out across the river to Pest and its near copy of our Houses of Parliament on the other side.

Civilisation became sparser as we made our way south through Hungary. Here and there, small villages appeared along the banks, but largely there was nothing around except the flat and empty Hungarian plain known as the Puszta. The Danube became quieter too. We passed the occasional giant barge, but for most of the time we seemed to have the river to ourselves.

Since the Danube forms much of the northern stretch of the border between Croatia and Serbia and even cuts across from one country to the other in places, this can make immigration control on leaving Hungary confusing. We made our way towards a small boat on the right bank, manned by a tall, blond officer.

'You want Vukovar?' he asked us.

'No,' Ali replied. 'We're heading for Serbia, not Croatia.'

The officer pointed back up the river to a derelict barge we had just passed. 'That is Serbian immigration,' he said.

We motored over to it, and then had to wait a long time before the immigration official arrived. He was short and dark, the opposite of the Croatian officer we had just met.

'Bulgarian ship, big problem,' he said. 'You bring boat? Big problem. Many forms.'

He was right. We were driven in an ageing Yugo car to the road border control, little more than a tin portacabin, to pay $50 and then, after being allowed back to *Ribaleta*, we were told to wait for the customs inspection while they disappeared with our passports. The sun began to set. Beside us, three barges had stopped while waiting for clearance. We cooked and ate our dinner in silence as darkness fell, hoping the officers would return soon. When they did finally return, it was too late to continue, but we were relieved to know that we could be on our way the next morning.

Motoring down through Serbia, we came to an unexpected stop at Novi Sad. Our way was blocked by a pontoon bridge made from solid steel, a makeshift crossing put in place because all the bridges had been bombed in the war. We managed to find an official, who told us that it would not open again until ten o'clock that evening. With no choice but to wait, we decided to tie up to the floating pontoon of the *Zeppelin*, a nearby restaurant boat. As I came alongside it, Ali threw out a stern line, only to tumble forward as she did so, just managing to avoid falling overboard and landing on the engine cover instead. Thankfully, she was unhurt, and a Serbian waiter at the *Zeppelin* grabbed the line for us.

The memory of the Yugoslav Wars was still fresh in Serbia, as they had ended just three years earlier in 2001. We were expecting a decimated city in Novi Sad, but found instead a lovely town with well-preserved old buildings and modern shops. Since we had tied up to the *Zeppelin* restaurant boat, it seemed only fair to eat dinner there, and Sasha, the friendly owner, gave us a warm welcome and a bottle of good red wine while we waited for the bridge to open.

Finally, 10.00 p.m. came, and we boarded *Ribaleta* to pass through the crossing. Since it was so late, we wanted to find another place to moor as quickly as we could, although Ali admitted that, after what had happened that morning, she was nervous about tying up in the dark. Fortunately, we found a freighter which had been converted into a disco, and not only did the owner take our line and tie us up to it, he also invited us on board for a beer and a much-needed hot shower. The next morning, with typical Serbian hospitality, he gave us a breakfast of strawberries and delicious Turkish coffee, and in return we took him for a much-enjoyed ride in *Ribaleta*.

Feeling renewed from our stop, we continued down the Danube, making sure that we stuck to the main marked channel, avoiding the many small islands in the river, where fishermen cast their nets into the shallow waters. By the time we reached Belgrade, our priority was to find fuel. Unfortunately, nobody seemed prepared to sell us any as they wanted to wait until the following day when the price of diesel was due to increase. One of the locals told us that, if we carried on to Orşova, a port on the Romanian border, we would find a fuel ship which might supply us. As it seemed our only option, we set off.

We didn't have time to make it as far as Orşova, and as the sun began to set, we decided to stop at Veliko Gradište, a nice little town on the right bank of the Danube which faces Romania. The border police there were welcoming and friendly, inviting us to stay for dinner, but we wanted somewhere a little quieter, so we carried on further until we could anchor beside a small island. We opened Sasha's bottle of wine and drank it with our supper under the stars.

◎ ◎ ◎

'Allo? Allo?' The voice woke us both. I could tell from the light coming through the tent's windows that it was barely dawn.

'Allo?' the voice repeated, and then: '*Polizei!*'

We opened up the tent to find an officer staring at us. '*Documentos!*' he demanded. As we fumbled about looking for our passports, we realised what had happened. Overnight, we had strayed into Romania on the left bank. We were, in effect, illegal immigrants. Ali handed over our passports and explained to the officer what had happened, who accepted our apologies and let us continue on to the border control.

Beyond the border, we made our way towards the Iron Gates, a wide gorge which separates the southern Carpathian Mountains from the north-western Balkan Mountains. This was once an incredibly dangerous stretch of the Danube, and boats used to require a pilot to guide them through it. For barges travelling upriver, they had to be winched against the current with a cable tug. However, when the Djerdap power station and its massive lock complex was built on the other side of Orşova, this slowed the river and made it much safer. As we passed through one section of the Iron Gates, with its steep cliffs rising up on either side of us, the water remained calm and still. When I checked the depth sounder, I found that there were 157 feet of water below us.

When we arrived at Orşova, Ali was able to do the talking. Unlike the Slavic languages of many of its neighbouring countries, Romanian is a Romance language, and Ali's excellent Spanish meant she could master it. We cleared customs and set off in search of the fuel ship, for by now our reserves were becoming dangerously low. Unfortunately, the fuel ship refused to serve us because *Ribaleta* was too small. But Ali's language skills helped us find the solution. We were escorted to a Moldovan tug and supplied with 220 gallons of fuel with the authorities turning a blind eye.

Full of fuel, we continued on along the Danube, eventually reaching the Iron Gates lock complex in the early evening. We tied up to a tug which was pushing nine barges carrying 10,000 tons of sunflower oil. The captain invited us on board for the journey, and we asked him about the power station.

'The Iron Gates barrage and lock was the last major joint project of Tito and Ceauşescu,' he said. 'And now the hydroelectric system provides a large percentage of the energy needed by the two countries.'

When the lock gates opened, the captain said we could leave, but the thought of his 3,200-horsepower engines starting and throwing us against the lock wall was so terrifying that he allowed us to stay tied up until he and his barges were out of the lock and back into the river.

The next day, we motored down the river without interruption for ten hours. The Danube was calm, clear and a joy to navigate. There were many islands along the way with a variety of birds and white sandy beaches. The only people we saw on the land either side of us were fishermen pulling in their nets or farmers loading logs on to horse-drawn carts. The river begins to make its way east once more to where it forms the border between Romania and Bulgaria. We kept to the Romanian side on the left bank, hoping to enter Bulgaria at Ruse, and then changed our minds when a corrupt officer there demanded that we pay him $100. Instead, we headed back to the Romanian side and the town of Giurgiu. It faces Ruse over the river, and the reception we were given by the harbourmaster there was the opposite of what we'd received trying to enter Bulgaria. As we ate fried carp for dinner that evening, we agreed that we had made the right choice.

The following morning, we had lemon tea and jam pancakes for breakfast, and filled up with fuel from a Ukrainian tug. We set off downstream and all seemed well until, about 20 miles later, the engine overheat alarm began to beep, accompanied by a series of red flashing lights on the control panel. It turned out that a turbo cooling pipe had broken, losing most of the water. We considered our options. Turning round and heading back to Giurgiu on one engine, against a 5-knot current, was out of the question. Continuing on with the flow of the river would give us about 12 knots but we had no idea where the next town was. It can take a barge a full week to travel from Vienna to Constanța on the Black Sea, and twenty-five days to return, so we had to prepare ourselves for a long haul.

Fortunately, we weren't too far away from Bucharest, Romania's capital, and there we found a river cruise ship moored. Ali had marked 'I need a mechanic' in every language in her Eastern European phrasebook, and with that we managed to persuade the ship's engineer to help us out. He worked on *Ribaleta* while we had a drink in the air-conditioned bar. The pipe he fitted to tide us over was only plastic, but he did such a good job that it lasted us for the rest of the journey.

Pleased that our problem had been solved, we carried on. By 8.00 p.m. darkness had begun to fall, and ahead of us we could see gathering storm clouds and the occasional flash of lightning. We anchored by the riverbank and put up the tent. As soon as this was done, the storm reached us; strong winds howled while rain beat down on the tent. Worse than that, a cloud of mosquitos somehow found their way inside, far more than we had ever experienced along the Orinoco. We heated up a tin of chicken curry for dinner, doing our best to swat the mosquitos away as we ate.

By the following morning the storm had abated, and we motored on to Tulcea, an ancient Dacian harbour town which now serves as the gateway to the Danube Delta. We had been especially looking forward to this part of the adventure. The delta comprises some 2,200 square miles of rivers, canals, swamps and lagoons. We spent the next few days exploring it at our leisure, following the currents through the willows and reeds. Sometimes we would see the occasional fisherman, but mostly we were alone, with nothing for company except the ever-present birds: swans, geese, pelicans and herons. At night, we fell asleep to the croaking of the delta frogs.

Eventually, it was time to head towards the Black Sea. We stopped off at Mila 23, a small and unusual village only accessible by boat, which takes its name from its location on the river as it used to measure exactly 23 miles from this point to the river's mouth. The village was founded 200 years ago by the Lipovans, Eastern Orthodox 'Old Believers' who emigrated to this area from Russia in the eighteenth century. Their reclusive and self-sufficient nature was one of the reasons they were able to survive the Ceauşescu regime.

From Mila 23, it didn't take us long to reach Sulina, the easternmost point of Romania and, technically, the end of the Danube, although the delta had silted up around this area, and the old lighthouse was four miles inland. We stopped at customs and immigration so that we could be checked for any hidden drugs or stowaways. The harbourmaster was fascinated by *Ribaleta*. 'In all my twenty-five years here,' he said, 'I've never seen a boat like this.' This was our halfway point. With 1,400 miles of river behind us, it was now time to take to the seas.

◎ ◎ ◎

After stocking up with supplies, we made an early morning start. The shipping forecast predicted that the winds were due to change to south-east Force 4–5, and Ali was keen to start making our way south as soon as possible to avoid them. She had been reading the *Black Sea Cruising Guide* and was growing increasingly anxious about the notorious 'Death Swells' which batter the northern Bulgarian coast in the late spring. Fortunately, we only had to make our way through a few waves to reach the sea and, once behind them, the crossing was calm and we sped to Varna at 35 knots.

We arrived at the harbour yacht club, where the harbourmaster, Valentin, explained apologetically that, until we had been visited by port control, we would need to stay in the boat. It was an appalling place in which to wait, with its ugly apartment buildings and noisy cranes. But eventually we were allowed to disembark and make our way into Varna for the rest of the day. We spent some time in the archaeological museum, and then wandered amongst the interesting 'revivalist' buildings: a neoclassical kind of architecture which was used here in the nineteenth century to help encourage a sense of national identity once Turkish rule was over. Sitting down for a cappuccino in one of the many pavement cafés, we learnt about an anomalous Bulgarian custom. In Bulgaria, unlike almost every other country in the world, a nod means 'no' and a shake of the head means 'yes'. Dinner that evening was a casserole of lamb, peppers and herbs served with Bulgarian red wine, and was most enjoyable.

From Varna, we had to clear customs to leave, even though we were only heading down the coast to another Bulgarian town, Nessebar. Once we arrived, we were told that our stamp was incorrect and we were refused permission to land. The bureaucracy of it all was becoming maddening, so we carried on for another 30 miles to Burgas, the last major town on the Black Sea coast before the border with Turkey. Immigration control there was just as infuriating as it had been at Varna, but finally we were allowed through, and could return to Nessebar to visit its UNESCO-protected streets and sights.

The following day, we were late leaving Nessebar as Ali wanted to dry all the bedding before our return to Burgas where we had to obtain our customs clearance to leave Bulgaria. The wind I had tried to avoid with an early start was now blowing strongly as we began the long coastal run to the Bosporus. The conditions were much worse than they had been down the coast of Bulgaria; Ali was finding it difficult to avoid hitting various parts of herself on the aluminium console and she kept asking to go ashore. I had to explain that there were no entry ports on the coast so we needed to press on to Turkey. She became resigned to the discomfort until we saw the cliffs of the Bosporus, at which point we turned right, then the wind was behind us and the seas calmed down. Ali was thrilled to be with all the ships in this famous waterway and to see Asia on our port side. We carried on down the Bosphorus, enjoying the castles on the right until we reached Istanbul. This was totally chaotic with large ferries coming and going and as the port at Istanbul was no place for a RIB we headed on to the Ataköy Marina. We took a night off to stay at the Holiday Inn next to the marina. We went into Istanbul where Ali treated herself to a Turkish bath. I walked the streets, remembering the first time I had been here, some thirty years earlier in 1974. I was pleased to see that the Blue Mosque and the Grand Bazaar and the Hagia Sophia all looked much the same as they did then.

As we readied ourselves to leave the next morning, Ali noticed the couple in the boat next to ours taking pictures of us. It seemed that they were intrigued by our somewhat unorthodox starting technique without ignition switches, when I would lie on the port engine with the hatch up in order to short the solenoid, and then do the same with the starboard engine as Ali cast off. With the process complete, we waved goodbye to them and set off to cross the Sea of Marmara, passing through the Dardanelles Strait and tying up at Çanakkale in Asia, the fifth continent I had visited with *Ribaleta*.

It was time for us to enter the choppy waters of the Aegean Sea and make our way to Greece. As the light began to fade, we had to use eyeball navigation to pick out the islands as my Navionic chart plotter had failed. I was relying on the chart on the screen and eyeballing from that, eventually coming to a small and sheltered bay in Limnos. We grilled the fresh mackerel we had bought in Çanakkale and then fell asleep to the chiming of the bell from the nearby Greek Orthodox church.

Breakfast the next day was brief. Ahead of us lay days of island hopping, and we wanted to make a start. First, we motored from Limnos to Lesbos, tying up in Molyvos, a small fishing village with restaurants lining the quayside. We left the boat to walk up to the hilltop castle, but when we returned, we found the harbour police waiting for us. It turned out that Molyvos was not a port of entry and, since we had no papers, we were not supposed to be there. When we said we were having engine trouble and that it was now too late for us to find anywhere else, the police let us stay for the night, on condition that we did not leave *Ribaleta*. We agreed and then, once they had gone, sneaked off to a nearby restaurant for a dinner of baked lamb in herbs.

The police came back to see us again the next morning, informing us that we had to go to Mitilini on the south-east coast of Lesbos to go through the correct customs and immigration procedures. Fortunately, since *Ribaleta* is one centimetre under ten metres long, it was exempt from a complicated transit log, and we were cleared fairly quickly. Still concerned about the water-cooling pipe, I made a few calls to try and track down the Yanmar representative in Piraeus, but it was impossible to locate him. Ahead of us was the long open-water crossing to the Sporades, so we decided to rest for one more night and found a small and quiet bay to moor. We had our dinner at a table on the quay, eating souvlaki and dolmades and drinking wine while the fishermen mended their nets below. The chef of the restaurant took a shine to Ali, bringing her a posy of roses and herbs.

The next day, feeling refreshed, we set off to cross the Aegean, driving close to the coast of Skyros on the way. We anchored off a deserted island, and then followed the coast of Evia down to Lavrion. We continued on to Athens but, unfortunately, the main marina was closed in preparation for the upcoming Olympics. We were, however, able to tie up in a smaller marina. Visiting the Acropolis that afternoon was wonderful to see, even though it was covered in scaffolding.

After Athens, we made a whirlwind islands tour, from Hydra to Poros to Spetses and then, finally, to the entrance of the Corinth Canal. We tied up to complete all the necessary paperwork and wait for the eastbound traffic to clear. We then took advantage of an offer from a small truck to refuel. Once the final cargo ship had passed through, the road bridge reopened and, along with a local fisherman and an Australian couple yachting around the world, we entered the canal. I had sailed Caleta through here in the 1970s and now, on board *Ribaleta* and much closer to the water, the 300-foot walls looked even more impressive.

We came out into the Gulf of Corinth at around 3.00 p.m., just in time to be met by the afternoon wind, which whipped up the water into waves that broke over us. The port navigation light broke and I had to reduce speed to just 11 knots. When we rounded a flat and rocky islet off the coast of Galaxidi, the waters grew calm again and we moored at the town. Once more, the rough seas had made us keen to spend another night off *Ribaleta*, so we booked into a local pension. The overall beauty of Galaxidi, an old shipbuilding town where a hundred years earlier some of Greece's best sailing boats were built, encouraged us take a day off. We used it to visit the temple at Delphi and take in its views of Mount Parnassus and its green foothills.

We did not have long left in Greece before our northward leg up the Adriatic to Venice. So we left early the following day, stopping at Nafpaktos to visit its Roman port and then crossing into the Gulf of Patras to see Missolonghi with its famous salt marshes and fishermen's huts built on stilts. The Gulf of Patras led us into the wide Ionian Sea and we continued on to Ithaca and Cephalonia. We spent that night in Argostoli, famous for two things: as the home of *Captain Corelli's Mandolin*, and as the place where 9,000 Italian troops were massacred by their German 'allies' during the Second World War.

We spent time exploring the coastlines of Cephalonia and Lefkada, an area with lots of little bays and harbours. It is well known amongst the boating community as a wonderful place for both yachts and RIBs. Then we passed through the Lefkas Canal to stop for the night at Preveza where, astonishingly, I was stopped by a couple cycling along the harbour. 'Didn't we see you in Tunis in 2001?' they asked. 'Yes, you did,' I replied, amazed at the coincidence.

With just one day left in Greece, we stopped for lunch on the small island of Paxos before arriving at our final destination: Corfu. We tied up in the old harbour of Corfu Town and went out, wandering amongst the jacaranda trees and the charming old buildings, and then ate dinner in a quiet piazza, enjoying the warm Greek evening.

◯ ◯ ◯

The previous time I had sailed in the Adriatic it had been in *Caleta* in the mid-1970s, and back then I had made sure to give Albania a wide berth for fear of the mines listed as dangerous on my charts. Much had changed in that country since then, but it still didn't have a good reputation. When we arrived at the port city of Sarandë and were met by two police in a battered RIB with three Mercury 275s on the back, we both grew slightly anxious.

For two hours, we were at their mercy. The problem was that they weren't used to tourists arriving in their own boats and, as a result, they had no idea what to do with us. A number of times, various 'agents' came to give us advice and to demand payment. But we refused all their demands, and eventually we were allowed to go without giving anyone any money.

There was a small yacht in Sarandë harbour belonging to a German couple. We started talking to them and decided to share a taxi to Butrint, a UNESCO World Heritage site of ruins dating back to Roman and even ancient Greek times. From there, a narrow and winding road led us across the mountains to Gjirokastër: an Ottoman town with a well-preserved fortress, and the birthplace of Albania's former communist leader, Enver Hoxha. We saw several of the 750,000 fortifications that he built in his Stalinist fanaticism to protect his country from attack. They were usually in groups of four, with the commander in the top one at the back and the other three lower down the hill. The lower ones usually had three openings, two in the front to shoot through, and one at the back to get orders or possibly be shot at by the commander in the top one. The cost of all these impoverished the whole country to its present state.

We set off from Sarandë early the next morning, driving through thick fog which slowed us as we followed Albania's coast north. We had intended to stop at Durrës, the country's main port, but when we arrived, we found it to be a miserable and unappealing commercial shipyard, and not the kind of place where we wanted to spend the night. So, instead, we went back out to sea and continued north to the Buna River-Velipoja Protected Landscape, which lies on the border between Albania and Montenegro. This extensive reserve, of approximately 1,700 acres, is home to a great many migratory waterbirds, and forms a large wetland spreading out from the Buna River. Although we had no charts or guides, nor papers for either country, we decided to motor up the river. I was certain that, if I kept a close eye on the depth sounder, we would be fine. And we were. The river took us 20 miles inland, and as we glided along, we were surprised by the contrasting scenes on both banks. To the left, Montenegro looked quaint and rural, with farmers gathering hay and loading it on to carts; to the right, Albania appeared affluent with large and expensive-looking houses. When the river eventually became too shallow for us to continue, we turned round and headed back to the mouth of the Buna.

In 2004, Montenegro was not the independent country it is today, but was part of a federation with Serbia. Two years later, it declared independence after a referendum, the last of the ex-Yugoslav states to finally break its ties with Belgrade. Thus, we saw it in the final days of its long union with Serbia, it having changed little since I first visited in *Caleta*, when Tito was still alive and in power. We motored into the Bay of Kotor and moored beside the old town. Climbing up to the fortress which overlooks Kotor was not as easy for me as it had been in the 1970s, but the view from the top was just as spectacular.

Montenegro was able to declare independence peacefully, but for Croatia it had not been as simple. We left Kotor to drive north and stopped at the entrance to the old harbour in Dubrovnik, which had been bombed by the Serbs but was now restored. We couldn't enter the harbour as private boats were prohibited, but we found a more modern marina in a bay beside the city. We spent the rest of the day in Dubrovnik, walking round the walls of the old town and soaking up its history.

Like Greece, Croatia is perfect for island hopping. We made our way to the first island, Korčula, not far from the mainland and with its own Venetian walled town, similar to a smaller Dubrovnik. After walking along its cobbled streets, we came back to *Ribaleta* to find that the mooring line had broken. We had left it tied to an open quay, but the forward bow cleat had been torn out of the deck and had sunk to the seabed. It was fortunate that the captain of a nearby charter boat had seen it happen and had jumped aboard to stop *Ribaleta* drifting out to sea. We thanked him profusely after he explained what had happened. 'At certain stages of the tide,' he said, 'a surge rushes under the jetty and everything gets sucked under.'

We left Korčula and motored north to the tranquil island of Hvar. There we anchored in a small bay and, after checking everything carefully, left *Ribaleta* to go and explore the main town, with its Gothic palaces and marble streets free from cars. It is another example of a fortified Venetian town, showing how much of the Adriatic was under Venetian rule.

Heading back to the mainland again, we arrived at Split. The town quay was virtually empty and we had no problems tying up. We bought some delicious pastries from street vendors and then spent a long time exploring the remarkable fourth-century Diocletian's Palace. By this point, it occurred to us that we had seen rather a lot of historic sites, so we followed the coast round to Šibenik Bay and entered the inlet taking us towards the Krka National Park. The river entrance to the park itself was closed to private boats, so we anchored in a small bay near Skradin and then took a tour boat into the park. The tour was lovely, culminating in a waterfall which flowed over rocks and carved out deep plunge-pools.

Our final stop in Croatia was an island called Brijuni. It was in the north of the Adriatic fairly close to the Slovenian border, and we probably would not have chosen to go there at all if it weren't for the fact that Ali's sister, Kathron Sturrock, a classical pianist, was playing a concert there the following night. Brijuni is actually an archipelago of fourteen islands, and for thirty years it was known as 'Tito's playground', where he would often spend six months of each year living an extraordinarily luxurious lifestyle. When Tito died, Brijuni was turned into a national park. 'Rather like Richmond Park,' Ali's brother-in-law, Professor David Bennett, had said. 'Acres of green grass, broad-leaved trees and lots of deer. But Richmond doesn't have Roman ruins or peacocks.' David was a consultant neurologist and had brought a group of doctors to Brijuni who liked the idea of a ride on *Ribaleta*. When asked if they wanted a comfortable or adventurous ride, three chose the latter. They lay on the front bunk but after going over three waves which lifted and then crashed them back on to the bunk cushion, they decided to go for the comfortable ride, after which I slowed down.

Kathron, who had trained under Alfred Brendel, played a superb concert, which was a fitting end to our time in Croatia. The following day, we set off early towards Venice, our final destination. The morning was grey and overcast, with a fresh wind and small swells for us to bounce over. It took two hours for us to reach the breakwater and enter the main marked channel for St Mark's Square. We headed into the Grand Canal and then passed under the Rialto and Accademia bridges. *Ribaleta* was too big to go under the Bridge of Sighs, so named by Lord Byron in the

Ali and Charles in the Alps

nineteenth century. Weaving through numerous gondolas, we found a post to tie up to and walked along rickety boards to a canalside restaurant. The moment we stepped on to dry land in Venice, thunder sounded, followed by a torrential downpour.

Once the rain had stopped, we returned to the boat and headed out of the city in search of a marina. We found one on a peninsula ten miles away at Cavallino. It had a good slipway, which was important as we would be bringing the Unimog here to haul *Ribaleta* out of the water. We ate fresh fish for dinner, had a good night's sleep, and the next morning caught a ferry across the lagoon to the station at Venice. Our adventure was over, but there was still a long way to go before we arrived home. First, we had to take a train through the Alps to Austria and then a taxi to the Unimog itself, and then drive back to Venice and load *Ribaleta* on the trailer. It was covered in weed and slime as it had no antifouling. We had to scrub this off while it was wet and easier to remove. Finally, we drove the Unimog and *Ribaleta* on to the motorway up through Italy and into the mountains of Germany. The hills slowed us down to about 20 miles an hour on the motorways and, as HGVs are not allowed in the fast lanes, we held up the German economy for about two hours. The first truck to pass us was a 500-horsepower Greek truck; five miles further on we passed its driver talking to a police officer. We soon arrived at Calais and could look back with great satisfaction at having motored *Ribaleta* 3,500 miles and driven the Unimog only 300 miles to circumnavigate the Balkans.

CHAPTER THIRTY-SEVEN
RIBALETA AND THE RED SEA

I had begun to race *Ribaleta* more often with BIBOA, and in 2006 John Puddifoot, the race director of the Royal Yachting Association, told me that the RYA was organising a rally in the Red Sea. He asked if I would like to join and, as it sounded like fun, I agreed. It was, after all, free entry and free transport.

It was not until later that I learnt that the rally was actually a race, a race with a few minor modifications and reduced safety measures. Some of the smaller boats were 20 miles an hour faster than *Ribaleta*, and I was going to be put into the biggest and fastest class. It was all beginning to sound a little too crazy to me, so I suggested to the organiser that maybe I shouldn't enter as *Ribaleta* was too slow. Refusing to take no for an answer, John continued to encourage me, repeating how much fun it would be, until I eventually agreed to enter.

I trailed *Ribaleta* down to Southampton where it was loaded, complete with the trailer, on to a ship. At Cairo, the Egyptian organisers put it on a road trailer and drove down to our hotel at Sharm El-Sheikh. We then all flew out together as a group, and a bus collected us from the airport to take us to our first hotel. I had last been to Egypt eleven years earlier on my 1995 Unimog trip with Sarah, and it was good to be back. The bus ride taught me the strange signalling systems here, how the right indicator means 'I'm turning right' and the left indicator means 'Get off the road'.

It seemed a well-organised and luxurious bus ride, even by BIBOA's standards, and when we arrived at the hotel, I asked why we were being so well looked after. 'The Egyptians think you're a member of Parliament,' I was told. 'It's because of your title. They assume any 'Sir' must be an MP. If there's any trouble and a Member of the British parliament is involved, it would have a disastrous effect on the tourist industry here. So, you are being given VIP treatment.'

In Sharm El-Sheikh a notorious terrorist attack had happened just one year earlier, so when we arrived at the main gate of our hotel, we were carefully scrutinised both on the road and then again inside the hotel. It was rather tedious, but we were glad that such trouble was being taken with our safety.

The following morning, it was time to launch the boats. Because *Ribaleta* was the heaviest, I had to be nearest to the crane. We all went out for a test run, and it was then I realised that Paul Lemmer, my crew for the race, had put the propellers on the wrong engines. I had to take the boat out again to change them over.

On the first day of the race, as I made my way to the start line, one engine stopped because of water in the fuel. Fortunately, the organisers delayed the start while we cleared it and, once the engine was running smoothly, we could line up all the boats.

Line-up of racing boats with Ribaleta *to the left*

I kept *Ribaleta* well to one side as I didn't want any of the smaller boats hitting my wash. While *Ribaleta* was gathering speed, I couldn't see anything in front of me. Since my boat was so much heavier, I needed to be certain that no other boats strayed in front of me – if I hit them, it would be disastrous. Thankfully, all the boats started safely, and we were off.

The weather was quite rough and, as such, the smaller boats weren't able to reach their maximum speeds. This gave us an advantage, and soon *Ribaleta* was near the front, following a professional Greek boat and a smart English race boat. We headed from the Gulf of Aqaba across the Red Sea to mainland Egypt. We were doing well, but then unfortunately more water got in the fuel. Nevertheless, by the end of the first day, we managed to come third, which was very satisfying and much better than I had expected.

That evening, we stayed in a different luxury hotel, and once again were given five-star treatment, courtesy of the Egyptian government. When we set off for the second leg of the race the following day, the weather was still rough and the propeller safety clutch failed as a result of changing the propellers. I knew that Paul was going to have to get into the water to change it, but it was too rough.

'Use your powers to calm the sea,' I said to Paul, who was a Seventh Day Adventist and very religious. My joke made him rather indignant. 'Don't worry,' I continued, 'I'll calm it myself in half an hour.' This made Paul laugh.

I knew that my chart was good and I could see that there were reefs nearby. I drove *Ribaleta* behind a reef and, sure enough, the water was calm, as I had predicted. Paul got into the water and changed the propeller clutch.

All this delay made us late, yet we still managed to come third at the end of that leg.

The third day was even rougher. We were racing downwind and, even though I was concentrating hard, the irregular wave frequency caught me out. We went straight over one wave then through the next and under eight feet of water, submerging us entirely. It was even worse than the dive in the Caribbean with Ali. This time, Paul's visor broke and cut his forehead, and he was lucky to have survived, with seawater driving at 25 miles an hour into his face. I cleared the ton of water out of the boat in about 15 seconds as before and we were able to carry on, but went slower, zigzagging across the waves at an angle but still racing.

The next day was a lay day. Paul and I needed to spend time repairing *Ribaleta*. His wife Paula and Ali, who had come along for the ride, decided to go on a shopping tour in the port. They were accompanied throughout the tour by two men wearing thick suits which were absurdly unsuitable for the hot Egyptian weather. It turned out that the men were wearing the suits to conceal handguns in their belts – they were armed escorts. The VIP security I had been given as a Member of Parliament was clearly being extended to wives and partners.

Paul and I managed to repair the boat, which was a great relief. That evening, the BIBOA racing committee announced that, with the final race still to go, I had won the BIBOA World Championship. This was very special, especially as *Ribaleta* was a heavy cruising boat, two or three times the weight of any other boat in the race.

On our final day, the weather was fairly calm. Unfortunately, we still suffered water problems, perhaps caused by taking diesel from 40-gallon oil drums during the race. When we crossed the finishing line we were once more in third place behind the professionals, but I was still very pleased as *Ribaleta* was the first British boat to finish. We found out later that we had actually been penalised 500 points on the second day because the Egyptian organisers were sure we were going to hit a reef. I knew for certain that we were not going to hit the reef as I had seen it clearly, but it didn't affect the result. We had a wonderful party at the end of it all, where the Egyptian tourism minister gave a speech and we received a winner's garland. All that remained was to haul the boats out of the water the following morning.

As we made our way home, we agreed that it had been a wonderful experience, and very kind of the Egyptian government to put it all on for us and give us VIP treatment as well.

CHAPTER THIRTY-EIGHT
THE LAST RIBALETA TRIP

After exploring the Orinoco Delta, cruising down the Danube and racing in the Red Sea, it seems appropriate that my last trip in *Ribaleta* was across the English Channel.

Launching from Lymington, I had a calm and sunny ride across to Sark, where I picked up a mooring in the bay and took my little dinghy to tie up to the steps to climb on to the island. I took a lovely walk along the top of the island, enjoying the fact that there were no cars. I looked down at the beaches, but the descents were far too steep to tempt me down. Sark seemed to me to be unique, in that it was a British island totally free from traffic with lots of sunshine and little shops selling drinks and ice cream.

The next morning, I set off, hoping to make my way through the Minquiers. Just south of Jersey these are a group of 365 islands at low water and 52 at high water due to the 14-metre tide. I had been through them before, following a local guide in a RIB. I hoped that, this time, I could do it on my own, but by the time I arrived the tide had begun to fall too fast with a strong possibility that I could end up aground. Instead, I tried to find a route round a little islet amongst the rocks. Keeping a close eye on the depth sounder and the movement of the sea around the rocks, I was able to avoid the underwater rocks and make it through. This was satisfying as not only was my route uncharted, but it also saved me a long trip out and around the islands.

Deep water took me across to the Chausey Islands off the coast of Normandy. I headed for a wide but shallow pass that had just enough water and then crossed into a passage on the western half of the biggest island, coming past Grande-Île, the main town to a little anchorage at the top of the channel. I took the dinghy to the rocks, climbed over them and, there before me, where just two hours before I had been driving *Ribaleta*, were 300 yards of yellow sand. The 14-metre tide had dried the wide sea channel to become a large beach. Local men walked across it, digging in the sand for worms and shellfish.

When the tide came in, I made my way down to the Brittany coast, where I passed through a lock at Dinard and then up a canal towards Dinan. The water was not what I had expected; the tide should have been coming in, but it was still low. I saw a notice board at the top of a wall so climbed up to have a look. It seemed that the waterway I had driven up was within a tidal barrage on the River Rance and, since it was designed to produce electricity, it was planned so that the tide was high enough outside before opening the gates to ensure maximum power from the turbines. Therefore, the tide heights were not natural but were, in fact, controlled by the electricity board.

I spent the night there, and was lucky not to have fallen down on the concrete, as there were no lights or barriers to protect people from the 20-foot fall into the water. When the gates opened in the morning, I drove along the canal through the French countryside to stop below Dinan, a lovely, fortified town. I went up to see the local church as I had been told that there was a medieval stained-glass window there which depicted one of my distant French cousins.

Back in *Ribaleta*, I continued further up the canal into rural countryside but decided to turn back at the picturesque village of Évran. I spent the night in the canal waiting for the lagoon to fill up before the lock opened the next day. A French boat was next to me, and the skipper told me that the forecast for the following day was bad. The winds were south-westerly Force 6 backing north-westerly 7 to 8. It sounded so terrible that I had to make a choice. I could go to a hotel in St Malo for a few days and wait for it all to pass, or I could risk a hazardous drive back. As I've never overcome my aversion to hotels or rain-soaked French towns, I decided to risk the latter option.

With my dry suit on, I headed north towards England. I hoped *Ribaleta* and I could manage the weather, but if it became too bad, I knew I could at least run downwind to Cherbourg. The Alderney Race, the strait that runs from Cap de la Hague in Normandy to Alderney, was luckily quite calm, but once I cleared Alderney the full Force 6 wind and seas hit me. I headed north-west and stayed upwind in case it became even stronger. I managed to maintain about 20 knots, but I was being passed slowly by the Channel ferry to Poole and I couldn't turn east until it had gone ahead of me. The wind and the waves increased as I turned downwind towards the Solent. I was short of power on the port engine and the waves were too steep for me to go straight up the back of them, so I had to go up at an angle and then speed up as I went down the face of the waves. This happened repeatedly until finally I neared the Needles and the waves became small enough to climb them. I headed straight into the Solent with a Force 8 gale behind me.

At Lymington, I tried to turn round, but it was impossible to go into the wind and I realised then just how strong it was. I had been lucky to make it back in such conditions. It made me really appreciate just how great a boat *Ribaleta* was. The cruise contained all the best types of RIBbing in one trip. I had seen summer sunshine, little Channel Islands, French countryside and culture, and then bad weather and an exhilarating ride home; no other boat could have handled such a varied adventure.

I hauled *Ribaleta* out of the water at Lymington and put it on to the trailer. At this stage, I had to go through my routine of jacking up the wheels on each side and finding out which bearings had the most play. I then took that wheel off the hub, took the hub off and replaced it with my spare hub, which had had a new bearing fitted at the farm with my 50-ton press. Then, finally, I tightened up the hub with a three-foot-long bar. Once that was done, I was able to start the Unimog and begin the slow drive home.

After towing a five-ton trailer with no working brakes for five years, I felt my luck might soon run out. When I arrived home, I weighed the trailer and discovered that all the axles were 25 per cent overloaded and that the brakes had been corroded by salt water. It was clear that I had to upgrade the trailer, but this was easier said than done. My submersible axles were the heaviest available in Europe so I looked online to see if I could find in America the perfect set of disc-braked axles. I did, but no supplier in America would ship such axles to England. Eventually, I found a friend who was due to travel to America and who would order them to be sent to his American address, from where the axles could be shipped to me in England. Then, with my guidance, my farm mechanic could rebuild the axle frame to fit my chassis and convert them from electric to air operation to conform with English law.

Twice, before I started checking the bearings for each trip, wheels had come off while I was driving on the road. Luckily, they did not hit anything or anyone. I had to cut the axles in half and bolt them together so that, if one hub broke, I was able to change half an axle with the boat on the trailer. Otherwise, the boat had to be taken off the trailer by a crane to enable the whole axle to be removed and replaced. I count myself lucky not to have had any inspections with my modified axles or to have hit anybody with high-speed self-steering wheels.

PART VI:
FURTHER ADVENTURES

With Clare on motorbikes on the Dalton Highway

CHAPTER THIRTY-NINE
EARTHWATCH

In the early 2000s, I began to work quite closely with an organisation called Earthwatch. An international environmental charity, Earthwatch is dedicated to conserving the planet by teaming up various people to conduct expeditions and research together. Since I had been a scientist at school and university, I found their work appealing and decided to offer my help. I was keen to get involved in wildlife research if I could do anything useful; Earthwatch would also give me the opportunity to visit places that were out of bounds for private individuals and tour companies.

The first expedition I joined was a project to monitor the survival of the crocodiles which live in the Zambezi River. Our objective was to ensure that the natural population of crocodiles was healthy and continued to grow, while also allowing the local people to collect their eggs. Both elements were important: the locals relied upon the money they made from selling the eggs to crocodile farms, and it was crucial that they kept it sustainable and didn't endanger the future of wild crocodiles.

To monitor the reptiles, we would set out on the Zambezi at night, taking small boats along its tributaries and looking out for baby crocodiles to catch. We had a researcher on board our boat, and it was up to her to ascertain whether the crocodiles were less than two-and-a-half feet long. If so, the students were allowed to catch them by hand. If they were any bigger, then the researchers needed to use a noose.

The catching followed a pattern. First, we would creep up on the crocodile as we dazzled it with our light, and then one person would grab it behind the neck, snatch it out of the water and bring it into the boat, where another person would tape its jaws shut. Following that, we had to weigh and measure it, sometimes taking samples from the gut to see what it had been eating. Finally, we would clip off one of the spikes on its tail to show it had been caught before releasing it back into the water.

It was a good system and generally worked well, until one day one of the fellow volunteers on my boat dropped his crocodile before we had a chance to tape its jaws. All of a sudden, we were faced with the danger of a snapping crocodile in the boat. I came very close to putting my foot on it, but fortunately another of the volunteers was quick to take control of the situation. He was the reptile curator of a zoo and neatly picked up the crocodile, being used to this sort of thing. I was grateful he was with us, although there had been other times when I found him rather strange. Once, he told us that a snake had bitten his cheek and that he knew that, as long as he was patient, it would eventually let him go. Another time, he spoke passionately about his concern for the environment and his belief that overpopulation was going to ruin us all. To prevent him helping this process at 19 years old he had been vasectomised.

It was interesting to be so closely involved with the crocodiles, and I enjoyed working with them. What was less enjoyable were the swarms of insects everywhere. These existed in such quantities that whenever I tried to take photographs they came out as a blur of insects. We didn't have any protection so hoped that none of the mosquitos carried malaria.

One day, we spent hours with two car springs, trying to bolt them together with rudimentary tools to set a trap to catch larger crocodiles. We heard the trap go off twice during the expedition, but we never did catch a large crocodile. I was relieved, as if we had caught one, I had no idea what we were supposed to do with it. The smaller ones we caught on the boat were powerful enough.

At the end of this particular expedition, I made a few safaris in the Okavango Delta in northern Botswana. These included flights to each of the lodges, which were built clear of the ground, since part of the tenancy agreement was that they left no impressions when removed. I stayed in magnificent rooms in the trees, surrounded by glass with a view of the plains, so high up that nobody could see inside.

Each of these lodges, which were only accessible by air, offered superb game drives. Also, excellent food was served, although after dinner you had to be escorted back to your room as all the walkways could easily be accessed by big cats and other wild animals. Even buffalo often slept under some of the covered walkways. It was a far more luxurious holiday than I was used to, but the cost was surprisingly low. Three weeks earlier, on the 11th of September 2001, two terrorist planes had crashed into and destroyed the Twin Towers in New York, following which nobody wanted to fly to tourist destinations.

○ ○ ○

LEFT: *Ali standing in the Peruvian jungle having used dug outs in the flooded jungle.*

RIGHT: *Preparing to go exploring in the dug outs.*

My second expedition with Earthwatch took me to the Peruvian Amazon, specifically to the Lago Preto Conservation Concession on the Yavari River. This is situated in one of the remotest areas of the Amazon, and is home to the red uakari monkey. I took Ali with me as she could speak both Spanish and Portuguese.

We flew to Iquitos, the gateway to the jungle, and then made a two-day boat trip down the Amazon on a restored cruising boat originally built for the rubber barons of the nineteenth century who had a monopoly of the trade and, with rubber money, built the famous opera house in Manaus. They lost their monopoly when a brave Kew Gardens botanist sailed to Manaus to collect seeds of the rubber trees and was reputed to have made the customs officers so drunk that they signed off the cargo, enabling a new rubber industry to form in Malaysia. Moored on the banks of a small creek, the old rubber boat was our accommodation, with cabins down below and a deck above over which stretched an awning where we relaxed in the evenings watching the river and enjoying all the wildlife choruses. We took dugout canoes daily into the rainforest. It was the wet season, and the river had flooded over its banks to flow between the trees. There were various islands on higher ground in the forest where the ground-dwelling wildlife stayed until the dry season returned and the waters receded. We paddled for 2 miles in our dugouts between the islands, counting the numbers of monkeys and birds on each.

It was great fun conducting research about the uakari monkey and counting their population. We had many opportunities to take trips down the river, where we would find spectacularly coloured green and red macaws feeding on the salt cliffs and saw, on a couple of lucky occasions, river dolphins.

After the research was finished, we began to head back up the Amazon. Suddenly, a gunboat approached, demanding that we stop. It occurred to me that this was the part of the river which formed the border between Brazil and Peru, and I noticed that the soldiers who boarded our boat to question us were Brazilian. As Ali spoke Portuguese, she knew what they were saying and assured me that the gunboat was just stopping us out of curiosity. They did not stay for long and we were able to resume our way on the river.

Unfortunately, the organisers realised that our boat was going too slowly against the current, and was not going to bring us back in time for our flights. We changed boats at Leticia and we took a speedboat all the way upriver to Iquitos. As we sped back up the river I kept my dream alive of building a steel dugout in England in three sections with a waterjet engine in the stern and fuel and accommodation in the other and shipping it out to Iquitos in a container where it could be assembled and launched. The dream would take us down the Amazon up the Rio Negro into the Casiquiare which connects to the Orinoco to Trinidad. It was fun to dream, but I soon realised it would be far too risky and expensive, and that adventure never became more than a dream.

◎ ◎ ◎

My third and final Earthwatch trip, also with Ali, was to the African savanna, where we were to observe the ecology and behaviour of the lions which lived in and around the Tsavo National Parks. Both Tsavo East and Tsavo West are national game parks, but we camped on a private conservation area to the south of Tsavo West. During the nights we drove two old Land Rovers inside the conservation area, scanning with searchlights and recording everything we saw. It was great fun and,

LEFT: Our rubber baron boat in which we cruised down the Amazon

RIGHT: Locals crossing the river in an Amazon sunset

undisturbed by the tourists, we could drive over all the area at night, searching mainly for lions but recording all the wildlife we saw. The bush babies were the easiest to spot, for although they had small bodies, they had large reflective eyes which lit up under our searchlights. Elephants, on the other hand, were virtually impossible to see. Even at a distance of 30 yards we often missed them, as their pure grey colour did not reflect the light.

The lead researcher on our expedition was called Dr Bruce Patterson. He shared a surname with Colonel John Henry Patterson, author of the book *The Man-Eaters of Tsavo*. He was no relation, but there were a number of connections between the two men. For one, Bruce was the curator of mammals at the Field Museum of Natural History in Chicago, where the two man-eating lions from the book are currently displayed. Similarly, Bruce had actually written a book about that book, called *The Lions of Tsavo*.

The original book, which came out in 1907, recounted Colonel Patterson's experiences of a pair of man-eating lions which, at the time, were said to have been the only things halting the expansion of the British Empire. Patterson had been overseeing the construction of a railway bridge between Mombasa and Nairobi when the two lions began eating his Indian workers, devouring them after pulling them out of their tents. It is said that, in total, these two lions ate 135 people. Those who were not attacked refused to work while the lions were still at large, stopping the construction of the railway. It was only when Patterson finally killed both of the man-eaters, after waiting up for them many nights beside a tethered goat, that the work resumed.

One of our lions had been radio-collared, and we searched the savanna with a radio antenna to see if we could find it; sadly, we never did. We never found out whether it had moved out of the territory or was dead. Nevertheless, we still had some exciting night drives through the dry African bush trying to follow other lions who seemed undeterred by our presence. Once, we were able to watch them with our searchlight as they drank together from a water hole.

The area adjacent to the reserves we searched at night was privately owned by two brothers who had different ideas about how to manage their land. One was keen on conserving the wildlife, whereas the other brother just wanted to make money by allowing cattle to graze there. The cattle herders who came on to the land were Somalis. They had little respect for the law and herded their cattle into *bomas*, a kind of enclosed compound surrounded by thorn bushes. One night, we passed one of these *bomas* to see three semi-naked Somalis banging tin cans and waving hurricane lamps to try and drive the lions away. It was a rather primeval sight.

We had some wonderful experiences searching for these wild lions and watching them so close. One night, we followed a pride through the forest for three hours before returning for supper. It was incredible seeing them in the night without their being disturbed, living their normal pride lives.

Another night, we followed two lions after driving them through the bush towards a water hole where we watched them drinking side by side in the searchlight. After too much use of the searchlight our truck refused to start when we wanted to return to the camp. The lions were just 20 yards away, and none of us were prepared to volunteer to push the truck when the lions were so close. The other truck was able to start, so it reversed towards us, backing up until the spare wheel on its back door touched the spare wheel on our back door. With a push from the other truck, our truck started. After that, we made sure to keep our engine running when we had our searchlights on.

A big yawn from a lioness in the Tsavo Park in Kenya.

We were right to be fearful of the lions, and when close to them, we never left our vehicles, being well aware of their stealth and strength. At one point, we spotted a lion in the grass about 20 yards away. We looked away but when we looked back, we could no longer see it. We knew it was still there, but it had completely disappeared. It was amazing to see how well lions could hide in fairly short grass.

Towards the end of the expedition, we were given a day off, and used it to visit the Tsavo East Park. It was then that we saw just how badly it was being run. There were vehicles everywhere, and as soon as a guide spotted a lion a call would be put out on the radios and all the vehicles would desperately try to move in front of each other for a better view. It was a distressing sight, and it made us all appreciate how fortunate we were to be able to observe these wild animals at night, often at unusually close quarters. And we were particularly lucky to have been a part of that Earthwatch expedition. Not long afterwards, conflicts with the cattle eventually drove the lions out of the area and, sadly, the research project came to an end.

CHAPTER FORTY
SCIENTIFIC EXPLORATIONS
PART I: IN SEARCH OF RAJA GAJ, NEPAL

As well as Earthwatch, I have also been involved with the Scientific Exploration Society (SES) for many years. This is a British charity which sends scientific expeditions around the world; I have been fortunate enough to join a few. The society was started by Colonel John Blashford-Snell CBE in 1969 after he had organised the first navigation of the Ethiopian Blue Nile. In 1972 he completed the first North to South American land journey across the Darién Gap, testing the then-new Range Rover.

My first expedition was in 2001 to Bardia National Park in Nepal. This involved a week of river-rafting on the Kanali River and then another week riding elephants. Unfortunately, just before I left England to fly out to Nepal, Maoist terrorists killed a government minister and several civil servants in the town from which we were planning to raft. Therefore, not surprisingly, the area was suddenly deemed too dangerous to visit.

Nonetheless, I still flew out to Nepal before the SES expedition began and made a short trekking trip followed by a rafting trip. The amount of equipment the porters had to carry just for my trip was daunting, even more so when my guide casually threw his backpack on top of the porter's load. Despite this, it turned out to be a wonderful trek and I wanted to repeat it. I then had three days of white-water rafting and camping on the riverbank, which was exciting with its inevitable capsizes and the joy of being in really wild places.

After my rafting trip, I joined the main group at a camp which had been built specially for us just outside Bardia National Park. It was an incredibly complex and luxurious base for all sixteen of us to stay in. The hot showers were proof of that. Half-oil drums were placed over open fires and filled with water. The water was then scooped up into the shower bucket and cold water added to give the perfect temperature. The bucket was then hoisted up a tree and the valve turned to give a luxury shower. Since we would be travelling by elephant, additional facilities needed to be

provided for them, as well as for their mahouts and handlers, whose job it was to collect food for the elephants and generally ensure that they were well looked after. And, of course, there were the camp cooking staff, who were the ones that ensured we were well looked after.

On the first morning, we set out from the camp with four people in a howdah, a sort of carriage, on each elephant's back. Behind the howdah was the guide, and in front of it, the mahout, the rider, sat on the elephant's neck, controlling the animal with his bare feet. Unfortunately, the mahouts also carried steel spikes in their hands if they needed to reprimand the elephants. Needless to say, I preferred it when they just used their feet.

LEFT: *With Colonel John Blashford-Snell enjoying an evening meal in Bardia National Park.*

RIGHT: *Our expedition party riding elephants in Bardia National Park*

Watching the local wildlife whilst riding elephants in Bardia National Park

The whole Raja Gaj team mounted on elephants.

We were on a quest to find local elephants. One in particular, known as Raja Gaj, which translates as 'King Elephant', was famed in these parts, and stories about him had an almost mythical quality. The largest Asian elephant in modern times, he was 11 feet 3 inches tall and had a massive body weight. Many thought he was in fact a mammoth, although this was later disproved; he was just an exceptionally large elephant. He had two large domes on his head, unlike any other elephant, which gave the impression of a mammoth, but which after his death were accepted as just growths. He lived in Bardia National Park, and is believed to have been about seventy years old when he died in 2007.

It soon became clear that Bardia was a land of huge elephants. As we tracked one large bull, our guide moved too close, provoking him to charge us. Fortunately, our mahout was able to stop the attack by turning our elephant away in submission. It was important to be aware of just how wild elephants can be. In many of the game parks and wildlife reserves, there are often problems between the elephants and the locals, which in Bardia are sometimes fatal. We were told about one such recent death when a rogue elephant had wandered into a nearby village, taken an unsuspecting child from the top floor of a house and then killed him. We went to the village to offer our condolences and see if we could do anything to help. When we met the mother, we were rather surprised at how little concern she showed for the loss of her child. Being English, it

was difficult for us to come to terms with the fact that local families are so large that not all children are expected to survive to adulthood.

Although some elephants, especially lone males, can be dangerous, they can also be kind and even playful. One day, we rode our elephants across a river, which was deep enough to rise halfway up their sides. I began to grow concerned that the river would become so deep that we all might fall into the water, but fortunately it didn't happen, and we reached the other side safely. Once across the river, we went to visit a local school. It was modern and had been built to typical English-schoolhouse standards, with four walls, a roof and small windows. The school was so hot that it was impossible for the children to keep cool. What they needed was a building of open walls with a roof to allow plenty of light and airflow.

It was during our visit to the school that we saw just how wonderful elephants can be. To entertain the children, we arranged for them to sit up on the elephants' backs while the animals played football with each other. One of the mahouts, knowing this was going to happen, had spent a long time training his elephant to pick up a ball and throw it down the pitch. After the game, we gave the children books and other little gifts. We hoped the whole experience would help them to appreciate elephants. The growing tourism industry in Nepal needed children to see elephants as kind and gentle animals and not as pests who ate and trampled their crops.

Crossing back over the river, we saw a rogue elephant not far away. We stopped and watched it, wondering if the situation was dangerous. Would it become aggressive towards us, or would it accept us and walk back into the forest? Luckily, it must have decided that our four elephants should not be attacked and vanished into the trees.

LEFT: *Ali shows off a contraption used to cut hay into chaff*

RIGHT: *Charles and Ali feeding the elephants under their sheltered huts*

ABOVE: *Raja Gaj, King of Elephants, Bardia National Park.*

BELOW: *A close encounter with an elephant, mock-charging us in Bardia National Park*

We continued with our trek, always keeping one eye out for the legendary Raja Gaj. As we continued through the jungle, our elephant suddenly smelt a tiger in the bushes. We stopped as the mahout wanted to flush the tiger out for all the riders of our other elephants to see it jump out and back into the bush after we had left The elephant was unwilling to comply and this meant that we had to watch the mahout trying to drive it on by hitting it on the head with his steel spike. However much it hurt, the elephant wouldn't go any closer to the tiger. Instead, it began to back determinedly into the jungle. (We later found out that it had once been attacked by a tiger and refused to go near another.) In the howdah, we were quite worried by this as the guide was standing on the elephant's back and in grave danger of being crushed or knocked off by its determination to back into the trees to get away from the tiger. We radioed the other guides to tell them we had found a tiger. They were able to flush it out but regrettably we were gone by then.

Because of the Maoist killing of the government minister, we were camped a long way out and had to take vehicles to reach the other side of the park as it was too great a distance for the elephants to walk. Once we arrived, we continued on foot. I was happily strolling along watching what was going on, when a message was passed down from the leader that Raja Gaj was following us. I looked round and, sure enough, there he was, just 30 yards away, this enormous and famous elephant walking past me in complete silence. It was a truly amazing sight, to be so close and on the ground with no guide accompanying me. I couldn't quite believe my good luck and we all agreed that we were glad we had done nothing to upset the legendary Raja Gaj. He moved so quietly that, had he wanted to attack us, he could have done so without us hearing him. He stayed beside us for a while before disappearing off into the forest. Seeing Raja Gaj was the most memorable event of the expedition.

We continued on and, finding a herd of elephants, stopped to watch them. We spent so long observing them that we even saw one of them fall asleep. We then moved on to a clearing where we came face to face with a younger elephant watching us. We stopped where we were, very near to him, observing him quietly and patiently so as not to disturb him. It was a wonderful experience being so close to this wild elephant, with us watching him and him watching us.

Then one of the women in our group did something peculiar. She was rather elderly and she wore a singlet which revealed her extremely white skin. For reasons completely unknown, this woman suddenly threw her arms up in the air, exposing a large expanse of flabby white flesh. The elephant, spooked by the sight, trumpeted loudly and stampeded off in the opposite direction. It was a shame because I could have watched him for longer, but I was at least grateful that he had chosen to run away from us – had he charged towards us, there were no trees that could have protected us and stopped him.

Back at the camp that night, I told this story to John, who had trekked elsewhere during the day. He laughed and said it reminded him of something which had occurred on a previous trip. 'There was this large American woman on one of the elephants,' he said. 'She was riding along when suddenly a tiger appeared below them. She completely panicked and, for reasons only known to her, jumped off the elephant. Do you know where she landed? Right on the back of the tiger. Luckily for her she was so big and heavy, that the tiger chose to run away, and quickly too.'

CHAPTER FORTY-ONE
SCIENTIFIC EXPLORATIONS
PART II: WHITE-WATER RAFTING DOWN THE BLUE NILE

I joined SES again for a major adventure. It was white-water rafting, through very inaccessible terrain on the Blue Nile, and would feature all the unknown dangers of one of the longest rivers in the world, more than half of which flows through Ethiopia. To be as fully prepared as possible, the team all met up on the best Welsh white water beforehand. This is a fortunately predictable run of water: the sluice gates from the dam at Llyn Celyn are opened for the day to allow the agreed amount of water to flow down the River Tryweryn.

We started with learning how to walk across a fast current with a team of six in a V formation, with one person leading and five others following behind, so as to give a strong feeling of security. We then practised turning over Avon rafts and righting them. I tried hard but could not right mine and could not understand why it was so difficult, until I went round the other side to find the instructor holding it down. We had excellent lectures from a former SBS commander, Major Ram Seegar, about possible rafting dangers, all of which we hoped never to see.

LEFT: *In deep white water rafting training for the Blue Nile trip*

RIGHT: *Preparing white-water rafting kit for the Blue Nile scientific exploration*

Fully prepared, we landed in Addis Ababa and went to our hotel to see all our equipment spread out over the hotel car park. We were split into boat teams of five and we set about checking all the equipment that Ethiopian Airlines had brought out for us. Special terms had been organised with the airline by Colonel John Blashford-Snell, the leader of the expedition. Each raft had to carry the paddler's personal kit in semi-waterproof bags and a share of the expedition kit. We then loaded it all into a truck and 4x4 pick-ups. All was ready by mid-afternoon when we set off for the British embassy for afternoon tea with the ambassador and his staff. This was a great honour and also a chance to meet the first secretary, a charming lady who was going to join us on the river.

Next morning, we set off to join the Bashilo River, one of the main tributaries of the Blue Nile. The Blue Nile has its source in Lake Tana and used to flow over spectacular falls. It still flows over the Tisisot Falls, but the spectacle is limited by water going through the hydroelectric station. We drove on to the gravel of the dry river bed to unload and inflate the rafts and stow all our equipment. Our vehicles were positioned upriver with a rope to each raft to prevent any early departures of partly filled boats. We then took the usual departure photograph before clambering into our rafts, ready to be cast off by the drivers. All were released together but none of us moved. We all climbed out and started pushing before jumping back aboard. This was going to be a common occurrence on this wide, shallow tributary. There were soon some narrow fast sections with much back-paddling and many collisions with the vertical rock faces, but fortunately without damage. Our lead canoe, skippered by our ex-SBS officer Ram Seegar, soon found a suitable sandy campsite for the night.

Getting ready to launch on the Beschillo tributary which joins into the Blue Nile

It was then that our helmsman discovered that he should have packed our bags with the opening at the top and not laid them flat, as only the bottom was waterproof. I was lucky that his was at the bottom and that mine was stowed on top.

We split the chores of cooking and water gathering. The latter was new to us all and involved collecting buckets of muddy river water to fill our large 20-litre container and then adding a coagulant which had been specially imported to coalesce all the mud particles so that they dropped to the bottom. We then put the clear water into a hessian filter that drained into a plastic jerry can and added iodine and taste remover to have good clear drinking and cooking water. This was tedious but there was no space for bottled water and it meant that we had no worries about plastic waste where none was visible on the river. It was a truly wild area. I was tasked with videoing the expedition so had tripods and extra equipment in my bag which made hauling it up the sandy beach with a bad back hard work. I ended up twisting my back so badly that one leg was half an inch shorter than the other. I went to see the expedition doctor who could not do much except prescribe ineffective pills. I was not impressed, even though he had the highest CV as a former Falklands paramedic for the Second Battalion of the Parachute Regiment at the Battle of Goose Green. Time had moved on and he had joined us to see if he could manage six dry weeks. My back soon healed, but the paramedic left the expedition to resume his drinking.

We were a scientific expedition so after three days we had a research day with our scientist. I joined him to help set up pitfall traps: buckets dug into the sand with the top level with the surface so any insect walking past fell in to be caught next day and then identified and recorded. We also set mouse traps baited with cheese and Nutella on shrubs and animal tracks to see what lived in the area for later analysis.

Even with some local help it was slow work dragging the rafts over the shallow sections. One day, a few days later, we found ourselves beside such a shallow rocky section. Our scout canoe went over easily and was waiting quietly below the rocks while we stopped for our basic lunch: two people sharing a tin of pâté and a packet of snack biscuits. As we cleared the rocky section, we heard a radio call from Ram: 'Just been punctured by a crocodile heading for the shore need assistance.' They just made the shore before all the air from their raft was lost. The crocodile's jaws had missed Ram's backside by only four inches. We thought the sudden splash of the paddles must have woken the animal up, causing his instant reaction.

After emery-papering and sewing up the hole, we glued a patch on the tear and started paddling again. Soon the river widened, dividing into two channels, when the scout canoe took the wrong fork, forcing them to drag the boat back. We stopped and waited until I suggested that our younger paddlers run back to help instead of just watching, which they did. One was a young man who disliked doing any chores and just wanted a continuous adrenaline adventure.

After the canoe was back on track and some way ahead, we heard a couple of shots and soon after another radio call from Ram. 'We've just been held up by gunfire and told we are not allowed to continue. Please come as soon as possible.' John showed no concern and carried on paddling at the same speed until we rounded the corner to reach the site of the shooting. Our liaison lieutenant was the only Amharic speaker and asked what the bandits – or *shifta* as they were called locally – wanted, translating for John. We had little money with us and even if we had had more they could have run over the gravel at the side of the river faster than we could paddle, so could demand more further down the river. We asked to see their *shifta* chief but were told he was four or five days away. They decided to let us go but, just as we paddled away, they changed their mind. They finally agreed for us to go to a place where we could camp and talk further.

We asked them to bring their chief while we settled into our camp routine, but with a slight difference. John got his satphone out and called the ambassador with whom we had had tea and our lieutenant called his colonel. They talked and arranged a meeting with the interior minister, who called the police chief. The latter, confident of his rank, asked to speak to the *shifta*. He ordered them to let us go but they refused point blank. We guessed our ambassador and the minister had insisted that we should be freed promptly. The police chief said he had no transport, so we offered him our support Land Cruiser with driver and our land party leader, Simon Hampel. He must have felt a very small police chief by that stage. He called a sergeant who got into the Land Cruiser with Simon to lead the rescue, and they set off into the night to a small village. The sergeant knocked on a door, which was answered by a policeman: a roughly dressed man with good military boots and his regular issue AK47, who joined the team. This happened six more times until the Land Cruiser was full. They drove along the top of the escarpment until they arrived opposite our camp, then started the 3,000-foot descent to the river until they could see fires. A satphone call to John to ask him to flare up our fire to make sure they were heading for the correct camp and could continue to make their final plans.

I woke soon after dawn. All was quiet so I went to investigate and was soon shouted at to lie down in strong military language by a recently returned officer from Afghanistan. I immediately complied. But I kept my head up and a few minutes later a policeman with an AK47 at the ready ran through the camp. Five minutes later the cry went up. 'All over!' The *shifta* had all been surrounded and taken by surprise, and the possibility of twelve AK47s all being used together had gone. We could see all the *shifta* squatting down handcuffed with their rifles. I was told they had all been unloaded but they would have to carry them back to the top of the bank. I saw one policeman casually walk past one of them and swipe him across his face with the side of his boot, knocking him over. I tried to imagine what life would be like in an Ethiopian jail. We all lined up for victory photographs with the police competing for their best action pose with their guns.

Our guide with the Police gunmen who captured the Shifta who had kidnapped our party

A relieved team returned to the river glad to have such a good leader in John with all the right equipment and planned backup. He told us towards the end that, including our large team, only 83 people had ever rafted the Blue Nile – about a fifth of the number who had climbed Everest at that time – and of these only five had done so without shots being fired. During an earlier army expedition in 1968 his team had two serious fire fights with the *shifta* and had to make a rapid escape in their boats, leaving all their food behind. Hungry soldiers are not happy, but they are resourceful. Being fully armed they soon saw, shot and skinned a crocodile. The expedition was using outboards and had nice clean engine oil with which to cook the crocodile.

We soon reached the Blue Nile itself, which was much wider, deeper, faster and saturated with mud which would test our freshwater system. It coped perfectly, just taking a little longer to sediment the mud. Now we were in deep water, we could take advantage of the fast current. Good food was running out, so we were glad to reach our resupply point, arriving to see a small herd of donkeys which had just unloaded their panniers. We quickly transferred all our supplies from cardboard boxes to our waterproof boat containers.

I had a good meal that night for a dawn start to make the 3,000-foot ascent over ten miles to the plateau so I could do my videoing job. It was the hardest trek I had ever done but I was well supported by a young doctor called Alice Mavrogordato and reached the top after ten hours to find the young dentist on the expedition hard at work pulling out teeth to give much-needed relief to local people. It was one of the regular jobs of these expeditions to help the tribespeople with skills to which they did not have easy access. Next day we drove along the flat, grassy plain to a large village to visit the local hospital. As we expected it was very basic with dirty wards and dirty linen and blood-spattered walls. We went to see the power supply and found two quite new generators which were broken purely through lack of instructions on how to maintain them. So they requested new ones from another aid agency or the government. Our engineer spent an hour and repaired one of the generators, for which they were extremely grateful. We wanted to put some pressure on them to improve what they had been doing, so I set my video up for Simon to ask their chief lots of difficult questions which we told them would be sent to the minister of health. We hoped it might encourage them to maintain their hospital and equipment to a better standard. We visited several villages to look at their clinics, which were much the same. We then camped for the night in wonderful wild places entirely out on our own, able to enjoy magnificent desert sunsets and lie under bright stars with no other lights visible. Unfortunately, one night I left a small opening in my tent and woke the next morning to find it full of mosquitos. I hadn't heard them but was bitten a few times. Luckily, the bites were not too painful. I was taking Lariam – known as the honeymoon killer, because that is the effect it has on lots of people. But that wasn't a worry for me as I was glad to have the best protection against malaria.

We were soon due to raft down a treacherous section full of rocky gorges that John had found difficult during his previous military passage. He was worried about us older and less fit paddlers and wanted to fly over it with the helmsmen of all the rafts. This plan unfortunately coincided with Eritrean army aggression on Ethiopia's northern border, which caused riots in Addis Ababa. This forced Ethiopia to fully mobilise its forces to demonstrate their determination to prevent any loss of territory, meaning all their helicopters were needed for their defence. But the helicopters were also our ultimate support should we have any serious medical or other emergency. With no back-up we dared not take thirty paddlers into rocky, inaccessible territory. There was no alternative other than for all of us to come off the river and make a dry-land camp for a week. We chose a beautiful flat grass field on a cliff beside a river and a waterfall. We were also within walking distance of a substantial village that contained a good clinic. It had dusty clay streets but at the back of the clinic was a small laboratory with the ability to do blood tests to identify malaria. This was extremely useful as John's deputy leader, a Colombian economist called Yoli Cipagauta, was becoming quite ill and we were able to have her tested. The results were worrying: she had both cerebral and vivax strains of malaria. Living in a malarial country, she thought she was immune, but she was not immune to the African variants. Her condition worsened but, luckily, we had two doctors who could do continuous shifts of twelve hours each for five days. She became so unwell that she felt she had passed the point of no return before her death. Fortunately, she did recover sufficiently to be sent to Addis Ababa and then fly home to Colombia at the end of the expedition. If we had been on the river she would not have survived.

Four weeks after I returned home, I developed the symptoms of a bad cold, had a hot bath, and retired to bed. During the night, I became feverish and sweaty, followed a short while later by feeling freezing cold. This was repeated during the night. I knew it was not a cold, so I went to the doctor for a blood test, who confirmed malaria. He prescribed five pills and after three I felt fully cured with no recurrence. Another member of our team contracted malaria but took a month to recover. I had a sailing friend who did his National Service in Malaya and caught malaria there. He was cured but 30 years later it flared up again. I was incredibly lucky.

When the Eritreans stopped being aggressive, we resumed our trip. We had been prepared for some mountain climbing so had all the climbers' ropes and carabiners. This proved essential as we headed back to the river. The mountaineers rigged their ropes and carabiners so we could lower all our boats and kit down to the river from a 150-foot-high bridge to save a difficult muddy descent. We naturally wanted to take some good photographs of our rafting from such a wonderful vantage point. The Ethiopian police watched us take the photographs and made sure we never included the bridge in our pictures. This gave us a good idea of what the river would be like if in full flood going over the rocks. We were shown some photographs of John's military expedition from 1968 with fit soldiers, but to me they looked more like Belsen survivors. How body shapes have changed with healthy food over the years. This part of the river was deep enough so that no pushing was needed and gave us more time. I was given the job of surveying the river with my hand-held depth gauge. It was mostly five to seven feet but to our great surprise I recorded a hole 150 feet deep over a length of 300 yards. It was the first time the river had ever been surveyed and was a useful addition to our scientific knowledge.

We soon had our next resupply point but this time the donkeys arrived on the opposite side of our camp. Such was the impatience to have our new luxuries that the land and river parties just loaded the cardboard boxes into the wet rafts. This meant that all our stores including batteries had to be dried out.

The fishermen and scientists enjoyed an evening fishing which was both productive and interesting. One of the fish caught surprised everyone as it was an electric fish which gave a massive shock to all who touched it. Even when it was landed and multimeters used, it still produced over 300 volts. The scientists and the cooks studied the catch, with the former deciding which was for science and which was for supper. The electric fish and two others were unknown in the area, and one was not known outside South Africa. We also saw an antelope being chased by a pack of wild dogs, also not known to exist in the area.

Next day we saw a hippo, one of the most dangerous wild animals and a killer of many tribesmen in the riverside bush. Rafts full of people are at great risk as they cannot paddle fast enough to escape. But as usual John was well prepared with a high-pitched hooter, the sound of which the hippo clearly didn't like. It was so agitated that it remained on the far bank.

We had another long stop on an island where by chance the team, digging at the back of the campsite, found a collection of broken pottery from prehistoric times which they sorted and brought back to give to the Addis Ababa Museum. John had also heard of an ancient village on the other bank so a search party was organised to see if they could find any trace of it. There were six in the party with Alice, the doctor, and they set off into high elephant grass in the middle of the day to cut a path. One of the trekkers – Alastair, a big man over six feet tall and weighing about 18 stone – found the hot, windless walking hard going and needed lots of water. He kept stopping to rest and drink but the heat and exercise were too much for him, causing him to suddenly collapse unconscious. He was far too heavy for the small team to carry so they radioed for help. John quickly organised a rescue party with plenty of water to cross the river to recover him. All went well until they lost the track and, with eight-feet-high grass, could not see anything. But the practical young Ethiopian soldier in the party came up with a solution. He would fire his revolver into the air so that the rescuers would know the location of the casualty. With radios they could give directions. It is the only time I have heard of a firearm being used to save a life. When they reached Alastair, he was filled up with water and soaked with it as he regained consciousness. Using nearby wood and the expedition's canvas stretcher six men carried him back. When they reached the riverbank, he could stand so I took what video I could, but it was too far away for me to see what I was taking. They just stood there holding Alastair, who, when I later looked at the footage I had captured, was urinating continuously. Very embarrassing. They all came back across the river so that the doctors could help Alastair to make a full recovery.

Loading the rafts and gear onto the four wheeled drive truck to return to civilisation

Back on the river, paddling with thick jungle on either side, we were surprised to see a hunter on the riverbank. He was the only other person we had seen in a week. There are few places you can travel on land where humans are so rare. The river widened and slowed so we had to use our little outboard engine to keep up the pace for our pre-planned departure from the river. We reached our exit point and then had to drag the rafts up a muddy track with all our equipment. We deflated them and then packed everything on to an old four-wheel-drive truck with cart-spring suspension that gave us a very rough ride. With just a short pause to tie up the broken tailgate that we were sitting on before we were deposited in the dirt, we soon reached a good dirt road where normal buses waited to take us back to our hotel for a big clean-up and a farewell dinner to celebrate a memorable and successful scientific expedition.

CHAPTER FORTY-TWO
SCIENTIFIC EXPLORATIONS
PART III: THE HEAD-HUNTERS OF NAGALAND

I n the north-east of India, squashed between Assam and Myanmar, is the state of Nagaland. Well known as a difficult place to travel to, it usually requires numerous permits to enter. When the British ruled India, the extent of their power effectively ended at the flat plains of Assam. They never controlled the hills of Nagaland. Since partition, the state has been rife with insurgency and demands for independence, demands which continue to this day. This has led to violence across Nagaland, which is why permits can be so difficult to obtain.

Fortunately, John Blashford-Snell was friendly with John Edwards, also in the SES, who had good contacts in India and was able to obtain the necessary permits. We made our way there and, on arrival, stayed in a traditional village house, where we lived with locals whose tribal and family traditions were centuries old. The tribe needed to rebuild their main community house, so several villages had joined together, working as a team to rethatch the building with palm leaves.

Once the work was complete, a celebratory meal was held to which we were invited. The villagers dressed up in their traditional costumes with special headdresses and performed their tribal dances. It was wonderful

Local natives constructing the roof of the community hall with woven palm leaves

to see these long-standing traditions which had been in place since before the beginning of Christianity.

We knew that another ancient custom in this area was the practice of head-hunting. The locals wouldn't talk about this very much, and we couldn't establish when it had come to an end. However, in the village there was a memorial to the late king which said that he had five wives and had taken 35 heads in his lifetime. He had died only ten years before we arrived. After much persuasion by our guide, the villagers showed us a small cave where they still had a large number of heads which we were allowed to inspect. A member of our party, a doctor whose wife was a dentist, explained that one of the skulls showed an extremely rare double tooth.

The head-hunting naturally fascinated us, so eventually the villagers decided to tell us more. First, they showed us an old dugout canoe covered with a cloth. Removal of the cloth revealed around 100 heads hidden inside. Then, we were introduced to two old men who had been head-hunters in their youth. They greeted us in their traditional headdresses. We had a translator with us, and after much persuasion they finally told us some of their story.

Head-hunting had been banned by the British in the nineteenth century, but it was still widely practised in Nagaland as late as the 1970s. Since then, the practice had declined, although the two men were some of the very few alive who had continued to head-hunt until the 1990s. They refused to tell us any more.

Both men had been born in the 1930s. For them, head-hunting was a rite of passage. They grew up in a world where it was expected of them and, as such, they never questioned whether it was right or wrong. It was just something men did to impress the women they wanted to marry. Women didn't take part in the actual practice of head-hunting, but they encouraged and took pride in their husbands' 'collections'. One of the men admitted that his wife had refused to marry him until he had brought back his first head. 'It was', the translator said, 'like a kind of dowry.'

I asked the man if he could describe what it was like to take that first head. After my question was translated, he shrugged, as if it was no big deal. He could not remember exactly how old he had been, for it was a long time ago, but he was young. Joining his father, his uncles, his brothers and cousins, they raided a nearby village whose men were known to be weak. Perhaps it had been chosen specifically for his initiation into the

custom of head-hunting. They knew the fight would be an easy one. The man tackled one of the villagers to the ground and then removed his head with a machete. When they all returned to their village, he held the head proudly out before him. People praised him and called him a warrior. He was married soon after.

The head would have eventually been taken to the morung, the 'skull house'. Every village had a morung. The number of heads a warrior took indicated his power, and the number of heads in the morung indicated the village's collective power. To preserve the heads, the flesh and hair were boiled off. Before being placed in the morung, the skulls would be displayed outside their hunters' houses. Those with the greatest number of skulls held the greatest prestige and married the most prestigious women. As such, head-hunting became a form of competition between the village's men, and they sought out further raids and battles with other villages purely to collect more skulls. These two men had grown up in a time of perpetual war between villages.

When they had finished their story, we thanked the two men for sharing their history with us. They accompanied us outside as we left. In front of the house stood a totem pole, and I asked if it symbolised anything. The translator directed my question to the men, and they discussed it between themselves for a minute or two. Eventually, the translator turned back to me.

'After a raid,' the translator said, 'sometimes they would bring a man back to the village, alive, a captive. He would be tied to this pole. There was a tradition that if the captive escaped, then his village and the other would be united in friendship. But that rarely happened.'

LEFT: *An elder head hunter who took heads in his youth now wearing his traditional headdress in Nagaland*

RIGHT: *One of the village headhunters*

On our final day in Nagaland, we went to an old ceremonial house which lay across the border of Myanmar and India, with the main part of the house in the former and the rest in the latter. That day, we had lunch in Myanmar. Then it was back down the mountains and into Assam where we wanted to stop at Kaziranga National Park on the banks of the Brahmaputra. Said to be the biggest and best park in all India, Kaziranga gained notoriety when a certain video appeared on YouTube. A wildlife officer tourist riding on an elephant was filming the grass in the park when, all of a sudden, a tigress sprang out unseen from the long grass, made a huge leap at the mahout on the head of the elephant and took a swipe at him, tearing his arm and shoulder. They were trying to drive her and her cubs back into the reserve when she attacked. I've watched the full and unedited video a few times, and it never fails to amaze me how that tiger was able to creep up, undetected even from the height of an elephant.

We were riding exactly where that video was shot but we did not see any tigers, although we saw lots of other wildlife. Much like Bardia in Nepal, we travelled across Kaziranga on the backs of elephants, riding silently through the mist and long grass. There were several small Asian rhinos in the park, and we were fortunate enough to see them up close, having the unique experience of looking down on a rhino from the back of an elephant. Similarly, there were plenty of deer and water buffalo, and we saw lots of them.

Riding elephants through Kaziranga Park, in the fields where a tiger had hid previous to attacking

CHAPTER FORTY-THREE
SCIENTIFIC EXPLORATIONS
PART IV: MEGHALAYA

Another SES expedition I joined was to install a solar-powered water pump in a very remote village, in 2003. On the road to Meghalaya, in north-eastern India, we stopped for the night in Shillong, an old British hill station where Assam tea planters used to stay in order to escape the extreme temperatures of the Indian summers. Our hotel was built for old-fashioned comfort and still retained it. I particularly enjoyed its typically old-English characteristic of having a real fire in the bedrooms for when it was too cold. Now little more than a tourist attraction, it was nevertheless a wonderful place to stay, a relic of life from the British Raj, and still the best hotel in town.

Beyond Shillong, Meghalaya became much more rural and tribal, sharing its southern border with Bangladesh. Our destination village was deep within the state's interior. It used to take three or four days to walk to this village but, the year before, the villagers had cut a wide track through the jungle directly to it, so rather than walk we were able to climb into the back of four-wheel-drive coal trucks and be driven down the track. As night fell, we reached a river, where one of the trucks was stuck. Since it was now dark, we agreed to camp beside the river for the night and free the truck the next morning. Happy with our decision, we fell asleep to the sounds of the jungle, entirely on our own in the middle of it.

In the morning, we worked together to collect wood and build ramps so that the trucks could cross the river and drive up into the jungle on the far side. Once we had crossed successfully, we continued on through the virgin jungle until we reached another river. We again used wood and rocks to give the trucks traction as they struggled through the mud. Finally, we arrived at the village, where we were given a warm welcome and washed off all the coal dust.

Some of the villagers led us away from the village to show us where they currently obtained their water. A steep and muddy track took us to an opening where the water flowed out of the mountainside. The villagers

The opening of a newly installed well by the Just a Drop *charity*

would collect their water there and then carry it on their heads back up the track. It was hard work even in the dry season. In the wet season, it would have been a completely different story. The village was situated only a few miles away from Cherrapunji, which holds the distinction of being the second-wettest place in the world, with more than 400 inches of rain a year. We went to Cherrapunji and, with the aid of a pair of binoculars, I looked down at the Bangladesh plains below. All I could see were acres and acres of water with a few telegraph poles sticking out from them. When the wet season began in this village, the steep track became a waterfall of mud, and carrying water up it would have been extremely difficult.

The water charity Just a Drop had bought a solar panel and pumps for the village, and we were here to install it. We had a water engineer with us to ensure it all functioned. He set it up, but it did not work properly, so I tried modifying the collection point, raising it up a little and changing some of the wiring. This helped and, soon, it was up and running. The water was pumped from the bottom of the pit where it came out of the side wall up to a halfway tank, and then another pump filled up a second tank near the village. The villagers were delighted with their new supply, but I felt sad to see that they had spent a lot of money on these plastic tanks. Back on my farm, I had similar ones which used to contain imported orange juice and which, had I known, I could have given them for free.

With the new water system complete, we were invited to go for a trek into the scrub and jungle. Apparently, someone from the village had seen rare wild cattle not too far out in the jungle, and we hoped we might find some tracks or signs of them. It was also a good opportunity to camp out and sling our hammocks between the trees.

We found a perfect campsite where the trees were 15 feet apart. I had discovered this was the correct distance to avoid the very common deep sag in the middle of a hammock. We put ours up and then placed waterproof bashas over them to ensure we stayed dry through the night. We had a wonderful camp meal and then set out into the jungle in search of the rare beast which the villagers had seen.

As we walked out, the guide, Mike, suddenly stopped, turned and looked at us. 'Can you all climb trees?' he asked.

We stared at each other. Could we? I had no idea. It had been a long time since I had even attempted to climb a tree. Luckily, the trees around us were fairly low and scrubby, and we did not have to climb too far up them. We sat in the branches staying silent as an hour passed, and then another, and then yet another. Unfortunately, no wild animal, rare or otherwise, ever appeared. It remained a mystery.

I was not too upset by our failure to see any rare creatures. We returned to our hammocks for a wonderful night camping out in completely wild jungle. This experience was enough to make the trek a great success for me. We slept well and then hiked back to the village the following morning where the water pump was still working well. We found out that there had been one in place previously and that, in fact, it had been even more sophisticated than this one, with galvanised pipes which had run up the hill. Unfortunately, the elephants had not liked this intrusion into their territory, and had torn all the piping out.

Another jungle expedition was announced. They were going to go in search of a bear. It sounded like a lot of fun and I was keen to join, but Mike forbade it. He believed that I couldn't climb trees quickly enough, and laid down an ultimatum that if I went on the expedition, he wouldn't. Since he was the guide, I had little option other than to remain in the camp while they set off.

When they returned, they didn't look happy. They carried with them a black bear which Mike had spotted up a tree as they were hiking. It had climbed down to the ground and then attacked them, leaving him no alternative but to shoot. This was, of course, very sad for the bear, and Mike was especially upset because this was a conservation area and he was the chief warden. But it had been a necessity. If he hadn't shot the bear, it would have attacked the whole group. I realised then that one's ability to climb a tree counts for nothing when a bear is on the attack. Even bear spray I doubt would have been effective.

CHAPTER FORTY-FOUR
LIFE ON TWO WHEELS

Though the bulk of my travelling has been done by boat or in the Unimog, I've always had a fondness for motorbikes. Even when I was a teenager in the Young Farmers' Club, I became friends with a dairy farmer through our mutual enthusiasm for bikes. That was when I bought my first ever motorbike: a Triumph Tiger Cub which I used to play with on the little farm tracks. It was great fun and soon my friend and I entered a small scramble event. This was not successful as I had a totally unsuitable bike and a cork helmet, and I was soon banned.

This spurred me on to try again with a more appropriate bike. Though I had little experience, I bought a Cotton, which ran on methanol and Castrol R. It made a magnificent sound and smelt lovely, but it needed far too much maintenance. I did a few events but was not particularly successful and, at one, I crashed. Since my friend could not drive, my mother had to come and collect me and the bike and take me to hospital. I was diagnosed with early arthritis so had to stop. As I was the only driver, my mother could not be expected to come and collect me again.

I gave up motorcycling after that. Soon, I left for Australia, and then, besides getting married and farming full time, my travels and adventures centred on *Caleta* and then *Caleta II*. My married life at that time was not especially conducive to motorbikes, and I did not own another until the Unimog came along, when I invested in the Kawasaki to put up on its front carrier. All those journeys out in Africa and the Middle East, when I would park the Unimog and go off exploring on the bike, reignited my love of motorcycling. Over the years, I traded up to a Suzuki DRZ 400 with an electric start after a very hot day trying to kick-start the Kawasaki in Venice. I took Ali to ride up the Outer Hebrides in typically Scottish weather. She was carrying our clothes in a rucksack on her back. One day was so wet and windy that all the CalMac ferries were cancelled. We then realised that a Suzuki with Ali and me with one backpack was far too limiting.

In 2009, I was driving back from a shooting trip in Wales when I passed the Birmingham National Exhibition Centre while the International Motorcycle Show was on. I had both the time and the inclination, so I stopped for a visit. The exhibition was incredible, and two things in particular caught my eye. One was a two-day BMW rider training course and the other was a motorbike expedition down to Dakar. I booked both of them.

First was the BMW course, which was to be in Wales. I drove there in the Unimog, having put the KTM on the front. Of course, my KTM was different to the BMWs which everyone else used. The instructors were excellent and I had an enjoyable two days. One of them was Patsy Quick, the first British woman to finish the

Unimog with Kawasaki on front carrier

Dakar Rally. At the end of the course, I loaded my KTM back on to the Unimog and drove back to bid them all farewell and show them the bike on the Unimog. I later wrote to Patsy to thank her for the help she had given me at the training. She remembered me well, which was, I think, thanks to my somewhat unusual entrance and exit in the Unimog.

I went back to the BMW school a few times after that to build up my experience. One of the instructors was a man called Clive Town, usually known as Zippy. He had been a co-rider with Patsy when they both finished the Dakar Rally and, when I told him I had trained with her, he called her to tell her I was there. That was how I received the great honour of being invited to Patsy's Pyrenees Party.

I was placed in a team with a woman called Tamsin Jones, who had also been an instructor at the BMW school. Tamsin and I set off together and, just outside the camp, were stopped by the police.

'What's the problem, officer?' Tamsin asked.

He pointed at our bikes. 'No mirrors,' he said.

'These are off-roaders,' Tamsin replied. 'Off-roaders don't have mirrors. They break.'

The policeman continued to insist that we needed mirrors, and we had to call Patsy to bring some out to us. Another rider, Bill, was in our team. He had brought his own bike from England which also did not have a mirror. As we waited, the police called in a recovery truck and, before we knew it, Bill's bike was loaded on to it. I had flashbacks to the era of Franco.

After a lot of discussion, the bike was finally released and we made good time, effectively following Tamsin on the trails since she was so much faster than us that she could stop and read the instructions before we caught up.

It was such a good weekend, that I was invited to go to Morocco with Patsy. She took me on a private tour, which was extremely kind of her. I had the same bike which, unfortunately, had no lights. This made the last part of the tour rather difficult for me, so Patsy and I swapped; she rode my bike out in front, while I followed on hers with a light.

○ ○ ○

After spending so much time with all these bikers, many of whom had ridden the Dakar and told exciting stories about it, I began to grow fascinated by the prospect of the famous rally. I asked Patsy how I might be able to see it first-hand. She invited me down, explained the various options and recommended that the best one for me would be to become a full member of her team and drive a support vehicle. Not only was this a great privilege for me, it was also extremely kind of her to take me on, and I happily accepted the offer. It enabled her to have two support vehicles and, if Patsy rode with me, she could get some sleep in peace and we would be able to get a good parking space in the new bivouac each day.

The whole experience was incredible. We started at about 4.00 a.m. when the bike riders left, clearing up all their tents and open gazebo shelters. Then, while Patsy slept beside me, I drove her Nissan Patrol for 400 miles or so to the next bivouac, where all the truck drivers and bikers met and had their food. This was a secure compound where the competitors would park and have all their maintenance, repairs and servicing done. In the evening, the organisers would build a big fire, put on a splendid French gourmet meal and then give out all the navigation information for the following day, including the route book and the verbal warnings of any dangers. Since I was the driver for Patsy, my main job while the mechanics serviced the bikes was to collect cold bottles of Red Bull – the only cold drink available – for all the drivers and mechanics. Being part of this amazing event was extremely exciting. I especially enjoyed seeing the huge Russian Kamaz and Dutch trucks as they were worked on.

The bikes set off early the next morning. They always left first: this was to ensure they completed the day's course before the cars and trucks and, as a result, were less at risk of being run over by them. The rally lasted fourteen days in total, with one day earmarked for rest. This was most welcome, and it was good to sleep in a hotel and get clean. The other days were filled with excitement. It was great to see how all of our team were getting on, especially Tamsin. She was amazingly tough and had one incredible day which, after all the breakdowns she endured and then fixed, took her twenty-one hours to complete. When she arrived at the compound, it was in the early hours of the morning. Patsy and her team had to get up, service her bike and get it ready while Tamsin stole a brief sleep. Three hours later, with her bike checked over and repaired and her road book done, she set off again.

The other rider I knew was Craig Bounds. He did well at first, but unfortunately his clutch went in the second week, and he had to pull out of the rally. He was disheartened by his failure to finish, but soon joined in with the general sense of camaraderie which was one of the good things about our team.

The rally ended at a series of immense sand dunes, one of which was 2,000 feet high and ran right down into the bivouac. It was so impressive to watch all the bikes, trucks and cars as they raced down this dune towards the finishing line. I was lying down in a place which I thought was well clear of the track, when suddenly I had to roll away to get clear of a car driving wide. There was such wonderful enthusiasm from all the South American supporters, who crowded at the sides of the roads, cheering everyone on and trying to touch all the drivers as they passed. On the last day there were no difficult sections so we could wait for Tamsin and the other team riders to finish and receive their well-deserved finishers' medals. She was the second British woman after Patsy Quick to complete the Dakar. All in all, it was a tremendously exciting time, and I was keen to do it again.

Celebrating with Tamsin Jones after completing the Dakar Rally, 2010

CHAPTER FORTY-FIVE

BIKING FROM LONDON TO BEIJING

When the opportunity to ride my motorbike from London all the way to Beijing came up, I could not resist it. The team of fourteen had already decided they would each ride a BMW. This was a logistical decision: if any bike broke down during the expedition, they would need only one supplier to send out parts. It all seemed like a marvellous idea to me, so I bought a brand-new BMW F800 and became the fifteenth member of the team.

I asked Ali if she would like to come along. By now, we had enjoyed many adventures together, most of them on water, and I thought that perhaps she might appreciate a long overland trip, the kind we had not yet undertaken in each other's company. She loved the idea, but unfortunately only had the time to accompany me for the first leg through Europe. I was happy to have her riding pillion, and we both looked forward to the opportunity to revisit some of the areas we had seen from the deck of *Ribaleta*.

The team gathered at the Ace Café in London, an old transport café which has since found fame amongst bikers, many of whom use it as their

With Ali preparing to set off to Beijing from Ace Café, London.

starting point for grand and exciting expeditions. We ate our greasy-spoon breakfasts, posed for numerous photographs and set off. The team leader for the expedition was Kevin Sanders, who rode with his wife Julia. There was also a professional photographer, Adam Giles. The support van was a Ford Transit which could carry two bikes and was driven by Jeff Condon, a New Zealander. The riders were: Alex and Ann Frick from the USA, Simon Callender, Robert Czerucki from Poland, Colin Moss, Ed McMullen, Max Richard, Michael Cowen, Aoran Sprague from the USA, Lorraine Johnstone, Edwin Langford and Mark Hamilton. Aged seventy, I was the oldest of all the riders.

After an easy ride to the Channel Tunnel, we boarded the train for France. It was my first time, and I was pleasantly surprised at how simple it all was. As we crossed, I talked with the other riders about how we would navigate. Jeff – the support van driver and mechanic – said he liked to use a combination of GPS and road book. It seemed to me that using both only complicated matters so, when we rode off the train and into France, I stuck to the GPS. It took us along motorway after motorway and I soon realised the benefit of the road book – with that, we could ride the smaller, more interesting roads.

Europe passed in a blur and before we knew it, we were entering the former Yugoslavian countries. Ali and I took a quick detour so that we could see the Danube from land, reminding ourselves that, just a few years before, we had motored down that same stretch of water in Ribaleta.

We crossed the border into Turkey and rode into Istanbul to stay at a hotel in the centre. Since Ali and I had already seen most of the city's tourist hotspots, we left the rest of the team to their sightseeing and went for a superb dinner and catch-up with Ali's friends. It was a shame that Ali had to leave the next day to fly home, although she admitted that she did not mind missing out on the more difficult roads which lay ahead.

After taking Ali to the airport, I rejoined the others as we travelled deeper into Turkey. When the trip was first suggested to me, I had been pleased to learn that the team did not intend to simply plough through the miles with their sights only on the destination, but instead were hoping to stop here and there at interesting places. Our first that day was Yassıhöyük, site of the famous Gordion: the capital of the ancient Phrygian Empire and the place where Alexander the Great cut the Gordian Knot. The legend stated that whoever could achieve such a feat would go on to become king of all Asia. Alexander did not quite manage that, but his conquests were nevertheless impressive. Gordion is also where we saw the tomb of King Midas, a huge burial mound which we entered through a modern tunnel to see the well-kept burial chamber; and then after that we spent some time enjoying the Gordian Museum over the road, which was filled with fascinating finds from the area.

Just over 200 miles south-east of Gordion is another well-known Turkish place: Cappadocia. We booked into one of the hotels which had been built into the rocks. Many of the locals who had lived in these cave-dwellings had been told to leave over the years as the residences were unhygienic and old-fashioned, but we were pleased to see that our hotel had been fitted out to a high standard and still maintained a traditional look.

Cappadocia is most famous for its fairy chimneys: numerous columns and conical towers with hard tops which protect the volcanic ash underneath from the rain. We took a hot-air balloon flight over the magnificent landscape and the pilot, who was exceptionally skilled, managed to land on one of the towers. Then we were back up in the air again, where the visibility was tremendous – we could see the smaller cave entrances clustered here and there as well as the bigger hills behind them all. The flight was soon over and as we started to descend several ropes were thrown out of the basket and caught by a group of men on the ground who, co-ordinating perfectly with the pilot, manoeuvred the basket to land on its trailer, where it was immediately strapped down before the canopy collapsed or the basket turned over and spilt us on to the ground.

The ride from Cappadocia to the underground city of Kaymaklı took us across desert made from centuries-old volcanic ash. From the road, Kaymaklı appeared to be just desert with little on the surface, but when we descended underground, we suddenly found ourselves in a complex maze of passageways and rooms dug out of the volcanic ash which plunged down for four storeys. The townspeople had built it all to protect themselves from marauding tribes. Should invaders have discovered the underground city, they still would not have been able to penetrate it, for the passageways were blocked by round stones like millwheels that were rolled across each entrance.

As we continued east, the roads steadily worsened. I fell behind a little and then, coming round a corner, found a 50-foot-wide river blocking my path. On the other side, Jeff and a few of the riders who had made it across had set up a camera, hoping that they could catch us falling in. Luckily, I crossed the river without losing my balance, but the youngest rider,

Max, hit a hole and crashed. He was unhurt apart from a slightly bruised ego – Jeff and the others had known about the hole but hadn't told Max precisely because they hoped he would hit it! The cameraman made a short film featuring Max's fall, reversing it and replaying it over and over on a loop, which we all found amusing, even Max.

I hadn't fallen in the river, but I did soon have my own accident. We were riding through livestock country when suddenly we came across some of the biggest dogs I have ever seen - an Anatolian Shepherd dog. One crossed my path and, unluckily for the dog, I did not have the time to swerve out of the way. I hit him square on. I didn't come off the bike and managed to keep going, though I was unable to turn around and see what had happened to the dog.

One of our final stops in the east of Turkey was the small spa town of Masoudi, where we enjoyed the hot springs and thermal pools. Amongst the attractions were the fish which populated the pools. As you swam, they would swim with you and nibble at your skin, supposedly eating away any diseases or ailments you might have on the surface of your body. It was a strange and not entirely pleasant sensation.

We reached the eastern border of Turkey and I had time to walk around an old fort overlooking Armenia. I found a battered church, its walls badly pock-marked with shell holes. I wondered if this may have been one of the sites where the Ottomans had massacred Armenians almost 100 years earlier as part of the 1915 Armenian genocide, when over a million Armenian people were expelled from the empire and sent on death marches to the Syrian desert.

Crossing over into Azerbaijan, we knew we would soon come up to the Caspian Sea. We had already decided that – rather than forge north through Russia or south through Iran – we would cross the sea from the modern, oil-rich port city of Baku to Turkmenistan by the vintage rail freight ship which made the crossing. It was extremely old and filthy, but it ferried us across without incident and for that we were grateful.

Now that we were in Turkmenistan, we could join the legendary Silk Road along the Iranian border to Ashgabat, the capital, where the dictator Saparmurat Niyazov had erected a giant memorial to himself, and then north across the Karakum Desert to a wild, sandy campsite where we set up our tents. At nightfall we were taken by bus to see the Darvaza gas crater, the remains of a Soviet-era gas drilling site that exploded in the 1950s, leaving a burning crater 50 feet deep and with a diameter of 330 feet.

Posing in front of the 1,000 degrees Celsius Darvaza gas crater, otherwise known as the "Gates to Hell". Karakum Desert, Turkmenistan

It is also known as the Gates to Hell, and it is easy to see why. It was spectacular and we were lucky the wind was behind us as, if it had been blowing towards us, we would have breathed in all the toxic gases.

Further along the Silk Road we entered Uzbekistan and the magnificent city of Bukhara. We visited the notorious Bug Pit, a rat-infested dungeon 13 feet deep, accessible only by rope, where in the 1830s Colonel Charles Stoddart had been confined. He had been jailed for little more than arriving at the emir of Bukhara's castle on horseback rather than on foot, and for neglecting to bring a gift for the emir. After three years alone in the prison, Colonel Stoddart was joined by a Captain Connolly, who had been sent to Bukhara to negotiate Stoddart's release. Connolly failed to secure his release and was also thrown into the Bug Pit. The two spent the next year in the pit before being beheaded under order of the emir, whose nickname, rather aptly, was 'The Butcher'.

Samarkand was just as beautiful as Bukhara, and we enjoyed sights far less nasty than the Bug Pit: the magnificent mosques and madrasas with their superb, coloured tiles; the huge undercover markets made with old stone walls and pillars, filled with nuts, dates and other exotic produce from which my lunches were made for several days; and the large public square of the Registan, the heart of the city.

Crossing from Uzbekistan into Tajikistan marked the halfway point of the journey, and we allowed ourselves a day of rest. Jeff fitted off-road tyres to our bikes ready for the Pamir Highway, the second-highest road in the world which traverses the Pamir Mountains as it makes its way through central Asia.

With the Wakhan River beside us and passing the ancient Yamchun Fort which had been built some 2,000 years ago to guard this junction between the Hindu Kush and the Pamir Mountains, we set off up and along the highway. Stopping at a basic hotel – really a homestay, so basic it did not even have hot water – we were told that there was a dangerous hole in the road ahead. Kevin, the team leader, and a few of the hardier riders went forward to inspect it, and when they returned it was to tell us that the road had been completely washed away down the cliff. The locals with their 50cc bikes could get round it, but only by dismantling them and carrying them across. To do the same with our BMWs was impossible.

With no other choice, we had to turn back the following day. I took advantage of the slow and relaxed ride to watch the passing Afghans as they made their way along the hillside and pushed their donkeys up the steep hills. Some of the roads were so steep that ropes had been placed alongside the track to help the travellers climb on their way.

At one point, I stupidly ignored a small red flag at the side of the road, only to hear a bang and see a rock flying downwards from the Afghan side to hit my back wheel. Later, we came to a difficult waterfall crossing where one of the riders, Simon Callender, fell off his bike and filled his engine with water. Kevin tried to start it but with the cylinders full of water the engine refused to turn over and the starter casing broke. Both bike and rider had to go in the truck. Worried that the same might happen to me, I took all my gear out of my panniers and walked them across so that at least they would keep dry. And I am thankful that I did, for when I tried to ride the waterfall crossing, I fell in. All of which, of course, was filmed and uploaded to YouTube – to the delight of the rest of the team.

Riding through the valleys of Tajikistan

We had put the difficult waterfall crossing behind us, but the issue of Simon's bike still remained. When we reached the next village, we asked around for help and, with the aid of a guide, learnt that there was possibly a European motorbike in the village, left there by a previous traveller. After lots of questions we tracked it down – a Yamaha Ténéré which Simon pushed back to the hotel and which, amazingly, Jeff got running. Simon was able to ride the Yamaha all the way to the Kyrgyzstan border, from where a local rode it back to the village.

Kyrgyzstan is an extremely poor country and, at the time of our visit, was dangerously unstable. We were advised not to go to the capital. So instead, we rode to a little village called Sary-Tash, following a narrow grassy track to find a basic and cold hotel. Beds were crammed together into the tiniest of rooms and the stove was unlit. Two of the riders took their boots off and placed them on top of the stove, and we all began to anticipate a miserable night ahead, when the owner invited us for supper in the hotel's yurt. The difference between the two spaces was astonishing. The yurt was warm and comfortable, filled with woven carpets and cushions which circled the fire in the centre. We ate a pleasant meal of boiled meat and bread and were enjoying a quiet evening when the owner offered to show us the clear sky above. He opened the top of the yurt, but the freezing air which rushed in was too much to bear, so we all fled back to our room, where we found that the stove had been lit and the boots left on top of it had begun to melt. The two riders weren't best pleased, but at least we all had a warm night.

We woke to find two inches of snow on all the bikes. The track itself was completely covered over. We scraped the snow from our bikes and, knowing I would fall in such conditions, riding back down the snow-covered track, I put on my waterproof gloves. Alex Frick told us to follow him and, missing the track, we set off across the grass and on to the slushy road with no trouble.

Though we were back on the road, we still needed to take it easy. Not far along, a large artic began to follow us and, as we let it past, it covered us in a cloud of freezing spray. Then the road began to climb, and the packed snow grew thicker. Several of the riders in front of me fell off. I switched to the left-hand lane to avoid the ruts they had hit and had an easy ride for a while until I got stuck behind a six-wheel truck towing a trailer which continually spun its chain-enclosed wheels as it fought for traction. I rode carefully past it, ploughing on through thick snow, until I had to stop altogether because of another blockage.

Alex pulled up beside me, and I was delighted to learn that I had been the first biker to arrive, and not the usual last. It was impossible to pass the blockage, so we chatted with the Chinese drivers who had also stopped and shared what food we had between us. They were kind and friendly – perhaps a little too kind and friendly, for one of them even offered me a bed for the night.

Observing the Chinese army on manoeuvers from the border of Tajikistan

Kevin was also worried that we might not make any progress for the rest of the day, and he had begun to consider camping in the snow in our desert tents. It was an unappealing prospect, and very much the last resort. I was extremely grateful when I heard the heavy diesel rumble of a 1950s vintage bulldozer as it trundled along the empty carriageway beside us, its blade leaving about two feet of snow on the road. A short while later, thick black smoke belched from its stack as the noise of the engine rose to a deep roar while it cleared the blockage. The traffic finally started to move again.

I was relieved that I would not have to spend the night in a Chinese truck for, as I made my way up the ten-inch ruts, I soon fell over. The wheel went on top of the ruts and I couldn't pick the bike up, so I just lay down in the road waiting until my Chinese driver came into view and stopped to pick it up.

Back on the saddle and still climbing up the mountain, I began to grow concerned about what might happen when I reached the top and had to go down the other side. I dared not touch the brakes as they would have locked the wheel, and trying to use my feet instead would have been even more dangerous. So, when I made it to the top, I was enormously relieved to see that the snow had melted and it was just wet gravel. Alex was already there and had stopped at a café and I waited with him for everyone else to catch up. Once the entire team was complete, we shared our stories about the day behind us, discovering that, between the 15 of us, there had been 42 falls in just four hours. Thankfully, there had been no damage.

We made it over the Yamchun Pass and soon arrived at the Chinese border. However, once I had completed all the entry forms, my bike would not start. Jeff tried, but to no avail, so it went into the van, as did I. When we reached Kashgar, Jeff discovered that the problem was the fuel injection pump. I was a little perturbed that it had become faulty after only six weeks of riding, but was also grateful that it had made the pass. Things could have been much more treacherous if it had packed up along those frozen and isolated roads.

In Kashgar, we knew we had to collect our full Chinese papers and that this would take some time, so we used the opportunity to give ourselves – and our bikes – a rest. Travel in China is always a bureaucratic nightmare, and this time was no different. Our bikes needed Chinese licences, and to qualify we each had to pass a sight test and buy individual Chinese plates for each bike. With plenty of time to spare, we took a bus down the Karakoram Highway towards Pakistan, enjoying the spectacular Himalayan views.

Once all the paperwork was done, we set off to climb the 13,000 feet up and on to the Tibetan Plateau. I was taking Diamox to prevent altitude sickness – as were all the other riders, with the exception of Max. He was young and fit and decided that he did not need them. A week later, after suffering serious health problems, Max was driven at maximum speed in the second support vehicle we had brought for such an emergency to Lhasa. Our plan needed 8 days at high altitude. An impossible or lethal time with altitude sickness, while all of us old riders remained absolutely fine.

As we rode through Tibet, the landscape around us became increasingly wild and rough with huge open spaces and tiny, poor villages dotted here and there. We stayed at one, where the village had the implausible-sounding name of Reed Willow Beach. We quickly learnt that the beach was half a mile away and the hotel not worth a one-star rating.

Nevertheless, dinner that evening at the all-night diner next door was an interesting experience. Since we were special guests, we were treated to duck soup – after watching the duck being chased and caught. As the oldest person, I had the honour of the duck's head in my soup. Then it was back to our room, which featured twelve beds all pushed up against each other; to get into them we had to climb over the foot of the bed. There was continuous cooking and chatter from the diner all through the night, but it did not bother me in the slightest: I simply slept on my left side, never so grateful to be deaf in my right ear.

Back on the road the next day, we found ourselves frequently passing vehicles stuck in the deep muddy holes made by the construction gangs. Some of them were using modern diggers, while others did it the old way, with two men carrying their loads on poles held across their shoulders – probably how the Great Wall was built. Further along, the road was in better condition, but the bridges had not yet been constructed, so each time we had to detour down to the plains and then back up on to the road again. On one of these occasions, I followed Alex's tracks, only to realise that we were riding through some worker's vegetable garden.

In the south-west of the Tibetan Plateau is Mount Kailash, a 21,778-foot peak considered to be the most sacred mountain in Tibetan Buddhism. People from all over undertake the pilgrimage to Kailash to circle its base and reap its spiritual benefits. We rode on towards the Himalayas, which were growing ever closer, and soon passed under the sign welcoming us to

Waiting for the lorry to move as they continue with construction work on Tibetan Highway

LEFT: *Taking a moment at the sign for the Everest base camp turn off*

RIGHT: *Capturing a rare clear sky moment showing the strong winds over the peak of Mount Everest*

A fun switch-back road snaking it's way up to Everest base camp

the Qomolangma National Park – Qomolangma is the Tibetan name for Mount Everest – to take a picture.

We began the long zigzag climb up to the viewpoint, where a group photo was taken with the great mountain in the background, and then down another zigzag road past the highest monastery in the world to a large, flat gravel site: Everest Base Camp. It was not an attractive place to begin one's climb. I rode on towards the highest point I could reach, when suddenly my engine stopped and refused to restart. I had a temporary panic – I was, after all, off the main road – but I was able to push the bike around and freewheel it back down the mountain and about half a mile from the main road it started again.

Making our way north, we joined the Friendship Highway, the new and well-maintained road which runs from the Nepali border all the way to Tibet's capital, Lhasa. Lhasa is a beautiful city, but it is being continuously repopulated with Han Chinese, many of whom are soldiers who shelter under Coca-Cola umbrellas on street corners. I took a tour of the Potala Palace, which is truly amazing, but it is incredibly sad that no new monks are admitted. The old ones have been allowed to stay and continue their traditional lives, but once they all die so will Buddhism in the Potala Palace.

From Lhasa, it was a long road down, leaving the Tibetan Autonomous Region and crossing over into Sichuan Province, where we stopped in Chengdu and went to visit the Panda Base. This is China's principal research centre for panda breeding, and we saw lots of giant pandas eating bamboo shoots and playing with each other, as well as the red pandas, which are much smaller and more active, and also the symbol of the Firefox browser.

Riding out of the city, the bikes were supposed to form a single-file line with all of us following the leader. It was a six-lane highway and I didn't see the rider in front make a right turn so I continued on. I soon realised that I was alone, but rather than turn round or wait for them to catch up, I decided to continue on and follow the GPS, hoping we would meet up. This is not the easiest thing to do in Chinese cities as, for some reason, in China your GPS position is put about 400 yards away from where you actually are. This, coupled with the very high levels of traffic in Chengdu, meant that I was relieved to find a quieter, little-used road which appeared to be going in the right direction. All was well until the road came to its end: the entrance to a motorway, controlled by a barrier. Motorbikes are not allowed

Watching the giant pandas feast on bamboo, a key staple of their diet as a rich source of fibre, proteins, carbohydrates and essential vitamins and minerals.
Panda Base, Chengdu, Sichaun

on Chinese motorways, and I was unsure what to do. A policeman manned the barrier and came up to talk to me. Neither of us could speak the other's language, but it was all very jovial. I decided I should try and load my bike on a truck to reach my destination. I was having a great deal of difficulty explaining this, when a police pick-up parked in front of me. One of the officers got out and told me to follow them. The driver drove through the barrier and the officer in the back jumped out again and held the barrier up for me. We carried on and this happened twice more before we reached a busy road. The policemen then told me that this was my road. They then very kindly asked me if I would like to join them for lunch. I would have loved to accept, but unfortunately, I had a long way to go before dark. So instead, I thanked the officers and set off, grateful that they had been so helpful. They were the kindest, most helpful policemen I have ever met.

I finally met up with the rest of the team at the correct hotel just before dark to be harangued by Kevin for not calling him when I was left behind. We then rode on to Leshan, where we took a boat ride to see the famous Giant Buddha: a 233-foot-tall stone statue carved into a riverside cliff face at a junction of two giant rivers and covered in lichen. From there, we began the ride north-east to Xi'an, China's ancient capital. Along the way we passed through a large town. The traffic was heavy and, as I rode round a six-lane roundabout doing my best to dodge between the cars, my pannier accidentally brushed up against one. I could see that it wasn't serious and rode on, but the driver of the car had other ideas. He swerved round and began to follow me. When the traffic next stopped, he jumped out of his car, ran over to me and grabbed my key. In response, I grabbed his hand. Stalemate. Jeff arrived on the scene and he and another rider were able to force the Chinese man away from my bike and sit him on the ground. By then, the police had also arrived. They took some photographs and videos and an English-speaking officer explained that I had caused some minor injuries, but with a small fine it was all settled and we were on our way. Once again, I found myself impressed by the Chinese police, and decided there and then that I rated them much higher than their English counterparts.

Xi'an was a beautiful and fascinating stop-off. I especially enjoyed its huge defensive wall that is big enough for a car to drive along. It was bombed by the Japanese during the war, another example of the long list of conflicts between the two countries which has contributed to their still-strained relationship. I was also deeply impressed by the Terracotta Warriors lined up in their hundreds, each with an individual face.

Taking a hike on the Great Wall of China, a series of military fortifications which took over 2000 years to be constructed, starting in 220B.C. and continuing up to the Ming dynasty (1368-1644)

From there, our next stop was the Great Wall, which was much more impressive in real life than it is in the pictures. It was far too steep and the weather far too hot for me to climb much of, but I enjoyed what I saw – all well restored and in perfect order. The wall had regular forts along it. We finally made it to the outermost of Beijing's six ring roads, at which point motorbikes are forbidden to pass, but luckily for us the head of BMW China happened to be the brother of the area police chief, so we rode in with a police escort in great style for the final ceremony in front of the BMW dealership.

The end of the London to Beijing biking adventure

A view of The Forbidden City, the home to 24 emperors, their families and servants during the Ming (1368-1644) and the Qing (1644-1911) dynasties.

A visit to Tiananmen Square, where students led demonstrations in the June Fourth Incident in 1989 which ended in tragedy after military force was used to clear the square leading to deaths of civilians estimated anywhere in their hundreds to thousands

With the expedition now over and the rest of the day ahead of me, I decided to take the opportunity to see a little of Beijing, and went to visit the Forbidden City and then Tiananmen Square. It was in the latter that I met two local girls. I wanted to find out more about the massacre from them but learnt very little and instead somehow ended up in a karaoke bar – my first experience of one. It was a fun and interesting night.

The following day we rode the bikes to Tianjin, left them there, and boarded the bullet train. As the speed increased to 200 miles an hour, we agreed that it had been a wonderfully successful, and enjoyable, adventure. We ended our trip with a farewell dinner of Peking duck. During the three months of the trip, I had ridden 13,000 miles from London to Beijing through ten countries from deserts into snow-covered passes to Mount Everest Base Camp, all without serious mishap.

CHAPTER FORTY-SIX

HEROES LEGEND: THE RALLY FROM PARIS TO DAKAR 2010

During my previous time in the Dakar bivouac, talk had mostly been around bikes and bike rallies past and future. One future rally mentioned was the Heroes Legend, which was for cars and bikes, that ran from Paris to Dakar – mostly on the old classic route, but slower and less stressful. I kept asking more about it as it sounded so fascinating. Patsy was very enthusiastic and her partner and his friend were planning to join when she suggested that I should do it too. I said I had no suitable vehicle so she offered to sell me the Nissan Patrol that I was driving between bivouacs. This sounded perfect so we agreed the deal. It was an old French model fully modified for the job as it had done the original Dakar. As the Heroes Legend approached, I had still not managed to find a navigator, so she offered Zippy, who had trained me at the BMW school. He had also been Patsy's buddy when she finished the real Dakar in Africa.

We drove together to Paris to get our start photographs, with the Eiffel Tower in the background, before heading to Alicante for the official launch party and the prologue. This was a large flat field with holes dug in it. They were clearly steep-sided so low-range gears would be needed and I would just have to do my best between the holes. Zippy was not happy and wanted normal high-range gears. It was not an auspicious start and showed signs of trouble, but I proved correct and there were very steep holes to drive in and out of.

This was a Dutch-organised rally with Dutch support trucks and lots of Dutch drivers, many of whom had large American 6-litre Dodge Rams on huge tyres which they drove hard and fast. But they were not much good at the navigation. After crossing the Strait of Gibraltar, we drove down through Morocco to Nador for the start in the order that we had completed the prologue.

The road book gave us the detailed route and emphasised the dangers, and furthermore, Zippy was a very good navigator. Car navigation is so much easier than on a bike where riders have to navigate at high speed over difficult terrain. This terrain was mostly sand covered by varying amounts of camel grass and several dry, rocky river beds.

My Nissan was a 3-litre turbo diesel with a 40-gallon fuel capacity. It was amongst the lower-powered vehicles, so we were often near the back and we constantly had to decide quickly whether to follow the leaders' tracks in heavily churned sand or try a new route over virgin – and therefore firmer – sand. Some you win, some you lose. That meant either digging the sand out from in front of the wheels and putting sand ladders down or, if that didn't work, lowering the tyre pressure. Then we had to make the judgement as to whether there was more sand or not. That is: do you pump up the tyres soon or leave them for a bit longer and risk tyre damage and a puncture? There were lots of timed sections that had to be completed in the stated time. Points were lost for both early and late arrival so it was difficult to get it correct and make sure you found the end of the section, which was often hidden from the route.

Each night we stopped at a bivouac, which was usually a large Berber tent with colourful woven carpets spread on the desert floor with cushions on top. It was all very relaxing after a competitive day, and good Moroccan food was served before a night in pop-up Quechua tents. We managed quite well, even winning one section, much to my surprise. But I felt a bit embarrassed the next day being the first to start with a gentle take-off. No spectacular wheel spins for us. We soon arrived at the Mauritanian border from Morocco, having had to follow a strict narrow track through a minefield, with destroyed vehicles still visible on either side, and turned east to run parallel to the rail line that transported one of the longest trains in the world carrying phosphate to the port. This was one of the most isolated desert areas I had ever been to, but it had important Muslim holy sites and cities like the sand buried Chinguetti, now near derelict, from the days when it was green and heavily populated.

We were crossing some scrub desert when we came across a racing buggy tipped on its roof. Zippy got out quickly as he was a trained first responder for motorbikes. I stayed with the car and pressed the emergency button on our safety radio to call for a helicopter with its doctor. Zippy had found no serious injury so provided comfort until help arrived. The buggy had flown 18-metres though the air and somersaulted. The navigator only suffered bruising to the knee even though he had not been wearing his safety harness. The driver was not so lucky but was not seriously injured and went back in the helicopter, leaving the navigator to await recovery.

Back in 2008 the real Dakar Rally was cancelled the day before the start because of a terrorist threat. Morocco has large desert areas, but Mauritania is all desert except for two coastal ports and fishing communities. Tourism is virtually non-existent, but they dream about it and plan for it. At one camp we had a visit and speech by the minister for tourism asking if we could encourage more tourists. We could not see what they would come for. Bad news would be a total disaster for them so to prevent any attack they had deployed their army to protect us. Anytime you went out of your tent, it was comforting to know that night patrols were always visible. They were also often visible in the distance during the day.

Several of the entries were former Dakar classic cars that wanted to have another attempt to enjoy the past and the true desert experience again but with a good back-up system. We came across an old Porsche which had broken down so we were asked if we could tow it. I said I would try and we managed it for a few miles in the sand before my engine started to overheat. I dropped the tow and drove round for a few minutes until the Nissan had cooled down and then towed it again until we reached a town. The driver, a Frenchman, did not even offer us a drink.

We had several punctures but as we had two spare wheels we always managed to arrive at the camp before having to repair them. I had been advised to put tubes in tubeless tyres in case we blew a tyre off the rim and could not reseat it in the desert. In fact, it was the labels left on by the tyre fitter which caused the punctures.

One day near the end as we were approaching the bivouac, a bike came up behind us, planning to overtake. I put my hand out to the left to stop it overtaking but as we slowed to look for the bivouac entrance it disappeared from my mirror, then crashed into the right side of my vehicle and was flung down the road with its rider. I called the helicopter immediately. Soon the doctor arrived and started stabilising him. We held a towel up to keep the sun off them. He was soon safely up and away. This was my third medical emergency with the same action: 'Call the helicopter.' I hope I never have to deal with any emergency again.

Soon we approached the famous Lac Rose. This was the magical end to the original Dakar and this Dakar, and my third visit after my Unimog and KTM trips. We drove up the sand dune and stopped for photographs with congratulations under the inflatable finishing arch. Zippy and I had achieved a totally unexpected third place. It had been a truly wonderful rally in unbelievably beautiful and wild country.

CHAPTER FORTY-SEVEN
SOUTH AMERICA:
THE DAKAR RALLY 2011

By the following year, Tamsin Jones and Craig Bounds had become partners. After the bad luck he had experienced with his bike on the rally the previous year, Craig was keen to try again. Tamsin decided that she would go and support him, and asked if I would like to join their team. They had a German supporter on board and Tamsin had organised a car and two Yamaha bikes. The plan was for her to ride one of the bikes, as she had a bad back, and for the German and me to alternate the other bike and the car between us. It sounded like a good plan, and I gladly joined the team.

Tamsin and I started off on the bikes on the first day. We watched Craig begin the rally and then headed for the bivouac. I began to grow tired and kept seeing huge thunderstorms up ahead. I suggested to Tamsin that we stop, but she persuaded me to carry on. We finally arrived at 11.00 p.m. and were so exhausted from the day of riding that we just had a quick camp meal before heading straight to bed.

The next morning saw another early start. We had a long day ahead of us, but at least we knew that we only had to carry our day kits and other basic stuff on the backs of our bikes. The car would take our camping gear and everything else. We rode 550 miles in 24 hours to the next bivouac, but when we arrived it was to find that the car was not there. Since Patsy was running her team, we could at least get visitor's tickets and access to the bivouac, but we had no change of clothes or anything else. Time passed, and still the car did not arrive. By late evening, we realised that we needed to sleep, even though we didn't have any tents or sleeping bags. We just had to make do with what we had on us. Since the bivouac was a truck stop, it was mostly hard surfaces, none of which looked at all comfortable. I managed to find a small strip of grass, and eventually fell asleep on it. At two o'clock in the morning, I was suddenly awoken by a tremendous noise. It took me a few moments to understand what was going on. The grass strip I had bedded down on was the roadway out, and

six-wheel-drive support trucks were zooming past just a couple of feet from my head. I stood up rather quickly.

Since it was still so early, I was able to see Craig off and then, with nothing else to do, Tamsin and I set out on the next day's ride. It was supposed to be my turn to drive the car, but it still hadn't turned up, and we needed to be there for Craig at the next bivouac. So, deciding to just continue and hope for the best, we rode for the next 300 miles.

Along the way, we came to a petrol station and I pulled in to fill up. I saw Tamsin on the road waiting to go out. Once I had refuelled, I set off after her. There were some guards there, but I just waved and rode past them, desperate to see if I could catch Tamsin so that we could ride together. I was confident that she would wait for me. However, as I rode on, there was still no sign of her. I was sure I could catch her up and didn't want to turn back, so I kept on riding. But Tamsin was nowhere to be seen.

A little later, I saw a group of three BMW bikes with Belgian number plates. I stopped beside them and we started talking. I asked if I could follow them, and they said it was no problem. We carried on together for a while and then stopped for a drink in a café. They explained that they had prepared the road book for the support trucks. I realised that this meant that they knew all the routes, so I asked them for all the waypoints for each of the bivouacs. I was relieved to know them as now I was no longer reliant on anyone. If I got lost or if Tamsin disappeared again, I could find the bivouacs for each day.

Armed with my new knowledge, I rode on with much more confidence. At the next bivouac, I found Tamsin waiting for me. It turned out that the guards had forbidden her from leaving the garage on to the road that I had

LEFT: *The Nissan Patrol support truck driven by Charles giving Patsy the chance to sleep*

RIGHT: *Tamsin and Patsy on the finishing line*

last seen her on, so she had had to make her own way. As she described it to me, I realised how difficult her improvised route must have been, and doubted if I would have managed it myself. That she had succeeded in getting to the bivouac by herself showed how strong a rider Tamsin was.

The next day's riding passed without any problems and, when we arrived at the next bivouac and entered the main compound in our full off-road riding gear, we were treated almost like competitors, with everyone trying to shake our hands. Our support truck eventually turned up. We talked to the German, who was driving, and found out that there had been an incident the previous night. The Kiwi owner/driver had tried chatting up a girl. Not only did she reject his advances, she also called the police. Nine officers arrived on the scene, pinned the Kiwi to the floor, gave him an injection and then carted him off for psychiatric help. Needless to say, we never saw him again.

With this change in our circumstances, we decided to ensure our self-sufficiency for the rest of the rally. Patsy lent us some tents and we took all our gear with us. This way, our travelling could be self-contained and our accommodation under our own control.

Feeling much happier with this new state of affairs, we set off the following day. Things were going well until Craig had an accident. He had had a problem with his bike earlier and, when the mechanic had repaired it, he had not fixed the suspension properly, tightening it up too hard. This meant that the bike was not performing as it should, and when Craig hit a bump, the suspension was too hard and threw him off. He injured his shoulder so badly that he was forced to quit the rally and go to hospital.

I went to visit him. His shoulder was mending, but he was upset that he could not finish the rally. I decided to confide something personal to him. At the beginning of the rally, I had been given some bad news myself. I was told that I had pancreatic cancer. Craig was the first person I told, and he was very supportive. He told me I would be all right, which was a comfort and so it proved to be.

Since Craig was not fit to carry on, he had to be flown home. Tamsin opted to return with him as she wanted to look after him and the German rode her bike back. I, on the other hand, was keen to continue, so I followed the rally on my bike. Stopping at a section where the riders came close to the road, I parked my bike in the sand and walked up to watch them all pass. While I was there, I briefly chatted to a tourist and his guide who were there for the same reason but would be going back to Buenos Aires soon. When I returned to my bike, I found it was stuck in the sand. My new friends kindly helped me push it out, and I rode off to the next bivouac.

The following day, I continued on my own. We had to cross the Andes over the San Francisco Pass, a particularly challenging part of the route. I reached the customs post between Argentina and Chile only to discover that I did not have the correct stamp in my passport. This baffled me. I had entered the country with Tamsin and all had seemed to be in order, and yet here I was without the necessary stamp. Fortunately for me, the customs house staff eventually decided I could leave the country.

I set off up the steep and sandy incline towards the pass. On one especially tight hairpin, an artic could not get round it, and I had to give it a wide berth in order to get round the hairpin myself. The road was very sandy, and I have never been happy in sand.

To this day, I still cannot tell you what happened, but the next thing I knew I was being put inside a Dakar truck ambulance.

'Don't worry,' I heard. 'We'll get the bike back to Buenos Aires for you.'

In my semi-conscious state, I realised that these were the men who had pulled me out of the sand. I also realised how incredibly lucky I had been for them to find me, for I had been riding alone and without support. They had been in the queue behind the artic.

The ambulance set off up the horrible track, and I had to persuade the driver to give me a pillow to make it slightly more comfortable. Eventually, after what seemed like a very long time, we reached the other border post on the Chilean side and my passport was stamped. I found out that the two posts were 75 miles apart, as neither country wanted a border post right at the top of a mountain. If the Dakar truck had not found me, any ambulance sent out to get me would have had to get clearance to leave Argentina to go across the border and come back again, and it was unlikely that they would have had passports. I had been really lucky.

The truck took me to the nearest hospital, which was basic and ill-equipped. There was nothing they could do, so the next day I was transferred to a bigger hospital. There, X-rays were taken to identify the problem. My leg, I was told, needed to be pinned. But the hospital did not have the necessary equipment. If I wanted it done, they would have to apply to the government to get everything sent in. This would take two weeks to get the permission and then the equipment.

I was coming out of my dazed state and, rather than waiting for all that, I knew I had to contact my insurance company. Later that day an air ambulance flew me to Buenos Aires where I was transferred to a modern Swiss-owned hospital. Once there, I was very well treated. They X-rayed me again, agreeing with the earlier diagnosis that my leg needed to be pinned. However, they believed that my shoulder also required the same. They had the equipment in the hospital and could do it the next day, a Sunday. I felt both glad and lucky to have the operation and, after a few days of recovery, arrangements were made to fly me home. A travelling nurse was assigned to accompany me. Since she was not allowed to sleep on the journey, she had 24-hours' rest in Buenos Aires beforehand. The insurance firm was efficient and extremely well prepared – perhaps this was not so surprising, as I later learnt that I was the 63rd person they had repatriated from the rally.

The flight home was comfortable and free of problems. When we arrived, I was met by an ambulance, which drove me from the airport to my house far faster than I have ever managed to do it. Ali was there, as well as some friends who had come for a shooting party. I was relieved to be home and able to join them for the wonderful dinner that Ali had cooked.

Back in England, I had access to the NHS once more. I was given lots of help and support, but in spite of all the specialist treatment my leg did not seem to be healing. Finally, the doctors decided that I should have a bone graft. The operation was a success, but I was not able to walk again for the next ten months.

CHAPTER FORTY-EIGHT
BIKING WITH FRIENDS: ETHIOPIA

If I am in England at the time, I often attend the Adventure Bike Rider Festival. In 2012, I met a young woman there called Clare Southern. She had a stand which showed the round-the-world trip she and her partner, Sam Farah, were planning to take. Beginning in North America, they intended to overland right down to the southern tip of South America, and then ship across the Atlantic to do the entire length of Africa. The adventure was in support of several charities including the Welsh Air Ambulance.

I talked to Clare for some time that afternoon. She was twenty-seven years old and living in Weston-super-Mare. I found her to be charismatic and a good speaker, and I was impressed and envious of the trip they were planning. To help them on their way, I gave them some money. They were so grateful that they decided to come to Suffolk to visit me. They did just that, and we all got on well – so well, in fact, that when they invited me to join them for a portion of their trip, I accepted.

Unfortunately for Sam and Clare, they had a run of bad luck. Various problems and unforeseen complications arose, delaying their trip until eventually they had to postpone the Americas section altogether because the seasons were wrong. Instead, they decided to ride down through Europe and Africa. We were still regularly in touch, and they repeated their invitation for me to join them. We agreed that I would meet them in Ethiopia, and from there we would see how far we could ride together.

As Sam and Clare set off for the European leg of their adventure, I busied myself with trying to find a rental car in Ethiopia. It was trickier than I thought. Most businesses in the country only rent cars with a driver, and I wanted a self-drive car. I eventually found an old Mitsubishi that had been imported from Scandinavia and, once it was booked, I flew out to Addis Ababa to collect it. In the plane, I thought about Sam and Clare and wondered how they were getting on. By this point in the journey, they should have been crossing Sudan, a dangerous portion of their route. They told me later that, because the American ambassador was assassinated while they were in Libya and thus the borders were closed, they had to be snuck into Egypt in the footwell of a catering truck. It is probable that they were two of the last foreign nationals to make it through the land borders during that war-torn period.

Landing in Addis Ababa, I went to pick up the Mitsubishi. It was a little older than I had expected, but it seemed to drive all right and coped well with Ethiopia's rough roads. I drove it to Bahir Dar, where I found a lovely little hotel on the edge of Lake Tana. It was a popular stop-off for travellers, and I met some interesting people who were on their way north. From there, I carried on to the Sudanese border and waited in the town of Metema for Sam and Clare to arrive.

Keeping cool under the trees as Sam changes the inner tube to his tyre. Lake Tana in Ethiopia

They soon appeared and we were all pleased to see each other. Their KTM 690s still looked in good condition, albeit with melted, sandy and warped decal stickers from the staggering 55°C Sudanese desert heat, but they had prepared them well. They were fully laden with luggage and long-range fuel tanks. Once they cleared customs, I followed them as they rode into Ethiopia for the first time. We headed back towards Lake Tana to a campsite called Tim & Kim's Village which Sam and Clare had heard of. It turned out to be a lovely place under the shade of some trees, and despite our late arrival they prepared a beautiful meal for us of pasta, potato salad and a lemony-like tabbouleh. It was supposed to be a goat dish, but the meat had so little flesh on it that it was mostly just pasta.

Exhausted from their long ride across north Africa, Sam and Clare wanted a break so we decided to spend the following day at the campsite. The owners let us borrow a couple of canoes to go out on the lake and explore the islands. Sam and Clare took one and I took the other with a fellow camper called Brian. We all paddled out into the water together, making our way towards the nearest island. It was occupied by fishermen, but they had no market for their fish, so instead they strung them out to dry on wires around the island. We paddled across to another island, where we found a monastery. It would not allow women, so only Brian and I went in. It was a small place, and the two monks who lived there showed us where they prayed and slept. While we followed them round the monastery, Sam and Clare stayed outside. Their inflatable canoe had a hole in it and had begun to take on water, semi-submerging the front and making it impossible to steer. Clare found it hilarious and, after about thirty minutes of going round and round in circles and gradually sinking deeper and deeper into the hippopotamus-infested lake, Sam grew increasingly frustrated, eventually declaring that he wished he could marry Clare there and then just to divorce her. Unfortunately, the semi-sinking of the canoe washed the sun cream off Clare's legs and, since the doxycycline she was taking made her incredibly susceptible to the sun, she ended up with second-degree burns.

Back at the camp in the evening, we had a much better meal than the previous one. The night sky was beautiful and clear, and we fell asleep in our tents satisfied with a good day. The following morning, the skin on Clare's legs was tight and had started to swell severely from the sunburn. She could barely move, and by the time we were ready to leave it was clear that she was in no condition to ride. The only option was for me to take her bike and for her to drive the Mitsubishi. Fortunately, when Sam and Clare first asked me to join them on this trip, they had suggested I bring my motorcycle kit out with me so that I could occasionally have a ride. Hence, I was fully prepared. At first, I was a little nervous. The bike was completely new to me and the rather difficult potholed and corrugated dirt track which led from the campsite did not help matters. Soon, however, I became used to it, and we were on our way.

One of our first stops was the old city of Gondar where we could look at the ruins. We parked next to the entrance and climbed off the bikes. Suddenly, I heard my name called from the other side of our car. Feeling astonished that anyone should know my name out here in the heart of Ethiopia, I turned around to see Solomon, the guide from my SES expedition white-water rafting down the Blue Nile. I could not believe that he had recognised me, and since I was still wearing my helmet and he had not seen me, he must have done so by my voice alone. It had been four years or so since I had last seen him. When our group came off the Nile for a week, Solomon and I had taken a walk along the river. On that walk, we had seen something incredible: a brown snake eagle flew past us with a snake in its talons. The snake was doing its best to bite the eagle, but the speed of the bird flying through the wind prevented the snake from striking it with its fangs, and the eagle managed to kill it with its beak in mid-air.

After reminiscing with Solomon, I said goodbye and then the three of us set off again, eventually coming to a stop at a small town called Debarq. There we found a very basic hotel with no running water and a shortage of toilet roll. The staff were rather unfriendly, but we had a good night's sleep and, feeling refreshed, set off the next day. Sam fell off his bike trying to ride over a log on the track out of the hotel, but luckily was unhurt. We were heading for the Simien Mountains but were turned away at the entrance gate since we did not have the proper permits, or a guide and a guard with us, which was required. We briefly returned to the town where we discovered a local guide, Yeshi, who helped us acquire the permits and a guard, then advised us to take a different route to the

Watching as a group of Gelada's native to the Simien Mountains and otherwise known as the bleeding-heart monkey, crosses the mountain tops

mountains up a sandy track near a quarry. I was a little daunted at taking the track, but Sam rode on ahead – straight into the dust of a big quarry truck coming down the track. When it was clear, I followed. The sand was difficult but passable, and I was glad when we passed the quarry and climbed up into the mountains. High on the rugged plains, we saw a huge troop of gelada monkeys, which are native to the Ethiopian highlands. They are famous for being the only ground-dwelling monkeys that avoid their predators by sleeping on steep cliffs in the mountains, and we felt privileged to have seen so many of them all together like that.

Together we rode and drove to the highest point we could: a quite literally breath-taking 14,032-foot elevation. After taking a short walk and lapping up the rolling mountainous views, the sun was beginning to lower in the sky and, with such a sandy, rocky and somewhat dangerous mountain road to return on, we hastily travelled back while it was still light to a flatter section in the Simien Mountain where there was a pretty basic but incredibly beautiful campsite with stunning views. A few gelada monkeys were around, so one of the soldiers lent Sam a rifle. We were all glad that he did not have to use it.

Clare's legs werc still severely swollen and blistered, so we agreed she would keep driving the Mitsubishi and I would carry on with her bike. We continued and, by the time late afternoon came around, we realised that Clare was no longer behind us. Sam and I stopped the bikes to wait for her, agreeing that she had probably just fallen behind and would catch up with us soon.

Another car approached us, and as it slowed down, I recognised my friend Solomon inside. The car stopped and he leant out of the open window. 'I think you've got a problem with your Mitsubishi,' he said.

'Can you take us to it?' I asked.

'Sure. Follow me.'

He turned the car round and we rode after him to where the Mitsubishi had come to a stop. We opened up the bonnet to inspect the engine and soon discovered the problem. The cambelt had broken and bits of valve gear could be seen under the rocker cover. The Mitsubishi couldn't go anywhere.

Sunset dinner in the Simien Mountains campsite.

Solomon waved down a local truck and asked the driver if he could help. The driver said that he would, but first he had to drop his passengers off. True to his word, he returned an hour later with an empty truck. Precariously, he drove the truck down a steep track beside the main dirt track, and then reversed it up so that its back was level with the main road. We pushed the Mitsubishi towards it and up its tailgate, but the weight of the car caused the tailgate to collapse. Searching for an alternative, we found some rocks and stones to put underneath it and managed to heave the Mitsubishi on to the truck.

By now, it was beginning to become late, with dark, ominous clouds looming in the direction of our return. A rumble of thunder chorused through the valley, causing a sense of urgency and concern to get moving, knowing we had a difficult section of the road ahead. As the Mitsubishi was now in place and only needed to be ratcheted down, Sam and I decided to make headway and set off in an attempt to make it off the mountain before nightfall and the incoming storm hit. We managed to make it through a good portion of a rough section with me upfront, riding as fast as I dared in order to cover as much ground as possible before the storm broke. When it eventually did, the rain came down in torrents. Darkness settled in with it, and despite upgraded halogen lights on the bikes, the weather was so horrendous our vision was reduced to mere feet. With thunder ricocheting through the valley, lightning was striking all around, momentarily lighting up the track, now a muddy waterway, beneath our tyres. There were rivers of water gushing across our paths over the track down the sheer cliff edges into pure darkness. I slowed right down as the conditions worsened, hoping we would soon find a hotel so that we could get to safety. Sam took the lead so I was able to follow him, which was much easier. We found a hotel on the mountain and checked in, relieved to be off the road.

Solomon was already at the hotel, and we thanked him for all his help that afternoon. Eventually, Clare arrived with the truck driver. She was so relieved to see us and told us all about the terrifying drive she had endured. At one point, the road and weather became so bad that the driver insisted all the passengers get out and walk up the hill. This was not particularly easy for Clare with her swollen and burnt legs, but then the driver explained why. He was worried that the truck would slide off the edge and he didn't want to take all the people with him. After a number of failed efforts to slick and slide up the track, the truck ended up dangerously fishtailing and eventually jack-knifing before sliding back down into the paths of Yeshi, Clare and the guard. With a sheer cliff edge on one side and a steep rocky climb on the other, they had no choice but to grapple and push their way up the rocks and mud to avoid being hit, causing her to tear off the skin of her blistered legs and bleed profusely. The driver fortunately managed to gain control and finally made it up the worst part of the path. Upon returning to the cab, drenched and covered in mud and blood, the rest of the journey off the mountain was filled with desperate songful prayer from the guard, and with them all keeping their eyes glued to the path to ensure that there were still two bike tracks in the mud and that neither Sam nor I had been washed off the edge in the flash flooding. Whenever the tracks disappeared into a washed-out section, the praying would intensify until their re-emergence and the whole cab would cheer.

LEFT: *One of the 11 medieval monolithic rock hewn Catholic churches in Lalibela, carved over a period of 24 years within the seventh and thirteenth centuries.*

RIGHT: *The top of one of the Lalibela churches where it was surmised that the Archangel Gabriel carved within 24 hours.*

We were all pleased to have made it to the hotel. The truck driver agreed to take our Mitsubishi and drop it off at the next big town where we could collect it. After cleaning up the wounds and some rest and recovery following a somewhat stressful night, we made our way there the next day and were met by the Mitsubishi's owner, whom Solomon had called from the hotel. He was angry with us and demanded lots of money to compensate for the damage. Clare, who was a former police officer, was having none of it, and spent a long time persuading the man that it was his fault, having failed to change the cambelt when he should have. She won the argument and the owner accepted it was his fault. While we were in the town, Clare went to the hospital to have her legs checked. They confirmed she had suffered second-degree burns and dressed them accordingly.

Once we had sorted it all out, we headed off down to Addis Ababa and then the Bale Mountains, with Sam and me riding the bikes and Clare following in a taxi. The roads were not easy. We frequently had to avoid various livestock. Most of these were stubborn donkeys which refused to move, and I nearly hit one because the mischievous children who owned it gave it a shove towards my bike just as I was approaching. This is a common trick in Ethiopia and other surrounding countries: for locals to purposely throw themselves, or an animal, in front of vehicles in the hope that they might be hit and will be offered financial compensation. More often than not, this is done with old and lame animals which are no further use to them.

Eventually, we reached the Bale Mountains. We wanted to go right up to the top to see if we could find any Ethiopian wolves, but Clare's taxi was too slow and, in the end, we did not have time. It was a shame, as I was due to return home soon. Sam and Clare still had the rest of Africa to complete so, as I made my way back to the airport, they continued on with their long journey down to South Africa. From Cape Town, they planned to ship their bikes to New York and keep the adventure going from there. As we said our goodbyes, they told me they hoped I would be able to join them on the far side of the Atlantic, and I agreed that I would see them somewhere out there.

There was nothing left to do now but make my way home. Unfortunately, after all the problems with the car, I missed my flight. I contacted my travel agent, who was able to have me rebooked. I explained to my insurance company what had happened. At first, I thought they might not believe me but, when I showed them a photograph of the Mitsubishi on the back of the truck, they accepted my story.

CHAPTER FORTY-NINE
BIKING WITH FRIENDS:
NORTH AMERICA

I had been dreaming of riding a bike across Canada to Alaska for some time, and with Sam and Clare heading out that way, it seemed a perfect opportunity. I had also bought a KTM 690 and fitted it out with panniers and large fuel tanks, everything it would need for adventure travel.

In the early summer of 2013, I flew my bike to Halifax in Nova Scotia. When I arrived, I was pleasantly surprised that it only took me two and a half hours after landing to have the bike cleared through customs and back to the hotel. The following day I rode through pouring rain to Saint John to meet Sam and Clare. Reunited but soaked, we left our kit to dry while we explored the local area, visiting the famous Reversing Rapids, where the Bay of Fundy meets the Saint John River and creates a turbulent series of whirlpools and white water.

The rain did not stop, and so we pressed on regardless, biking towards Alma through the Fundy National Park along a beautifully paved road lined with forests of balsam fir trees and bog-ringed lakes. Alma was a picturesque fishing village famed for its lobsters, and that night we ate dinner at the local Harbour View Restaurant, where Sam and I had freshly caught lobster and Clare chose the clam chowder.

From there, we rode to Moncton and then east to Truro, where I had my first 3D cinema experience watching *World War Z*: a somewhat chaotic introduction to the 3D world. The following morning, Clare's bike wouldn't start. We called KTM Basel in Switzerland, who made the suggestion that we simply spray some WD40 in the ignition button. We followed their advice and were relieved to discover that it worked. However, Clare's problems were not to end there. Soon, her clutch began playing up and her rear brake was not working adequately. In Halifax, we visited a local bike shop, which quoted over a thousand Canadian dollars for the job. Thankfully, a British mechanic in the area fixed it all quite easily by tweaking the brake to release the piston and adjusting the clutch lever – it had become pressed up against the hand guard. He was a very kind man and did not even charge us.

With Clare's bike fixed, we could get back to our journey, and made our way to the Cabot Trail. It was a magnificent road with long mountain climbs and incredible views. We were able to join a whale tour boat off the coast of Cape Breton, where we were followed by a pod of pilot whales who played around us. There were even minke whales swimming off in the distance and seals sunning themselves on rocks. We felt very fortunate to have seen such sights.

Unfortunately, our luck was about to turn again. As we made our way across Nova Scotia, we found a little gravel track up a mountainside which looked fairly easy and fun to ride. It quickly became narrow with some rather steep sections. My bike did not seem to be behaving properly and, since I wasn't sure how it would respond to the throttle, I felt a little nervous about the steep parts of the track. Sam offered to ride the section and it turned out that I had been right to be nervous, for when he rode Clare's bike along it after mine, he crashed.

Once we were all finally off the gravel track, we stayed the night in a motel and then, the next day, Sam and I spent the morning working on my bike. Nevertheless, no matter what we did, it still kept cutting out. Since the next part of our route was the Trans-Labrador Highway – where hundreds of miles can pass without any signs of civilisation – we decided we needed to get the bike fully sorted, and so travelled back to Halifax. I contacted KTM Canada, but they could not help. Instead, they suggested the small mechanic who had modified the bike for me in England, which was clearly not helpful while we were in Canada. Plenty of arguing ensued, until eventually KTM admitted that they had put an ignition programme in which was two versions out of date.

It was a great relief when the bike was finally fixed and we could proceed with the ride. We took the ferry to Newfoundland, which was especially memorable for its abundance of lobsters from the island's rocky shoreline. We visited a shop with dozens of lobsters both dead and alive for sale including one which weighed 16 pounds. We rode all the way round Newfoundland and then took the ferry across the Strait of Belle Isle to Labrador. There, a gravel road took us to Cartwright to join Route 516, east Canada's most northerly road. I rode down it quite carefully as it was my first time on main road gravel but enjoyed the feeling of being in pure wilderness as the pine trees rose up on either side of us. It was the least populated area I have ever seen. One big road sign said: 'Check your fuel – 350 kilometres to the next gas station.'

Eventually, we reached the town of Happy Valley-Goose Bay, the home of one of the biggest air bases in the north. Surprisingly, it had no security whatsoever and we could ride freely around the base. Sam knew about a 1950s Vulcan bomber which his uncle had worked on but it could not be made airworthy and, thus, had been left in Canada rather than taken back to England. We were free to inspect it without any kind of restrictions, seeing all the covers opened from the ground, allowing us to inspect all the wiring.

Returning to the road, we continued towards the immense concrete Manic-5 dam across the Churchill River. The dam supplies much of New York's electricity, but the river has been diverted to fill it, just leaving a small trickle. We then took a ferry across the St Lawrence River to ride around the Gaspé Peninsula on the edge of the Gulf of St Lawrence. We found a lovely campsite where we met some French Canadians. Since we were British, they spoke to us in English. However, if we had been Canadian, they assured us that they would have spoken only in French.

We had hoped to go to Montreal, but because of all the delays caused by the problems with my bike we no longer had the time, and so we bypassed it and rode straight down to Toronto. Sam and Clare had friends there and I needed to return home because my BMW had been shipped to Tucson in Arizona, ready for my 15-week ride down through Central and South America to Ushuaia in Argentina.

◎ ◎ ◎

Taking a breather after some deep gravel riding on the Trans-Labrador Highway.

The following year, I flew back to Toronto. On my own, I rode across the Great Lakes, round and up northern Canada to Flin Flon, and then through as much of the northern forests as possible before hitting the prairies. Eventually, I arrived in Calgary where, once again, I had arranged to meet Sam and Clare. After leaving me in Toronto last time, they had tried to continue on to Prudhoe Bay in Alaska, but delays and bike problems had spoilt their plans, and by the time they reached Fairbanks the roads were too icy and the air was well below freezing. They then had to hire a truck, load the bikes and return frozen to Calgary, where Sam had a friend.

It had been a year since we had last been together, and it was wonderful to see them both again. To celebrate, we went to see the Calgary Stampede, an annual festival famous for having one of the largest rodeos in the world. We watched a huge procession of Old West vintage vehicles and then a tank that, astonishingly, spun round in the street without moving its gun, which remained always pointed forwards. Rubbish carts had been dressed up to look like bulls, girls rode enormous horses by standing upright on the saddles and one man even rode a bull. We ate fast food which, although we were in Canada, was distinctly American. Instead of chicken, we bought turkey drumsticks so big that they lasted us the whole day. At the rodeo itself, the performances were staggering, with bull riding, bronco riding and even steer wrestling, which they called calf bulldogging. The competitors would aim to ride for about ten seconds as part of the competition. When that time was finished, the support

Overindulging on the smallest available turkey legs for lunch at the Calgary Stampede.

riders would ride up beside the animal, enabling the competitor to grab on to them and so get off the still-bucking animal and get safely on to the ground. Then the support riders would reach out to remove the very tight belt around the animal's stomach which had made them buck so violently and which, went it was removed and the competitor had climbed off, made the animal calm once more. There were clowns who purposely got butted by the bulls. Possibly the most exciting of all was the chuckwagon racing. Wagons pulled by four horses completed a figure of eight around a succession of barrels before madly racing each other around the circuit with their support horses joining in. It was all extremely close racing with solo horse riders having difficulty keeping up with the chuckwagon and many drivers losing their Stetsons in their enthusiasm to push their four-horse team to the front. There was also an Indian village where many tribes showed off their culture and traditions.

Once we had our fill of the Calgary Stampede, it was time for us to start riding north into the Rockies. We spent the night camping at Lake Louise, the first campsite in my life to have warning signs saying 'Be Bear Aware'. There were plenty of black bears in the local surroundings, and all food had to be put away in lockers outside the campsite so as not to attract them. We never saw the bears on the site itself, but we saw several on the road, as well as the silly people who tried to take selfies with them.

Soon, we made it on to the Icefields Parkway, one of the most spectacular roads I have ever ridden. Glaciers reached right down near to the roadside. It was possible to go up on to them, but we chose not to. The ends of the glaciers were just muddy gravel, and we preferred to look at them from a distance, where they looked shiny, clean and white. We carried on over the Rockies to the Stewart-Cassiar Highway, which we followed up through British Columbia to Watson Lake in Yukon. There, we found a park where visitors left various tokens of their presence, such as a plaque with their vehicle number plate, or simply their names carved or painted on a plaque and nailed to a tree – which is what we chose to do. A group of motorcyclists had made it there on totally unsuitable road bikes, one of which had a broken cast alloy wheel. It was beyond repair, and they were forced to abandon it.

On we went to Whitehorse. This was very much the north, and we followed the Yukon River to Dawson City where it meets the Klondike River. The second-largest town in the territory of Yukon, Dawson City is most famous for being the principal town of the nineteenth-century Klondike

Gold Rush. Starting out as a poorly equipped boom town, miners had to carry everything up the snow-covered passes of the Chilkoot Trail from the Pacific coast. As it was in Canada it was policed by the Mounties, who insisted that all miners entering Canada had to have at least 1,000 lbs of food and supplies. Often it would take a miner three months making thirty to forty journeys to haul all of this on his back up the Chilkoot Trail. Nevertheless, Dawson City became a thriving hub of prospectors. The town's streets and buildings were mostly the original from the Gold Rush era. It retained the pioneer feel. Some of the old houses which were built during the mining era were situated on ground above permafrost, but the many years of keeping them warm in the region's subarctic climate have melted the permafrost below, causing these houses to slant like the Leaning Tower of Pisa.

I took a short ride up some of the old creeks. Gravel had been dredged out of the river by huge bucket dredgers and put over the large gold-panning table. Most of the dredgers were owned by the Guggenheim family. They dredged the whole river leaving behind huge piles of stones. Beside one creek, I came across a man shovelling loads of gravel over a little portable machine in the hope of finding some gold. The dreams of the prospectors, it seemed, had continued on into the twenty-first century.

Crossing the Yukon River by ferry, we joined the Top of the World Highway, named so because much of it runs along the crests of the mountains, affording sensational views across the peaks and into the valleys below. A terrifying hailstorm forced us to stop and seek shelter under some diggers parked by the side of the road. From there, we rode on to the Alaska Highway and made our way to Fairbanks, on the way passing through a town called North Pole, which featured plenty of signs for 'Santa's Grotto'. Arriving at Fairbanks, we found ourselves a small hotel where we could leave some of our equipment before tackling the Dalton Highway, which has a bad reputation for muddy gravel and fast, heavy articulated trucks that will never slow down.

As we set off from Fairbanks the following day, the roads began well, but it was not long before they started to deteriorate. We crossed the Yukon River once more and then stopped at the town of Coldfoot, the midway point between Fairbanks and our ultimate destination, Prudhoe Bay. We were now in the far north, where there are two seasons: the freezing season and the muddy season. As such, all the bunkhouses in this region provide their guests with plastic pull-on slippers to stop them traipsing mud into the rooms. We happily obliged with the practice, putting them over our muddy boots as we checked in.

The next day, well fed and rested, we set off for our wild ride to Alaska's north coast. It was by now late July, and yet there were still six-inch icicles hanging from the rocks and a light sprinkling of fresh snow on the ground as we climbed and went over the Atigun Pass. The pass was closed for two days after we rode over it. Trucks passed us regularly, spraying mud everywhere. Eventually, the land levelled out and we reached Deadhorse, the town of Prudhoe Bay, where we were surprised to see a small herd of shaggy musk ox at the side of the road.

The hotel we checked into for the night looked more like a prison with its stencilled 'F BLOCK' on the door. Of course, there were also the inevitable plastic shoes to put on. Parked outside, amongst the light drifting snow, were an array of huge agricultural Case crawler tractors, each having 600 horsepower, with four tracks and a train of four very large sledges behind them. This was the slack season, and the tractors would be going nowhere until the winter. They were all waiting for the government to decide when it would be safe to drive on the tundra and over the frozen lakes again.

Deadhorse exists purely for the oil companies, their staff and the drilling support businesses who work at the enormous Prudhoe Bay Oil Field, the largest oil field in North America. We met some workers whose firm was being paid over a million dollars to make an aerial survey of the area and measure the depth of the pools. The weather had been so poor that they

The Trans-Alaska Pipeline, a remarkable 800-mile long above ground pipe to protect the permafrost. It runs from Prudhoe Bay to Valdez, Alaska and has shipped over 17 billion barrels of oil as of 2015.

had only 15 per cent flying days. The shallow pools freeze completely and therefore have nothing living in them. The deeper pools, however, are often able to sustain life so must not be damaged by supply trains.

Sam, Clare and I wanted to see the Arctic Ocean itself. We were not allowed to ride there as it is all private land, so we took a bus out to a BP concession, where we were told we could see the largest drilling rig in the world, all fully encased, although the guide admitted we were not meant to look at it. We were told it could drill five miles deep. One of our party volunteered to swim, but the idea seemed like madness to me. I remained wrapped up, taking photographs of icebergs offshore.

There was little else to do in Deadhorse. The town was just a series of large oil supply equipment depots, where all the equipment was available to rent. We passed the Alaska pipeline, which was mounted above ground and capable of carrying two million barrels a day but averages 1.6 million, just above the UK usage of 1.4 million. We met a fellow biker at the hotel and were astonished to learn that he had ridden here on a scooter. That was how he did all his travelling. It was incredible to discover that he had come so far north on such an unsuitable bike.

It was time to leave Prudhoe Bay and begin making our way back down south. We passed roadworks after roadworks but were fortunate that motorbikes were allowed to go to the front of the queue and not have to wait behind lines of trucks spewing out mud. We arrived back at Coldfoot for the night and, the next morning, I was ready first so set off ahead of Sam and Clare. A bridge climbs over the Yukon River and, despite the

LEFT: *Standing at the northern most motorable point next to the Beaufort Sea and the site of BP's world's largest oil drilling rig. Prudhoe Bay, Alaska*

RIGHT: *A narrow bridge crossing over a gnarly river on the Trans-Labrador loop. Canada*

sign prohibiting it, I decided to stop to enjoy the view of the river and surrounding tundra from a high vantage point. The Yukon is, after all, one of the principal rivers in the world. I saw a boat launch ramp into the river and a car park behind it, and the idea occurred to me that this would be a fantastic place to go boating.

Sam and Clare arrived, indicating that I shouldn't have stopped on the bridge, so we rode onwards to Denali National Park where we took an afternoon tour bus into the reserve to see the nation's highest peak. There was plenty of wildlife to be seen, including a coyote, elks and bears. Loving the location, we decided to stay in the nearby town of Healy for a couple of nights where we found a beautiful hotel with a most eccentric and loopy

On the Denali River, white water rafting in dry suits with the gold medal USA Olympic swimming team. Denali, Alaska

owner. Every morning, amidst a room brimming full of his hunting trophies, he delighted in regaling us with tales of the wilderness followed by a guitar-strumming session of Beatles songs, while drinking a series of mid-morning Bloody Marys. During our stay, Sam and Clare surprised me with a white-water rafting afternoon where we took to the waters of the Denali River in dry suits. It was great fun, with stretches of icy cold waters and mild rapids. Amazingly, we discovered that our rafting group included America's Olympic gold-medal swimmers.

Onwards, we made our way south towards Anchorage. During a stop, we ended up chatting to some locals who kindly offered a stay at their home-built log cabin a few miles off our route. We happily accepted and spent an evening with them enjoying conversations around an outdoor open fire while fighting off mosquitos with electrified tennis rackets. As they had to work the next day, they left us to settle in for the evening, showing us where the guns were in case any wildlife came wandering by in the night. We found it somewhat baffling to be entrusted with their holiday cabin and guns having just met them a few hours before. The following morning, we left a thank-you note, locked up and headed into Anchorage. As it was the last two days before Clare and Sam caught a flight home, I decided to surprise them with one final adventure – a trip to see wild bears via a seaplane.

The flight was incredible, with a stone-skipping take-off across the ocean in our prop plane before taking to the skies. We spent most of our time marvelling at the scenery before descending and landing smoothly on an enclosed lake where we were greeted on shore by our bear-and-boat guide for the day. A cup of hot chocolate later, we all piled on to a small boat where we made our way to the far edges of the forest. We could see huge shoals of salmon in the waters, having made their way upstream to lay their eggs. The shorelines had multiple brown bears taking advantage of the salmon-filled breeding grounds. We watched them jumping and diving head first into the lake, emerging 30 or 40 seconds later with a flapping salmon in their jaws. There was a mother bear and three cubs also trying their luck to catch fish, although the cubs were distracted play-fighting with each other. Spooked by a much larger grizzly, they ended up dashing into the brush where we watched the bushes and saplings rustle as they barged their way through, perfectly camouflaged. In most cases, we were as close as 30 feet to the bears although they seemed completely oblivious to our presence.

The day passed quickly and at the end of the afternoon and after some fantastic lake-sourced salmon for lunch, we returned to the seaplane. Having been tipped off by the boatmen that the pilot was an aerial acrobat and loved to visit the volcanoes, Clare asked him if we could take the more scenic route home, hinting at some aerial fun along the way. He smiled mischievously, asked if any of the six passengers were prone to travel sickness, then proceeded to blast Lynyrd Skynyrd's 'Free Bird' song through our headphones. He then took an almighty swoop up the mountainside and suddenly nosedived into a neighbouring volcano. From there, he roller-coasted us through the skies, before gliding low across the plains where we could see the eyes of a moose galloping through the marshes. It was fantastic and utterly terrifying with Sam and Clare saying it was a most exciting and exhilarating end to their trip. They were sorry to have to head off but so happy and proud having succeeded in seeing Prudhoe Bay, which was a big achievement for both of them as it had been Clare's second attempt and Sam's third. I agreed to hire a U-Haul van, put all three bikes in and drive them down to Calgary, where I could leave them with Sam's friend.

We said our goodbyes. They were grateful to me for taking their bikes and for the company on the road. I was grateful that they had let me join them for what had been a magnificent ride further north than I had ever

LEFT: *Demonstrating using a hand thrown arrow used by Indians to kill the wounded buffalo after they have been driven over a cliff.*

RIGHT: *An American buffalo also known as a bison, the largest mammal in North America, weighing up to 2,000 pounds.*

travelled before. They left to fly back to England, and I continued on south, with the dream of the Yukon River going round and round my head. After unloading their bikes and returning the U-Haul I got back on my KTM 690 with all my camping gear and headed to the south of Alberta. There, not far from the Canadian–US border, is perhaps the most unusually named UNESCO site in the world, Head-Smashed-In Buffalo Jump. A buffalo jump is a steep, rocky cliff edge where Native Americans would kill buffalo or, to give them their correct name, bison by driving them over the edge. Prior to the kill, they would quietly drive the herd towards the cliff where fellow tribesmen hid behind shelters and would suddenly appear making loud noises that helped to start them stampeding towards the cliff and jumping over to their subsequent deaths. Those that didn't die from the fall would be finished off by the tribesmen waiting at the bottom of the cliff with spears and hand-thrown arrows. The name is a translation from Siksiká, the language of the Blackfoot people, and comes from the story of a young Blackfoot man who hid under the cliff to watch the buffalo fall from below. Unfortunately, the buffalo fell directly on to him and, when he was later pulled from the pile of dead animals, his head had been smashed in.

The site was my last stop in Canada before crossing the border into America. I continued on into Montana, which has many visitors in the summer and hardly anyone at all in the winter. As I rode, I could not stop thinking about my dream of travelling down the Yukon by boat. Every time I crossed a new river, I wondered if it was navigable, and if I could get to it from the Yukon. I kept looking for boats in any shops I passed, but nothing suitable appeared.

I crossed into Idaho and decided to stop at Yellowstone National Park, the oldest national park and the centre of a huge volcano. The other great attraction for me were the bison: I wanted to take pictures of them. A little recklessly, I stopped the bike by the side of the road. There was a herd of large bulls and, confident that they were tame, I began to take photographs of them from about eight feet away. Then, I went down a little side road where there was a lone bull heading slowly towards the road. I stopped to watch it. By the time it had reached the road, there were about ten large pick-ups behind and in front of me, and so the bison started heading directly towards the smallest object it could see: me. This was clearly not a good place to be. With no other option, I rode – quite illegally – across the park to avoid being trampled by the bison.

Yellowstone is one of the largest volcano craters in the world but is unlikely to erupt as the whole crater floor is covered with hundreds of small geysers and thermal pools which allow the pressure to escape. The most famous is affectionately called Old Faithful, thanks to the fact that it consistently erupts on schedule. Its cold water closes the vent and builds

Yellowstone River

up a pressure head of steam, which then bursts 60 feet up into the air before dying down again. Alongside Old Faithful, there are numerous other steaming lakes, possibly the biggest in the world, with multi-coloured rocks and life-forms which are somehow able to survive in this superheated atmosphere. I followed the wooden walkways which crossed over the pools, allowing me to look directly down into them.

Happy with my Yellowstone experience, I rode further into Idaho, stopping in the city of Pocatello, where I found a camper and boat dealership called Park-A-Way and met 'Ol' Bob' the salesman, who had a small jet boat for sale. It seemed to be exactly what I was looking for so I bought it. Ol' Bob also had an old Tioga campervan for sale which I could use to tow the boat and the bike. He invited me to stay with him at his wooden lodge in the forest where he kept the van. I spent the weekend up there, sleeping in the van and spending the days with him and his family. Amongst their bikes were some quad bikes and side-by-sides, and we took them out for a 50-mile ride through the forest. We met no one along the way, and it was an indication to me of the huge and wild public areas that were available for off-road adventure travel in America.

The boat needed some work before it would be ready to use. I was able to complete a few of the jobs myself, and Ol' Bob gave me the name of a mechanic called Robert Phelps who could do the other modifications. While this took place, I returned to England. Back at home, I was able to set myself the task of working out how to carry both the bike and the boat behind the campervan. I decided that the bike could be put on the trailer with the aid of a hydraulic ramp. I flew back to Idaho, gave my plans to Robert, and we worked on it together. It turned out to be a great success, so much so that Robert had to show everyone who came to the workshop what it could do. Unfortunately, he ended up doing that so many times that he broke it.

Nevertheless, I could manage, so I took the boat off to try on some of the local rivers and lakes. I still distrusted a single engine from back in the early RIB days, so I had a small outboard fitted as well. The first running in was great fun, so I took the boat out on a bigger lake. For some reason, this time the engine failed and I had to come back on just the little outboard. I then tried a river, which went well and which I could take quite fast, but it became too shallow and I was carried by the current into even shallower water. Luckily, a nearby fisherman saw me and offered to help. A friend of his was out boating, so the fisherman called him, and he gave me a tow

A unique way of launching the Gatortrax boat over a jetty, utilising the knuckle boom lorry crane

back out into deep water. I realised then that I still had a lot to learn about the currents and shallow waters.

Rather than another river, I decided to take the boat out on a big lake and, once again, the engine didn't work. As I couldn't find the cause I called the dealer and he told me to bring it in so he could have a look. One of the problems with travelling in America is just how vast it is. I realised that going back to the dealer would be a two- or even three-day trip, which was most inconvenient. I managed to find out that the builder and the main engine agent were both based in the same town, Lewiston, which was much closer, so I took it to them instead. They were able to diagnose the problem and replace the broken part.

Glad that all was in working order again, I took the boat out on the Snake River, a well-known 2,000-mile-long white-water river. I motored up it to see how far I could get and soon reached a rapid. I tackled it on full power, but it was so strong that, when I looked at my GPS, it showed I was doing just one mile an hour. I had to look at the bank to see if I was actually moving forwards or backwards. Fortunately, it was the former, so I kept on, slowly progressing up the rapids amongst the waves without touching the throttle.

When I finally came clear, I was able to speed up to 30 miles an hour with the same throttle setting. It had all been very exciting, and had made me understand why people had said the boat wasn't powerful enough for the Snake River. Further up, an even bigger rapid appeared that was clearly far too dangerous for me so I turned back down the river. I was later told that I would need a special strengthened cabin to withstand those waves.

The next day, I drove down the river to Clarkston, the town opposite Lewiston. The pair of towns are named after Meriwether Lewis and William Clark, who were the first white Americans to travel from the Mississippi across the Rockies and to the Pacific Ocean. The Snake River has now been dammed many times before joining the mighty Columbia River. Both rivers have a lock system along them so that ocean-going ships can navigate to the inland cities where they collect grain. I continued on down the Snake River, into what was effectively a lake held up by a dam, where I heard a strange noise. I looked round and saw that there was steam coming from all the engine vents. Immediately, I stopped the engine and lifted up the hatch. The water filler had completely blown off the header tank and the top-up tank was still full. I had no idea how it had happened, so I kept the engine turned off and used the little outboard once again to motor back.

It occurred to me that, so far, on only four trips out of ten had the main engine kept running. Once I made it to land, there was luckily a good boatyard and an engine mechanic who did his best to fix the problem. The first attempt failed and they had to fit a completely new engine with a redesigned cooling system. By this time, I had lost confidence in the boat. I explained this to the manager of the repair yard, and he told me that they also built boats. I was persuaded to buy a new one. This time, I succumbed to a V8 engine, which everyone had been telling me I needed. Leaving them to build my new boat, I towed the old one back to Pocatello, where I hoped to get a good price for it.

CHAPTER FIFTY

JET-BOATING IN NORTH AMERICA

I left the boat and campervan with Robert, the mechanic who had originally fixed the bike on the trailer. By now, I had known him for two years and trusted him to sell the boat on my behalf. He always closed his workshop while I was there and worked exclusively on the boat and the van, never charging too much and always being extremely helpful and kind. I felt confident leaving both vehicles with him while I returned to England.

Not long after, I received a message at home. 'Have you heard the news about Robert? It's not good.' I made some calls and found out what had happened. Robert had been in the petrol station opposite his garage filling up his car. One of his mechanics – whom I remembered well: he had lots of rings in his face and had always seemed a little strange to me – produced a gun in the petrol station and shot Robert in the head and killed him stone dead. Then, as if he knew that he was going to be caught anyway, the mechanic just hung around in the petrol station until the police came. Loren, who had sold me my campervan and was now a neighbour selling from the used-car lot next to Robert's garage, saw and heard the whole thing happen. Robert's body, he said, was just left there on the ground in the garage for the next five hours until it was collected.

I was astonished by the news, and followed it as closely as I could from home. The mechanic was convicted of pre-meditated murder. The more I looked into it, the more I realised how shady the whole affair was. Robert, I discovered, was not the man I had thought him to be. He was deeply in debt. When I had left the boat with him, he had convinced me that everything would be much simpler if he put it in his name to sell. When the IRS discovered he 'owned' the boat, they took it as payment for his debt. There was nothing I could do about it. I was thankful that, at least, Loren the car salesman quickly took my campervan away and put it in his son's storage yard – especially when I heard that the night after Robert's death his workshop was broken into and anything of value was stolen,

*The first American RV –
a large-sized Tioga RV
with a Ford V10 engine
with the KTM and jet boat
on a trailer behind.*

including the documents for seventeen vehicles, mostly Ford Mustangs in bits, but also my Tioga. The next day a local Shoshone Indian from the nearby Fort Hall reservation arrived with my Tioga registration document to say he had come to collect his vehicle. Luckily, Loren was there and told him where to go. He still has the document, but Loren, who recently bought the vehicle back off me, has been happy to deal with the problem as his wife used to work at the vehicle registration department and could get new documents. If not, I never would have been able to sell it.

I thanked Loren personally when I next returned to America. It was all such a tragic mess, and I was glad to collect my camper and leave. I drove down to pick up my new boat. The builders warned me that it might be a little underpowered, and kindly offered to put in a newer, more powerful V8 engine as well as a Hamilton jet-drive unit. All this they would do with no charge for the labour for changing them round; just the cost of the engine and jet unit. After everything that had happened with Robert, this helped to restore my faith in the American business world.

The owner gave me a demonstration drive up the river so that I could become used to the boat. He knew the waters extremely well, but I couldn't help feeling a little nervous – especially whenever he shouted into my ear: 'We're sinking, we're sinking, go faster!' The boat drew about three times as much stationary as it did on the plane, so I was very much relying on his knowledge of the river.

Feeling much more confident with it, I then went back to take the boat out on my own for the weekend. As soon as I left the marina, it stopped.

I called the workshop and the mechanic came out to me. He discovered the problem immediately. The owner had turned the fuel switch the wrong way. I was lucky the engine had stopped so close to the workshop. Any further out, and I might not have been able to obtain such quick help.

Finally, it was time to press on. I loaded the boat on to the trailer and towed it behind the campervan as I drove north, making my way to Seattle, where I hoped to try the boat on the sea for the first time. When I arrived there, I realised the sheer scale of American boating. Just this one marina had eight launching ramps and eight recovery ramps, so that large numbers could be launched simultaneously.

I spent a few days exploring Puget Sound, where the beaches were covered three feet high in driftwood logs which had been swept down the river. From there, I carried on north, up into Canada, exploring more rivers and creeks along the way. Finally, I reached Alaska, where my dream of boating the waterways of North America had begun on that bridge over the Yukon years before.

My first experience of Alaskan water was a small creek which, unfortunately, was too shallow. I went aground on a sandbank. I had enough power to refloat, but the engine overheated in the process because there wasn't the necessary water flow. I was learning the hard way. When I headed back slowly down the river, I noticed many of the pine trees, some over 12 inches in diameter, had been cut off very roughly about three feet above ground level. After seeing a lot of these on the outside of the river bends, I realised that they had been cut down by the huge floating icesheets

Having travelled down a narrow mountain track with burnt out forests either side, Charles had to tow fallen trees out of the road to continue onwards.

that appeared as the river started to melt in the spring and destroyed all before them. The local people built a large tripod on the Tanana river and connected it to a clock on the bank. They then laid bets on the date and time that the thaw would occur and when the tripod would trip the clock. It can vary by over six weeks from early April to the middle of May.

I found a bigger river, but it was also shallow, extremely muddy, and flowed at about 8 knots. With its strong current, numerous sandbanks and no other boats in sight, I decided that it was far too dangerous for me.

I drove on, intending to camp out somewhere for the night before reaching Fairbanks, but the van's transmission began to sound ominous, and I reasoned that it would be safer to go all the way to Fairbanks without stopping. Once I arrived, I visited the local Ford dealership. It was an enormous place, but they quickly told me that they would not be able to help, and sent me on to another garage. They were busy, but after two days of waiting they were able to take a look. The gearbox had seriously overheated and the van was in need of a new one. Since it was a Ford, I did not imagine this would be much of a problem, and yet they were unable to find one. If they could find a new one, it would have to come from the Lower 48 and would cost $500 for carriage alone and take a week. Instead, they said they could rebuild the gearbox themselves. When they finished on a Friday afternoon, they took it for a test drive. The gearbox jumped from first into reverse. They had not rebuilt it correctly. I was back to square one.

To make matters worse, Labor Day weekend – a three-day holiday – was about to begin and, with it, the start of the hunting season. The four mechanics at the garage were all going off moose hunting for the weekend. My van would be stuck in the garage for the next three days. This left me not just without transport but also without accommodation, so I decided to take the motorbike and see some more of Alaska that way.

I set a course for Circle, a town on the Yukon River about 150 miles north-east of Fairbanks. On the way up, I passed large car parks full of various vehicles with trailers for UTVs (utility terrain vehicles). I realised that they were all parked there so that their owners could take their UTVs out moose hunting. I hoped they all wore high-visibility jackets to protect themselves from trigger-happy hunters. I did not stop as, by now, it was growing extremely cold, and I wanted to check into a hotel in Circle and have a hot meal. I warmed up a little as I drew closer, which was lucky for me as there were no hotels. Riding through the town, I came to the Yukon River. Two men and two young girls were launching a small boat into the river.

They were off hunting; I counted at least five guns in the bottom of the boat. I made a point of remembering this place. My dream all along had to been to take a boat along the Yukon, and here was another viable place to launch.

I rode round the town a little more and on one street I came across lots of cars beside the road. I turned round, rode back the same way and counted them. There were approximately 100 cars lined up in four rows, with the ones nearest the houses behind four-inch-diameter trees. These houses all belonged to the local Indian tribe, who used the government money they were given to buy new cars. The old ones were just left to rot outside their property.

There was only one universal shop in the whole of Circle and nowhere at all to stay, so I headed back. As I rode, the bike began to make nasty noises. I hoped it would make it back, but suddenly it stopped. The valve gear had broken. It was clearly not going to go again. I had just passed a small hotel and, as I started to push the bike back towards it, a pick-up stopped beside me. The driver and passenger – a father and son – offered to help. The father was the local priest who was on his way to take a service in Circle. I asked him about all the cars I had seen there, and he laughed.

'Can you believe there's only 80 people living in that town?' he said. 'They all own several cars each.'

The son helped me to push the bike back towards the hotel. Then another pick-up coming towards us stopped and the driver offered to help. He had a large piece of wood in the back of his truck which we could use to push the bike up and into the pick-up. I did not need to ask why he was carrying this large piece of wood around, for I already knew the answer. Just like my mechanics in Fairbanks, he was off moose hunting for the Labor Day weekend, and he planned to use this board to drag any of his kills into his truck.

We eventually loaded the bike on to the pick-up, but there was no room in the front for me. Fortunately, yet another truck pulled up. Its driver had just been out hunting with what I considered to be a rather unusual companion for a moose hunter: his three-year-old son. He just needed to drop his son off and then he could take me back to Fairbanks while the others transported my bike. I was very grateful to them all.

As we drove, the hunter was full of warnings and advice. 'You need to be prepared out here in the winter. If anything goes wrong while it's minus 30 Fahrenheit, you have to be ready for it. Round here, when we park our cars, we keep them connected to the mains electricity. That way, the engines stay warm and they'll start up whenever you want. Last thing you need here is a frozen engine, or a puncture. Changing a tyre in minus 30 degrees is no fun at all.'

Eventually, my campervan was repaired. Because of all the delays, I was now three days late, so I had to drive back down through Alaska and Canada on my way to Idaho as quickly as possible – bearing in mind all along the way that the Ford transmission was not capable of towing my boat. I looked at some bigger trucks as I went, but they were all huge mobile homes the size of a bus and completely unsuitable for what I wanted. When I finally made it to Idaho, I left everything with Loren's son Brett, who had space beside his house. It was time for me to fly home and to think about the future.

Back in Suffolk, I thought through the problem. What I really needed was a commercial truck engine and transmission. I could, I decided, get a Mercedes truck and put a body on it, and with that I should have commercial reliability. Unfortunately, I soon learnt that European trucks are not allowed into North America, in much the same way as American trucks aren't allowed into Europe, even though we both consider ourselves as having high environmental standards.

The only remaining option was to buy an American truck with a commercial transmission, build the body for it in England and then ship it out to America. This was a fairly drastic solution, but not impossible –

Farm tractor towing the truck body to the paint shop to be sprayed to match the colour of the truck. Suffolk,

The seating area to the interior of the American International truck.

I had a commercial tenant who could do the steel bodywork while his landlord, who was a cabinet maker, could build the interior. That was how it came to be built in my barn. Using the measurements of an American truck, we built it on an old farm trailer and, when it was finished, took it behind my farm tractor to be painted at the commercial body shop that built my Unimog. After it was completed, we had the nerve-wracking job of winching it into a 40-foot shipping container. Once all that was done, it was taken down to the docks and loaded on to a container ship to Miami.

On arrival in Miami, the trailer was taken to the truck yard. As it was dragged out, it looked rather like a large animal being born. The truck had a Palfinger lorry crane on the front and the body was then put on behind it. By now, I knew that my boat was not really suitable for small rivers – it was a sea boat – so I also bought a lightweight duck-hunting boat with

LEFT: *One tractor and two forklifts taking the truck body out of the shipping container in Miami.*

RIGHT: *With the body now mounted onto the truck, the cross America journey begins at Key West, with the flat bottomed boat on top of the roof.*

The truck, towing the jetboat with the Gatortrax boat on the roof.

LEFT: *Stopping off at The Arches National Park in Utah which has over 2,000 red hued natural stone arches and hundreds of pinnacles, rock fins and giant balanced rocks.*

RIGHT: *Damaged boats after Hurricane Irma, Florida Keys*

an outboard jet drive engine which only drew about four or five inches and was light enough to manhandle. This would sit on top of the camper body. When all was completed, I drove it down to Key West, a few weeks after Hurricane Irma tore through the Florida Keys leaving a trail of destruction behind it. When I drove the truck down the Keys I passed piles of palm leaves, roofs and other debris, 25 feet high and 300 yards long, that had been torn up by the 180mph winds of the hurricane. Contractors had come from the northern states to clear the debris from around the houses creating these temporary piles before final removal. Dozens of yachts were thrown up on the land awaiting assessment for the damage by insurance companies. I could see where the eye of the hurricane was by seeing where all the leaves of the evergreen mangrove trees had been stripped off by the force of the winds over a distance of 25 miles.

Only then could I start my planned journey from the most southerly point to as far in the north-west as possible, hoping to reach the Yukon again and Yellowknife and Inuvik. I did several trips into the Everglades and the west coast of Florida. On the way back, I could not resist seeing Elvis's home in Memphis: Graceland. I was very surprised at how modest it was compared to modern stars' palaces and was glad to have taken the opportunity to join the pilgrimage for the legendary rock star. Then I headed back via the monuments of Utah to leave the truck with Brett.

◗ ◗ ◗

The jet boat with its 400hp V8 petrol engine

The following year I returned after Covid and drove up to Alaska. The round trip to Skagway and back, which I made in my ten-ton International truck covered just over 7,000 miles. I had built the body in our workshop in Suffolk and had a friend make the beautiful teak interior. It was then shipped in a container to Miami where it was mounted onto the chassis. The truck spent a few years at my base in Idaho from where I travelled to explore the Puget Sound, the gateway to Seattle, and up to Prince Rupert in Canada for short trips in the Pacific and round the deserted offshore Haida islands.

With more time on my hands, I continued my crossing of North America and Canada all the way up to Skagway. I was towing a boat which I launched there to cruise the inlets and view from the sea several glaciers high up the rocky and snow-covered mountains. It was to Skagway in 1898 and 1899 that the Klondike gold prospectors came and started dealing with the loan sharks who had by this time proliferated in the region. To reach the main gold deposit in Dawson City, they had to buy food and equipment weighing 1,000 lbs. They had to pack it into wooden cases and carry it on their backs to climb 3,000 feet for 33 miles up the very steep Chilkoot Pass in deep snow in temperatures of minus 50 degrees Fahrenheit. They then left their equipment in piles watched over by the Royal Canadian Mounted Police who would not let them enter Canada, where the gold was, unless they had their 1,000 pounds of equipment and food to last for a year.

Travertine terrace at Mammoth Springs, Yellowstone National Park

LEFT: *Sculpture of gold prospectors with their packs ready for one of 10-20 climbs up the Chilkoot trail*

RIGHT: *Snowplough on the Chilkoot railway*

Until I went there, I had not realised that the British had been forced to agree the border with the Russians whose territory it was until they sold it to America in the 1867 at 2 cents per acre without, of course, knowing of the presence of gold. The potential miners had to cross rivers and lakes to reach Dawson City, their final destination. By then most of the richest claims had been taken. I had been to Dawson City on my motor bike nine years earlier and had seen the old dredgers used by the Gulbenkian family, when dredging the rivers on which they had claims, to a depth of ten to twelve feet just leaving piles of ugly stones.

Skagway is just a small town of which only an area about four streets wide and six streets deep is of interest to tourists; the rest is residential.

On every day of the summer, this little town 'entertains' all the passengers of three or four cruise ships each having eight to ten decks. All the entertainment such as the train up the mountain and the helicopter flights has to be booked in advance and all the 2025 cruise ship visits had already been booked. I had to be careful to avoid the cruise ships' tenders each having up to 190 passengers going to the shore.

I saw a plaque which said that an old cargo 3-masted barque had been 'wrecked' and abandoned by its captain and crew. A tug boat skipper thought it had some value, towed it to a safe anchorage and went to Juneau, the capital of Alaska, to claim salvage. When he returned to his prize, he was met by an angry captain who welcomed him with a revolver! As there was no escape from Skagway other than by the long and difficult Chilkoot trail or by ship, the captain was soon arrested for threatening the tug skipper with a revolver.

I climbed the steep hill and left Alaska, continuing on into the Yukon and the North West Territories of Canada to Fort Liard. It was a very lonely road and I started worrying that I had seen no cars coming towards me for well over an hour and that there was a lot of smoke in the air which was becoming increasingly thicker. I became concerned that the source of the smoke might have closed the road and wondered what I should do. I couldn't turn round towing a boat and had no idea of a possible alternative when suddenly a car came towards me and I knew that all the road was safe. I reached Fort Liard where I was shown the slipway. One look from the top made it obvious to me that it was far too steep and gravelly for my truck, let alone when towing a boat. Even my Unimog would have struggled.

LEFT: *A bull bison crossing the road*

RIGHT: *The truck below volcanic pillars*

I thought I had better check the road and fire conditions with the RCMP. The door of the police station was locked and I pressed two buttons with no result. I had returned to my truck when a man appeared, called me back, showed me into the waiting room, locked the outside door and then called his boss. I was told that the road was open and I was let free to go. I headed back to the main road which had fire-smouldering trees on either side of it. It was a beautiful road, wild and empty for 240 miles where I saw only six cars. But I had the great joy of seeing three herds totalling about 70 buffalo and three black bears all in the scrub between the road and the forest. I had never seen any wild animals like the black bears with colours so contrasting to their surroundings.

I found the Alaska Highway stunning with 40 shades of green going up the mountain to bare volcanic rock and coming down to dark blue rivers and lakes. It was a good road with little traffic and plenty of stopping places, all with Canadian standard-bear-proof rubbish bins.

I stopped to fit a new tyre on my trailer at Watson Lake and went into Sign Post Forest, so called because travellers in years gone by had left their names or car license plates on trees. This practice carries on till this day. Sam, Clare and I had left our names on our motor bike trip in 2014 but I could not find them. The place was now more regimented with lots of new posts having been put up.

At the end of the Canadian section, 960 kilometres long, is Dease Lake. The whole road was built in a big rush using black-American troops in 1943 and 1944 to protect this massive wilderness and swamp from a possible Japanese invasion.

The Sign Post Forest at Watson Lake

Neither North America nor Canada does any checks on outgoing traffic; they only check and stamp incoming passports and goods. North American customs confiscated a half a tomato and a bag of grapes that I had bought on the way up!

I was now in Washington State, which advertises itself on its car number plates as 'the evergreen state.' All I saw was about 20 miles of pine trees and the rest was endless miles of yellow dry grass and ripe cereals and stubbles. I must not say 'corn' as that is green and we call it maize!

The pump room of the The John W. Keys III Pump-Generating Plant at the Grand Coulee Dam, with 200,000 horsepower of pumps

Finally, I reached the small town of Grand Coulee, famous for its colossal dam which backs up the Columbia River to the Canadian Border. This 150-mile-long lake is called Lake Roosevelt because President Franklin D. Roosevelt had it built to provide 10,000 jobs in the depression and to appease farmers who were complaining about the drought. The scale is totally massive and used 12.5 million tons of concrete, enough to build a road from Seattle to Miami. The dam's water can irrigate 675,000 acres of farmland. The pump room contains 12 pumps, eight at 16,500 horse power and four at 17,000 horse power pumping through 12 eight-foot diameter pipes. The dam is nearly a mile long and 300 feet high. There are three generating units producing enough power for four million homes. This vast amount of electricity was an essential ingredient to power both the aluminium smelters in Seattle, to enable Boeing to mass produce enough aircraft to sink the Japanese fleet in the Second World War and to power the atomic-bomb research.

LEFT: *Dry Falls plunge pool*

RIGHT: *Steam Boat Rock, Grand Coulee cut by the ice flow from the ice dam*

Unlike our green-energy plants, their hydro-electric plants don't need expensive lithium battery backups. They only need another reservoir higher up which can be filled with surplus water and reused downhill again to regenerate power for other uses.

A little further on was a site called Dry Falls, too much of a curiosity to pass by. The name refers to a time 20,000 years ago during the ice ages. Huge ice sheets built up to the northeast with an ice dam 30 miles long, two miles wide and half a mile high. This enormous structure held a lake of 500 cubic miles which would probably cover the whole of Wales to a depth of 100 metres. When global warming caused the lake to melt and breach the dam, this mass of water carrying large icebergs, weighing hundreds of tons, would smash into the banks and cause rocks to break away and cause more damage downstream, creating the Grand Coulee. On a previous boat trip to Alaska, I saw 12-inch-diameter pine trees cut off about two feet above the ground on the outer curve of the river. It took me quite a while to realise that this was what the winter ice does when the river starts to flow in the spring. The large sharp icebergs form when the river ice breaks up and are carried down by the current on the outside of the bends with sufficient power and speed to sever the pine trees cleanly. Dry Falls still has large plunge ponds created by the ice age torrents.

I came off the plateau down the 2,000-foot steep decline to Lewiston, where my boat was built, for a few repairs to my boat and my trailer brakes. 6,000 miles with no trailer brakes on steep hills needs a lot of concentration. Lewiston is beside Snake River with its twin town Clarkston on the other bank. As mentioned previously these two towns are named after the two famous American army captains Meriwether Lewis and William Clark who made their Corps of Discovery Expedition, commissioned by

President Thomas Jefferson in 1804 to 1806. The principal aim of the expedition was to discover an all-water route to the Pacific Ocean. They used boats as far as The Rocky Mountains and then used Indian ponies to go over the top until they found the Clearwater River. They followed it down until they found some trees large enough to make canoes to navigate the rapids of the Columbia River, hoping to reach the Pacific, where they camped for the winter. Finally, with the help of some Indians, they returned over The Rocky Mountains to be congratulated by President Jefferson. The most helpful Indians were the Nez Perce who still have their headquarters at Lapwei next to Lewiston.

Boulder left behind by retreating glacier

The roads I have driven on have largely followed routes travelled by Lewis and Clark, the Wagon Train Pioneers on the Oregon Trail, and the Nez Perce Indians. The latter had a homeland of 17 million acres before continuous reductions by the American government reduced it to 750,000 acres. After the second reduction in 1855, 700 Nez Perce rebelled and took 2,000 horses and all they could carry, including many of their elderly, and headed to freedom in Canada. They set off from Lewiston over The White Bird Pass, now an eight-mile descent which was built as recently as 1975. Half way down is an observation hut overlooking a massive five-to-eight-mile-wide valley. At the bottom of this valley the Nez Perce camped and put out sentries. At dawn a large troop of American soldiers approached and the Indians came forward with a white flag. Somehow shots were fired and soon after the soldiers retreated in total disarray having had 34 men killed and only wounded three Nez Perce who then collected a largequantity of rifles and ammunition.

The Indians knew the soldiers would return. They continued their flight with five more battles during 15 months when they covered 1,700 miles. They crossed the Yellowstone geyser land before it became a National Park and kept ahead of the soldiers after all the battles until they reached North Dakota. When only 40 miles from Canada, a new American army unit finally caught up with them, armed with machines guns. Even after 15 months of being pursued during their flight from America, the Indians showed kindness to give water to the injured soldiers.

Next year on to the Yukon River!

EPILOGUE:
NAMIBIA TO KENYA 2019

The Unimog at a gateway to the Skeleton Coast National Park. 2012

Parked up for the night beside a lake in Zambia

My whole life has been one prolonged search for excitement. I had originally intended to conclude this account of my travels around the world with the stories of my journeys by motorcycle and jet boat through north-west America. But now I have decided by way of an epilogue to write about the expedition I made by Unimog through Africa to celebrate my 80th birthday, so as to give true meaning to this book's sub-title: *Sixty Years of World Travel*.

If at first you don't succeed, try, try again. So goes the saying which I recall hearing from as long ago as my childhood, and which is still very true today. Despite my three failed attempts to reach East Africa by Unimog, and having had to turn back due to border closures in Algeria, the Democratic Republic of Congo, and finally between Egypt and Sudan, the dream never faded. At the age of 79, I decided to give it another go. The floor of the Unimog's shower cubicle had rotted away, so I had a new one made and refitted, and then drove down to Canvey Island, where I handed over the shipping papers and in less than five minutes left the Unimog on the dock to await the ship which would take it to Walvis Bay in Namibia. Unfortunately, I had to leave its keys with it for the customs check, which meant that any of the dockworkers could have entered my cabin.

Once the Unimog was loaded on to the ship and on its way, I organised my own journey south: first on a flight to Windhoek, the capital of Namibia, and from there on a bus to Walvis Bay. I had a relaxing stay at a hotel on the coast and, during a very good breakfast the next morning, my agent arrived to collect my papers and, just one hour later, returned to announce that the Unimog was waiting for me outside. I could not have asked for a simpler process.

Feeling very enthusiastic to be driving in Africa again, I was brought down to earth as soon as I set off. The steering was ridiculously heavy; it was obvious I had no power steering. After a quick stop at a garage for some fluid, all seemed well again, and I set off past a large salt-drying plant to a quiet campsite by the sea. But then, the following morning, the problem returned. Once more, the Unimog had only manual steering. After a laborious 12-point turn in the sand – and only just keeping out of the sea as I performed it – I headed back to the port for a proper repair.

Finally the pipe was welded, and I set off along a little-used gravel track to Luderwitz, an old German mining town. Diamonds had once been excavated here and it seemed that the equipment they use now was only slightly better than the basic tools they had used over a century earlier. The road out of Luderwitz was rough – too much, in fact, for the rear tyre, which pulled the tread off on a particularly rocky patch. I drove off the road to investigate whether I could change the tyre myself on such

The Unimog on the "main road" in the mountains in Malawi which took almost two days of travel averaging at 9mph

uneven ground as I had only ever done it before on a hard surface. Since each wheel weighs over 200 pounds and is 40 inches tall, a lot of leverage is needed to get them under the hub and to get all the holes lined up. I decided to try. First, I had to take the spare off the back. Just as I was doing so, the first vehicle I had seen in over an hour appeared. To my great delight, it was a tyre repair truck. The two men took over, changing the wheel for me and putting the old one on the back. Had they not helped, I would have had to resort to my basic plan of lowering the front bike frame, ratchet-strapping the wheel to the bull bar and then winching it back up until I reached a garage.

I carried on past Walvis Bay to Swakopmund, Namibia's adventure capital, where I intended to fulfil a lifelong dream: sky-diving. It was the perfect day for it, with clear, clean, warm air. The instructor spoke with such a broad Afrikaans accent that I could barely understand a word he said, but his checks were thorough and comprehensive and I felt confident alongside him. We stepped into the little Cessna, where my harness and I were strapped to him, and then slowly climbed to 10,000 feet. I grew steadily more and more nervous as the ground disappeared below us. Finally, I pulled my goggles on, edged towards the open doorway, and was pushed out into the airstream to free-float downwards. It took a while for me to let go of the harness and put my hands out for the guide to control us, but I eventually did – taking not just his hand but also that of the photographer, who took pictures of us as we plummeted downwards. All too soon, the parachute opened. I enjoyed the immense peace around me as the desert slowly came closer, culminating in a gentle landing on the runway. It was a truly magical experience, in a truly magical country.

〇 〇 〇

Taking a daring day out to experience a first sky dive over the deserts of Namibia

It was time to make my way north. Somewhere up that way was the site of a large colony of seals that had been my dream destination ten years earlier when I had ridden my BMW F800 GS from Zanzibar across the hot desert. Back then, the thought of a cooling swim in the Atlantic had encouraged me forward. Sadly, on that trip the closer I came to the Atlantic, the colder the weather had become, so that by the time I reached the ocean all thoughts of a swim had vanished.

This time, I arrived in the national park late in the evening and parked the Unimog amongst some very hard dunes. The night was beautiful and quiet, with an incredible starlit sky above completely unaffected by any light pollution. I slept well and was up bright and early the next morning. The park office was due to open and so I walked into it and bought a ticket. Between the office and the sea was a flat area where tourists could walk to reach the rocky shore. It was here that some 200 seals had chosen to sleep for the night. At the sight of me approaching, they all started to bark aggressively. The big bulls were the loudest and most ferocious. As they were clearly in charge, I had no desire

The Cape fur seal colony by their hundreds at Cape Cross, Namibia

to challenge them. Finally, after I had waited a while, they all waddled off into the water. This gave me the opportunity to step up on to the walkway and watch thousands of seals swimming, riding the breakers into shore or sunbathing below the rocky cliff. It astounded me how they could clamber over the rocks to dry land unharmed with such large waves crashing over and around them.

Leaving the seals in peace, I headed further north, to drive deeper into the Skeleton Coast along the salt road, taking regular detours across the sands to scout for the fabled wrecks. I saw several old hulls with their wooden ribs sticking out of the sand, as well as one intact modern steel trawler which had been driven on to the shore. I could not help but think of those poor sailors who, having survived the beaching of their disabled ship, would have waded ashore, relieved to have survived the sea, only to find out that the land they had come to was even more hostile. This was, after all, the Skeleton Coast, and its name was apt. With no food or water anywhere to be found in this dry scrub desert, they would have walked, using up any supplies they might have salvaged, and grown more and more desperate when they could find nothing to sustain them on their trek. With only this barren hamada desert for over 70 miles in every direction, they would have died soon after from lack of water and food. Many years ago, German colonists, fully aware of how inhospitable this area was, used it to exterminate the native Himba tribe when they resisted the takeover of their ancestral lands. They simply drove the spear-wielding tribesmen westwards into this barren area and posted guards to make sure they could never return. The Himba all died of thirst and starvation. Maybe a precursor for Nazism!

I continued north, towards Etosha National Park with the fence on my left. Suddenly, three giraffes burst out in front of me, running frantically. They had heard me long before I saw them. I stopped to let them cross the road when, ahead, three Harley-Davidson motorbikes appeared, filling the air loudly with their characteristic rumble. The poor giraffes were now trapped by the fence and caught between two monsters: the Unimog and the bikes. They must have decided that the less frightening were the bikers, for they dashed past them as quickly as they could.

The park was huge and, 600 miles in, I came to an area south of the great Salt Lake, which at that time was sand-coloured on top but muddy below, allowing antelopes to walk across it, their hooves sinking in by some three to four inches. There was a lot of thick scrub which made sightings difficult. However, one benefit of the area was the numerous artificial waterholes, where I watched elephant herds come to drink and play. The best of the waterholes near the lodges were floodlit and I was fortunate to see several black rhinos and elephants coming for an evening drink, the giraffes and their fellow grazers standing well at the back until the stronger animals had drunk their fill and vanished off into the night.

◎ ◎ ◎

A small, rough signpost pointed the way to a village of San bushmen, so I turned off the road and headed towards it, greeted by a spread-out collection of thatched huts and a welcome sign. I was told to park by the only large tree and wait until someone came to take me to the village. Soon, a very short, thin, wire-haired elderly man came to lead me through the bush to the traditionally built huts. A small group of topless women sat around chatting. My guide explained that the San used to be nomadic, regularly moving from place to place for fresh lands and hunting opportunities. Yet all this had ceased 20 years before, when they were forced to settle.

The guide sat me down and showed me how they made their fires. He selected a round stick and rapidly rotated it between his palms, pressing the pointed lower end into the depression of a piece of hard wood. I was amazed at how quickly smoke was produced, and when small fibres from cow dung were placed beside the smoke, flames magically appeared.

After that, the women kindly performed a native fertility song, and then my guide led me further into the forest to show me where and how they set snares to catch small animals. We came to a forked tree; water had

collected at the join and could be drunk with the aid of a straw. Finally, the man produced his bow and gave a demonstration of how he would creep through the bushes to shoot his prey. It had been his way of life for thirty years, and was thoroughly realistic. I felt very honoured to have met him: a San bushman determined to keep the culture he grew up with alive.

◎ ◎ ◎

My time alone in Africa was now coming to an end. I made my way back south to Windhoek, where I had arranged to meet Steph Jeavons, a good friend who had kindly volunteered to be my crew navigator and companion for the main trip. Steph is one of the most adventurous travellers I have ever met. For four years, she rode her 250cc Honda solo around the world's seven continents, including Antarctica. We first met because of our mutual love of off-road motorbike travel. I was a client on one of her Welsh trail-riding days, the kind of riding which simply cannot be done in flat Suffolk. When we started talking, we realised that she had ridden through 53 countries and I had ridden through 55 countries.

It was lovely to see her again and, after greeting her from the plane, we immediately went to fill the Unimog's large fridge and deep freeze from the best supermarkets we were likely to find for the next few weeks and then, once we were suitably stocked up, headed south to Fish River Canyon, the second deepest on earth after the Grand Canyon. It was hot and dry and, even with binoculars, all we could see were pools of stagnant water deep down in the rocky gorge.

We drove on towards the Kgalagadi Transfrontier game park, which spills over the border from South Africa to Namibia and Botswana. It is fairly flat with lots of good acacia cover and a river down the middle.

LEFT:
Three generations of Himba women in Namibia

CENTRE:
The Kalahari sand bushmen in Namibia

RIGHT:
A Kalahari sand bushman setting a traditional snare in Namibia

We were extremely lucky to come across a large pride of some 15 lions, all lying on the road beside a bank, and had the rare and absorbing opportunity to watch the cubs chase each other about, free from the disturbance of any tourists except us. It was the largest pride I have ever seen.

It was time to leave Namibia, and we pushed on into South Africa, heading east across the plains towards Kimberley. Though we arrived late in the afternoon, we still had to wait until sunset for the campsite to open. When the manager finally showed us where we could camp, he followed it up by propositioning Steph, and so we made sure to park pointing towards the exit, just in case he had any funny ideas during the night.

Kimberley is famous for the Big Hole, the deepest hand-dug mine in the world. It was originally operated by the De Beers brothers, whose farm it was on, as a diamond mine between 1871 and 1914. Approximately 50,000 men dug the pit without machinery 800 feet deep, excavating almost 2.8 tons, or 14 million carats, of diamonds. When the mine was closed down at the start of the First World War, it silted up and filled with green-algae-covered water to a depth of 230 feet.

We then headed south-east, skirting Johannesburg and entering the 19th-century battlefield area, containing such infamous sites as Isandlwana and Rorke's Drift. The former was where the overconfident Lord Chelmsford suffered defeat to a well-organised and very brave Zulu army. The latter was quite the opposite: Rorke's Drift was the site of a great victory, by a small Welsh regiment over the same Zulu warriors. We were given a detailed and enthusiastic description of the battle by the nephew of a local historian, who had been murdered in his own house, despite the guards and electric fences.

On the 22nd of January 1879, when Lieutenants Chard and Bromhead heard of the defeat inflicted at Isandlwana, they immediately set about improving the defences of their own little outpost. It had a five-foot stone wall on one side which they reinforced with bags of 'mealie', or corn, and biscuit boxes. Then they strengthened the doors of the hospital and the storehouses and opened and readied the ammunition boxes. They were armed with the latest Martini-Henry rifles, which fired a high-velocity .45 bullet. A good soldier could fire one of these at 12 rounds per minute. They were also fitted with 15-inch bayonets, enabling the soldiers to outfight the Zulus, who had much shorter spears. While all this was going on, over at Isandlwana there were 3,000 to 4,000 Zulu reserves keen to share in the rewards that their fellow victorious warriors would receive when they returned home. The Welsh at Rorke's Drift, who numbered only 150 infantry soldiers, must have seemed an easy target. However, the mealie bags and superior firepower prevented any breach at the front, and the Zulus began to grow disheartened, especially when they realised that their spears, their main weapon, were no match for the bayonets of the British. Seeking a different path to victory, some of the Zulu warriors crept around the back and set the thatched roofs alight. The hospital patients had to be removed to the main battle compound. The store rooms, also set alight, were valiantly defended at the doorways. The Welsh soldiers used their bayonets to break holes in the internal mud walls so they could retreat and slaughter any Zulus who tried to follow them. Eventually, the Zulus retreated, taking most of their wounded with them and leaving about 350 dead. The British only lost 17 men, but they won 11 VCs – the most in any action in the history of the British army.

◐ ◐ ◐

To the north lay Kruger National Park, one of the largest and most diverse parks in the world. We were so eager to visit it that we spent a whole week driving through it, seeing wonderful varieties of wildlife in all their different habitats. One of the most memorable featured a rhino father, mother and baby wallowing together in a small waterhole.

We continued on, right to the northern border between South Africa, Zimbabwe and Mozambique. This area is known as 'Crooks Corner' because of the ease with which crooks from any of those three countries could cross the border into another and disappear into the jungles from the pursuing police. We kept going, crossing the northern part of South Africa, back into Botswana, where a good friend of Steph's had organised a luxury bush camp for us. We had the good fortune to meet there a fellow guest called Tim Liversedge, a cinematographer most famous for his IMAX film *Roar*, for which he had camped in lion territory. There he had managed to capture close-up footage of a lion killing a springbok ten feet in the air – all just within a few feet of where he stood. The luxury camp's lodges were exceptional, and we could eat our dinner looking out over the waterhole. Unfortunately, I seemed to spend much of my time there trying to get the air conditioning fixed.

A Rhino wallowing in mud in Kruger National Park

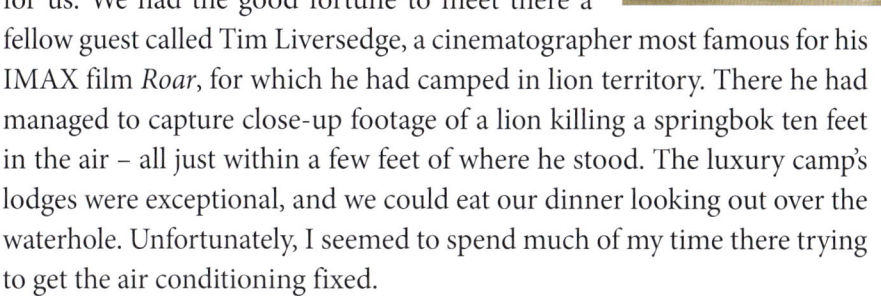

LEFT: *A loving elephant embrace at an Etosha watering hole*

RIGHT: *A baby elephant running around joyfully*

We moved on to the Elephant Sands lodge, arriving just in time to see around 30 elephants drinking and playing at the waterhole. We camped overlooking the site and then walked to the terrace viewing area. On our return to the Unimog, we had to keep a careful watch about us as the track we had to cross was a regular elephant route – we were told that they would become visible just 15 yards away, and that they walked surprisingly fast.

A short but heavy storm flooded the terrace, forcing us to take shelter. And then, as soon as it stopped, the sun came out and the biggest elephants came right to the edge of the terrace. They put their trunks over the balustrade to drink the fresh rainwater pouring back out into the sands. We were well within touching distance of them, but were safe in the knowledge that just outside our terrace were pyramid-shaped concrete blocks that the elephants could not stand on. After the storm abated, they all disappeared off into the bush, and we felt extremely lucky to have seen them so close.

A drought had been ravaging the area over the previous months, and we were told that Victoria Falls had completely dried up in October. When we arrived there, no water was coming over the main fall, but we heard that there was a trickle on the Zimbabwean side. We decided to cross over into that country, arriving at the Hwange National Park, where we saw very little game but where we at least had a spectacular campsite on the edge of a cliff with great views of the plain below.

We drove on through Bulawayo. It was an old-fashioned town with wide streets and little traffic. I later learnt that the Unimog was too big and we should not have been allowed to drive through the centre, but the police had caused us no trouble when we did so. We pushed on to Harare. A friend of mine ran a new plastic factory there – one which had been designed specifically for Zimbabwe. This meant that, to be efficient, it required its own generator in order to be independent of the local mains supply, which often only worked at night and weekends – unless, of course, you were lucky enough to have a house or factory on the same supply line as a minister's house. My friend's factory was fully fenced with ten-foot-plus walls followed by four to five strands of electric wire on top. Since levels of problem drinking in Harare are high, the factory's gatekeeper had to breathalyse every single person who entered, including the managing director himself. My friend explained that pricing was notoriously difficult: all imports were in US dollars and yet all local work was done in Zimbabwean dollars, which, when we were there, were inflating at about 700 per cent. Once, Steph changed US$50, only to become convinced that she had been robbed and supplied with worthless paper. We were lucky that one of the shops we tried accepted her money for our groceries. It took the cashier ages to count over 400 notes for our few supplies. The Zimbabweans always use a mobile phone app to pay instead of rapidly devaluing cash. The government tried to ban it but all commerce ceased as nobody could pay for anything. Possibly the only setback the Zimbabwean government has ever had.

It was time to leave Zimbabwe and make our way to Zambia. We passed the Kariba Dam, the last big project before independence. The water was more than 30 feet below its optimum level and was therefore producing much less current than expected, even before the various governments took their cut. We crossed the river on a vintage ferry boat that ran beside a new bridge. The bridge itself was ten years behind schedule, and so the ferry was still operating ten years beyond its expected life.

When we finally reached Zambia, we stayed with some more of Steph's friends, a lovely Dutch couple called Remco and Marianne. Remco was a former Dutch policeman who, fed up with locking up drunken Dutchmen every night, decided to change his working life by volunteering for the Zambian police wildlife crime unit. He would take his well-trained dogs to sniff out bodies or even just parts of wild animals, which were often trafficked on buses. Marianne had been fully supportive of Remco's decision and now ran a pangolin rehabilitation centre. Pangolins cannot be artificially fed and must be taken to find their own food, and when we went to visit them they were just back from their morning walk, where they had found and eaten their fill of large numbers of ants. Then they were weighed. Marianne explained that this happened before and after the pangolins' walk to ensure they were putting on weight. When they reached a certain weight,

Letting the Pangolin out for a walk at the rehabilitation centre. Zambia

they could be released into a protected area. We felt grateful to have seen them – pangolins are now so rare that this is one of the few places where they can be found.

Malawi was the next country on our journey. We had both been there before on motorbikes. Indeed, we had both ridden exactly the same lakeside road, and so this time we decided we wanted to see the highlands. This meant driving the Unimog up above the treeline on a road which was little used but which gave superb views over the whole country. It was, however, very slow going, with lots of deep water gulleys. Over two ten-hour days we only managed 180 miles. Nevertheless, it was thoroughly enjoyable and totally devoid of tourists. When we came down from the mountain, the roads greatly improved all the way into Tanzania, where we found a beautiful campsite beside Lake Malawi. It was there that we celebrated Christmas and my 80th birthday by swimming in the warm, calm lake. It was a unique experience, and one to be treasured.

◎ ◎ ◎

There was just one more border crossing: into Kenya. Steph had to fly home from there, but I still had some time before I needed to return to the cold and wet of England, so I decided to pay a visit to Tsavo West National Park, where I had last been with Earthwatch almost 20 years earlier.

I pulled up into the car park. Beside me was a battered Toyota which looked as if it had been rolled, although how anyone could have rolled a car in a game park with a 40km/h speed limit was beyond me. I looked closer and was horrified to realise that the body and engine were pierced in more than ten places by holes with a 4–5-inch diameter, clearly from the tusks of an elephant. I later learnt that the elephant had rolled the car at least twice and that the female ranger driving it had been killed. I was left wondering how an experienced ranger had let an angry elephant get so close. Once before I had been presented with a similar situation, and I knew it was safer to back the Unimog out of the way immediately.

Leaving Tsavo, I drove further north past the Rift Valley lakes and took a boat ride on Lake Naivasha, where a five-star hotel had been built on its shore. My boat driver took me through the gates at the bottom of the hotel's lawn to show me five hippos standing with their heads just above water. The water in all the Rift Valley lakes has risen some nine feet over the past years and it was now 650 yards nearer the building. As a result, the hotel had been abandoned.

In the middle of the lake stood a rather unusual island. Zebras, giraffes, wildebeest and gazelles lived there – possibly the only island like it in the world, where grazers such as those could live peacefully without predators. This had not happened naturally. The ancestors of these animals had been brought to the island for the filming of *Out of Africa*, and they had lived there happily ever since.

I drove further north to Marsabit, the last town before Ethiopia, where I was stopped by the police. They wanted me to take two of them back to the town. In general, I do my best to oblige the police as I find it usually pays off later. We passed what appeared to be some sort of rough and possibly disused marketplace, but the policemen informed me that it was in fact the camp of the Chinese workers who had just built the road to Ethiopia. He explained that their living conditions were far below those of the locals.

To the east of Lake Turkana are the real outback areas of Kenya, and I was keen to see them. Unfortunately, the roads were very poor and, for the first time ever, I found myself on roads that were not on my GPS. The countryside around me was entirely volcanic lava. There was no sign of any grass, just scrub bushes, and yet somehow the locals managed to feed large herds of camels and goats. Everyone lived in very old-fashioned domed huts covered in animal skins which I guessed had remained the same for centuries. Many seemed to prefer to live in communities of just two to four huts far away from any villages. In the larger villages, there were sometimes one or two shops and always a liquor store. It seemed astonishing to me that just two hours' drive from these remote communities was the frantic pushing and shoving of normal Kenyan towns.

My next stop was Ol Pejeta: a 140-square-mile wildlife conservancy that was once a large cattle ranch owned by Adnan Khashoggi, the multi-millionaire Arabian arms dealer, in his rich days. It is now not-for-profit and used almost entirely for conservation, especially for rhinos. It has made great progress in reducing poaching. I was particularly moved by the large

A baby rhino charging in defence of his mother. Kenya

tree which had been made the centre for the graves of 25 poached animals shot or trapped or even, in the case of one, killed by bows and arrows. I was glad to see that poaching numbers had fallen dramatically in recent years. One grave was for Sudan, the last male northern white rhino in the world, who was euthanised in 2018 to save him from extreme pain. He left behind a daughter, Najin, and her daughter, Fatu. I had the privilege to enter the 600-acre paddock where Najin and Fatu lived. Accompanied by a guide, I was able to drive the Unimog in. I sat watching these unique animals for a while when Najin approached the Unimog, rubbed, or perhaps polished, her horn on my back locker, and then walked right under my window so I could photograph her from above, before she went forward to rub her horn again on my front bumper. Incredibly, my guide did not realise what was happening until it was all over. After all, this was not the sort of thing that they wanted to happen to the usual new tourist-owned Toyota Land Cruiser.

It was sad to think that Najin and Fatu are likely be the last of their kind as there are no male northern white rhinos left alive to make them pregnant. In their previous home, the Dvůr Králové Zoo in the Czech Republic, where they had lived with Sudan, they suffered damage to their hind legs by standing on freezing concrete all their lives, leaving them unable to carry calves to birth. Still, attempts to preserve the species are being made. Eggs from both Najin and Fatu and sperm from Sudan have been taken to Padua in Italy for IVF treatment. The hope is that they will be able to fertilise the eggs and insert them into surrogate Southern White rhinos living in the same paddocks. So far, this has come to nothing.

There was, however, some good news. Over 100 black rhino calves have been born at Ol Pejeta. These special animals spend their nights in a fenced enclosure with armed guards watching over them until the morning. It is hoped that, with conservancies like this, we will not lose forever the northern white rhino as a species.

◎ ◎ ◎

It was now time to end my journey. I headed back into the chaos of Nairobi, where it seems as if they are permanently building roads at the same time as congested traffic is trying to use them.

Impressive sized horns on a black rhino, Kenya.

In Nairobi traffic jams, buses tend to know the best way. At one junction, I watched a bus drive up the pavement on the left before cutting right across three lanes of traffic. I followed it, crossing the central reservation to confront the oncoming traffic before recrossing to force my way into six lanes which were having to merge into just one.

I finally reached Jungle Junction, a well-known base for overlanders that offered accommodation for bikers, a restaurant and first-class repair service from a very skilled German mechanic. He had a large garden of one-and-a-half acres to store vehicles. The garden dated right back to the days when the city was laid out by the men of the British Empire and was in the best part of Nairobi, an area called Karen, which is named after Karen Blixen, who rose to fame as the author of *Out of Africa*. She created a farm there before the war. Now, it is home to wealthy Kenyans with gated houses and ten-foot-high walls with the obligatory five strands of electric fence on top – homes which are reputedly owned by those with lots of money to hide. I knew my Unimog would be safe there while I returned to England.

It had been an incredible journey. I could happily say that, to mark the occasion of my 80th birthday, I had driven my Unimog for 10,000 miles through ten African countries.

When I returned to England in early 2020, it was to find that a new challenge awaited us all. Covid-19 had brought the world to a standstill and, with it, my travels. But, as I said at the start of this epilogue, the old saying is still true: if at first you don't succeed, try, try again. I will be back on the road again soon: to drive the Unimog overland to Namibia and eventually ship it back to England.

A bit of off-roading in the Unimog in the Malawi mountains

The summary of my travels by country and by distance is as under:

	Countries	Miles
Caleta	54	55,000
Ribaleta	39	18,000
Unimog	61	120,000
Motorcycle	63	60,000
American truck	2	27,000
Total		**280,000**

Five hundred years ago, before Vasco da Gama discovered the all-sea route to India in 1498, Portuguese explorers, to use Shakespeare's phrase, 'put a girdle around the earth'. I have visited 166 countries by air, land, river and sea and my travels to them have amounted to more than 280,000 miles. Assuming the girdle of the earth to be 25,000 miles, I have circumnavigated the world the equivalent of ten times. I have crossed the seven continents of the earth's surface in modes of travel that would have astonished explorers of the past. However, unlike some of the great explorers, notably Captain James Cook and Ferdinand Magellan, I have survived my travels and have withstood every kind of danger. I have explored difficult terrains, hitherto unnavigable rivers, arid deserts and unfriendly seas. I have always known that it has been mankind's gift to be inquisitive and to overcome great challenges. Some of these challenges I have met within the framework of well organised expeditions and others I have met with the support of members of my family or with intrepid friends. It is mainly as a personal tribute to the latter that I have written *By Power and Sail: Sixty Years of World Travel.*

ACKNOWLEDGEMENTS

I would like to thank Ross Dickinson for his initial work in helping to prepare an early draft of the book.

Particular thanks are due to Louise Millar, who has designed the book with skill and excellence.

I am also most grateful for the editorial and management role played by Alan Gordon Walker.

I would like to thank my very good friend, and the best expedition leader, Colonel John Blashford-Snell CBE, and the organisation he founded, the Scientific Expeditionary Society (SES) and for letting me join three of his expeditions. Also thanks to John Edwards for allowing me to join his SES expedition.

I would also like to thank Earthwatch, which allowed me to join four expeditions, two tracking lions at night, another catching crocodiles on the Zambesi and one for being paddled in a dugout among the trees of the flooded Amazon jungle, looking for Uacari monkeys.

INDEX